International Treaties (*Mu'āhadāt*) in Islam

Theory and Practice in the Light of Islamic International Law (*Siyar*) according to Orthodox Schools

Labeeb Ahmed Bsoul

University Press of America,® Inc.
Lanham · Boulder · New York · Toronto · Plymouth, UK

4501 Forbes Boulevard
Suite 200
Lanham, Maryland 20706
UPA Acquisitions Department (301) 459-3366

Estover Road
Plymouth PL6 7PY
United Kingdom

British Library Cataloging in Publication Information Available

Library of Congress Control Number: 2007936069
ISBN-13: 978-0-7618-3898-2
ISBN-10: 0-7618-3898-8

TABLE OF CONTENTS

Abstract v

Acknowledgments vii

Introduction ix

Chapter One: The Islamic Law of Nations: *Siyar* 1

Chapter Two: Muslim-*Dhimmī* and Muslim-*Musta'min* Relations 39

Chapter Three: International Treaties *Mu'āhadāt* 107

Chapter Four: Selected Treaties 151

Appendix 183

Glossary 185

Bibliography 189

Biographical Note 217

Abstract

An intrinsic branch of the Sharī'a, *siyar* deals with the notion of mutual relations between Muslims and non-Muslims during times of war and peace. This study seeks to explain Islamic international law legal theory (*siyar*) regarding treaties (*mu'āhadāt*) with non-Muslims. The varying nature of *siyar* and its changing interpretation throughout Islamic history have captured the attention of a number of jurists and historians from both the classical and modern times. In the course of classical and pre-modern Islamic history, treaty-making continued to evolve and contributed to shaping both political and social relations between Muslims and non-Muslims. Non-Muslim residents in Islamic territories (*dār al-Islām*), such as the *ahl al-dhimma* and *ahl al-amān*, were dealt with as existing identities within Islam and were also dealt with by the means of contracts (*'aqd*), which determined their status under *siyar*. Relations between Muslims and non-Islamic territories (*dār al-ḥarb*) were determined by the conditions of peace and war, and treaties between the two were regulated according to the precedent set by *siyar*. The treaties selected for this study cover the full spectrum of what Muslims and non-Muslims could do to develop and protect the interest of their communities. Thus, this study aims to shed some light on a relatively untouched branch of Islamic law, while also elucidating the social ramifications of legal theory and practice.

Acknowledgments

In the Name of Allah (God), the Most Gracious, the Most Merciful

Many people must be thanked for contribution to the successful completion of this study. I would first of all like to express my gratitude to Professor Uner Turgay, former Director of the Institute of Islamic Studies at McGill University, and Professor El Obaid Ahmed El Obaid, Professor of the Law Faculty at McGill University, for their guidance, encouragement and comments. I would like to take the opportunity to extend my deep thanks to the faculty and staff of the Institute, each of them assisted me in a variety of ways, especially by their example of scholarship in the course of my studies and through their support on both personal and academic levels. The Institute's office staff deserves special thanks, particularly Dawn Richard and Ann Yaxley, whose moral support and encouragement I will never forget; my deepest gratitude goes to both.

I am also grateful to many personal friends who aided me with moral support and scholarly discussion. It would take many pages and much space to thank all those who were part of my life and dear and true friends for many years. I must thank also those many friends whose names are not mentioned here, but who have contributed in one way or another to the completion of this study.

I would like also to express my deep gratitude and thanks to my colleagues in the History department at Saint Mary's University-Halifax, namely Drs. Jim Morrison, Michael Vance, Michael Earl, and fellow graduate student and then Dr. Karly Kehoe, as well as (and especially) Marlene Singer, for their moral support and encouragement. Thanks are due also to Drs. Jamal Badawi, Marguerite Abdalmasih, Bruce Andrew, Mahmoud Mohammad and David Heckerl for their friendship and encouragement. I would like to acknowledge Professor-Tom Faulkner, former Chair of Comparative Religion Department at Dalhousie Universitys, as well as Dr. David Sutherland and Cynthia Neville former chairs of Dalhousie History Department Dr., who supported and encouraged my work throughout. Also special thanks goes to Drs., Jamil Brownson, Ali Idrisi, Robert Reid, James Ayers, Dennis Leavens and the faculty members of the History and Archeology Program in the United Arab Emirates University for their friendship and special thanks for Mr. Mahmoud Sabri the history program secretary for his technical support. Special thanks are due to late Drs. Dwight James Simpson, Hank McGuckin, Jr., Aguibou Yan Yansane and Ted Keller from San Francisco State University for their advise, support, encouragement and valuable discussion throughout my academic career. Many thanks also to my students at Saint Mary's University, Dalhousie University, United Arab Emirates University, and Qatar University with whom I was inspired to share my knowledge and from whose interesting discussions I benefited immensely.

I would like to express my gratitude and appreciation to Steve Mellier for editing my work, as well as to Ahmad al-Hasan, Yasmin Badr, Lisa Alexandria, who read and offered valuable suggestions for improvement.

I owe thanks to the University Press of America for helping me bring this manuscript to completion. In particular I would like to thank most heartily the UPA staff and editors, Mr. Brian DeRocco, Ms. Patti Belcher, Ms. Catherine Forrest-Getzie, and Mr. Ryan Quick for their dedication, hard work, professionalism, distant corresponding and their persistent on fixing the formatting and measurements of this work according to the best and professional standard throughout the final stage of this book. I alone am I responsible of any errors of fact or interpretation that may remain in this book

Finally, I am especially grateful to my wife Sana Ashour for being beside me throughout the difficult period while I was working on this study and other research, as well as for providing the atmosphere to do research and study. Her patience with me while I was spending so much time doing research in libraries and traveling was exemplary. The same goes for my beloved sons Ahmed, Muhammed and Yousef, may God be pleased with them always. My special gratitude and thanks go to both of my families: the Bsouls in Palestine, my brothers and sisters and their families, and to my in-laws the Ashours, in Canada. Lastly, may God confer His blessings upon those who have assisted me in whatever capacity in my work and to those who devoted their lives to providing support for those who need it most.. Last but by no means least, I would like to thank those scholars and individuals who have contributed and continue to do so to improving lives and understanding throughout the world, in order to make it a better place for all. AMEN!

Introduction

This work aims to shed light on a particular area in the field of Islamic international law (*siyar*): international treaties. It addresses such treaties both theoretically and historically and highlights their continued relevance to the contemporary world. Not only is there a lacuna in scholarship concerning such treaties, but it can also be argued that the failure of international legal theorists to study and integrate the Islamic treaty system into the body of modern international law has contributed to frequent misunderstandings and even conflicts between Muslim and non-Muslim countries. This study aims to demonstrate and re-iterate the importance of understanding this crucial yet neglected subject.

Part of the reason for this neglect is the fact that the Islamic law of nations has itself received little attention from modern scholars. Several completed studies have deal with the subject of Islamic international law, but none have focused exclusively on the formulation of treaties and their legal and juristic aspects. It is hoped that this work will provide fresh analyses and shed new light on this important subject.

What they have written on *siyar* in general and on treaties in particular will be considered in this study, but as the references will show, much of the information on this topic must be obtained from the original sources - - few of which have ever been exploited for this purpose. The opinions of modern researchers and scholars of Islamic law shall serve as a secondary focus of study.

This study begins by examining the theoretical bases for treaties in Islamic law. Although many classical jurists consider the normal relationship between Muslim and non-Muslim communities to be one of natural hostility, others insist that it is not inconsistent with Islam's ultimate objective that a peace treaty be concluded with the enemy, whether for purposes of expediency or because Muslims have suffered a setback. According to Islamic teachings, making treaties with non-Muslims is permitted by divine legislation.[1] Explicit Qur'ānic verses enjoin Muslims to seek accords with non-Muslims in order to eliminate conflicts. They oblige Muslims to respect the letter and the spirit of treaties once concluded, even when it may seem expedient not to do so.[2] The Qur'ān thus views the written agreement as a religious duty and not just as an act of political necessity (Q. 16:7,91, 17:34, 9:4, 8:72).[3]

Traditionally, the Muslims' duty to implement treaties, external or internal, was derived from Qur'ānic verses as well as Prophetic words and deeds. Islamic legal theory in this area also drew on precedent, which is why a principle focus of our study will be the written treaties concluded by the Prophet and the four Rightly Guided caliphs (Rāshidūn): these agreements became models for other treaties in later Islamic practice. Classical Muslim jurists collected these treaties, which can be found embedded both in general works on the points of law (*fiqh*) and in particular works devoted to the conduct of the Islamic state (*siyar*). Certain jurists, however, showed a particular interest in the study of diplomacy and international law, and wrote on it under a variety of subject headings. Among the chief works in this discipline are Mālik ibn Anas's (d. 179/796) *al-Muwaṭṭa'*, Abū Yūsuf's (d. 182/798) *Kitāb al-Kharāj*, al-Shaybānī's (d. 189/804) *al-Siyar*, al-Shāfiī's (d. 204/820) *al-Umm*, Abū 'Ubayd's (d. 224/837) *Amwāl*, Balādhurī's (d. 279/893) *Futūḥ al-Buldān*, Ibn Qayyim al-Jawziyya's (d. 751/1350-1) *Aḥkām Ahl al-Dhimma* and al-Ṭabarī's (d. 310/922) *Ikhtilāf al-Fuqahā'*, besides many others.[4] Their comments on these treaties, particularly the treaty of Ḥudaibiyya (concluded in 6/628) and the agreements reached by the four Rightly Guided Caliphs in their dealings with sovereign non-Muslims communities, contributed generally to the development of Islamic international law (*siyar*). For this reason, considerable attention is paid in the present study to these treaties, especially the treaty of Ḥudaibiyya, which in a sense forms the backbone of its arguments. This work also examines the works of historians such as Ibn Hishām and al-Ṭabarī, as well as of modern scholars such as Muḥammad Hamīdallāh and Majid Khadduri, particularly in reference to the Ḥudaybīyya treaty.

The book is divided into four chapters. The first chapter introduces the subject of *siyar* (Islamic international law) and sketches its historical development and significance. It also provides an overview of the jurists' reflections on *siyar* in all four Sunni schools of thought regarding to *dār al-Islām* (the Abode of Islam) and *dār al-ḥarb* (The Abode of War). The second chapter discusses Muslim-*dhimmi* (Non-Muslim who are protected by a treaty of surrender) and Muslim-*musta'min* (Enemy alien who has been given the promise of security and safe conduct by Muslims) relations, including *ahl al-dhimma* (non-Muslims subjects of the Islamic State); *ḥarbī* (enemy alien); *musta'min* (enemy alien who has been giving security to safe conduct by Muslims); *jizya* (poll-tax); *kharāj* (land etax levied on lands); *'ushūr* (tithe, tax levied on lands held in absolute ownership); *'aqd al-amān* (pact of safeguard) and *'aqd al-dhimma* (contract of protection). The third chapter discusses the Islamic legal theory regarding international treaties, particularly their definition, conditions, duration, and termination. The fourth chapter discusses in detail five selected treaties concluded by rulers from a variety of periods. It shows how, when and by whom the treaties were concluded, as well as presenting their particular outcomes. My analysis of these treaties and their influence, the opinions of jurists from the four Sunnī schools will be discussed, since there is disagreement among them concerning the interpretation and the consequences of the treaties that were concluded by Sunni rulers during earlier times. The works of the classical jurists provided their successors with precedents that enabled the latter to conclude and ratify further treaties during their own time.

Under the Umayyads (41/661-132/750), ʻAbbasids (132/750-657/1258), Ayyubids (564/1635-1169/1238), and Ottomans (680/1281-1342/1924), jurists framed treaties to a greater or lesser extent on earlier patterns, and debated whether they fit Islamic legal criteria or not. To examine this question, four treaties completed during the Umayyad, ʻAbbasid, Ayyubid and Ottoman eras have been selected for special consideration. Changes in their approach and substance are analyzed, and the reasons for these changes are identified and discussed. The aim is to understand how the different needs and purposes of Muslim rulers at various periods in Islamic history and at different stages of dynastic political and military power influenced the drafting of such agreements. An understanding of these factors: social, political and economic, sheds some light on the endorsements of these treaties by contemporary jurists.

The first treaty in the post-Rāshidūn era that will be analyzed is the one that the fifth Umayyad caliph, ʻAbd al-Malik ibn Marwān (d. 86/705), concluded in 70/689 with the Byzantine emperor Justinian II. In it ʻAbd al-Malik agreed to pay a tribute in exchange for cessation of hostilities. At the time, ʻAbd al-Malik was faced with a strong insurgency in Iraq and riots in his capital. Arriving at an understanding with the Byzantine emperor allowed him to secure his northern flank while consolidating his power over the center of the Empire.

The second treaty to be examined was the one signed between the second-century ʻAbbasid caliph Hārūn al-Rashīd (d. 193/809) and the Empress Irene of the Byzantines (d. 187/802) in 182/798. In this treaty the Byzantines were the weaker party; they were forced to pay annual tribute to Baghdad as well as to end their frequent violations of the ʻAbbāsid frontier.[5] This study examines this treaty in terms of the juristic legitimacy accorded to it by the jurists of his day–an endorsement that was critical to its validity, as will be shown–and the socio-economic factors that might have influenced their thinking.

The third treaty for examination is the one concluded between al-Malik al-Kāmil (d. 636/1238), the fourth Ayyubid sultan, and Fredrick II of Germany in 1229 A. D. This treaty ceded control of Jerusalem and several other Palestinian towns to the Christians. Al-Kāmil faced a predicament similar to ʻAbd al-Malik's and chose to placate the Christian/Crusader, thus enabling him to turn his attention to his brother's rebellion in Syria. This major treaty presents an interesting insight into the process of legitimating by jurists of the time.[6] On the face of it, ceding sovereignty over the holy city of Jerusalem would seem to run contrary to Muslim sentiment if not doctrine itself. But once again, the hard realities of the prevailing political climate and a realistic assessment of the strengths and weaknesses of both parties seems to have allowed jurists to accord legitimacy and support to this treaty.[7]

The fourth treaty selected for examination was concluded between the Ottoman Sultan Suleiman The Magnificent (d. 974/1566) and Francis I, King of France, in 1535 A.D. This treaty differs from theses mentioned above treaties in terms of mutual recognition and emphasis on the permanent nature of the agreement. At the time of the conclusion of this treaty, Ottoman power was at its zenith, and many historians have attributed a degree of "magnanimity" to it.[8] Moreover, it received full support from the *Shaykh al-Islām*, Abū Su'ūd (d. 982/1574) Grand Muftī of the Ottoman Empire.[9] However, this treaty was to prove a landmark in Ottoman-European relations. Once Ottoman power declined, other treaties of this nature allowed the European powers a greater degree of control over Ottoman lands through the infamous "capitulations".[10]

These four treaties were selected to cover the broad spectrum of the Islamic history of diplomacy after the treaty of Ḥudaibiyya. They also cover the various periods of Muslim state strength vis-a-vis their Christian opponents. It is clear that the conduct of diplomacy by the aforementioned rulers differed according to their positions of relative strength and immediate necessities. This study aims, in part, to determine whether Islamic jurisprudence evolved to accommodate these changes, drawing correlations between historical and juristic developments.

As stated earlier, the study makes extensive use of available primary sources. It also identifies areas of *ijmā'*(consensus) and *ikhtilāf*(disagreement) between members of different legal schools related to this topic. The areas of disagreement usually involve the issues of treaties duration, time limits, and other conditions. An attempt is made to determine how these differences came about and to identify the factors that caused them. At the same time, we will see that consensus was reached on the importance of strictly adhering to a treaty once it has been concluded. This dissertation then evaluates the argument that considers abiding by agreements not simply as an act of political necessity but also as a religious obligation dictated by Qur'ānic and Prophetic injunctions.

---

1 Majid Khadduri, *War and Peace in the Law of Islam* (Baltimore: Johns Hopkins University Press, 1955) 202; Abū Yūsuf, *Kitāb al-Kharāj*, 207; al-Ṭabarī, *Kitāb al-Jihād*, ed. J. Schacht (Leiden: E. J. Brill, 1933) 14-15; Hanse

Kruse, "al-Shaybani on International Instruments," *Journal of the Pakistan Historical Society,* 1(1953) : 90-100.

2 Q. 16: 91-92.

Fulfil the Covenant of Allah when you have made a covenant, and do not break oaths after making them.... be not like her who unravels her yarn, disintegrating it into pieces after she has spun it strongly.

All quotations from the Qur'ān used in this dissertation are from the translation of its meaning entitled *The Noble Qur'ān,* into the English language by Muḥammad Ṭaqī al-Din al-Hilālī and Muḥammad Muḥsin Khan (Riyad: Dār al-Salām, 1996).

3 Q. 2: 281. The significance of this verse for contracts and, by extension, treaties, will be discussed more fully below in chapters two and three.

4 See bibliography, especially the primary sources.

5 Hārūn al-Rashīd also concluded several *fidā'* (ransom) treaties with the Byzantines to secure the release of prisoners of war by mutual exchange and the payment of an agreed upon sum of money. Majid Khadduri, *War and Peace in the Law of Islam,* 217; regarding the legal and linguistic meaning of the term *fidā'* see Sarakhsī, *Mabsūṭ,* 10: 139; Kasānī, *Badā'i' al-Ṣanā'i',* 9: 4349-4350; *Sharḥ al-Siyar al-Kabīr,* 4: 1592; Abū Yūsuf, *Kharāj,* 212; Shāfiʿī, *Umm,*4: 170; Rāghib al-Iṣfahānī, *Mufradāt al-Qur'ān,* 374; Muṭarrizī, *al-Mughrib,* 2: 127; Fayyūmī, *al-Miṣbāḥ al-Munīr,* 2: 465.

6 Muḥammad Sallām Madkūr, *Madkhal al-Fiqh al-Islāmī* (Cairo, 1964) 93-111; Ṣubḥī Maḥmaṣānī, *Falsafat al-Tashrī' fī al-Islām* (Beirut, 1961) 198-219; Elie Salem, "Arab Reformers and the Reinterpretation of Islam" *The Muslim World* 55(October 1965) :311-320.

7 See R. Stephen Humphreys, *From Saladin to the Mongols: The Ayyubids of Damascus, 1193-1260.* (Albany: Sunny Press, 1977); Claude Cahen, "Ayyubids," *Encyclopedia of Islam,* second edition, vol. I: 796-807; M. C. Lyons and David Jackson, *Saladin: the Politics of the Holy War* (Cambridge: Cambridge University Press, 1982).

8 See for example, Bernard Lewis, *The Middle East: 2000 Years of History from the Rise of Christianity to the Present Day* (London: Weidenfeld and Nicolson, 1995); U. Heyd, *Ottoman Documents on Palestine: 1552-1615* (Oxford: Oxford University Press 1960).

9 Joseph Schacht, *An Introduction to Islamic Law* (Oxford: Clarendon Press, 1964): 90-91; idem, "Abu 'L-Su ūd," by J. Schacht, in *The Encyclopaedia of Islam,* new edition (1960) 1:152; Uriel Heyd, *Ottoman Documents,* 59-61. For further information regarding the life, work and conduct of Abu Su'ūd please ses the work of Colin Imber, *Ebu's-Su'ud: The Islamic Legal tradition* (Stanford: Stanford University Press, 1997).

---

10 G. Veinstein, "Suleyman," *The Encyclopedia of Islam*, new edition (1997) 9: 832-842; Albert Hourani, *A History of the Arab Peoples* (Cambridge: Harvard University Press, 1991) 258-259.

Chapter One

The Islamic Law of Nations: *Siyar*

The first question that must be raised in connection with our topic is: From where does Islamic legal theory of treaties derive? In order to answer this question, it is first necessary to explore the bases of Islamic international law, known as *siyar*. An understanding of *siyar* is essential, since in it lay the principles underlying the whole process of treaty-making. Knowledge of the definition, sources, and historical development of *siyar* as an important category within the field of Islamic law is likewise important. As a matter of clarification, treaties in Islam are not considered a part of worship; rather they are viewed as an obligation that falls under the rubric of *mu'āmalāt* (legal relations of Muslims with others or with other nations).

I. Background

Siyar is a significant branch of Islamic law: its roots lie deep in the history of the latter. Essentially, the concept of *siyar* evolved from its lexicographical meaning, in particular from its connotation of behavior or conduct. *Siyar* the plural of the noun *sīra*, which means literally a "path", "way of walking". *Sīra* in the singular came to be used by chroniclers in their narrative accounts to mean life or biography, i.e., the conduct of an individual. The most famous work by this title is the *Sīra* of Ibn Hishām (d. 218/833), which relates the life of the Prophet Muḥammad. In its plural form, though, it also came to be used by jurists to denote the conduct of a state in its relations with other communities.[1]

Four basic and interrelated concepts of Islamic international law determine the relations of the Islamic state with the external world. These principles are: *jihād*; *dār al-Islām* (the territory of the Islamic state); *dār al-'ahd* (the territory of covenant); and *dār al-ḥarb* (the territory of war). Because of their importance, these terms are defined below in detail at length, and their origins examined both in terms of the period of their emergence and their incorporation into Islamic law in the formative period is examined.

Other technical terms also represent the types of relations with non-Muslim states and their subjects, such as *hudna or muwāda'ah* (truce), *ṣulḥ* (armistice or treaty), *amān* (safe passage), *mīthāq* (covenant or pact), *dhimmī* (non-Muslim subject of the Islamic state) and *'ahd* (covenant or pledge). All these relations are forms of *'aqd* (contract) that are considered binding, provided that they do not stipulate anything that contradicts Islamic law. These contracts or treaties can be either written or oral, depending on the circumstances under which they are concluded.

Indirectly, this study is also a part of the debate on the nature of relations between Muslim and non-Muslim political entities in the contemporary world. By examining the *modus vivendi* that existed between Muslim and non-Muslim powers in the earlier periods, we can identify the conditions that made such accommodation possible. It may show that a balanced and equitable relationship can only come about once Islamic values are understood and accommodated in the international political order. Ignoring them in favor of strictly European secular ideals will only lead to continued misunderstanding between Muslim and non-Muslim states.

From a historical perspective, Islamic civilization is no different from other civilizations it developed systems for regulating various aspects of social and economic life. There came into being Islamic Laws or codes of conduct that govern not only governed inter-personal relations, but also communal and inter-civilizational relations. Like the products of other civilizations Muslim powers dealt with their neighbors in a way that served their interests and represented their system of values and what they deemed to be acceptable behavior. In general, conventions emanated from a variety of sources such as religion or social custom. What was needed above all, however, was a legal framework regulating such relations, one that created legal obligations among nations in times of either war or peace. This, in the course of time, crystallized into a law of nations.[2] Even among primitive societies, various rules and precepts governed mutual relations between sovereign entities long before they were developed into a coherent system governing the relations of civilized nations.[3] Each of these nations had a law of nations.[4] Islamic civilization too developed such a law, although it was in many respects independent of the trends that preceded it.[5]

It is important, in connection with the above-mentioned points, to understand that Islam views itself as a universal and all-encompassing creed based on a profound consciousness of monotheism.[6] Islamic law, in all of its branches, is believed to emanate from four sources: the Qur'ān as the word of God and the Sunna of the Prophet as attested by reliable narratives of Prophet Muḥammad's words and deeds, consensus (*ijmā'*) and analogy (*qiyās*). Therefore, Muslims jurists view the Islamic law of nations as derived from the eternal truth and justice that God had bequeathed to humanity through His messenger. Thus, in theory, almost no weight could be given to previously established conventions, no matter how deeply entrenched. Nor could political and diplomatic norms be respected if they contradicted the words of God in any way.[7] However, in practice, the existing structure of diplomacy was partly incorporated by the Umayyad state.

Another important feature of the Islamic law of nations is the emphasis it places on the universal brotherhood of mankind.[8] The significance of this brotherhood is that it annuls all racial and material differences between human beings. According to Islamic tradition and practice, Islam does not recognize nationalities since it does not regard itself as an assembly of citizens but rather as a community of believers. Many verses in the Qur'ān suggest that the rest of the world be regarded as a community of non-believers and, therefore, not necessarily as an enemy *per se* but rather as potential subjects for submission to the divine law. Thus, the history of Islamic international law is, first of all, a history of ideas.[9]

International law operates between independent and sovereign states; it deals with relations between nations.[10] Each nation possesses its own internal law and exercises an authority subject to no restrictions save those imposed by the law of nations.[11] International law, in the Islamic state, or *siyar*, was derived from what are seen as infallible religious sources. In its application it has always operated within the spirit of *Sharī'a*, i.e., Islamic law. Its rules were respected and observed by Muslim rulers as a branch of divine law and were rarely violated.[12] *Siyar* was thus a binding force and not merely a convention existing by the consent of the state, nor was it obeyed because it was the alternative to anarchy. It was part of Islamic religion and based on divine law; thus, violation of *siyar* was considered to invoke divine punishment. This implied, by necessity, that honoring principles set forth in treaties was a religious duty.[13]

The term *siyar* did not refer as much to the concept of international, interstate relations in the early classical period *per se* as it came to do from the medieval period onwards. The term was not necessarily used in this sense by Muslim jurists of the classical period. It is a modern term, but this does not mean that simply because Muslim jurists did not use it as a technical term that it did not exist as a concept within the sphere of Islamic jurisprudence. Muslim jurists simply identified international law under a different rubric. Thus, in early works jurists/scholars generally discuss the relations of the Muslim state with other states under the rubric of *jihād*, *siyar* (conducts) and *maghāzī* (military campaigns of the Prophet), while other jurists treat similar issues under the categories of *kharāj* (land-tax) and *siyāsa shar'iyyā* (administrative state organization and public institutions).[14] The legal rulings that arose from these cases later became known as *siyar*. Not surprisingly Islamic rulings on the topic in the early period dealt mostly with the law of war, since the Muslims faced major threats from the beginning and were surrounded by many enemies. They therefore had to develop laws and regulations to communicate with other states. However, the field gradually expanded to cover international political relations in general, a natural progression to the outcome of *jihād* and the expansion of the Islamic state.[15] Some modern scholars, such as Ḥamidullāh, contend that Muslim jurists and scholars were responsible for the invention of international law as a whole.[16]

A. Early usage

The first scholars to use the term *sīra* were the *muḥaddithūn* (collectors of *ḥadīths* or traditions). They used the term to refer to the Prophet Muḥammad's conduct: deeds, sayings and actions in his lifetime.[17] In effect, the term *sīra* became synonymous with *maghāzī*, which encompassed the biography of the Prophet, his battles/raids and his conduct. It became common among the Muslim jurists and *muḥaddithūn* to list these topics, *al-Jihād wa l-Siyar* and *al-Maghāzī*, along with other topics, such as faith (*īmān*), *'ibādāt* (religious observances), *adab*, *akhlāq* (morals) and *mu'āmalāt* (mutual relations) under the heading of *sīra* in their *Ḥadīth*, Law and the biography of the Prophet books.[18]

The literature on *sīra* and *maghāzī* is concerned above all with the biography of the Prophet and his Companions. It includes reports transmitted about his conduct by arranged according to the year and the place and authenticated by *isnād*, or chain of transmitting authorities.[19] These methods came to be employed by both the *ḥadīth* experts and historians in the decades and centuries to come.[20]

The term *sīra* was first used by Ibn Hishām (d. 218/833) in his *al-Sīra al-Nabawiyya*, an abridgement of an earlier work by Ibn Isḥāq (d. 151/768). In applying it to the Prophet's biography he established a precedent that was followed by later historians;[21] who eventually applied it to the entirety of Prophet Muḥammad life, including accounts of his *maghāzī*.[22]

Maghāzī, strictly speaking, denotes battles and wars. Especially in the early years of Islam in reference to, the wars in which the Prophet and his Companions had participated. Because of the perecined centrality of these battle in the Prophet's mission this term consequently took on the sense of the Prophet's biography as well. Initially, it referred to the portion of his life in Medina, because that was where he was the most involved in the warfare out of which the Islamic state emerged. Later, the term was expanded and used of the Prophet's entire life story,[23] almost synonymously by jurists, and biographers. For example, Ibn Kathīr in his *al-Bidāya wa al-Nihāya* uses the two terms interchangeably, referring to Ibn Hishām's recension of Ibn Isḥāq's book on the one hand as "*Sīrāt Ibn Isḥāq*" and on the other as "his *Maghāzī*."[24]

The *sīra* works themselves depended on an emerging body of data known as *ḥadīth*. The concern to sort out authentic from fabricated narrations was felt by both historians and *muḥaddithūn* (*ḥadīth* collectors). The former were diligent in evaluating their sources, but, more often than not, determined authenticity on the basis of a connection between *ḥadīth* reports and Qur'ānic verses. The *muḥaddithūn*, however, were developing at the same time, in the second half of the second century more systematic approach to *ḥadīth* criticism.[25] Historians, who until then had tried to determine whether or not Medina was the birthplace of this historical methodology of *sīra* and *maghāzī*, based on the authentication of *isnād*, as first expressed in the works of Abān ibn 'Uthmān (d. 105/723) and 'Urwāh ibn al-Zubayr (d. 94/712). The leading figure in this field was Muḥammad Ibn Isḥāq (d. 151/768), whose *Sīra* of the Prophet is the culmination of the historical trends that existed in his era.[26]

In the second phase of the evolution of the term *sīra*, it was used to refer to the biography of anyone and not only of the Prophet. This became evident at the end of the third century H., when Aḥmad ibn Yūsuf al-Miṣrī (d. 340/951) became the first writer to employ it for the biography of another individual in his work entitled *Sīrat Ibn Ṭūlūn*.[27]The second instance of this usage comes from al-Balawī,[28] in his treatise entitled *Sīrat Aḥmad ibn Ṭūlūn*.[29] In the fifth and sixth centuries H., this usage of *sīra* gained wider currency in the Muslim world; it came to be applied to the biographies of scholars and caliphs. Examples include Ibn al-Jawzī's (d. 597/1201) treatises *Sīrat 'Umar ibn al-Khaṭṭāb* and *Sīrat 'Umar ibn 'Abd al-'Azīz*, and al-Rāzī's (d. 660/1261) treatise, *Sīrat al-Shāfi'ī*, or *Manāqib al-Shāfi'ī*.[30] Some scholars even wrote biographical encyclopedias using this term. For example, al-Dhahahī's (d. 748/1347-8) work is entitled *Siyar A'lām al-Nubalā'*.[31]

The third phase in the development of *sīra*, or more properly, the plural *siyar*, as a technical term denoting international law arose from the jurists' use of the term *siyar* in direct reference to certain areas such as *maghāzī* and *jihād*, as well as relations with non-Muslims, such as the Ahl al-Kitāb (People of the Book).[32] For example, Ibn Isḥāq reported that the Prophet ordered Bilāl to pay a sum of money to 'Abd al-Raḥmān ibn 'Awf (d. 32/652)[33] at the battle of Dawmat al-Jandal,[34] saying: "Fight in the path of Allah. Fight the unbelievers. Do not commit treachery, nor depart from the right path. You must not mutilate nor kill a child. This is the covenant of Allah and the conduct [*sīra*] of his Prophet for you."[35]

The Prophet's teaching on worldly affairs was carried on by the later caliphs, such as 'Umar ibn al-Khaṭṭāb. who advised his generals: "Allah has revealed into you everything which is permissible in some cases except two: the *'adl fī al-sīra wa l-dhikr*"(justice of conduct and glorification).[36]

A similar approach was followed by Caliph 'Uthman ibn 'Affān, who issued commands to his deputies saying:

Allah has ordained the leaders of the community to be responsible and to look after the interest of the people under them. Allah did not ordain them to collect money from the people under their control. The heart of Islam is to be responsible and protect the interests of the people and this is the ultimate duty and obligation of the leaders. If the leaders stray from this path they will mark the end of trust, loyalty and modesty. Therefore, the best conduct [*a'dal al-sīra*]: is the fulfillment of duty beholds upon you and to look after the interest of the community as well as to be kind to the enemy.[37]

The foregoing examples show how the term *sīra* evolved as a term denoting an individual's life/conduct and abstract notion of conduct. This was the foundation on which the concept of *siyar* was to be based, as we shall see in the following section.

B. Technical legal term

The term *sīra*/*siyar* come to be used in the medieval period in reference to several kinds of relations between Muslims and non-Muslims, including: *maghāzī*, *jihād*, *murtaddūn* (apostates), relations with polytheists, *musta'mins* (enemy aliens who have been given *amān*, the promise of security and safe conduct, given to an enemy by Muslims), dealing with the *ahl al-dhimma* (non-Muslims subjects of the Islamic state), and war and peace.[38] In the following paragraphs the gradual evolution of this concept is surveyed in summary form.

Sarakhsī (d. 483/1090), the word *siyar* represents the plural of *sīra*, of which he offers in his *Mabsūṭ* a more precise definition of *siyar*.

It describes the conduct of the believers in their relations with unbelievers in enemy territory, as well as with people with whom the believers have made a covenant, temporary (*musta'min*) or permanent (*ahl al-dhimma*); with apostates, who are considered the worst of the unbelievers since they adjured after they accepted Islam, and with rebels (*bāghīs*), who are not counted as unbelievers, thought they were ignorant and their understanding of Islam is considered to be inadequate.[39]

Najm al-Dīn ibn Ḥafṣ al-Nasafī (d. 537/1132) defines *siyar* in his *Ṭilbat al-Ṭalaba* as:

> Siyar is the campaign of conquest, similar to the ceremonies of pilgrimage, and it is the plural of sīra. It is the verbal noun of sāra, yasīru sīra. Sīra, likewise masīra and sayr is the method, way or path. The majority of these terms were named as such, because they referred to the movement to conquer enemy territory.40

Kāsānī (d. 587/1191) went so far as to name one of his works *Kitāb al-Siyar*, because it propounded the theory and process of conquest of the enemy.[41] Mutarrizī (d. 610/1213) also explains that the term *siyar* is derived form the word *sīra*, but adds that it became known in legal circles as a term referring to the conduct of *maghāzī* and related matters.[42] The term *siyar* then spread throughout the Islamic Empire, bearing with it this connotation. Similarly, *jihād* acquired the meaning of striving against the unbelievers.[43]

Nawawī (d. 776/1374) acknowledges that *siyar* is the plural of *sīra*, and adds that the books on *siyar* were given this title because they dealt with all of the rulings that were transmitted from the Prophet in his *ghazawāt* (battles and military campaigns). Books of *siyar* also discussed the rules of *jihād*.[44] Some other authors, in their writing on the subject of *siyar*, included chapters entitled *Kitāb al-Jihād*, *Kitāb al-Tanbīh* (the Book of Warnings) and *Bāb Qatl al-Mushrikīn* (Chapter on The treatment of polytheists).[45]

Some scholars expanded the definition and meaning of *siyar* to contain the biography and conduct of the companions of the Prophet. For example, 'Aynī (d. 855/1451) defines *siyar* as the plural of *sīra* and said that it meant 'way' or 'method' such as in *Sīrat al-'Umarayn* (*Sīra* of the two "'Umars"Abū Bakr and 'Umar) concentrates on their conduct of public affairs.[46] Furthermore, 'Aynī asserts that works on *siyar* contained guidance for Muslims on how to conduct themselves with others, modeled on the conduct of the Prophet and his Companions in their dealings with non-Muslims.[47]

In the twelfth century *hijra*, al-Tahānawī defined *siyar* as the plural of *sīra*, and interpreted it to mean either "method" or "conduct" pertaining to a Muslim's dealings with unbelievers, wrongdoers, the *ahl al-dhimma*, *musta'minīn* and apostates. According to Tahānawī, this is fully in accordance with the Sunna of the Prophet and his Companions. Some principles are derived from the Companions' practice of imitating the Prophet: "*sāra Abū Bakr bi-sīrat Rasūl Allah*" (Abū Bakr imitated the Prophet's conduct). For example, he cites the phrase, i.e., "*Sayr* Zayd" in order to describe the individual's conduct in conquest and dealing with unbelievers as practiced by the Prophet.[48]

Modern Muslim scholars, such as Abū Zahra, define the field of *siyar* as a set of rulings on the subject of *jihād* and war, on what is prohibited and what is permissible in the conduct of war, and on the granting of *amān* (protection) and with whom it is permissible. Furthermore, it deals with booty, ransom, slavery and other matters that are related to warfare. In general, *siyar* is the body of laws that concerns relations between Muslims and non-Muslims in times of peace and war, although the classical literature mostly deals with their relations within the confines of *dār al-Islām*.[49] Other scholars define *siyar* more in terms of the conduct of Muslims with others in regards to treaties, rulings, foreigners inhabiting the *dār al-ḥarb*, the *Ahl al-Kitāb*, and people who have been granted *amān* (temporary safe-conduct), i.e., *musta'mins*.[50] *Siyar* is thus seen as applying not only to relations between nations, but also to the obligations of Muslims with respect to individuals residing in *dār al-Islām* as well.[51]

C. *Al-Qānūn al-Dawlī al-Islāmī* (The Islamic law of nations)

The early and medieval Muslim jurists never used the term "international law" (*al-qānūn al-dawlī*) as such; this term belongs to the modern period and was developed as a concept in the West.[52] For many centuries, Muslim jurists used the term *qānūn* (law) as a singular noun in referring to legislation on a variety of subjects, including theology, jurisprudence and civil matters. For example, a treatise of al-Māwardī (d. 450/1058) entitled *Qawānīn al-Wizāra*,[53] dealing with *siyāsa shar'iyya* ('policy', administrative justice within the limits assigned to it by the Sharī'a), is more of a manual for *wazīrs* (deputies or ministers) and not a work of law *per se*.[54] There is also the treatise of Abū Ḥāmid al-Ghazālī entitled *Qānūn al-Ta'wīl*, but here too the term *Qānūn* is used to mean guidance and regulation on the usage of the Qur'ān.[55] Moreover, the judge Abū Bakr ibn al-'Arabī (d. 546/1151), in his book likewise entitled *Qānūn al-Ta'wīl*, also deals with the fundamentals of the study of the Sharī'a.[56] The Egyptian administrator As'ad ibn Mammātī (d. 606/1209), who held the post of minister under the Mamluk sultans, discusses in his book entitled *Qawānīn al-Dawāwīn*, the regulation of the state.[57]

Naṣr al-Dīn Qāsim ibn Yūsuf al-Ḥusaynī Samarqandi (d. 556/1161) in his treatise *al-Qānūn fī al-Furū',* a member of the Ḥanafī school, uses *qānūn* to designate a corpus of rulings.[58] The Mālikī jurist Muḥammad ibn Aḥmad ibn Juzayy al-Gharnāṭī's (d. 735/1334) treatise *al-Qawānīn al-Fiqhiyya* or *Qawānīn al-Aḥkām al-Shar'iyya,* contains in part an introduction to the Malikī school and its disagreements with other schools of law.[59] Likewise, in *Qānūn al-Islām fī al-Faḍā'il al-Islāmiyya* by Ja'far ibn Sharīf 'Alī al-Qurayshī al-Hindī, *qānūn* is used to refer to the customs of Muslims and provides an account of their various rites and ceremonies in India.[60]

In the twentieth century, scholars in the field of Islamic jurisprudence have chosen to use the term *qānūn* (law) in all branches of the Sharī'a. This was due in part to their attempt to compare *siyar* with modern international law, especially by those with a keen interest in the literature of Islamic jurisprudence. Therefore, some modern scholars have defined Islamic international law (*siyar*) in such terms. For example, Muḥammad Ḥamīdallāh defines *siyar* as a body of rulings and as *'urf* (custom) according to the usage of a particular society or state, one of whose main purposes is to guide the drawing-up of treaties between the Islamic state and other states.[61] Najīb Armazānī defines Islamic international law as a collection of rulings that provide guidance to Muslims with regard to their relations with non-Muslims, whether they be *muḥāribūn* (combatants) or *musālimūn* (non-combatants), or whether they be states or individuals residing within the *dār al-Islām* or outside it. These rulings also apply to apostates, highwaymen and the *bughāt* (rebels).[62] Similarly, 'Abd al-Karīm Zaydān defines Islamic international law as the corpus of rulings in the Sharī'a that guide the Islamic state's relations with non-Muslim states.[63] In addition, Muḥammad Ṭal'at al-Ghunaymī defines *siyar* as a collection of rulings observed or arrived at by Muslims in the early period that represent Islamic teachings and that are acceptable in the field of international relations.[64] By the same token, Majid Khadduri defines *siyar* as a compilation of rulings and customs that organize and normalize the relations of Muslims with other nations.[65]

Among scholars writing on the topic today is Ja'far 'Abd al-Salām, who disagrees with the definitions of his contemporaries. In his view modern scholars fail to address the genuine meaning of *siyar,* and so he calls upon Muslims to look at how the Sharī'a deals with the questions raised by *siyar* in their original terms, and not to assume that *siyar* has the same meaning as that found in modern, foreign terminology. Only in this way can valid comparisons be drawn, in the correct framework of interpretation.[66]

D. Historical evolution of *Siyar*

The expansion and addition of newly conquered territories to the Islamic state had a significant influence and effect on the *tadwīn* (recording) of the rulings on international relations with non-Muslims, whether these qualified as *ḥarbīs* (enemy aliens, those belonging to the *dār al-ḥarb*), *dhimmīs* (non-Muslim subjects of the caliph who are protected by a treaty of surrender) or free non-Muslims within the *dār al-Islām*. Muslim jurists began producing and compiling a number of works related to the field around the second half of the second century.

The common interest of these scholars was to determine the rulings of *siyar*, drawing on the Prophet's conduct and relations with non-Muslims in matters of conquest and peaceful agreements. Some approached the subject from a chronological, historical aspect, while others strove to study the principles of Sharī'a as they applied to the situation. They produced a vast amount of literature and treatises, which acquired great significance with the passage of time.[67]

The first generation of jurists tended to discuss topics related to *siyar* in the context of such subjects as *jihād*, *maghāzī* (raids), *ghanā'im* (booty), *ridda* (apostasy), *'ahd* (covenant), *amān* (safe conduct) and *jizya* (poll tax). Among those who wrote on these issues were 'Āmir ibn Sharāḥīl al-Sha'bī (d. 103/721), Awzā'ī (d. 157/774), Thāwrī (d. 161/778) and Fazārī (d. 186/802).[68] Complementing the efforts of these jurists, Abū Ḥanīfa and his disciples contributed greatly to the field of *siyar* themselves, as well as gaining recognition among later jurists.[69]

'Āmir ibn Sharāḥīl al-Sha'bī, one of the most prominent Kufan jurists and *muḥaddithūn* (*ḥadīth* expert),[70] was an advisor to the Umayyad caliph 'Abd al-Malik ibn Marwān, and ambassador on his behalf to the Byzantine court. Many *ḥadīth* sources refer to him as having been one of the most knowledgeable regarding the Prophet's conduct in his campaigns and therefore an expert in the practical as well as theoretical aspects of international relations.[71] Similarly, Abū 'Amr 'Abd al-Raḥmān ibn 'Amr ibn Yuḥmad al-Awzā'ī (d. 157/773), a prominent scholar of Syria, was among the leading *mujtahidūn* of his day and eponymous founder of his own school of *fiqh* (law), which spread all over the Near East and was introduced into Andalusia before finally vanishing in the middle of the third century *hijra*.[72] Awzā'ī had a special interest in *siyar* as is demonstrated by his teaching, writings and commentaries. He produced a work on *siyar* that was written in response to the opinions expressed on the subject by Abū Ḥanīfa, and was destined to have a profound influence. In fact, when this treatise reached Abū Ḥanīfa's disciple Abū Yūsuf, the latter wrote a refutation of al-Awzā'ī's opinions in a treatise known as *al-Radd 'alā Siyar al-Awzā'ī*. Later, a second Ḥanafī jurist, Muḥammad ibn Ḥasan al-Shaybānī, responded to al-Awzā'ī's formulation of *siyar* in a work entitled *al-Siyar al-Kabīr*.[73] Furthermore, Shāfi'ī, in his large legal work *al-Umm*, discusses al-Awzā'ī's opinion on the subject, with reference to the *Radd* of Abū Yūsuf.[74]

Another prominent scholar in the field was Sufyān ibn Sa'īd ibn Masrūq al-Thawrī (d. 161/777), who was an expert in Qur'ānic recitation, a *ḥāfiẓ* (one who knows the Qur'ān by heart) and a prominent jurist of his era. He was one of the leading *mujtahids* (one who exercises *ijtihād*, i.e., independent legal reasoning) of his time and had many disciples. The author of a treatise entitled *al-Jāmi'*, he had a special interest in *siyar* in terms of the nature of relationships between Muslims and non-Muslims in time of war.[75] In the same century, Abū Isḥāq Ibrāhīm ibn Muḥammad ibn al-Ḥārith al-Fazārī (d. 186/802), one of the leading scholars and *ḥadīth* experts of Kufa, wrote a treatise on *Siyar*, [76] in which he dealt with the subjects of *maghāzī*, *siyar*, *jihād* and other rulings. In addition, he analyzed the nature of the relationship between Muslims and non-Muslims, including *ahl al-dhimma* (inhabitants of territory protected by a treaty of surrender) and *muḥāribīn* (non-Muslims dwelling in the *dār al-ḥarb*). Shāfiʿī praised al-Fazārī and said "nobody has written a treatise on *siyar* as good as that of Abū Isḥāq al-Fazārī."[77]

However, the first jurist to compile a treatise on *siyar* was Abū Ḥanīfa al-Nuʿmān ibn Thābit (d. 150/767). His work was much praised by many later scholars. Abū al-Wafā' al-Afghānī reports:

The earliest jurist to compile a treatise in on *siyar* is the Kufan author Imām Abū Ḥanīfa al-Nuʿmān ibn Thābit, who dictated it to his disciples Abu Yūsuf (d. 182/798), Zufar (d. 158/774), Asad ibn ʿAmr al-Ḥasan ibn Ziyād al-Lu'luʾī (d. 204/819), Ḥafṣ ibn Ghiyāth al-Nakhaʿī, Muḥammad ibn al-Ḥasan al-Shaybānī, and ʿAfiya ibn Yazīd.[78]

Many of the above -named jurists based works of their own on Abū Ḥanīfa's or edited his work and systematized and classified his teaching. For example, al-Ḥasan ibn Ziyād wrote a work entitled *Kitāb al-Siyar*, and Muḥammad ibn Ḥasan al-Shaybānī wrote a work known as *Kitāb al-Siyar al-Ṣaghīr*.[79]

Muḥammad Ḥamīdallāh says that the first jurist to use the term *siyar* in the technical sense was Abū Ḥanīfa in the second century, and that it was developed and spread by his disciples. It was in fact through the works of Abū Ḥanīfa's disciples that the term *siyar* became so widely used in later centuries to represent this area of the law.[80]

The last work that needs to be mentioned in this survey of the origin of the term *siyar* is the treatise attributed to Imām Zayd ibn ʿAlī ibn al-Ḥusayn ibn ʿAli ibn Abī Ṭālib (d. 122/738). Zayd ibn ʿAlī was a jurist and *ḥadīth* collector whose teachings were compiled by one of his disciples in two books known as *Majmūʿ al-Ḥadīth* and *Majmū' al-Fiqh*. These works were later combined into one book known as the *Majmūʿ al-Kabīr*, by his disciple Abū Khālid al-Wāṣiṭī al-Ḥāshimī (d. late second century).[81]

This work was edited and translated into Italian some eighty years ago by Eugenio Griffine under the title *Corpus Iurus di Zaid ibn ʿAlī*. Its chapters and other headings are arranged in the same way as in traditional books of law. Thus it begins with *ṭahāra* (ablution) and goes on to discuss *ʿibādāt* (rituals), *buyūʿ* (sales transaction), *sharāka* (partnerships), *shahādāt* (testimonies), *nikāḥ* (marriage), *ṭalāq* (divorce) and *ḥudūd* (punishments), before at last coming to a chapter on *siyar*. This chapter itself includes several sections, beginning with *ghazw* (raid) and *siyar*, followed by sections on *jihād*, *shahāda*, *qismat al-ghanā'im* (division of booty), *al-ʿahd wa dhimma* (covenant), *al-alwiyya wa 'l-rāyāt* (banners and standards), *al-khums wa al-anfāl* (fifth of the booty and spoils), *al-murtadd wa al-ghulūw* (apostasy and immoderation), *qitāl ahl al-baghy* (fighting rebels) and finally *ṭā'at al-imām* (obedience to the ritual leader) and *quṭṭāʿ al-ṭuruq* (highway robbers).[82]

Scholars have disagreed regarding the authenticity of *al-Majmūʿ*. The majority of Sunni scholars have accused Abū Khālid al-Wāṣiṭī of fabrication and stated that he was not trustworthy. On the other hand the Zaydi school has always accepted his authority and his works as authentic.[83] Because it represents one of the earlier treatment of *siyar*, it would be useful to establish its authenticity. To do so, we may ask: How was *al-Majmū'* recorded? Did Imām Zayd himself compile it or did he dictate it to his disciple Abū Khālid or narrate to him both treatises of *Majmū' Aḥādith* and *Fiqh*? If not, who then recorded and systemized it?

Abū Zahra replies to this question by summarizing the opinions of scholars, pointing out that all of them have in the past regarded the *Majmū'* as a genuine expression of Imām Zayd's doctrine. Moreover, because Zaydī scholars accepted it without any *dalīl qaṭ'ī* (conclusive evidence), he also feels certain of its authenticity. The lack of a traditional *isnād* might arouse suspicion, however, so Abū Zahra favors the opinion that Abū Khālid received the narration of the *Majmū'* from Imām Zayd and then recorded and systemized it.[84]

The opinion of Abū Zahra, however, has not been that widely accepted in the tradition. Many authoritative Sunni scholars of the science of *al-jarḥ wa al-ta'dīl* (the evolution of *ḥadīth* transmitters character) rejected the claim of the *Majmū's* authenticity. Their reasoning was that Khālid al-Wāṣiṭī's narration of the *Majmū'* was not valid because he was judged untrustworthy, and thus the work might be considered fabricated.[85] Furthermore, Ibn al-Nadīm, despite his special emphasis on Shī'ī scholars in general, does not even mention al-Wāṣiṭī in his *Fihrist*.[86]

If we compare the *Majmū'* with other treatises such as the *Muwaṭṭa'* of Mālik ibn Anas, or even early Ḥanafī treatises like the *Āthār* of Shaybānī, the *Majmū'* suffers from the comparison in a number of ways. In the first place, the latter work is not as accurate as the treatises of the scholars of medieval Iraq. Secondly, the material included in the work appears to have been influenced by the Iraqi schools and not the other way around, rendering its contribution less original. The *Majmū'* seems to represent collections by Shi'ī jurists who were not sufficiently trained, and who derived their material from the available Sunni sources. The only additional information it provides is in the form of materials that are not considered authentic. Nor does the work mention the opinion of any of the major jurists of his era, with minor exceptions. But most telling is the fact that the latest material in *al-Majmū'* dates from the second half of the second century and Zayd had died much earlier. Moreover, it is common knowledge that the second half of the second century saw the emergence of prominent Iraqi jurists such as Abū Ḥanīfa (d. 150/767), Abū Yūsuf (d. 182/798), Shaybānī (d. 189/805), Thawrī (d. 161/778) and Awzā'ī (d. 157/774),[87] who accepted the authenticity of *al-Majmū'*.

E. The Nature of Islamic International Law

Islamic international law was not the product of an attempt to discover the rules actually observed and practiced by states in their mutual intercourse, as is the case generally with modern systems of international law. Instead, its origins lie in what are perceived to be infallible religious sources, so that its application and observation had to operate in accordance with the spirit of those general rules. Islamic international law from the outset was neither an *a priori* inquiry into what the rules of international intercourse ought to be, nor was it a historical investigation of what they truly were. It proceeded from divine revelation, from which were deduced most of its provisions, and these were considered generally conformable to justice and humanity. They were applied to cases in keeping with the spirit in which they were derived.[88]

What makes the rulings of Islamic international law (*siyar*) different from modern concepts of international law is the fact that *siyar*, like any branch of Islamic law, has always carried with it the added weight of religious sanction. The rulings of *siyar* were derived not from human but from divine sources, i.e., the Qur'ān and the Prophet's traditions. In addition to these sources, there were the treaties themselves ratified by the caliphs and the consensus of jurists. It is not, therefore, subject to arbitrary change or replacement.

What is more, Islamic international law places individuals and other nations on an equal footing,[89] unlike modern international law, which does not recognize individuals. Nevertheless, its predominant focus is on sovereign states and on deriving rulings on matters affecting nations in peace and war.[90]

F. Sources of Islamic international law

The rulings of Islamic international law are seen as being derived ultimately from revelation. This is a very important consideration, for it lends to this branch of the law the same authority for Muslims that other branches of the Sharī'a enjoy by virtue of their grounding in the Qur'ān and the Prophet's Sunna.[91] The Prophet's Sunna is of equal importance as a source, since, according to Muslim scholars, the Prophet regulated all his decisions on the basis of the revelations he received, including those affecting the day-to-day existence of Muslims, as individuals and as a community. Thus, he often ruled on the conduct of the Muslim state, or what we call rulings of international relations. It is obligatory for all jurists of succeeding generations to base their opinions on these sources.[92]

Ibn Khaldūn, in his *Muqaddima*, indicates that, with regard to the rulings of God, those scholars who undertake to interpret and to express their opinions must ensure that these are based on the revelation. As long as they do so, these opinions deserve to become part of law.[93] Given the status of revelation as a criterion in both the formation and application of Islamic law, [94] it seems spurious to argue that *al-Tashrī' al-Islamī* "Islamic legislation" is based equally on revelation and positive law, as some scholars do.[95] Indeed, some modern scholars divide the system of Islamic constitutional law into two types: first, that derived from the Creator *'Ibtidā'* (form the very beginning, religious observances) and second, that derived as *Ibtinā'* (establish). The latter introduces human agency, acknowledging that people have the right to determine jurisprudentially the application of Sharī'a, but that they have no right to make their own legislation.[96]

It is this that distinguishes the rulings of Islamic international law from any other non-Islamic legislation based solely on positive law, whether practiced in ancient or modern times. The distinction lies, as we have seen, in the role of revelation, i.e., the Qur'ān and in the Prophet's traditions, which were highly respected, memorized, interpreted and observed in principle by Muslims throughout the ensuing generations.[97]

Islamic international law (*siyar*), therefore, based as it is on the Qur'ān and Sunna, enshrines certain major ethical principles that are incumbent upon Muslims. Just as individual Muslims are obliged to observe certain ethical principles, so are nations. Throughout Islamic history, ethical principles have governed the conduct of Muslims in their relations with other individuals or states both in peace and in war. Indeed, in the eyes of Muslim jurists, any system of human relations not based first and foremost on ethical principles loses all significance.[98]

II. Relations between Muslims and Non-Muslims

After thirteen years of hardship, torture, agony and collective and individual suffering on the part of the Muslims in Mecca, the Prophet decided on emigrating in order to protect and safeguard Muslims from harassment and persecution. The place he chose as refuge turned out to be Yathrib (later called Medina), where the Prophet and his followers began to conduct their lives in accordance with the political and religious edicts of Islam.[99]

Islam established the foundation of relations between people on the basis of whether they are believers or non-believers.[100] It has been stated by 'Abdallāh ibn 'Abbās that the unbelievers in Yathrib were divided into two categories in terms of their relations with the Prophet and the believers: the first category were the *mushrikū ahl al-ḥarb* (unbelievers from among the people in conflict), while the second group were the *mushrikū ahl al-'ahd* (unbelievers from among the people of truce). Essentially, the division was between those who fought constantly against the Prophet and those who did not.[101]

Ibn Qayyim, in his *Zād al-Ma'ād*, indicates that relations between the Prophet and the unbelievers remained ill-defined until a portion of *surat* "al-Tawba", (Q. 9: 1-4) in the Qur'ān was revealed,[102] dividing unbelievers into three groups: *muḥāribūn* (those in a state of war with Muslims), *ahl al-'ahd* (people in a treaty relationship with Islam), and *ahl al-dhimma* (non-Muslims who are protected by a treaty of surrender). In essence, therefore, the non-Muslim opposition to the nascent Islamic state could be divided into two: the *ahl al-'ahd* and *ahl al-dhimma* on the one hand, who had reached an agreement with the Muslims, and the *muḥāribūn* who maintained hostile relations. Hence, the Prophet always had three groups of people to deal with: believers who accepted him as Messenger of God, known as Muslim *mu'minūn* (believing Muslims), those who were *musālim āmin* (those who were not Muslims but were securely at peace), and the *khā'if muḥārib* (fearful combatants).[103]

These relationships lay at the heart of the system of relationships that the Prophet developing and that emerged in subsequent decades as the bipartite division of the world into *dār al-Islām* (the territory of the Islamic state) and *dār al-ḥarb* (enemy territory). At the same time it had to address the status of people who did not fully belong to either territory. This points to the special character of *siyar*, for the Islamic law of nations applies both within and without *dār al-Islam.* According to Muslim tradition, Islam is one truly universal religion that addresses all people, and its rulings should apply to all peoples without distinction between tribe, nation or race. The goal of the Sharī'a is to establish one human society that follows one system.[104] This goal, however, has never attained its final state, since Islam had no control over other nations, nor has the Sharī'a become the religious code of the entire world. Given existing political and social circumstances, the Sharī'a could only be applied in places where Islam was the dominant religion, or where the majority of the people submitted to Islam and accepted its rulings.[105]

On that basis Muslim jurists divided the world into two "worlds," one known as the *dār al-Islām*, encompassing all of the *bilād al-Islām* (Muslim world), where the rulings of the Sharī'a apply, and the other made up of all the nations where law is based on rulings other than the Sharī'a, called *dār al-ḥarb* (territory of war) in recognition of the state of hostility that characterized Muslim non-Muslim relations in the first centuries of Islam[106] The legal term *dār* refers to a territory or region, or the states that form part of these according to constitutional and international law. [107] Ibn 'Ābidīn, for one, defined *dār* as a specific territory that is subjugated by Islam after being wrested from unbelievers. However, it does not necessarily mean a territory where mainly Muslims reside.[108]

Perhaps the most extensive treatment of the issue is that of Shaybānī, who looks at the division of the *dār* in detail in a series of treatises on Islamic legal rulings. The following pages attempt to clarify the meanings of *dār al-Islām* and *dār al-ḥarb* and the rulings that those differences imposed. This inquiry will be divided into two parts, the first dealing with the legal definition of *dār* and the second focusing on the differences between the two *dārs*.

A. *Dār al-Islām* (The Territory of the Islamic State)

1. Definition of dār applied by early jurists to dār al-Islām

Since Shaybānī is the chief architect of *siyar*, I intend to rely on his work regarding the reference to legal definitions of technical terms that serve the objective of study. According to Shaybānī, *dār al-Islām* can be a region that comes under Islamic authority, or one where Islamic rulings are dominant,[109] or one where Muslims live in a state of protection. This allows for cases where non-Muslims reside in Muslim territory (the *ahl al-dhimma*), retaining their identity but living in a full state of subjugation.[110]

Following Shaybānī's explanation in his *Siyar al-Kabīr* and the commentary of Sarakhsī on that work, we observe that a region which is *dār al-ḥarb* can became *dār al-Islām* under any one of the three following conditions: first, if the people in a city at war with Islam become Muslims, and yet remain residents of that city - - in which case the city would became a part of *dār al-Islām*,[111] or second, if a city or territory within the confines of *dār al-ḥarb* comes under the authority of *dār al-Islām* and the people remain non-Muslims - - in which case the city will yet again become part of *dār al-Islām*; or third, if the city had been under the influence of *dār al-Islām* but came under the influence of *dār al-ḥarb*, and then the Muslims redeem it.[112] In essence, if Muslims conquer any territory in the course of war and declare the authority of Islam and apply its rulings there, it becomes part of *dār al-Islām*,[113] although the territory of war does not became *dār al-Islām* if the authority or influence of *dār al-ḥarb* is not fully dismantled.[114]

A territory can become *dār al-Islām* despite the status of its inhabitants. In *dār al-Islām*, furthermore, when the rulings of Islam apply, "People of the Book" or non-Muslims who possess a scripture (*ahl al-Kitāb*)[115] become *ahl al-dhimma*, and Islamic rulings apply to them.[116] Shaybānī takes the extreme position and insists that, even if all of the inhabitants of a territory were non-Muslim, but the authority belonged to Muslims and Islamic rulings were applied, then the territory would be defined as *dār al-Islām*. Shaybānī gives the example of a situation where a Muslim army enters *dār al-ḥarb* with the permission of the caliph, and in taking possession of a city, finds that the inhabitants refuse to accept Islam. In this case the caliph will ask them to pay the *jizya* (poll-tax), and if they accept, then they may demand an *'ahd* (covenant) allowing them to stay in their homes without any fear of threat or attack. If Muslims reside along with them in the same place in order to continue fighting with *ahl al-ḥarb* and the inhabitants of that place do not intervene, then there is no penalty if the commander changes their status to *ahl al-dhimma*. So long as they accept the condition of application of Islamic rulings, their place, city or territory will become an Islamic city. In the event that a Muslim commander cannot apply the principles of Islamic rulings without the cooperation of the *ahl al-dhimma*, then the commander ought not to sign or conclude an agreement, i.e., an *'aqd al-dhimma*.[117] For if the Muslims are not capable of applying the rulings without the acceptance of the *ahl al-dhimma*, then the territory or the city cannot be considered as *dār al-Islām*.[118]

If Muslims are subjugated by the *dār al-ḥarb*, after having lived under *dār al-Islām*, this does not change the status of their territory. Shaybānī explains in his *Kitāb al-Siyar* that this region cannot become *dār al-ḥarb*. Even if the *ahl al-dhimma* violate the *'ahd* (covenant), declare war against Muslims and conquer *dār al-Islām*, the Islamic rulings state that this *dār* does not become *dār al-ḥarb* so long as the Muslims are protected, as they were under *dār al-Islām*.[119]

Sarakhsī, for his part, comments that any place where Muslims are subjected to a threat is a part of *dār al-ḥarb*. Since *dār al-Islām* designates a locality, place or post under the Muslim control and influence, the inference is that authority or influence is necessary for Muslims to feel secure.[120]

Scholarly consensus sided with Shaybānī regarding the definition of *dār al-Islām*. For example, Kāsānī indicates that there was no disagreement among his fellow Ḥanafī jurists (*aṣḥāb*) on the question of whether *dār al-kufr* (the abode of infidelity) (Kasānī sometimes uses this term *dār al-kufr* in preference to *dār al-ḥarb*) might become *dār al-Islām* whenever Islamic rulings are enforced or implemented there.[121] The Mālikī jurists similarly define *dār al-Islām* as the region where Islamic rulings are enforced and practiced.[122] Shāfi'ī jurists express a similar definition, saying that *dār al-Islām* is where Islamic principles are applied without *khafīr* (guards), grants of *ijābah* (asylum) and without paying *jizya*. Furthermore, if the principles of Islamic rulings are implemented with respect to the *ahl al-dhimma*, and as long as the *ahl al-bid'a* (people of heterodoxy) do not apply compulsion on the *ahl al-Sunna* (people of tradition), then it is *dār al-Islām*.[123] Lastly, any place where Muslims can implement the principles of Islamic rulings without any kind of fear becomes *dār al-Islām*.[124] The Ḥanbalī jurists defined *dār al-Islām* as the region where the majority of rulings are Islamic in nature as opposed to rulings of *kufr* (infidelity).[125] Thus Ibn Qayyim al-Jawziyya states that the *dār* of migration in the time of the Prophet was *dār al-Islām*, and that when the inhabitants of that place became Muslim, the entire territory became *bilād al-Islām* (Islamic territory).[126] He also indicates that *dār al-Islām* is the region where Muslims reside and Islamic rulings are applied and that if the rulings of Islam are not implemented, then that region is not considered *dār al-Islām*. This is so even in the case of a neighboring city, such as Ṭā'if, which was close to Mecca when it came under Muslim rule but did not become part of *dār al-Islām* until some time later.[127] In the Zaydī school, *dār al-Islām* is defined in terms of the implementation of the promotion of Islamic principles and its rulings under Islamic authority, along with acceptance of other rulings such as those regarding *dhimma* and *amān*.[128]

2. Definitions applied by modern Muslim scholars to dār al-Islām:

According to 'Abd al-Qādir 'Awdah, *dār al-Islām* includes the territories where the principles of Islamic rulings are enforced or where Muslims are able to practice the legal rulings of Islam.[129] Thus any place or territory populated by a majority of Muslim residents, or any place that is conquered by Muslims and ruled by them (even if the majority of its inhabitants are non-Muslim), as well as any place that is conquered and ruled by non-Muslims but where the Muslim residents are free to implement Islamic rulings, is *dār al-Islām*.[130] 'Abd al-Wahhāb Khallāf, on the other hand, defines *dār al-Islām* as the *dār* where Islamic rulings are enforced on all its residents and the protection of Islam is extended to them, i.e., Muslims or *dhimmīs*.[131] Abū Zahra defines *dār al-Islām* as a state that is ruled by Islamic authorities and that maintains the full capacity to enforce or forbid all orders or rulings.[132] Finally, Muḥammad Rashīd Riḍā defines *dār al-Islām* as whatever territory is encompassed by the Islamic realm and where Islamic rulings are implemented and practiced.[133]

The above definitions of *dār al-Islām* demonstrate a basic agreement among most schools of jurisprudence. Modern scholars, along with their classical and medieval predecessors agree in principle that *dār al-Islām* is the territory that is under the full control of Muslims and where all submit to Islamic rulings, in contrast to the *dār al-ḥarb*, whose character we will analyze in the following section. Some scholars would, in addition, extend the definition of *dār al-Islām* to include those territories where Muslims are allowed to practice their faith unhindered, whether or not Muslims are in full control of the civil authority.

B. *Dār al-Ḥarb* (enemy territory)

1. Definitions Applied by Early Scholars to Dār al-Ḥarb:

According to Shaybānī, *dār al-ḥarb* (enemy territory) is the territory where rulings based on non-Islamic principles are authoritatively implemented and enforced.[134] Shaybānī furthermore says that, even if a region was part of the *dār al-ḥarb* and the Muslims living there came to an agreement with the non-Muslims to the effect that the rulings of the *dār al-ḥarb* would not apply to them, it would still be considered *dār al-ḥarb.*[135] Sarakhsī, on the other hand, maintains that in this case the region/territory would become *dār al-Islām* , but only if Islamic rulings are applied within the *dār*/territory. If Islamic rulings are not applied, then the region/territory would continue to be *dār al-ḥarb*, based as it is on a non-Islamic legal structure.[136]

The safety of Muslims is a very important consideration in determining the status of a particular territory, according to Muslim scholars. Shaybānī explains that if the place of residence is not safe for Muslims, then it is to be considered *dār al-ḥarb*, since the only place that a Muslim may feel safe and protected is a territory under Muslim control.[137] Whenever a place where Muslims reside comes under threat, and where rulings based on polytheism or a non-Islamic legal system are imposed on them, then, according to the majority of the Ḥanbalī jurists, that place is defined as *dār al-ḥarb.*[138]

The scholars of all the other schools reached a consensus regarding the definition of *dār al-ḥarb*. For example, Mālik asserts that at the time when Muslims were living in Medina, prior to the capture of Mecca, Mecca was considered *dār al-ḥarb*, because the system of law there was based on *jāhilī* (pre-Islamic) customs.[139] Mālik expresses himself vehemently on the question of whether relations with the people of *dār al-ḥarb* are allowed, and maintains that Muslims should not visit or have commercial dealings with them in order to prevent the rulings of *dār al-ḥarb* from being applied to their transactions.[140] This is also the opinion of Abū al-Walīd Muḥammad ibn Aḥmad ibn al-Rushd (d. 520/1122), who defines *dār al-ḥarb* as the territory where the dominant rulings are based on polytheism and not Christianity, Judaism etc.[141]

The Shāfi'ī jurists took the same approach to the definition of *dār al-ḥarb*, with Abū Manṣūr al-Baghdādī (d. 429/1037) defining *dār al-ḥarb* as territory in constant opposition to *dār al-Islām*. Further, he says that *dār al-ḥarb* is the *dār* where Muslims are prevented from practicing their faith freely and where they cannot enforce the Islamic rulings on *dhimmīs* if there is a *dhimmī* presence among them.[142] The Ḥanbalī jurists also define *dār al-ḥarb* as a territory where the rulings of polytheism prevail.[143] They in fact hold an extreme view of *dār al-ḥarb*, defining it as the *dār al-tabā'ud wa il-baghḍā'* (territory of separation and hatred), taking the word *ḥarb* (war) in its most literal sense.[144]

2. Definition Applied by Modern Muslim Scholars to Dār al-Ḥarb

'Abd al-Qādir 'Awdah defines the *dār al-ḥarb* as the territory/region that includes all non-Islamic territories governed by non-Muslims where the laws enforced are based on non-Islamic sources. According to 'Awdah, whether these territories are governed by single or multi-party systems, and whether or not non-Muslims reside there, as long as the Muslims living there are incapable of enforcing Islamic rulings, this territory is part of *dār al-ḥarb*.[145] 'Abd al-Wahhāb Khallāf, another modern scholar, for his part defines *dār al-ḥarb* as the *dār* in which Islamic laws are not enforced.[146] Yet, he also defines as *dār al-ḥarb* a territory that has peaceful relations with the *dār al-Islām*, acknowledging perhaps that the word *ḥarb* (war) should no longer be taken literally in modern definitions of the term.[147] Abū Zahra nevertheless claims that there is a difference of opinion among scholars in terms of defining the *dār al-ḥarb*. One opinion, according to him, defines *dār al-ḥarb* as the territory/region exclusive of Islamic authority and therefore outside the reach of Muslim rulers; this territory/region also has no covenant with Muslims. The second opinion, he says, is that a lack of authority on the part of Muslim rulers does not automatically make a territory *dār al-ḥarb*. A region may be declared *dār al-ḥarb* in three situations: 1) power and authority in the region belong to non-Muslims; 2) the territory is settled by Muslims but there is an expectation of enemy attack; and 3) Muslims or *dhimmīs* who reside in the a territory formerly controlled by Muslims lack the protection that was afforded to them when it was part of *dār al-Islām*. Abū Zahra favors the second opinion over the first, and further explains that the third situation addressed in the second opinion is meaningless since, *a priori*, the relations between Muslims and non-Muslims are supposed to be peaceful.[148]

3. How the Legal Status of a Given Territory May Change

Dār al-ḥarb can become *dār al-Islām* when the Muslims conquer it and impose Islamic law.[149] As mentioned above, scholarly consensus in the medieval and modern periods holds that a territory becomes *dār al-Islām* whenever Islamic rulings are applied and enforced.[150] A question remains: Can a part of *dār al-Islām* become *dār al-ḥarb* in the event that Islamic authority is lifted? Many jurists define the three situations under which such a change of designation may take place: 1) if the *ahl al-ḥarb* defeat the Muslims and take full control of a given territory; 2) if the people apostatize from Islam and take full control of their territory and apply the laws of polytheism (*kufr*); and 3) if the *ahl al-dhimma* abolishes an existing covenant and are victorious in their struggle against Muslim authority.[151]

Shaybāni and Abū Yūsuf share the same opinion regarding situations when *dār al-Islām* may become *dār al-ḥarb*. According to both these Ḥanafi jurists, this may take place whenever non-Islamic laws are applied and enforced in a given territory. This is the case whether or not the territory is physically connected with *dār al-ḥarb* or whether or not Muslims or *dhimmis* remain there.[152] Furthermore, both Abū Yūsuf and Shaybānī express the opinion that, wherever the rulings of polytheism are enforced, the authority in that particular place has by definition come under a non-Islamic system and the place becomes *dār al-ḥarb*, just as wherever the authorities enforce Islamic law, that place becomes *dār al-Islām*.[153] They base their opinions on the legal device known as *qiyās* (analogy).[154] Since *dār al-ḥarb* becomes *dār al-Islām* whenever the Islamic legal rulings are enforced there, regardless of the presence of polytheists, and whether or not that territory/region is connected with *dār al-Islām*, the converse is true, by analogy, of *dār al-Islām*.[155]

Kāsānī, another Ḥanafī jurist, supports this opinion and demonstrates that the original concept of the two '*dārs*' derives from consideration of the fundamental, essential feature of Islam and polytheism. Any distinction between the two comes down to the types of rulings each religious system implements. Whatever the status of the territory in question it is the conditions or phenomena associated with the type of territory/region that define it. Kāsānī offers a few examples to illustrate this point, equating *janna* (paradise) with *dār al-salām* (the abode of peace), for example, because safety and security characterize it, and then contrasting this with *nār* (hellfire), called *dār al-bawār* (the abode of ruin) because it is characterized by perdition. Similarly, the presence of Islam or disbelief is reflected in the rulings that are enforced in a particular place. If the laws enforced in a territory derive from polytheism, then it becomes *dār al-kufr* or *dār al-ḥarb*, just as a territory will become *dār al-Islām* if genuine Islamic rulings are it implemented and observed there.[156]

The above-mentioned opinions of Ḥanafī jurists came into play later when jurists of that school engaged in *iftā'* (the exercise of issuing a *fatwa* or legal opinion by a *muftī*) regarding the Mongols' conquests of Islamic territory in the thirteenth century. Ibn Nujaym indicates that in his day, after the *fitna* (turmoil or socio-religious strife) of the Mongols, certain provinces of *dār al-Islām*, such as Khwārizm, Transoxiana, and Khurasan and its surroundings, were regarded as having become *dār al-ḥarb* because they were governed under the Mongol law of "*yāsā*",[157] even though the majority of the population was still Muslim.[158]

The opinion of Abū Ḥanīfa recorded by Shaybānī in his work *Ziyādāt*,[159] is that a territory may become *dār al-ḥarb* under three sets of circumstances. The first situation is the imposition of a legal system that leaves Muslims without recourse to Islamic judges, terminate Islamic laws, and imposes on non-Islamic law on. The rulings that are applied, in this situation, be contradictory to Islamic principles. For example, Islam forbids *ribā* (usury or unlawful interest proscribed by the Sharī'a law), whereas the predominant law in *dār al-ḥarb* permits it, just as the Qur'ān condemns *zinā* (sexual intercourse outside a valid marriage contract) while the new law of the land may permit it. The same thing may be said of laws on consuming alcohol, eating pork and gambling. However, according to Ibn 'Ābidīn, if the legal rulings of both Islam and polytheists become permissible, the territory may not be considered *dār al-ḥarb*.[160]

The second situation, according to Abū Ḥanīfa, is where the territory is adjacent or connected to part of the *dār al-ḥarb*, without any intervening Muslim province, the inhabitants of which would be capable of coming to the aid of their fellow Muslims. Thus, geographical communication with *dār al-Islām* can be a mitigating factor.[161] Moreover, if a non-Islamic territory or province surrounds an Islamic territory and yet has no *sulṭān* (supreme ruler or sovereign) set over it, the Islamic territory will not be considered *dār al-ḥarb*.[162] Ibn 'Ābidīn adds that the sea cannot be considered a barrier, nor can it be under the authority of *dār al-ḥarb*, because it cannot be physically subjugated.[163]

The third situation is where the territory offers no protection to Muslims or *dhimmīs* and where the only protection is that afforded by polytheist rulings. Polytheist protection of both Muslims and *dhimmīs* is unstable, and besides, local Muslims loyalties continue to belong to the Islamic state. They only continue to reside within the *dār al-ḥarb* under the covenant of the government of *dār al-Islām*. Hence their loyalties are not determined by their residence, even though they may dwell in territory outside of *dār al-Islām*.[164]

In his *al-Mabsūṭ* Sarakhsī addresses some of the disagreements between Abū Ḥanīfa and his disciples, especially Abū Yūsuf and Shaybānī, regarding the determination of the status of the a given territory. Abū Yūsuf and Shaybānī had categorized the status of a territory on the basis of whether or not the authority of Islam had been established. However, Abū Ḥanīfā placed great importance on the nature of this authority. This is because he believed that, once a territory was part of the Islamic realm, nothing could dismantle that achievement without one of three situations coming into play. For example, if the territory is not connected with *dār al-ḥarb*, and its residents are subjugated because they are surrounded by Muslims on all sides, this is true the residents whether Muslim or *dhimmi* are granted protection which does not indicate whether they were fully subjugated by them. Similarly, if the non-Muslims took the wealth of a Muslim in *dār al-Islām* which is impossible since it could not be accomplished that in their territory because the subjugation is not present.[165] Abū Ḥanīfa's opinion regarding the status of the territory is based on a theoretical rather than an actual model. This is because he considers it possible for Muslims or *dhimmis* to remain in *dār al-ḥarb*, where the law enforced is non-Islamic. For him it is not necessarily the case that Muslims or *dhimmī* remaining residents of that territory, will be forced to abandon the religious practices they observed before their territory become *dār al-ḥarb*. According to Abū Ḥanīfa, the territory will remain under the authority of *dār al-Islām*.[166]

A *fatwā* (legal opinion) on the status of *dār al-ḥarb* was issued by Ḥāfiẓ al-Dīn al-Bazzāzī, known as Ibn Bazzāz al-Kardarī (d. 827/1423), based on the opinion of Abū Ḥanīfa, at the time when the Mongols had conquered many Muslim territories.[167] In it, he reviews the history of opinion on this topic in the Ḥanafī school.

The fatwā concerned with the opinion of Abū Ḥanīfa, which was that the occupied territories remained part of dār al-Islam. This fatwā, issued in the fifth century (A.H.) by Ḥanafī jurists at the time of Mongol invasion, defined the occupied territories as still Islamic since they were not contiguous with the dār al-ḥarb (enemy territory) and because polytheist rulings did not prevail there. Another consideration was the fact that the judges there continued to be Muslim, just as the subjects under Mongol rule remained Muslim. Muslim governors were even put in charge of the civil government, despite the fact that necessary obedience had to be shown to the Mongols. Muslims were furthermore allowed to perform their religious duties, while any obedience to polytheists was undertaken out of maṣlaḥa (self-preservation) or dissemblance. Thus, as Abū Ḥanīfa indicated, as long as any part of an 'illa (effective cause) remained in force and the territories did not become part of dār al-ḥarb, a territory's status as dār al-Islām would prevail. In this case, since the Muslims were capable of conducting their affairs according to Islamic principles, the territory/region could not be called dār ḥarb. 168

A similar approach was adopted by 'Abd al-'Azīz al-Ḥulwānī (d. 448/1056), one of the leading Ḥanāfī scholars of his time. He indicated that a region would become *dār al-ḥarb* if polytheist rulings were implemented and no rulings there were based any longer on Islamic law (apparently acknowledging by this that Islamic law can only partially be imposed and yet still be said to create the conditions for *dār al-Islām*). Furthermore, if the territory contiguous with the *dār al-ḥarb* where neither Muslims nor *dhimmīs* remained under the protection of Islamic law, it would become *dār al-ḥarb*. It would, however, remain a part of *dār al-Islām* if any one of the conditions set out by Abu Ḥanīfa were not met in the case of subjugation by non-Muslims.[169]

According to Ḥanafī jurists, furthermore, once a territory becomes a part of *dār al-ḥarb*, the legal punishments prescribed by the Islamic laws (*ḥudūd*), would no longer be enforced; however, their application would resume once the territory were to revert to *dār al-Islām*. In the event that Muslim judges are assigned to enforce Islamic rulings and should Muslims receive a guarantee of protection, then the region will be considered *dār al-Islām*.[170] Shaybānī's opinion regarding this situation is that, whenever polytheists conquer Muslim territories, these territories will become part of the polytheist region.[171] Mālik, Shāfiʿī, and Ibn Ḥanbal favored Shaybānī and Abū Yūsuf's opinions over those of other jurists, holding that a territory would only become polytheist should polytheist laws come to override the Islamic rulings.[172]

However, some Mālikī jurists, such as Muḥammad ibn 'Arafa al-Dasūqī (d. 1230 H.), insist that a territory cannot become a polytheist region if Islamic rulings continue to be applied; the simple fact of polytheists taking over the government is not enough. Whether some or all or none of the Islamic rulings are applied, the region would still not become *dār al-ḥarb*.[173] A similar stance was taken by some Shāfiʿī jurists, who argued that a territory with a Muslim population conquered by polytheists who enforced their own laws would remain part of *dār al-Islām*, the conquest would not change its status. Zakariyyā al-Anṣārī (d. 926/1520), one of the Shāfiʿī jurists who advanced this opinion, states that Muslims must continue residing in a territory after it is conquered by polytheists and that Muslims are prohibited from leaving that *dār* regardless of the type of rulings applied so as to maintain the statues of that *dār* as *dār al-Islām*.[174] Ibn Ḥajar al-Haythamī (d. 364/974) indicates that whenever a region becomes *dār al-Islam*, it can never again become a polytheist region, even if it were conquered and controlled by polytheists.[175]

Shams al-Dīn al-Ramlī (d. 395/1004) expresses an opinion similar to those of his fellow Shāfiʿī jurists. He indicates that, for example, when a non-Muslim becomes a Muslim in polytheist territory and manages to separate himself from the *ḥarbīs* (those who belong to *dār al-ḥarb*), and yet cannot obtain Muslim aid and assistance to emigrate, then his status is acceptable because the territory in which he is currently residing becomes *dār al-Islām*. However, if he were to leave that place, then it would become *dār al-ḥarb*. Ramlī states furthermore, in regard to a similar situation, that if in any place Muslim converts residents abstain from and do not affiliate with *ḥarbīs*, the place becomes *dār al-Islam*. He supports his opinion by referring to a *ḥadīth* which reads, "*al-Islām ya'la wa-lā yu'lā*" (Islam is superior but nothing rises over it).[176] This particular *ḥadīth* was used and referred to whenever the jurists ran into a case similar to the conditional status of the a given territory. Many jurists from all schools favored the opinion that a territory would remain *dār al-Islām*, despite coming under the control of the polytheists. These included Abū Ḥanīfa, Kāsānī, Rāfiʿī, Ramlī and others. Al-Ramlī defended these scholars by saying that, when they (Abū Ḥanīfa, Kāsānī, Rāfiʿī) referred to the territory meant by *dār al-ḥarb* then the *dār* does not necessarily become *dār al-ḥarb*, *ipso facto*.[177] Ramli's *fatwā* refers to the case of the Muslims in Andalusia following the Spanish Reconquista. He states that it was prohibited for them to leave that territory because the people who would replace them were not Muslim and because, if they were to leave, the existing *dār al-Islām* would become *dār al-ḥarb*.[178]

Rāfiʿī al-Qazwīnī (d. 632/1226) sets forth three categories of regions that acquire the status of *dār al-Islām*: 1) a region populated by Muslims; 2) a region conquered by Muslims; and 3) a region populated by Muslims in the past, but subsequently evacuated so that it then came under the control of the polytheists. According to him, any one of these situation render a region as a part of *dār al-Islām*, even the third category, over which earlier and later jurists differed. However, he narrows the third category by setting some conditions. For example, he explains that, if the polytheists prevent Muslims from staying in the territory under their control, then it will become a *dār al-ḥarb*. However, if they do not force the Muslims to leave, then the region will remain *dār al-Islām* despite the fact that the political control of the region has been passed to non-Muslims.[179]

C. *Dār al-'ahd* and *Dār al-Muwāda'a* (Territory in a Treaty Relation with Islam):

As mentioned above, a region where Islamic legal rulings are accepted and enforced Islamic authority is upheld considered *dār al-Islām* according to the opinion of the majority of Muslim scholars. These same scholars hold that the status of *dār al-Islām* can be attained in any of the four following ways: 1) the residents of a territory become Muslim and remain in their territory; 2) the territory is captured by an enemy force but their government allows the Muslims to practice and enforce Islamic rulings; 3) the non-Muslim residents accept Islamic law under Muslim protection by becoming *ahl al-dhimma*; and 4) the territory is conquered under a peaceful agreement where by Muslims are allowed to settle and apply the *kharāj* (land-tax). In all other circumstances, the region will remain *dār al-ḥarb*. Furthermore, Muslim scholars have agreed that the world can only be divided into two parts, i.e., *dār al-Islām* and *dār al-ḥarb*; there is no third type of territory.[180]

However, the status of *dār al-ḥarb* can further be modified as a result of whether or not a covenant or agreement exists with Muslim authorities. Early jurists such as Shaybanī and some contemporary scholars and jurists thus distinguish between *dār al-ḥarb* (enemy territory) and *dār al-'ahd* (territory in treaty relation with Islam) or *dār al-muwāda'a* (territory in a peaceful treaty relation with Islam for a fixed period).[181] Shaybānī was among the first jurists to discuss this matter in his writings, though he sees *ahl al-muwāda'a* not as an independent region but as part of *dār al-ḥarb*. In his commentary on Shaybānī's work, Sarakhsī endorses this view.

Shaybānī maintains that, if any part of *dār al-ḥarb* reconciles with Muslims by paying them a yearly land tax (*kharāj*) or a fixed tribute in exchange for not applying the Islamic legal rulings and for not imposing *dhimma* status on them, and if one of its residents enters *dār al-Islām* with considerable wealth, then according to that reconciliation agreement he should be granted *amān* (be safe or protected). Sarakhsī justifies the opinion of Shaybānī by saying that in this case the man who enters *dār al-Islām*, even though a *ḥarbī*, is safe and does not become a *dhimmī*, because the Islamic legal rulings are not applicable to the people subject to *muwāda'a*. Moreover, the region does not become *dār al-Islām* under the terms of this reconciliation because it does not enforce Islamic legal rulings, and thus remains *dār al-ḥarb*.[182] Furthermore, Shaybānī elaborates that, if someone party to a *muwāda'a* kills another party to the same in the *dār al-muwāda'a*, he will not be subjected to *qiṣāṣ* (legal punishment), although, if he should kill a *musta'min* (anyone who has been given the promise of security or safe-conduct by Muslims) in *dār al-Islām*, *qiṣāṣ* will apply. This is because, according to Sarakhsī, the *ahl al-muwāda'a* (people who have a treaty or contract with Muslims) have no commitment to Islamic legal rulings under the reconciliation agreement, so their *dār* is considered *dār al-ḥarb*.[183]

Most contemporary scholars claim that *dār al-'ahd* is an independent category. It is to be distinguished from the other territory statuses *dār al-ḥarb* and *dār al-Islām*, and is thus a third status. Some scholars claim that Shaybānī and Shāfi'ī in his *al-Umm* already identified *dār al-'ahd* as a distinctive type of territory. Among contemporary scholars, Najīb Armanzānī insists that the relations between Muslim and non-Muslim nations in modern time are to be based on the *dār al-'ahd*.[184] Muḥammad Abū Zahra, in contrast, maintains that the status of *dār al-'ahd* is primarily a theoretical construct, but that it has existed in reality. He cites the examples of certain tribes and nations that did not submit fully to Islamic rulings and on whom these were not subsequently applied, because an *'ahd* had been concluded and was respected.[185] All of these jurists ultimately base their opinions on the position of the Ḥanbali jurist Abū Ya'lā (d.

458/1065).[186] However, other jurists claim that the *dār al-'ahd* should be considered *dār al-Islām,* because the Muslims never concluded any contract, while they were in a position of power and strength.[187]

The divergence in opinion between modern and medieval scholars regarding the status of the *dār al-'ahd* invites certain observations. First, as mentioned above, medieval Muslim jurists divided the world into two abodes: *dār al-Islām* and *dār al-ḥarb,* while modern scholars, particularly twentieth century jurists identify a third, independent abode, namely *dār al-'ahd.* The medieval jurists, if they recognized a *dār al-'ahd* at all, saw it as falling within the *dār al-Islām.* In their view, if there was an agreement making the People of the Book there subject population it would be *dār al-Islām.* Otherwise, the territory would by definition be part of *dār al-ḥarb.*[188]

Secondly, modern scholars claim that Shāfi'ī in his *al-Umm* saw the *dār al-'ahd* as an independent territorial status, but this is not strictly accurate. He does refer to a *dār al-ṣulḥ* (territory at peace with Islam) in this work,[189] but his reference to does not occur in the context of the division of territorial status, but rather in discussing the conditions of the *ahl al-ṣulḥ,* whether People of the Book in a given territory were to pay *jizya* and become a part of *dār al-Islām,* subject to Islamic rulings. In such a case, he claims, their territory *dār* would become *dār ahl al-dhimma.* But if they submitted to Islamic rulings and authority, they would become part of *dār al-Islām.* The intention of Shāfi'ī in stating this case has not fully been understood by modern scholars.[190]

Thirdly, modern scholars repeat the same claim that *dār al-'ahd* as an independent territorial status and ascribe it to the followers of Shāfi'ī. This claim is given special attention by al-Māwardī in his *Aḥkām.*[191] There, Māwardī refers to the division of territory conquered by Muslims, and he keeps to the standard definitions; in fact he refers to the possession of territory without mentioning any categories of territorial status.[192]

Fourth, the claim by modern scholars regarding the territorial status the opinions of early jurists such as Abū Ya'lā in one of his treatises is spurious, as he does not see a third territorial status existing alongside *dār al-Islām* and *dār al-ḥarb.*[193] However, modern scholars' appeal to medieval works in this context is an effort to fit today's realities, for the Muslim world after all has to deal with non-Muslims in foreign relations, trade, and boundaries that are no longer the same as they were during earlier periods of Islamic history. This is one sidelight to the general increase in the literature of *ijtihād* (independent legal reasoning engaged in by a *mujtahid*) on how to deal with new cases that have emerged in today's world and what the role of Islam is in this new cases.[194]

Lastly, the claim made that Shaybānī was one of the initiators of the third category of territorial status has no ground in evidence since the commentator on his treatises, al-Sarakhsī, indicates that the existence of *muwāda'as* with non-Muslims does not necessarily alter the nature of *dār al-ḥarb*: for *dār al-muwāda'a* is *dār al-ḥarb,* simply because Islamic rulings do not apply there. The opinion of Abū Zahra, who regards the United Nations as an example of *dār al-'ahd,* contradicts his own basic claim that *dār al-'ahd* is an independent territory. As mentioned above, the third status did not exist in the medieval period; it is only a product of modern scholars' personal interpretations. The only territorial statuses recognized by medieval jurists were *dār al-ḥarb* and *dār al-Islām.*[195]

Western scholars' definitions of *dār al-Islām* and *dār al-ḥarb* make no reference to the possibility of a third independent *dār al-'ahd*, although this last concept is discussed, usually in connection with particular early jurists' opinions. *Dār al-'ahd* was considered as a temporary and often intermediate territory between *dār al-Islam* and *dār al-ḥarb.*[196]

D. A priori relations between *dār al-Islam* and *dār al-ḥarb*:

Muslim relations with non-Muslims regardless of religion, color, race or language is not based a priori on hostile but rather on peaceful relations. According to one modern Muslim scholar, the relationship between Muslim and other nations is based on how the other nations perceive Islam.[197] If these nations have the intention of arriving at a peaceful agreement with Muslims such as a *muwāda'a*, then this would bring about peaceful mutual relations. Upon the establishment of such relations with given nations, Muslims are prohibited from taking any type of offensive action against them.[198] According to the Qur'ān: "Allah does not forbid you to deal justly and kindly with those who fought not against you on account of religion and did not drive you out of your home. Verily, Allah loves those who deal with equity."199

As this verse states, *ikrāh* (hatred) and *iqsāṭ* (equity) are contradictory states. Therefore, in order for Muslims to gain eternal reward, they have to abide by the command of God.[200] There should be no more hatred in religion than there should be compulsion.[201]According to Shaybānī, if Muslims meet with non-Muslims who are ignorant of Islam, Muslims should not consider fighting with them until the message of Islam has been conveyed to them first.[202] That is also what the Prophet conveyed to the Muslim army commanders:

Whenever there is a battle between Muslims and non-Muslims the Muslim, commander must first convey the message of Islam, because Muslim's ultimate goal is to convey the message of God. The unbelievers should realize that the Muslims' intention in fighting is not desire for wealth or to capture booty.[203]

The primary object was seen therefore as informing the "infidels" about the message of Islam, and if this was accepted, then the need for battle and loss of life and property would be obviated. Prior to all of this, Muslims should direct and conduct their *du'ā'* (prayers) or preaching with others under the principles of wisdom and fair preaching (*ḥikma wa maw'iẓa al-ḥasana*).[204]

According to the Ḥanafī jurist Abū al-Qāsim al-Simnānī (d. 499/1105), whoever is invited to convert to Islam should know to what he is being invited and understand its rulings and principles. If he becomes a Muslim, then he will be enjoy freedom of movement, though he should be invited to live in *dār al-Islām*. If he refuses to adopt the faith, he will be asked to pay *jizya* (poll tax or alms tax), and if he accepts that arrangement he will be left alone, unmolested. In the event that he refuses to pay *jizya*, he will be fought against, which is truly the last resort.[205]

A similar explanation is given by the Ḥanafī scholar al-Kāsānī (d. 587/1191), who indicates that the relations between Muslims and non-Muslims should be based first on fair preaching. Muslim should not fight against or attempt to conquer any territory without first inviting the people of that territory to accept Islam and preaching its message fairly "by the tongue".[206] It is essential, according to Kāsānī, that Muslims should not initiate or go to war without proper and fair preaching beforehand. Preaching in his view is of two kinds: *binān* (fighting) and *bayān* (exposition/eloquent discourse); the latter is far preferable since the consequences are less severe for both parties.[207]

The types of relations between Muslims and non-Muslims are subject to transformation in time of war. When the opponents rejected *jizya*, or are apostates or idol worshipers, then their only choice is to accept Islam. If they refuse, then they are subject to war.[208] According to Shaybānī, Abū Yūsuf was in favor of the opinion that from Arab idol worshipers, nothing is acceptable except conversion to Islam or war.[209]

Conclusion

This survey of the evolution of *siyar* and of its key concepts *dār al-ḥarb* and *dār al-Islām* shows how a highly complex legal structure evolved out of a very localized effort at dealing ethically with the enemies of the nascent Islamic state. The simplicity of the bipartite worldview belies the work that went into developing an ideal of coexistence that had at its core not just the preservation of Muslims' freedom to preserve and spread their faith, but to ensure fair dealings with other sovereign nations and national groups. A constant refrain in the debate over *dār al-ḥarb* and *dār al-Islām* is the overriding concern for "protection" or safeguarding not only of Muslim territory but also of communities of *dhimmīs* with whom Muslim leaders had entered into agreements. That such a commitment should have been paramount in the face of constant conflict and shifting boundaries, even if the discussion is largely theoretical, is testimony to the respect held for contractual obligations in Islamic law and culture. In the next chapter we will see how carefully Muslim jurists went into the legalities of the Muslim-*dhimmī* relationship, and for that matter, into every aspect of the legal status of aliens (or non-Muslims) within the borders of *dār al-Islām*. This will of crucial importance to our later examination of the legal aspects of relations with non-Muslims beyond its frontiers.

1 Muṭarrizī, *al-Mughrib* (Hyderabad, 1328/1910) 2: 272.

2 Micheal Byers, *Custom, Power and Power of Rules: International Relations and Customary International Law.* (Port Chester, NY, USA: Cambridge University Press, 1999) 3, 19; Baron S. A. Kroff, "An Introduction to the History of International Law," *American Journal of International Law,* 18 (1924) 248; Majid Khadduri, *The Islamic Law of Nations* (Baltimore: Johns Hopkins, 1966) 4.

3 Micheal Byers, *Custom, Power and Power of Rules: International Relations and Customary International Law.* (Port Chester, NY, USA: Cambridge University Press, 1999) 2-5; Majid Khadduri, *The Islamic Law of Nations,* 4.

4 Micheal Byers, *Custom, Power and Power of Rules: International Relations and Customary International Law.* (Port Chester, NY, USA: Cambridge University Press, 1999) 147-153; Baron de Montesquieu, *The Spirit of the Law* (New York: Appleton and Co., 1900) 1: 5.

5 Abdullahi Ahmed An-Na'im, *Toward an Islamic Reformation: Civil Liberties, Human Rights, and International Law* (New York: Syracuse University Press, 1990) 141-144.

6 Marcel A. Boisard, *Humanism in Islam* (Indianapolis: American Trust Publications, 1988) 149.

7 Abdullahi Ahmed An-Na'im, *Toward an Islamic Reformation: Civil Liberties, Human Rights, and International Law* (New York: Syracuse University Press, 1990) 19-29.

8 This is made clear in two verses of the Qur'ān; chapter 49: 11 and 13, which read,

O you who believe! Let not a group scoff at another group, it may be that the latter are better than the former, nor defame one another, nor insult one another by nicknames…; O mankind we have created you from a male and female, and made you into nations and tribes, that you may know one another.

9 Hans Kruse, "The Foundations of Islamic International Jurisprudence." *Journal of the Pakistan Historical Society,* 3, 4 (October 1955) 231.

10 Micheal Byers, *Custom, Power and Power of Rules: International Relations and Customary International Law.* (Port Chester, NY, USA: Cambridge University Press, 1999) 147-155; Muḥammad Ḥamīdullāh, *The Emergence of Islam,* ed. and trans. by Afzal Iqbal (Islamabad: Islamic Research Institute, 1993) 105.

11 Majid Khadduri, *The Islamic Law of Nations* 1.

12 Hosny M. Gaber, "The Early Islamic State, with Special Reference to the Evolution of the Principles of Islamic International Law, 632-750" (Ph.D dissertation, American University of Washington, 1962) 24.

13 Ibid., 24-25.

14 Ja'far 'Abd al-Salām, *Qawā'id al-'Alāqāt al-Dawliyya fī al-Qānūn al-Dawlī wa al-Sharī'ā al-Islāmiyya.,* 31; Subḥi Maḥmaṣani, *Falsafat al-Tashri' al-Islāmī,* 25; 'Abd al-Karīm Zaydān, *Majmū'at Buḥūth Fiqhiyya* (Baghdād: Maktabat al-Quds, 1396) 12-16.

15 Najīb Armazānī, *al-Shar' al-Duwalī fī al-Islām.,* 44-45.

16 Muḥammad Ḥamīdullāh, *The Emergence of Islam,* 107-109

17 Muṣṭafa al-Subā'ī, *al-Sunna wa Makānatihā fī al-Tashrī' al-Islāmī,* 47.

18 For example see the *Muwaṭṭa'* of Malik ibn Anas (d. 178 H), as transmitted by al-Kanawī, 3: 362; Bukhārī, *Ṣaḥiḥ al-Bukhārī* (d. 256 H), 6: 3-285; Muslim, *Ṣaḥīḥ Muslim*

(d. 261 H), 3: 1356; Taḥāwī, *Sharḥ Ma'ānī al-Āthār*, 3: 206; and al-Khwārizmī, *Jāmi' al-Masānīd*, 2: 281-298; as well as other books of Ḥadīth. See Sakhāwi, *al-I'lān bi al-Tawbīkh līman Dhamm al-Tārīkh.*, 518, in *al-Tārīkh 'ind al-Muslimīn*, ed. Rosenthal, trans. Ṣaliḥ 'Alī; C. Brockelman, *Tārīkh al-Adab al-'Arabī*, 3: 10; Muḥammad 'Abd al-Ghanī Ḥasan, *al-Tarājim wa al-Siyar* (Cairo: Dār al-Ma'ārif, 1955) 30-31. Horovitz, *al-Maghazi al-Ūlā wa Mualifūha*, trans. Husayn Nassar, 1 and Ḥusayn Naṣṣār, *Nash'at al-Tadwīn al-Tārikhī*, 27.

19 The root of the word *isnād* is *sanad* (pl. of *asnād*) which signifies a "prop" or "support" in the sense of a person who has transmitted a report. The *isnād* is the chain of transmitters responsible for handing down a given *ḥadīth*. See Ibn Manẓūr, *Lisān al-'Arab*, 6: 387.

20 Ibn Badī' al-Shaybānī, *Ḥadā'iq al-Anwār fī Sīrat al-Nabī al-Mukhtār* (Doha: al-Shu'ūn al-Dīniyya, 1403/1982) 3; Munīr Muḥammad al-Ghaḍbān, *Fiqh al-Sīra al-Nabawiyya* (Mecca: Ma'had al-Buhūth wa Iḥya' al-Turāth al-Islāmi, 1410/1989) 13.

21 Ibn Badī' al-Shaybānī, *Ḥadā'iq al-Anwār fī Sīrat al-Nabī al-Mukhtār* (Doha: al-Shu'ūn al-Dīniyya, 1403 H.) 3; Ibn Khaldūn, *Tārikh*, 2: 569; Abū Ja'far Muḥammad ibn Ḥabīb, *al-Maḥbar* (Beirut: Dār al-Āfāq, n.d.) 265.

22 Sarakhsī (d. 571/1175) *al-Muḥiṭ*, 25; Ibn Quṭlūbughā, *Tāj al-Tarājim*, 248-249.

23 Horoviets, *al-Maghāzī al-Ula wa Mu'allifūhā*, trans. Ḥusayn Naṣṣar. P. 1 and Hussin Nasṣṣār, *Nasha't al-Tadwīn al-Tārīkhī*, 27.

24 Ibn Kathīr, *al-Bidāya wa al-Nihāya*, 3: 242; Wāqidī, *al-Maghāzī*, 1: 19; Ibn Dayba', *Hadā'iq al-Anwār*, 5.

25 The subject of the authenticity of *ḥadīth* has attracted the attention of many scholars wanting to distinguish between authentic and fabricated *ḥadīth*. For this subject in particular, see the work of Muḥammad Muṣṭafā al-A'ẓamī, *Manhaj al-Naqd 'inda al-Muḥaddithīn: Nash'atuhu wa Taṭawwuruhu* (Riyadh: n.p., 1402/1981); Nūr al-Dīn 'Aṭṭār, *Manhaj al-Naqd 'ind al-Muḥaddithīn* (Beirut: Dar al-Fikr, 1401/1980) and Asad Rustom, *Muṣṭalaḥ al-Tārīkh*, third edition n.d.

26 Ḥusayn Naṣṣār, *Nasha't al-Tadwīn al-Tārīkhī*, 67-70.

27 Aḥmad ibn Yūsuf ibn Ibrāhīm al-Baghdādi al-Miṣrī, and Abū Ja'far al-Khāṭīb ibn al-Dāyah were among the most prominent authors in the field of history. The author of *al-Mukāfa'a*, *Ḥusn al-'Uqbā* and *Sirat Ibn Ṭūlūn*. See, *Mu'jam al-Udabā'* 2: 157 and Ziriklī, *al-A'lām*, 1: 272.

28 Abū Muḥammad 'Abdallāh ibn Muḥammad al-Madanī al-Balawī, see Ziriklī, *al-A'lām*, 1:140.

29 This work was edited by Muhammad Kurd 'Alī, (Damascus: Maṭba'at al-Taraqqī, 1358/1939).

30 Muḥammad 'Abd al-'Azīz Ḥasan, *al-Siyar wa l-Tarājim*, 28-29.

31 This work was edited by Shu'ayb al-Arna'ūṭ (Beirut: Mu'assassat al-Risāla, 1981), in 25

32 Al-Qunawī, *Anīs al-Fuqahā'*, 181; Tahānawī. *Kashshāf Iṣṭilāḥāt al-Funūn*. 1: 170; Kaffawī, *Kulliyyāt*, 3: 38; Ibn Humām, *Fatḥ al-Qadīr*, 4: 277; 'Abdallāh ibn Muḥammad ibn Sulaymān Dāmād Afandī, *Majma' al-Anhur Sharḥ Multaqā al-Abḥur*, 1: 631.

33 Daynūrī, *al-Ma'ārif* (Beirut: Dār al-Kutub al-'Ilmiyya, 1987) 137-138.

34 Wāqidī, *Maghāzī* 2: 560.

35 *Sīrat Ibn Hishām*, edited by Muṣṭafā al-Saqqā, 2: 632; see Ibn Sa'd, *Ṭabaqāt al-Kubrā* , 1: 283 regarding the Prophetic *ḥadīth Innahum Āminūn bi Amān Allāh wa-Rasūlih* (they are protected by the protection of Allah and His Messenger).

36 Ṭabarī, *Tārīkh*, 3, 585; Muḥammad Ḥamīdallāh, *Majmū'*, 233-234

37 Ibid., 4: 244-245.

38 Qūnawī, *Anīs al-Fuqahā'*, 189; Tahānawī, *Kashshāf Iṣṭilāḥāt al-Funūn*, 1: 170; Kaffawī, *Kulliyāt*, 3: 38; Ibn Humām, *Fatḥ al-Qadīr*, 4: 277; Dāmād Afandī, *Majma' al-Anhur Sharḥ Multaqā al-Abḥur*, 1: 63.

39 Sarakhsī, *Kitāb al-Mabsūṭ*, 10: 2.

40 Nasafī, *Ṭilbat al-Ṭalaba fī al-Iṣṭilāḥāt al-Fiqhiyya*, edited by Khalīl al-Mays (Beirut, 1985) 165.

41 Kāsānī, *Badā'i' al-Ṣanā'i'*, 9: 429.

42 Abū al-Fatḥ al-Maṭarrizī, *al-Mughrib fī Tartīb al-Mu'rib*, 1: 427.

43 Muṭarrizī, *al-Mughrib*, 1: 427; Zayla'ī, *Tabyīn al-Ḥaqā'iq Sharḥ Kanz al-Daqā' iq*, 3: 240; Ibn Nujaym, *al-Baḥr al-Rā'iq*, 5:76 Ibn Humām, *Fatḥ al-Qadīr*, 4: 277; al-Fayūmī, *al-Miṣbāḥ al-Munīr*, 1: 299; Ibn 'Ābidīn, *Majmū'at al-Rasā'il*, 1: 18.

44 Nawawī, *Tahdhīb al-Asmā' wa al-Lughāt*, 3: 159 and idem, *Rawḍat al-Ṭālibīn*, 10:204

45Shīrāzī, *al-Tanbīh fī al-Fiqh*, 134; Rāfi'ī, *al-'Azīz Sharḥ al-Wajīz*, 11: 337.

46 Badr al-Dīn al-'Aynī, *'Umdat al-Qārī' Sharḥ Ṣaḥīḥ al-Bukhārī*, 14: 87.

47 Badr al-Dīn al-'Aynī, *al-Bināya Sharḥ al-Hidāya* (Beirut: Dār al-Fikr, 1989), 5: 624.

48 Muḥammad 'Alī al-Fārūqī al-Tahānawī, *Kashshāf Iṣṭilāḥāt al-Funūn* (Cairo: Wizārat al-Thaqāfa wa l-Irshād, 1382/1962), 3:170-171 He refers to the Ḥanafī treatises *Fatḥ al-Qadīr, al-Kifāya* and *Jāmi' al-Rumūz.*

49 This is the introduction by Muḥammad Abū Zahra to the *al-Siyar al-Kabīr* of Muḥammad ibn Ḥasan al-Shaybānī with the commentary of Sarakhsī (Cairo: University of Cairo Press, n.d.) 33.

50 Muṣṭafā Kamāl Waṣfī, *al-Nuẓum al-Islāmiyya*, 280.

51 Muṣṭafā Kamāl Waṣfī, *al-Mashrū'iyya fī al-Niẓām al-Islāmī*, 49.

52 Ja'far 'Abd al-Salām, *Qawā'id al-'Alāqāt al-Dawliyya*, 31; Ṣubḥī Maḥmaṣānī, *Falsafat al-Tashrī' al-Islāmī*, 17-18. Maḥmaṣānī indicates that Muslim jurists rarely used the term *qānūn* (law); instead they used *Shar'*, *Sharī'a* and *al-ḥukm al-Shar'ī*. In a modern period, *qānūn* has known three meanings: the first and the most common is corpus or a collection of rulings; the second is in general reference to the *Shar'* or *Sharī'a*, and third it refers to civil conduct (in the absence of ritual), and this is what makes it different from Islamic jurisprudence.

53 Suyūṭī, *Ṭabaqāt al-Mufassirīn*, ed. 'Alī Muḥammad 'Umar (Cairo: Maktabat Wahba, 1976) 71-72.

54 Māwardī, *Qawānīn al-Wizāra wa-Siyāsat al-Mulk*, edited by Fu'ād 'Abd al-Mun'im and Muḥammad Salām (Beirut: Dār al-Ta'līf, 1993).

55 Abū Ḥāmid al-Ghazālī, *Ma'ārij al-Quds* (Damascus: Dār al-Albāb, 1989).

56 Abū Bakr ibn al-'Arabī, *Qānūn al-Ta'wīl*, edited by Muḥammad al-Sulaymānī (Jedda: Dār al-Qibla, 1406/1985).

57 Ibn Mammātī, *Qawānīn al-Dawāwīn*, edited by 'Azīz Suryāl 'Aṭiyya (Cairo: Maṭba'at Miṣr, 1943); see also Muḥammad 'Abd al-Ghanī Ḥasan, *al-Tārīkh 'inda al-Muslimīn*, 42.

58 See Ḥājjī Khalīfa, *Kashf al-Ẓunūn* (Baghdad: Maktabat al-Muthannā, n.d.), 2:13; Isma'īl Basha al-Bahgdādī, *Hadiyyat al-'Ārifīn: Asmā' al-Mu'alifīn wa Athār al-Muṣanifīn*. (Beirut: Dār al-Kutub al-'Ilmiyya, 1992), 6:94; Khayr al-Dīn al-Zarkalī, *al-A'lām: Qāmūs Tarājim li Ashhar al-Tijāl wa al-Nisā' min al-'Arab wa al-Musta'ribīn wa al-Mustashriqīn*, (Beirut: Dār al-'Ilim lil Malāyīn, 1986), 7: 149.

59 Muḥammad ibn Aḥmad ibn Juzayy al-Gharnāṭī, *Qawānīn al-Aḥkām al-Sharī'iyya*, 2-3.

60 Ismā'īl Bāshā, *al-Dhayl 'alā Kashf al-Ẓunūn*, 2: 219; Ja'far Sharīf, *The Customs of Mussulmans of India*, trans. Gerhard Andreas Herklots (New Delhi: Asian Education Service, 1991).

61 Muḥammad Ḥamīdullāh, *Dawlat al-Islam wa al-'Ālam*, 14.

62 Najīb Armazānī, *al-Shar' al-Dawlī fī al-Islām*, 44.

63 'Abd al-Karīm Zaydān, *Majmū'at Buḥūth Fiqhiyya*, 16.

64 Muḥammad Ṭal'at al-Ghunaymī, *al-Aḥkām al-'Āmma fī Qānūn al-Umam.*, 37.

65 Majid Khadduri, *War and Peace in Islamic Law,* 17 and 71. Khadduri however mixes the definitions of both modern scholars and the international court of justice with the Sunna and the customary practices prior to Islam, while failing to produce any evidence to substantiate his claims.

66 Ja'far 'Abd al-Salām, *Qawā'id al-'Alāqāt al-Dawliyya*, 31-32; see also the works of 'Abdullhi Ahmed An-Na'im, *Toward an Islamic Reformation: Civil Liberties, Human Rights, and International Law* (New York: Syracuse University Press, 1990) 31-33.

67 Majid Khadduri, *al-Qānūn al-Dawlī al-Islāmī Kitāb al-Siyar li l-Shaybānī*, 52-54.

68 Ibid.

69 Abu Yūsuf, *al-Radd 'alā Siyar al-Awzā'ī*, 1; Muḥammad ibn Zayhid al-Kawtharī, *Bulūgh al-Amānī fī Sīrat al-Imām Muḥammad ibn Ḥasan al-Shaybānī*, 18; Abū Zahra, *Sharḥ al-Siyar al-Kabīr*, 33.

70 Ibn Sa'd, *Ṭabaqāt al-Kubrā*, 6: 246-256; Khaṭīb al-Baghdādi, *Tārīkh Baghdād*, 12: 227-233; Ibn al-Na'īm, *Ḥilyāt al-Awliyā'*, 4: 310-338; Dhahabī, *Tadhkirat al-Ḥuffāẓ*, 1: 79-88 and idem, *Siyar A'lām al-Nubalā'*, 4: 294-319; Ibn 'Imād, *Shadharāt al-Dhahab*, 1: 126-128.

71 Khaṭīb al-Baghdādī, *Tārīkh Baghdād*, 12: 230.

72 Ibn Sa'd, *Ṭabaqāt al-Kubrā*, 7: 488; Ibn al-Nu'aym, *Ḥilyat al-Awliyā'*, 6: 135-149; Dhahabī, *Tahdhīb al-Tahdhīb*, 6: 216-219; Dhababī, *Tadhkirat al-Ḥuffāẓ*, 1: 187-185, Dhahabī, *Siyar A'lām al-Nubalā'*, 7: 107-134; Carl Brockelman, *Tārīkh al-Adab al-'Arabī*, 3: 307-308.

73 See Abū al-Wafā' al-Afghānī's introduction to Abū Yūsuf, *al-Radd 'alā Siyar al-Awzā'ī*, 3-4. Awzā'ī treatise is unfortunately no longer extant, and is only known to scholars through the extracts found in Abū Yūsuf's refutation.

74 Shāfiʿī, *al-Umm,* 7: 303-335; see also Ṭabarī, *Ikhtilāf al-Fuqahā'*, where he reports both opinions of al-Awzāʿī on the subjects of *jihād, jizya* and non-Muslims residing within the Muslim state.

75 Ibn Sa'd, *Ṭabaqāt al-Kubrā,* 6: 371-374; Ibn Abī Ḥātim, *al-Jarḥ wa'l-Ta'dīl,* 1: 55-126; Dhahabī, *Tadhkirat al-Ḥuffāẓ,* 1: 203-207 Abū al-Nu'aym, *Ḥilya,* 6: 356 and 7: 1-144; and Khaṭīb al-Baghdādī, *Tārīkh Baghdād,* 9: 151-174.

76 Majid Khadduri, *War and Peace in Islamic Law* , 29 and 54. Khadduri keeps repeating in the above pages that he was among the *aṣḥāb* of Abū Ḥanīfa and his disciple, but this is not accurate, since he had experienced a disagreement with them. There is no evidence regarding which school he belonged to.

77 Abū Isḥāq al-Fazārī, *Kitāb al-Siyar,* edited by Fārūq Ḥamāda (Beirut: Mu'assasat al-Risāla, 1408/1987) 78.

78 Abū al-Wafā' al-Afghānī, introduction to Abū Yūsuf, *al-Radd 'alā Siyar al-Awzā'ī,* 1.

79 Muḥammad Abū Zahra, *Muqaddimat Sharḥ al-Siyar al-Kabīr,* 33; Abū Yūsuf, *al-Radd 'alā Siyar al-Awzā'ī,* 1; *Bulūgh al-Amānī,* 18.

80 Muḥammad Ḥamīdullāh, *Dawlat al-Islām wa al-'Ālam,* 23-24. As mentioned above regarding the treatises of *al-Radd* by Abū Yūsuf and *Siyar* of Shaybānī, these treatises were heavily influenced by Abū Ḥanīfa's teachings.

81 Muḥammad Abū Zahra, *Tārīkh al-Madhāhib al-Fiqhiyya.,* 674 -657.

82 Imām Abū al-Ḥasan Zayd ibn 'Ali ibn Ḥusayn ibn 'Alī ibn Abū Ṭālib, *Majmū'' fī al-Fiqh,* edited by Eugenio Griffini under the title "Corpus Iurus di Zayd Ibn 'Ali (Milano: Libreria Della Real Cassia, 1919); see "*Musnad al-Imām Zayd,*" 349-362; Sharīf al-Dīn al-Ḥusayn ibn Aḥmad al-Siyāghī, *Sharḥ Majmū' al-Fiqh al-Kabīr.* 4: 608 and 5 (Ṭā'if: Maktabat al-Mu'ayad, 1388/1968) 7-34.

83 Joseph Schacht, *Origins of Muhammadan Jurisprudence* (Oxford, 1950) 262.

84 Abū Zahra, *Tārīkh al-Madhāhib al-Islāmiyya,* 674-677 and idem, *al-Imām Zayd,* 233-258; *al-Rawḍ al-Naḍīr,* 1: 66, and the introduction to *Musnad al-Imām Zayd,* 17-20.

85 Ibn Abī Ḥātim, *al-Jarḥ wa'l-Ta'dīl,* 6: 230; Bukhārī, *al-Tārīkh al-Ṣaghīr,* 139; al-Dhahabī, *al-I'tidāl,* 3: 257-257; Ibn Ḥajar al-'Asqalānī, *Tahdhīb al-Tahdhīb,* 8: 24-25.

86 Muḥammad Yūsuf Mūsā, *'Aṣr Nash'at al-Madhāhib,* 73-74.

87 Ibid., 72-73; 'Alī 'Abd al-Qādir Ḥasan, *Naẓra 'Āmma fī Tārīkh al-Fiqh al-Islāmī,* 182.

88 Hosny M. Gaber, *The Early Islamic State with Special Reference to the Evolution of the Principle of Islamic International Law, 632-750* (Ph. D. dissertation, The American University, Washington, D. C., 1962) 24-25; 'Abdullahi Ahmed An-Na'im, *Toward an Islamic Reformation: Civil Liberties, Human Rights, and International Law* (New York: Syracuse University Press, 1990): 185.

89 *Mīthāq al-Umam wa al-Shu'ūb,* 5-6; *Qawā'id al-'Alāqāt al-Dawliyya,* 35; Sulayman al-Ṭamāwī, *al-Sulutāt al-Thalāth fī al-Dasātīr al-'Arabiyya fī al-Fikr al-Islāmī* (Cairo: Dār al-Fikr al-'Arabī, n.d.) 382-385.

90 For further details see chapter II in Gaber M. Husni, 24; 'Abdullhi Ahmed An-Na'im, *Toward an Islamic Reformation,* 19-29.

91. Muḥammad Ḥamīdullāh, *Dawlat al-Islām wa al-'Ālam,* 108-109.

92 Muḥammad Yūsuf Musa, *al-Tashrī' al-Islāmī wa Atharuhu fī al-Fiqh al-Gharbī*, 60-61; see also by the same author, *al-Amwāl wa Naẓariyyat al-'Aqd*, 136-137; al-Kaffawī, *al-Kulliyāt*, 2: 80-82; Āmidī, *al-Aḥkām fī Usūl al-Aḥkām*, 1: 138-140; Manāwī, *al-Tawqīf 'alā Muhimmāt al-Ta'rīf*, 202.

93 Ibn Khaldūn, *Muqadimma*, 2 (Beirut: Dār al-Kitāb al-Lubnānī, 1981) 789.

94 There are many Qur'ānic verses that speak of how revelation is a mercy to all human kind. The Prophet's duty was communicate this revelation to its intended audience. See for example, Sura: 52 and 53; (Najm) 1-4, (al-A'rāf) 54; (al-Mā'ida): 67, (Yūsuf) 40, (al-An'ām) 106, (al-Qaṣaṣ): 5, (Nisā') 65, (Aḥzāb) 36, (al-Ma'ida) 44-47, (al-Baqara) 140, (al-Nūr) 19.

95 'Abd al-Ḥamīd Mitwallī, *al-Islām wa Mabādi' Niẓām al-Ḥukm* (Alexandria: Munsha'at al-Ma'ārif, n.d.) 11. Here Mitwallī argues that Islamic rulings are based on both positive law and revelation. On the other hand, 'Ābid al-Sufyāni refutes these claims that Sharī'a is based on positive law in his book al-*Thabāt wa al-Shumūl fī al-Sharī'a*, 96-99.

96 'Abd al-Wahhāb Khallāf, *al-Sulutāt al-Thalāth fī al-Islām*, 35 and 80; 'Ali Jarīshā, *al-Mashrū'yya al-Islāmiyya al-'Āliya*, 38. Among the scholars who adopt this interpretation is Ṭal'at al-Ghunaymī in *Qānūn al-Salām fī al-Islām*, 111-112. Ghunaymī explains that the original legislator of the Sharī'a is the Creator and that most jurisprudential interpretation reflects the desire of His servants, such as the state, which bears the responsibility to interpret these laws. The state is allowed to legislate within the range, sphere and framework of principles of these branches. Ghunaymī defines this source as being of secondary importance since it is derived and originates from authentic legislation that reflects the Creator's desire.

97 Shāṭibī, *Muwāfaqāt*, 2: 58-62; Ibn Ḥazm, *al-Aḥkām fī Usūl al-Aḥkām*, 4: 453; Zarqānī, *Manāhil al-'Irfān fī 'Ulūm al-Qur'ān*, 1: 289-337.

98 Majid Khadduri, *al-Qānūn al-Dawlī al-Islāmī*, 86-87. Ja'far 'Abd al-Salām, in *Sharṭ Baqā' al-Shay' 'alā Ḥalihi*, (p. 396), says that many western scholars lacks awareness of the benefits that can be derived from Sharī'a, and further indicates that these benefits can contribute to improving modern international law, especially in two areas: individual rights in international law and the inclusion of ethical principles in the system.

99 Ibn al-Athīr, *al-Nihāya*, 1: 236.

100 Sarakhsī, *al-Mabṣūṭ*, 10: 84-86; Abū Zahra, *Sharḥ al-Siyar al-Kabīr*, 1: 306; 'Abd al-Raḥmān 'Azzām, *al-Risāla al-Khālidah*, 156.

101 Bukhāri, *Ṣaḥīḥ al-Bukhārī*, 9: 417.

102 Q. 9: 1-4.

103 Ibn Qayyim al-Jawziyya, *Zād al-Ma'ād*, 3: 160.

104 Sarakhsī, *Sharḥ al-Siyar al-Kabīr*, 1: 21-24; Kāsānī, *Badā'i ' al-Ṣanā'i'*, 9: 4315-4318.

105 Ibn Qayyim al-Jawziyya, *Aḥkām Ahl al-Dhimma*, 1: 86; Sayyid Quṭb, *Fī Ẓilāl al-Qur'ān*, 3: 1559-1560; Najīb Armanāzī, *al-Shar' al-Duwalī fī al-Islām*, 67, 164; 'Abd al-Raḥmān 'Azzām, *al-Risāla al-Khālida*, 156-160;

106 Abū Ya'lā al-Farrā', *al-Mu'tamad fī Uṣūl al-Dīn*, 276; Ibn Mufliḥ, *al-Ādāb al-Shar'iyya*, 1: 213.

107 For further lexical meanings of *dār*, please see the following dictionaries where the term is defined in general and specific senses: *al-Ṣiḥāḥ*, 2: 659-660; *Mu'jam Maqāyīs al-Lugha*, 12:311; *Mufradāt al-Qur'ān*, 174, *Lisān al-'Arab*, 4: 295-300, *al-Qāmūs al-Muḥīṭ*, 2: 229-231; *al-Miṣbāḥ al-Munīr*, 1:202-203; *al-Tawqīf 'alā Muhimmāt al-Ta'ārīf*, 332 and *al-Mu'jam al-Wasīṭ*, 1: 202-203.

108 Ibn 'Ābidīn, *Ḥāshiyat Ibn 'Ābidīn*, 4: 166.

109 The verb *ẓahara* means to have authority or full influence; its original meaning is to give assistance, triumph or grant victory; for other meanings see the following references: *al-Mughrib*, 2: 36-37; al-Kaffawī, *al-Kulliyyāt*, 3: 172-173 and *Majma' Biḥār al-Anwār*, 3: 498-502.

110 *Sharḥ al-Siyar al-Kabīr*, 1: 249-250, 3: 1004-1006, 4:1253 and 1257

111 Ibid., 1: 249-250.

112 Ibid. This is also the opinion of members of the Shāfi'ī school; see for instance al-Māwardī, *al-Aḥkām al-Sulṭāniyya*, 137.

113 According to Ḥaskafī, in his *Durr al-Muntaqā Sharḥ al-Multaqā*, 1: 638, there is no disagreement that *dār al-ḥarb* may become *dār Islam* even if only a part of the Islamic rulings are implemented. A majority of jurists, however, disagree with Ḥaskafī on this particular point.

114 *Sharḥ al-Siyar al-Kabīr*, 3: 1004-1006 and 4: 1253-1257; Sarakhsī, *al-Mabsūṭ*, 10: 23 and 114; *al-Fatāwā al-Hindiyya*, 2: 232; *al-Fatāwī al-Bazzāziyya*, 3: 311-312 in the margins *al-Fatāwā al-Hindiyya*, and *Kashshāf Iṣṭilāḥāt al-Funūn*, 2: 256.

115 The term *ahl al-Kitāb* (People of the Book or Scripturaries) applied to all non-Muslims who possessed a scripture whether they resided within or without the *dār al-Islām*. However, their are tolerated communities within Islam or *dhimmīs* whom they accepted residence in any Muslim territory except the Arabian Peninsula, such as Christians, Jews, Majūs (Zoroastrians), Samaritans, and Ṣabians. See Abū Yūsuf, *Kharāj*, 128-129.

116 *al-Siyar al-Kabīr* with Sarakhsī's commentary 5: 216, 2191, 2197; Sarakhsī, *al-Mabsūṭ*, 10:23; *al-Fatāwī al-Hindiyya*, 2: 232; *al-Durr al-Mukhtār*, 4: 175; *Durr al-Muntaqā*, 1: 634. For the same opinions expressed by the Shāfi'ī school, see *Rawḍat al-Ṭālibīn*, 5: 433 and *Tuḥfat al-Muḥtāj*, 9: 269.

117 Ibn Qayyim al-Jawziyya, *Aḥkām Ahl al-Dhimma*, 2: 475-476.

118 *al-Siyar al-Kabīr*, 5: 2191-2193; *Majma' al-Anhur*, 1: 659; 'Ubayd al-Sufyānī, *Aḥkām al-Diyār*, 18-20. Similar cases can be found in the modern world. For example, there are several Muslim communities residing in the western world. They are allowed to perform their rituals, such as the feasts and the month of fasting Ramaḍān without any harassment or duress. Despite this fact, however, the western world cannot be considered *dār al-Islam*, because the governors or the leaders are not Muslim and the rulings of Islam are not enforced by Muslim authorities.

119 Shaybānī, *Aṣl*, 217.

120 Sarakhsī, *Sharḥ al-Siyar al-Kabīr*, 4: 1253; and idem, *al-Mabsūṭ*, 10: 93, 114.

121 Kāsānī, *Badā'i' al-Ṣanā'i'*, 9: 4374.

122 Ibn Rushd, *al-Muqaddimāt al-Mumahhidāt*, 2: 153.

123 Abū Manṣūr al-Baghdādī, *Uṣūl al-Dīn*, 270.

124 Ramlī, *Nihāyat al-Muḥtāj*, 8: 82; Zakariyyā al-Anṣārī, *Asmā al-Maṭālib Sharḥ Rawḍ al-Ṭālib*, 4: 204.

125 Abū Ya'lā, *al-Mu'tamad fī Uṣūl al-Dīn*, p. 276; Ibn Mufliḥ, *al-Ādāb al-Shar'iyya*, 1: 213.

126 Ibn Qayyim al-Jawziyya, *Aḥkām Ahl al-Dhimma*, 1: 5.

127 Ibid., 1: 366.

128 *Sharḥ al-Azhār*, 5: 571-572.

129 'Abd al-Qādir 'Awdah, *al-Tashrī' al-Jinā'ī al-Islāmī*, 1: 274-275; see also 'Abdullahi Ahmed An-Na'im, *Toward an Islamic* Reformation, 150 and 183.

130 'Abd al-Qādir 'Awdah, *al-Tashrī' al-Jinā'ī*, 1: 275-276, where the author makes reference to *Badā'i' al-Ṣanā'i'* and *Asmā al-Maṭālib*; see also Muḥammad Ḥāfiẓ, *Mabādi' al-Qānūn al-Duwalī*, 51.

131 'Abd al-Wahhāb Khallāf, *al-Siyāsa al-Shar'iyya wa Niẓām al-Dawla al-Islāmiyya*, 71; see also Ḥāmid Sulṭān, *Aḥkām al-Qānūn al-Dawlī fī al-Sharī'a al-Islāmiyya*, 112; 'Abd al-Karīm Zaydān, *Majmū'at Buḥūth Fiqhiyya*, 50; Wahbī Zuḥaylī, *al-'Alāqāt al-Dawliyya fī al-Islām*, 104-105; Muṣṭafā Kamāl Waṣfī, *Muṣannafat al-Niḍum al-Islāmiyya*, 285.

132 Abū Zahra, *al-'Alāqāt al-Dawliyya fī al-Islām*, 53; and idem, *al-Jarīma wa al-'Uqūba fī al-Fiqh al-Islāmī*, 1: 341-343.

133 Muḥammad Rashīd Riḍā, *Tafsīr al-Manār*, 10: 371.

134 Shaybānī, *al-Siyar al-Kabīr*, 1: 251, 4: 2070 and 2197; Sarakhsī, *al-Mabṣūṭ*, 10: 114; Kasānī, *Badā'i' al-Ṣanā'i'*, 9: 4375; *Durr al-Muntaqā*, 1: 634; *Mujama' al-Anhur*, 1: 659.

135 Sarakhsī, *Sharḥ al-Siyar al-Kabīr*, 4: 1253.

136 Ibid., 5: 2165; Sarakhsī, *al-Mabsūṭ*, 10: 114.

137 Sarakhsī, *Sharḥ al-Siyar al-Kabīr*, 4: 1253.

138 *Durr al-Muntaqā*, 1: 634; Tahanāwī, *Khashshāf Iṣṭilāḥāt al-Funūn*, 2: 256; al-Kaffawī, *al-Kulliyāt*, 2: 341.

139 Mālik, *al-Mudawwana*, with Saḥnūn's commentary, 2:22

140 Ibid., 3: 270.

141 Ibn Rushd, *al-Muqaddimāt al-Mumahhidāt*, 2: 151; *Fatāwī al-Shaykh 'Alīsh*, 1: 377.

142 Baghdādī, *Uṣūl al-Dīn*, 270.

143 Ḥajjāwī, *al-Iqnā'* with Bahūtī's *Kashshāf al-Iqnā'*, 3: 38; Mardāwī, *al-Muqni'* with the *Inṣāf*, 4: 121; Ibn Mufliḥ, *al-Furū'*, 6: 197, *al-Ādāb al-Shar'iyya*, 1: 213 and *al-Mubdi' Sharḥ al-Muqni'*, 3: 313.

144 Ba'lī, *al-Muṭli' 'alā Abwāb al-Muqni'*, 226.

145 'Abd al-Qādir 'Awdah, *al-Tashrī' al-Jinā'ī al-Islāmī*, 1: 277.

146 'Abd al-Wahhāb Khallāf, *al-Siyāsa al-Shar'iyya wa Niẓām al-Dawla al-Islāmiyya*, 71. The author summarizes the opinions of a member of scholars, for example see Ibn

Qayyim al-Jawziyya, *Aḥkām Ahl al-Dhimma*, 1: 366; and 'Abd al-Karīm Zaydān, *Majmū'at Buḥūth Fiqhiyya*, 51.

147 'Abd al-Wahhāb Khallāf, *al-Siyāsa al-Shar'iyya wa Niẓām al-Dawla al-Islāmiyya*, 77; a similar approach is defined by Ḥāmid Sulṭān, *al-Qānūn al-Dawlī fī al-Sharī'a al-Islamiyya*, 115.

148 Abū Zahra, *al-'Alāqāt al-Dawliyya fī al-Islām*, 53-54, and idem, *al-Jarīma wa al-'Uqūba*, 1: 340-343; Wahbi al-Zuḥaylī, *al-'Alāqāt al-Dawliyya fī al-Islām*, 105-106.

149 Kāsānī, *Badā'i' al-Ṣanā'i'*, 9: 4374; *Durr al-Muntaqā*, 1: 634; *Fatāwī al-Bazzāziyya*, 3: 312 and *Fatāwī al-Hindiyya*, 2: 232.

150 Ibid.

151 These three phases are outlined in the following treatises: Shaybāni. *Aṣl, Kitāb al-Siyar*, 217-220; Sarakhsī, *Sharḥ al-Siyar al-Kabīr*, 5: 1914 and 1941; *al-Jami' al-Ṣaghīr*, 249; *al-Mabsūṭ*, 10: 113-114; Kāsānī, *Badā'i' al-Ṣanā'i'*, 9: 4376; Ṭaḥāwī, *Mukhtaṣar al-Ṭaḥāwī*, 249, *al-Fatāwī al-Hindiyya*, 2: 232; *Fatāwī Qāḍī Khān*, 3: 584; *Ḥāshiyat Ibn 'Ābidīn*, 4: 174; *al-Baḥr al-Rā'iq*, 3: 230-231; Karābīsī, *Furūq*, 1: 340; Māwardī, *Aḥkām al-Sulṭaniyya*, 138; Ibn Hubayra, *al-Ifṣāḥ*, 2: 229-230; and Dimashqī, *Raḥmat al-Umma*, 352.

152 Sarakhsī, *Sharh al-Siyar al-Kabīr*, 5: 1914; and idem, *al-Mabsūṭ*, 10: 113-114; Kāsānī, *Badā'i' al-Ṣanā'i'*, 9: 4376

153 Kāsānī, *Badā'i' al-Ṣanā'i'*, 9: 4376

154 *Qiyās* is the method of systematic reasoning (analogy) that tries to identify the "*'illa*" (effective reasoning) in a given "*ḥukm*" (judgement) on the basis of the Qur'ān, Sunna and "*'ijmā'*" (consensus)

155 Shaybānī, *al-Aṣl Kitāb al-Siyar*, 217; Sarakhsī, *Sharḥ al-Siyar al-Kabīr*, 5: 1914; and idem, *al-Mabṣūṭ*, 10: 114; *al-Fatāwī al-Hindiyya*, 2-232; Tahānawī, *Kashshāf Iṣṭilāḥ al-Funūn*, 2: 256.

156 Kāsānī, *Badā'i' al-Ṣanā'i'*, 9: 4375; Abū Zahra, *al-Jarīma wa il-'Uqūba fī al-Islam*, 341; and *Fatāwā al-Imām Rashīd Riḍa*, edited by Ṣalāh al-Dīn Munajjid, 1: 373.

157 Such as in the "great *yāsā* of Ghengīz Khān," a comprehensive legal code laid down by the founder of the Mongol empire. See, "Yāsā" in the *Encyclopedia of Islam*, 11: 293-294.

158 Ibn Nujaym, *al-Baḥr al-Rā'iq Sharḥ Kanz al-Daqā'iq*, 3: 230-231; the term also appears in "Ḥāshiyat al-Shalabī", *Tabyīn al-Ḥaqā'iq*, 3: 285.

159 Shaybānī entitled this work *Ziyādāt* "additional", because he included additional cases as treated in earlier works, as well as cases where in it he deferred to Abū Yūsuf. It is known through the commentary works of Qāḍī Khān (d. 596/1199) and al-'Attābī (d. 586/1190). See Ḥājjī Khalīfa, *Kashf al-Ẓunūn*, 2: 962-963; Brockelman, *Tārīkh al-Adab al-'Arabī*, 3: 248-249; Fu'ād Sezgin, *Tārīkh al-Turāth al-'Arabī*, 3: 57-59.

160 Ibn Nujaym, *al-Baḥr al-Rā'iq Sharḥ Kanz al-Daqā'iq*, 3: 230-231; Ibn Qāḍī Samāwnah, *Jāmi' al-Fuṣūlayn*, 1: 13.

161 *Fatāwā Qāḍī Khān*, 3: 582-584.

162 Sarakhsī, *Sharḥ al-Siyar al-Kabīr*, 5: 1914; and idem, *al-Mabsūṭ*, 10: 114.

163 *Ḥāshiyat Ibn 'Ābidīn*, 4: 174-175.

164 Raḥbī, *Fiqh al-Mulūk wa Miftāḥ al-Ratāj al-Murṣad 'alā Khizānat al-Kharāj*, 1: 463.

165 Sarakhsī, *al-Mabsūṭ*, 10: 114

166 Ibid.

167 al-Bazzāz's opinion was transmitted from Muḥammad ibn Aḥmad b. Ḥamza b. al-Husayn al-'Alawī, known as Abū Shujā', one of the leading Ḥanāfi jurists of the fifth century H., and well known for his *fatwā*'s in that day. For further information, see *al-Jawāhir al-Muḍiyya*, 3: 28, and *al-Fawā'id al-Bahiyya*, 155.

168 Ibn al-Bazzāzī, *al-Fatāwā al-Bazzāziyya*, 3: 311-312, in the margins of volume 6 of the *Fatāwā al-Hindiyya*.

169 Ibid.; see also Tahānawī, *Kashshāf Iṣṭilāhāṭ al-Funūn*, 2: 256.

170 Ibn 'Ābidīn, *Ḥāshiyyat Ibn 'Ābidīn*, 4: 175; *al-Fatāwā al-Hindiyya*, 2: 232; Kāsānī, *Badā'i' al-Ṣanā'i'*, 9: 4376; *Mukhtaṣar al-Ṭaḥāwī*, 295.

171 Shaybānī, *al-Siyar al-Kabīr*, 5: 1957.

172 Mālik, *al-Mudawwana*, 2: 22; Ibn Rushd, *al-Muqaddimāt al-Mumahhidāt*, 2: 152; *al-Mughnī* with the *Sharḥ al-Kabīr*, 6: 403-404; Mirdāwī, *al-Inṣāf*, 4: 121; Bahūtī, *Kashshāf al-Qinā'*, 3: 38; Ibn Haybara, *al-Ifṣāḥ*, 2: 230; Dimashqī, *Raḥmat al-'Umma fī Ikhtilāf al-A'imma*, 352.

173 *Ḥāshiyat al-Dasūqī 'alā al-Sharḥ al-Kabīr*, 2: 188.

174 Zakariyyā al-Anṣārī, *Sharḥ Minhaj al-Ṭālibin*, 4: 244.

175 Ibn Ḥajar al-Haythamī, *Tuḥfāt al-Muḥtāj Sharḥ al-Minhāj*, 9: 268-269.

176 According to various *ḥadīth* collections, which preserve its *isnād*, this *ḥadīth* was narrated by Ibn 'Abbās. See al-Ṭaḥāwi, *Sharḥ Ma'ānī al-Āthār*, 3: 258; Ibn Ḥajar, *Taghlīq al-Ta'līq*, 2: 490; Bukhāri, *Saḥīḥ*, 3: 218.; Bayhaqī, *Sunan*, 6: 205; *Irwā' al-Ghalīl*, 5: 106-109.

177 Ramlī, *Nihayat al-Muḥtāj*, 8: 82 and 5: 454; *Mughnī al-Muḥtāj*, 4: 239.

178 *Fatāwā al-Ramlī*, 4: 53-54 in the margins of the *Fatāwā al-Kubrā* of Ibn Ḥajar al-Haythamī; see also *Nihāyat al-Muḥtāj* of Ramlī, 5:454.

179 Rafi'ī, *al-'Azīz Sharḥ al-Wajīz*, 6: 423-424; Nawawī, *Rawḍat al-Ṭālibīn*, 5: 433-434.

180 Abū Ya'lā, *al-Mu'tamad fī Uṣūl al-Dīn*, 267; Ibn Qayyim al-Jawziyya, *Aḥkām Ahl al-Dhimma*, 1: 475-576; Ibn Mufliḥ. *al-Ādāb al-Shar'iyya*, 1: 213.

181 See for example: 'Abd al-Karim Zaydān, *Aḥkām*; Wahbah Zuhaylī, *Āthār al-Ḥarb*; Abū Zahra, *al-'Alāqāt al-Dawliyya*.

182 Sarakhsi, *Sharḥ al-Siyar al-Kabīr*, 5: 2157 and 2165.

183 Ibid., 5: 1857 and 1893; Sarakhsī. *Mabsūṭ*, 10: 88-89 and 97.

184 Najīb Armazāni, *al-Shar' al-Dawlī fī al-Islam*, 50.

185 Abū Zahra, *al-'Alāqāt al-Dawliyya fī al-Islam*, 55; Wahbah Zuḥaylī, *Āthār al-Ḥarb fī al-Islam*, 157-156 and idem, *al-'Alāqāt al-Dawliyya fī al-Islam*, 107-108.

186 Muḥammad al-Dasūqī, *al-Imām Muḥammad ibn Ḥasan wa Atharuhu fī al-Fiqh*, 30; Majid Khadduri, *al-Qānūn al-Dawlī al-Islāmī: Kitāb al-Siyar li l-Shaybānī*, 22-23.

187 Abū Zahra, *al-'Alāqāt al-Dawliyya fī al-Islam*, 57; Wahbah Zuḥaylī, *al-'Alāqāt al-Dawliyya*, 108-109; 'Abd al-Ḥamīd al-Ḥājj, *al-Nuẓum al-Dawliyya fī al-Qānūn wa al-Sharī'a*, 183-184.

188 See Majid Khadduri, *War and Peace in the Law of Islam* (Baltimore: Johns Hopkins Press, 1955); 'Uthmān J. Ḍamīriyya, *Manhaj al-Islam fī al-Ḥarb wa il-Silm*, 58.

189 Shāfi'ī, *al-Umm*, 4: 103-104.

190 Ibid.

191 Māwardī, *al-Aḥkām al-Sulṭāniyya*, 137-138.

192 Ibid.

193 Abū Ya'lā, *al-Mu'tamad fī Uṣūl al-Dīn*, 276.

194 See for example the literature advocating reforms produced by modern Muslim thinkers, such as Muhammad Iqbal, *The Reconstruction of Religious Thought in Islam* (Lahore, Pakistan: Sh. Muhammad Ashraf, 1951); Malcolm Kerr, *Islamic Reform: The Political and Legal Theories of Muhammad 'Abduh and Rashīd Riḍā* (Berkeley: University of California Press, 1966).

195 Abū Zahra, *al-'Alāqāt al-Dawliyya fī al-Islam*. Therefore, since the countries of modern world belong to one organization which is the United Nations and all of its members are obligated to its rulings and concluded, Islamic nations are obligated under Qur'ānic injunction to accept and respect any treaties conducted with the United Nations members. According to other modern scholars, members of the United Nations are to be counted among *dār al-ḥarb* rather *dār al-'ahd*, 57; Wahbah Zuḥaylī, *al-'Alāqāt al-Dawliyya*, 108-109; 'Abd al-Ḥamīd al-Ḥājj, *al-Nuẓum al-Dawliyya fī al-Qānūn wa il-Sharī'a*, 183-184.

196 Halil Inalcik, "Dār al-'Ahd," *The Encyclopaedia of Islam*, new edition 2, (Leiden: E. J. Brill, 1965) 116; Majid Khadduri, *War and Peace in the Law of Islam*, Idem, *Islamic Law of Nations*; Hans Kruse, "Al-Shaybāni on International Instruments," *Journal of Pakistan Historical Society* (1953) 90-100.

197 Ghunaymī, *Qānūn al-Salām fī al-Islām*, 104.

198 'Abdallāh Ibrahīm al-Ṭarīqī, *al-Isti'āna bi ghayr al-Muslimīn fī al-Fiqh al-Islāmi*, 26.

199 Q. 60: 8.

200 Ghunaymī, *Qānūn al-Salām fī al-Islam*, 104; al-Ṭarīqī, *al-Isti'āna bi ghayr al-Muslimīn fī al-Fiqh al-Islāmī*, 26; Nādiya Maḥmūd Muṣṭafā, *al-Muqaddima al-'Āmma li-Mashrū' al-'Alāqāt al-Dawliyya*, 160.

201 Sarakhsī, *Sharḥ al-Siyar al-Kabīr*, 1: 75-76.

202 Ibid.

203 Khawārizmī, *Jāmi' al-Masānīd*, 1: 291-292; Zubaydi, *'Uqūd al-Jawāhir al-Munīfa fī Adillat Abī Ḥanīfa*, 1: 195.

204 *Jāmi' al-Masānīd*, 1: 291-292.

205 Sumnawī, *Rawḍat al-Quḍāt wa Ṭarīq al-Najāt*, 3: 1237.

206 Kāsānī, *Badā'i' al-Ṣanā'i'*, 9: 4304-4305; Juwaynī, *Ghiyāth al-Umam fī Iltiyāth al-Ẓulam*, 207.

207 Ibid.

208 Shaybānī, *al-Siyar al-Kabīr*, 1: 76-77 and 198; idem, *al-Jāmi' al-Ṣaghīr*, 248-249; Jaṣṣāṣ, *Aḥkām al-Qur'ān*, 1: 261; Qurṭubī, *Tafsīr al-Qurṭubī*, 16: 273.

209. Shaybānī, *Kitāb al-Siyar*, 222 edited by Majid Khadduri; *Sharḥ al-Siyar al-Kabīr*, 5: 1708.

Chapter Two

Muslim-*Dhimmī* and Muslim-*Musta'min* Relations

The legal aspects of relations between Muslims and non-Muslims within *dār al-Islām* had important theoretical and practical implication for the ways in which Muslim rulers dealt with their counterparts in the *dār al-ḥarb*, and particularly in regard to the law of international treaties and agreements. In *dār al-Islām* proper, a set of contractual agreements or, in a sense, a treaty, grew out of the need to regulate relations between former or potential combatants in newly conquered territory. This came to be known as the *'aqd al-dhimma* (a covenant of protection by a treaty of surrender to non-Muslims residing within *dār al-Islām*) referring to the covenant agreed to between Muslims and non-Muslims aimed at putting an end to hostilities and establishing civil peace within the borders of *dār al-Islām*. Those covered by the covenant were known as *dhimmīs*. At the same time, a practical arrangement, known as *amān* (pledge of security given to no-Muslims upon entering to *dār al-Islām* for fixed period of time), grew out of the real necessity for non-Muslims from the *dār al-ḥarb* to traverse Muslim territory–an arrangement that resembled in many respects the *'aqd al-dhimma*. Those who came under the protection of an *amān* were known as *musta'mins*. There are many parallels between the status of *dhimmī* and that of *musta'min*, but they are founded on slightly different assumptions and should be discussed separately.

I. Muslim-*Dhimmī* relations

A. Linguistic sense of *dhimma*:

The term *dhimmī* can mean a number of things, but for the purpose of this study it has a specific linguistic and legal significance. The lexical meaning of the term *dhimma* is engagement, undertaking, care as a duty of conscience or obligation, though depending on the circumstances it can signify *'ahd* (covenant), *amān* (temporary safe-conduct), *ḍamān* (liability), *kafāla* (suretyship) or *ḥaqq* (right or claim). In the phrase *ahl al-dhimma*, however, the term specifically designates those who have entered into a specific agreement to pay tribute to *dār al-Islām* in exchange for the safety and security of their wealth and lives. They are given this designation because they enter into an *'aqd* (contract) or *'ahd* with Muslims; therefore, they are also called *ahl al-'aqd wa al-'ahd* "the people of contract and covenant". The *amān* might be a contract of a fixed or open ended time period known as *'aqd al-amān* (pact of safeguard) or *'aqd al-dhimma* (pact of protection).[1]

The term *dhimma* is used in the Qur'ān to denote *'ahd* (covenant), *mīthāq* (pact), *ḥilf* (alliance) or *qarāba* (, affinity or blood relationship).[2] The following verse is an example: "How (can there be such a covenant with them) that when you are overpowered by them, they regard not the ties, either of kinship or of covenant (*dhimma*) with you." (Q. 9:8)

In this verse *dhimma* has the connotation of an *'ahd* (covenant) that stipulates certain obligations on the part of the two parties who have concluded it.[3] There are also Prophetic traditions which refer to *dhimmīs* in the above sense: the text of one *ḥadīth* reads, for instance, *yas'ā bi-dhimmatihim adnāhum* "The lowest of them is included in their pact". [4]

Some medieval jurists simply define *dhimma* as *'ahd*. For example, Fakhr al-Islam al-Bazdawī refers to *dhimma* as a case where a person or *raqabah* (bondsman) is party to a *dhimma* and *'ahd*. Many jurists have used the two terms almost interchangeably.[5]

1. Dhimma a legal term

In legal works, *dhimma* is most often defined as *'ahd* or covenant. For example, Shaybānī refers to *dhimma* as a covenant, whether it be temporary or everlasting.[6] However, Ibn Qayyim al-Jawziyya indicates that the concept of *dhimma* or *'ahd* originally referred to agreements that may be concluded with the *ahl al-dhimma* (people under the protection of Islam), the *ahl al-hudna* (people who have a treaty relationship with Islam) and the *ahl al-amān* (people who are given safe passage in *dār al-Islām*). Later, however, the term *dhimma* came to be associated exclusively with the *ahl al-dhimma*, and specifically with those people who are obligated to pay tribute (*jizya*). The latter have everlasting *dhimma* status in that but they are not eternal their communities have concluded the pact, which is automatically renewed.[7]

After defining the legal term *dhimma*, it is essential now to define *'aqd al-dhimma*. According to Ḥanafī scholars, *'aqd al-dhimma* refers to a particular legal contract, concluded either between two parties, individuals or a community, under certain conditions.[8] Shaybānī defines *'aqd* specifically as the pact that leads to the termination of fighting and the *'aqd al-dhimma* as the *dhimmīs*' acceptance of the precedence of Islamic legal statutes/rulings while continuing to reside in *dār al-Islām*.[9] Al-Kāsānī, in contrast, holds that *'aqd al-dhimma* refers to the termination of fighting between Muslims and non-Muslims as well as the everlasting *amān* that maintains this cessation of hostilities.[10] Al-Ghazālī for his part defines it as a pact enshrining the commitment of non-Muslims to dwell in *dār al-Islam* and the obligation on the part of Muslims to protect and defend them in return for their tribute and peaceful behavior.[11] Ibn Mufliḥ, a Ḥanbalī jurist, defines *'aqd al-dhimma* as the toleration of *dhimmīs*' maintaining their beliefs on the condition of paying a tribute and abiding by their commitment to Islamic rulings.[12]

Modern Muslim scholars define *'aqd al-dhimma* as the pact that is agreed between the Imām or his deputy on one side and the *dhimmīs* or their representatives on the other to terminate fighting on a permanent basis.[13] Furthermore, it is the pact that makes it possible for non-Muslims (among the *ahl al-Kitāb*)[14] to retain the right to maintain a permanent residence in *dār al-Islām* with full protection under the Sharī'a in return for paying tribute and the performance of some contractual and customary obligations.[15] Ghunaymī defines it as an *'aqd* that maintains the conditions of residency of non-Muslims in territories that have been conquered by Muslims. Nevertheless, as far as he sees it, while it provides general and specific rights for non-Muslims it does not require the paying of a tribute. Ghunaymī's opinion is clearly at odds with that of earlier jurists, whom he accuses generally of blind imitation.[16]

2. Definitions of *'aqd al-dhimma*.

The phrase *ahl al-dhimma* is in effect shorthand for *ahl dhimmat rasūl al-Allāh* ("people under the protection of the Prophet"), because the Prophet was the initiator of the first *'aqd al-dhimma* with non-Muslims in order to secure and protect their rights.[17] The phrase was used in contemporary documents, such as in the letters sent by the Prophet to the people of Najrān in the treaty that he concluded with the people of Maqnā.[18]

Classical Muslim jurists generally define *dhimmīs* as non-Muslims who pay tribute to Muslims in return for the protection of their wealth and lives.[19] Ghazālī define *dhimmīs* as male individuals belonging to the People of the Book who are mature, free, sound of mind, capable of fighting and ready to pay *jizya* (tribute).[20] The Ḥanbalī jurist Ibn 'Abd al-Hādī defines the *ahl al-dhimma* as non-Muslims who live under the protection of Muslims while paying tribute.[21]

Among modern scholars who have offered a definition of the term *dhimmī* is Abū Zahra, who says that *dhimmīs* are individuals residing among Muslims who possess the same rights and obligations as the Muslims.[22] Other scholars define the *ahl al-dhimma* as People of the Book who dwell with the Muslims under everlasting protection.[23] The consensus of modern scholars on the definition of *dhimma* can be summed up as non-Muslims residing within *dār al-Islām* perpetually under an *'aqd al-dhimma*.[24]

Most definitions of the *ahl al-dhimma* make it clear that an *'aqd al-dhimma* can only be concluded with the People of the Book, a category of non-Muslim that enjoys a special status in Muslim religious thought/law and are tolerated as *dhimmīs* by Muslim governments.

3. The legality of the'aqd al-dhimma:

The legal basis for the *'aqd al-dhimma* is said to lie in the Qur'ān, the Prophet's traditions (Sunna), the acts of the four rightly-guided caliphs and the consensus of jurists. In the following pages an attempt is made to trace these sources and analyze them one by one. The *'aqd al-dhimma* is mentioned in chapter nine, verse 29 of the Qur'ān

Fight against those who believe not in Allah, nor in the Last Day, nor forbid that which has been forbidden by Allah and His Messenger and those who acknowledge not the religion of truth (i.e. Islam) among the people of the Scripture (Jews and Christians), until they pay the *jizya* with willing submission, and feel themselves subdued. (Q. 9: 29)

This particular verse defines and specifies the relations between Muslims and the People of Book while at the same time illustrating the historical aspects of these relations. Furthermore, it reflects the nature of Islam and its differences with other religions.[25] The chapter was revealed after the conquest of Mecca in the ninth year of Hijra, and it was the last chapter revealed in uninterrupted form,[26] while verse 29 itself was revealed at the time when the Prophet and his companions were asked to prepare for the battle of Tabūk where they would confront the Romans and their allies, including the Christian Arab Ghassanids.[27]

Sunna also defines the *'aqd al-dhimma* as a pact that is concluded in exchange for tribute.[28] At the start of his mission the Prophet would preach in Mecca on the Oneness of God, without reference to fighting, but when he migrated to Medina he was asked to fight in the way of God against the unbelievers and those who waged war against him, making peace only with those who did not fight him. Then, when chapter nine of the Qur'ān was revealed, he was asked to fight all of the Arabs who refused to accept Islam. Of the people who fought, he was ordered to spare those who made a truce with him. He was asked to abide by such truces, although he was not at this enjoined to collect *jizya* from the non-Muslims. Indeed, he fought the Jews several times and won, without imposing *jizya* on them. Later, however, he was asked to fight the People of Book in order to impose Islam and to collect *jizya* from them. Some of them accepted Islam and others chose to pay tribute instead.[29]

A *ḥadīth* report narrated by Sulaymān ibn Barīdah from his father states that whenever the Prophet appointed military commander he advised him as follows:

If you meet with an enemy from the unbelievers, call upon them to do three things. If they comply with these demands then terminate the fight with them.

The first is to invite them to Islam. If they refuse, then ask them to pay jizya (tribute) If they accede to your request, then accept this from them, and if they refuse both, then fight them for the path of God. 30

Most of the *ḥadīths* related to the topic of paying tribute indicate that the Prophet took *jizya* from Zoroastrians, the Christians of Najrān and the Jews of Yemen.[31] The Prophet did not collect the *jizya* from the Jews of Khaybar because the verse regarding the collection of the *jizya* was revealed only after the Prophet had concluded a pact with them.[32] This is an added proof that the Prophet abided by his treaties, for despite the implication of the verse, which ordered the Prophet to collect *jizya* from the People of the Book, he did not abrogate his prior treaty. Thus, a pact of *dhimma* was sacred for Muslims, whether its conditions were seen as derived from Qur'ān or from Prophetic tradition. It had to be honored and enforced according to the conditions negotiated.[33]

According to Ibn Qayyim al-Jawziyya, the Prophet's traditions suggest that he did demand *jizya* from idol worshipers in the Arabian Peninsula. This seems unlikely, for as we have seen, verse 9:29 was revealed at the time of the Battle of Tabūk in the ninth year of *hijra*, at which time the people in the peninsula had accepted Islam and there were no idol worshipers left.[34]

The four rightly guided caliphs carried on the same practices in the early Islamic state, updating and renewing the contracts of protection (*'uqūd al-dhimma*), as Abū Bakr and 'Umar did with the Christian of Najrān.[35] Later, similar agreements were concluded with newly conquered territories by the army's generals. Under the caliphate of Abū Bakr, for instance, Khālid ibn Walīd concluded an *'aqd al-dhimma* and *ṣulḥ* with the people of Ḥira,[36] while under 'Umar, contracts of protection were agreed upon with the inhabitants of Iraq and Syria.[37] Eventually, pacts of this nature were concluded with the people of Iṣfahān, Rayy, Qūmis, Jurjān, Ṭabaristān and Azarbayjān.[38] 'Umar always ordered his generals to invite the enemy to accept Islam. If they refused, they were to be asked to pay *jizya*. If they accepted, they were to be protected and not asked for anything beyond their abilities.[39]

There was a consensus among Muslim jurists of the classical and medieval periods that it is permissible to conclude an *'aqd al-dhimma* and impose *jizya* collectively.[40] The general practice was that, when the Muslims intended to conquer new territories, they had to follow the practice of the Prophet and the Qur'ānic injunction regarding the *'aqd al-dhimma*. As Samarqandī writes, if Muslim forces encountered unbelievers, they had to invite them to Islam first, and if they met with refusal, the unbelievers were to be asked to submit to *jizya*. The last resort of course was to resume warfare.[41]

The purpose of the *'aqd al-dhimma*, according to Muslim scholars, is to avoid confrontation with the People of the Book, to prevent future hostilities and to allow them to practice their own faith. The advantage to Muslims is that, instead of fighting, they are better empowered to spread Islam among the *dhimmīs* and elsewhere. The Muslim obligation, on the other hand, is to treat the *ahl al-dhimma* with respect and understanding while they are living in *dār al-Islām*.[42] Furthermore, Muslims should strive to spread Islam and reduce the desire of non-Muslims to continue living in Muslim territory as well as to gain respect and dignity for Muslims.[43]

According to Shaybānī, an *'aqd al-dhimma* entails asking the people of the *ahl al-ḥarb* to become *ahl al-dhimma* by accepting the laws of Islam and paying *jizya* in exchange for protection of their wealth and their lives. If unbelievers ask the Muslim leader "Imam" to offer Islam to them, he must proceed as though they have asked for an *'aqd al-dhimma*. By complying with Islamic rulings in fulfilling the obligations of *ahl al-dhimma*, they (the unbelievers) may notice the merits of the Sharī'a, which would lead to their accepting Islam. This is considered the best and the most favored method of preaching.[44] Furthermore, al-Jaṣṣāṣ observes that when Muslims ask the *ahl al-dhimma* to pay *jizya*, they do so not because they condone non-Muslims beliefs, but rather as a sort of punishment for the unbelievers' insistence on persisting in their error.[45]

B. The Contractual Basis of the *'aqd al-dhimma*:

According to Ḥanafī jurists, the elements of the *'aqd al-dhimma* are similar to those found in an ordinary contract, i.e., offer and acceptance(*ījāb* and *qubūl*). The majority of scholars see the *'aqd al-dhimma* as composed of a number of features normally found in contracts: 1) *ṣīgha* (form), 2) the parties and 3) the content of the *'aqd*, which is the *jizya*.[46]

1. *Ṣīgha* (Form)

The form (*ṣīgha*) of the *'aqd al-dhimma* may vary, but it broadly consists of two types: contract voluntarily entered into, where the important aspects are the *naṣṣ* (text), and the *dalāla* (intended meaning or signification), or a contract entered into involuntarily by virtue of a dependency (*taba'iyya*) of some sort, such as by conquest or military victory. The voluntary *'aqd al-dhimma* takes on the form of a contract in the classical sense, in which elements such as the verbatim text (*naṣṣ*) and the intended meaning (*dalāla*) are of extreme importance. The text of the contract must be a declaration that reflects the true intention of concluding an *'aqd al-dhimma* and describes its content. Hence the contract may refer to a specific request from a *ḥarbī* or a group of *ḥarbīs* (or their representative) made to an Imām that he or they be allowed to reside in *dār al-Islām* under the provision of an *'aqd al-dhimma*.[47] In such a case, the imam is under obligation to answer a sincere request by accepting it.[48] Furthermore, the contract contains written articles stating clearly whatever was discussed and agreed upon by both parties and their representatives.[49]Shaybānī indicates that it is permissible to comply with the *ḥarbī*'s request to make a pact with him because, when the Prophet was asked to make an pact with the people of Najrān, he accepted and established a truce on the condition that they would pay a yearly tribute.[50]

The indented meaning (*dalāla*) required consists of actions that indicate the acceptance of *jizya* and the obligation to be bound by Islamic legal rulings.[51] This is best illustrated by the case of the *musta'min* (any one who has been given the promise of security or safe-conduct by Muslims), which will be described in great details below. The *musta'min* can demonstrate this intent either of by physical residency within *dār al-Islam* or by purchasing land within *dār al-Islam*. If the *musta'min* decides to live and reside within *dār al-Islam* and yet exceeds the period of time stipulated under the pact, the Imam/ Caliph ruler of the Muslim State will ask him to leave, or if he wishes to stay, he may do so by paying *jizya*. If he leaves after that time period, but before completing one year of residence, he may do so without paying *jizya*, but if he exceeds the one year limit, then the Imam will count him as a *dhimmī*, enforce the *kharāj* (land tax) upon him and prevent him from returning to *dār al-ḥarb*.[52] Shaybānī, states:

If the *musta'min* extends his stay in *dār al-Islām* then the *imam* will ask him to leave by giving him enough time to arrange for his departure, such as a year or less, and he [the Imam] should not place any burden on him which might result in his coming to harm.[53]

This is so because the Imam is obligated to look after the interests of both parties.[54] Thus, if the *ḥarbī* enters *dār al-Islam* through *amān*, he is not allowed to stay more than the specified time limit, unless he decides to stay and pay *jizya*. The reason for this, according to Shaybānī, is that if he were allowed to stay for a longer period, he might cause harm to Muslims by passing information to their enemies.[55] Therefore, he is allowed to stay for a fixed time. Should he violate that time limit, the Imam will then issue him a warning. While giving him enough time to leave, the Imam may warn him by saying that, should the time limit be exceeded, he would be counted among the *ahl al-dhimma*, and will become a *dhimmī*. Because the Imam is supposed to inform him of the conditions, the *ḥarbī* is always fully aware of the consequences.[56]Other Muslim jurists, including Awzā'ī, Shāfi'ī, and some Ḥanbalīs, state that the *musta'min* cannot stay any longer than one full year within *dār al-Islām* without paying the *jizya*. They allow that a *ḥarbī* may stay for four months within *dār al-Islām* without paying this tax, but that if he stays longer he must pay the *jizya*.[57]In the event that a *musta'min* purchases land within *dār al-Islām* and cultivates that land, according to the Ḥanafī jurists the state can impose on him *kharāj* (land tax). He automatically becomes a *dhimmī* and is obligated to pay the *jizya* as well. For by paying the *kharāj*, the *musta'min* demonstrates his intention to stay within *dār al-Islām*, and thus the Islamic legal rulings apply to him, making him a *dhimmī*.[58]

The *'aqd al-dhimma* entered into as a consequence of *taba'iyya* (dependency) occurs, for instance, when the *musta'min* becomes a *dhimmī* through marriage, birth or as a *laqīṭ* (foundling), as well as in the case of one who is a member of a conquered population.

In the case of marriage: if a *musta'mina* (female granted safe passage) or non-Muslim woman dependent on *dhimmī* parents marries within *dār al-Islam* to a Muslim or *musta'min*, she becomes a *dhimmiyya* through marriage and through dependency on her husband.[59] The Islamic legal rulings regarding *ahl al-dhimma* will apply to her. Because the wife depends on her husband for her residential status, she cannot leave without his permission, although this does not work the other way around.[60] By agreeing to marry a man living within *dār al-Islām*, she accepts the conditions and legal rulings acknowledge her status as a *dhimmiyya*.[61] However, if a male *must'amin* marries a female *dhimmī*, he does not in turn become a *dhimmī*, because the husband is not dependent on his wife for his residential status.[62] He may, for instance, divorce her and return to his own country, should he not wish to stay in *dār al-Islām*. Therefore, his wife's status does not make him a *dhimmī*.[63]

In the case of birth: Young children may become *dhimmīs* through either parent. As Shaybānī indicates, if a *musta'min* enters *dār al-Islām* with his children, then accepts Islam, the young children will become Muslim through their parents' conversion, while the older ones would have the choice of staying in *dār al-Islām* or returning to *dār al-ḥarb*. This is because they are mature and independent, unlike the younger ones and can make their own decision.[64]

The case of the *laqīṭ* (foundling):[65]If the *laqīṭ* is found within *dār al-Islām*, he will be considered a Muslim, but only if he is fostered by Muslims. In the case where he is fostered by a *dhimmī*, then he will be considered part of the *ahl al-dhimma*.[66] According to Ibn Mundhir al-Naysābūrī (d. 319/931), there was consensus among Muslim jurists and scholars that, if an infant was found living within Muslim territory, he should be considered a Muslim, and if he was found dead he should be buried in a Muslim cemetery. Should the infant be found in some other place, then his status would be determined by the locale where he was found.[67]

The case of *dhimma* status by conquest and victory: In non-Muslim territories that are conquered and come under Muslim authority and where the population is offered and accepts the option of paying the *jizya*, the inhabitants become *dhimmīs*. It is up to the Imam to determine the status of the *ahl al-ḥarb* and their lands. If they qualify as *ahl al-dhimma*, then he will leave the land under their control so long as they pay the *kharāj*, just as the caliph 'Umar did in the lands of Iraq and Syria.[68] Alternatively, the Imam might declare the land to be "booty," a place won by force of arms, and apply the *khums*, as the Prophet did with Khaybar.[69]The Imam therefore will determine the future status of newly conquered territories, deciding whether, if the inhabitants become *ahl dhimma*, he will impose *jizya* and or *kharāj* on their cultivated land, or apply the *khums*.[70] This is the standard Ḥanafite opinion, but it is also shared by Shāfiʿī and Ḥanbalī jurists.[71]

C. The Contractor (*al-'āqid*)

The person who is qualified to conclude an *'aqd* or *'aqd al-dhimma* specifically is the Muslim Imam or his deputy, since part of the Imam's obligation is to look after the interests of the Muslim community and to act as spokesperson on their behalf.[72] He is also responsible for enforcing the rulings of the Sharī'a and regulating the political conduct of Muslims.[73] The *imām* is entrusted with the interests of the community; he is authorized to take any measures for the interest of the community and prevent any occurrence that he deems harmful.[74]

The Imam is the one who issues the authorization for non-Muslims to stay in *dār al-Islam*, where the Islamic legal rulings prevail. According to Muslim jurists, Islam is a system based on a creed; it is a religion and a nationality, one that requires a united understanding and even solidarity, to which the presence of non-Muslims might pose a danger. The *imam* or his deputies have a very onerous responsibility in concluding an *'aqd al-dhimma*, taking into consideration the fact that he is the representative of his community.[75]

According to Shaybānī the Imam is the only one permitted to ask the *musta'min* who has overstayed his welcome in *dār al-Islām* to leave.[76] It is likewise the Imam's responsibility to renew the pact if he should so desire.[77] The Imam's deputies, such as the army commanders, can conclude the pact on behalf of the Imām in some cases. This may occur, for example, if, a general offers acceptance of Islam to the enemy at the time of battle and they accept. Should they reject it, and the general asks them to become *dhimmīs*, then they will be treated as *dhimmīs*.[78] There is a consensus among Muslim jurists regarding the responsibilities and obligations of the Imam in the case of *'aqd al-dhimma*.[79] The consensus of scholars therefore is that no one can conclude the *'aqd al-dhimma* apart from the Imam and his deputies. If any member of the Muslim community tries to do so, this pact is not valid, because ordinary Muslims can only conclude an *'aqd al-amān* (pact of safe conduct).[80]

D. The Contractee (*al-ma'qūd lahu or al-dhimmī*):

Shaybānī demonstrates that the *dhimmī* is the one who is eligible to conclude an *'aqd* or pact in return for a promise to pay *jizya*.[81] For not all non-Muslims were *dhimmī*, some non-Muslims were not even eligible for *dhimma*, such as the Arab polytheists and apostates. The people who are entitled to conclude an *'aqd al-dhimma* were the following.

1. Non-Arab People of the Book:

The term "People of the Book" refers to the Jews and Christians and all the peoples agreeing at least in part with the People of the Book, such as the Samaritans.[82]Furthermore, all of the various Christians sects, such as the Jacobites, Nestorians, Melkites, Roman Catholics and Armenians are referred to in the sources as eligible to conclude an *'aqd al-dhimma*.[83] However, there is disagreement among Muslim scholars over the qualification for the status of Ahl al-Kitāb by groups other than Christians and Jews. According to Ḥanafī jurists, whoever believes in a book of a Prophet, such as the (al-Zabūr) Psalms of David or Suḥuf Ibrāhīm (the Books of Abraham), belongs to the Ahl al-Kitāb. These, however, are not considered Ahl al-Kitāb by Ḥanbali and Shāfi'ī jurists.[84]

2. Zoroastrians (*Majūs*):85

It was believed by classical and medieval Muslims that the Zoroastrians originally possessed a scripture, but that it was taken from them;. Giving the benefit of the doubt in this case, Muslim scholars said the *jizya* was accepted from them. [86] Nor is any objection or prohibition against marrying or eating with the Zoroastrians mentioned in the texts. Nevertheless, according to Muslim jurists, Muslims should take precautions when it comes to marriage with or obtaining food from Zoroastrians.[87] It was however the practice of the Prophet and the rightly guided caliphs to conclude the *'aqd al-dhimma* with Zoroastrians.[88]

While, some Muslim jurists consider Zoroastrians as Ahl al-Kitāb,[89] the majority maintains that they do not belong in this category. The jurists base this opinion on the Qur'ānic verse which reads: "Lest you [pagan Arabs] should say: 'The Book was only sent down to two sects before us (the Jews and the Christians).'" (Q. 6: 156)

They argue that, if the Zoroastrians belonged to the Ahl al-Kitāb, there would have been a reference to three sects in this passage. Hence, they argue that no Muslim jurists can justify that the Zoroastrians were among the people of the Book. Furthermore, the Qur'ān mentions that all the Prophets received a Book that was revealed to them, and there is no mention of a Prophet being sent to Zoroastrians, nor any book, in spite of their numbers and power.[90] All the same, others point to a *ḥadīth* of the Prophet that reads *Sunnū bihim Sunnat Ahl al-Kitāb* ("apply to them [the Zoroastrians] the method of the People of the Book").[91] For them, this is an indication that the Zoroastrians were indeed originally part of Ahl al-Kitāb.

3. The Arab *Ahl al-Kitāb*

According to Shaybānī:

Some of the People of the Book are Arab and they are *ahl al-ḥarb*. If they decide to pay *kharāj* and become *dhimma* it is acceptable. [Shaybānī's opinion is based] on the Prophet's practice when he concluded an *'aqd* with the people of Najrān in return for payment of a thousand *ḥullas* (garments). They were Christian Arabs, and the rulings regarding them [were] applicable to the rest of the non-Muslims.[92]

According to the Mālikī, Shāfi'ī and Ḥanbalī schools, as well as Awzā'ī, Abū Thawr and Ibn al-Mundhir, it was the common practice of Muslims to accept *jizya* from Christian Arabs as well as non-Arab Jews and Christians.[93] Ḥasan al-Baṣrī, however, disagrees with the above-mentioned jurists in this matter. He claims that *jizya* could not be accepted from Arabs because they were honored to be among the kin of the Prophet.[94] Nevertheless it was the practice of the Prophet and his successors to accept *jizya* from the Christian Arabs, making no distinction between them and their non-Arab coreligionists.[95]

4. '*Abādat al-awthān* (idol worshipers)

There is a *ḥadīth* suggesting that the *'aqd al-dhimma* used to be concluded with non-Arab pagans or idol worshipers. It reads: "If you meet with your enemies from the polytheists invite them to the *shahādah* (testimony) that there is no God but Allah…in case they refuse, accept their *jizya*."[96]

This *ḥadīth* would extend *dhimmī* status to all polytheists in general and in particular the Arab polytheists.[97] For if the *jizya* could be accepted from the Zoroastrians, who are not generally recognized as belonging to the Ahl al-Kitāb, then *jizya* must not have been limited to the Ahl al-Kitāb alone, but accepted from all the non-Arabs whether they belonged to the Ahl al-Kitāb or were polytheists. Regardless, the *'aqd al-dhimma* could be concluded with all of them. This was the opinion of many jurists such as Abū Ḥanīfa, Abū Yūsuf, Ḥanbalī, Awzāʿī, Thawrī, Ḥasan al-Baṣrī and Abū 'Ubayd al-Qāsim ibn Salām.[98]

Shāfiʿī and Ibn Ḥanbal, and some Mālikī jurists such as Ibn Mājishūn, were of the opinion that the *'aqd al-dhimma* cannot be concluded with idol worshipers, whether they were Arabs or non-Arabs; nothing can be accepted from them except adoption of Islam or combat. The problem of the Zoroastrians was not a stumbling block for them, as they considered them to belong to Ahl al-Kitāb. Nevertheless, the opinions of the above-mentioned jurists were not in accord with the majority of the scholars.[99]

5. al-*Ṣābi'a*[100]:

The Ṣābi'a were also a subject of disagreement among classical Muslim scholars, because little was known about their true beliefs as a result of their secrecy. For this reason they could not agree on whether to classify them as part of Ahl al-Kitāb. Abū Ḥanīfa, for example, considers them as belonging to the People of the Book, judging them to be a Christian sect from what he could see of their beliefs. However, his disciples Abū Yūsuf and Shaybānī insisted that the Ṣābi'a could not be considered as People of the Book.[101]

Some Muslim scholars divided the Ṣābi'a (which still exists at present time in Iraq and southern Iran) into two groups.[102] The first group was considered to be a Christian sect, even though they differed from Christians in many ways. The second group, known as Ḥarrāniyyūn, were idol worshipers, had no Prophet and did not follow a revealed book. Therefore, the latter were not regarded as belonging to the People of the Book. Al-Jaṣṣās describes them thus:

They are not among the People of the Book, since they worship idols such as the seven planets as god. They are idol worshippers, [though] some consider themselves as a sect of Christianity. Many Muslim jurists cannot find a ground for their claims [to be a sect of Christianity] nor any evidence as to whether *jizya* was accepted from them in the past. Nothing can be accepted from them except for Islam or the sword. Their food cannot be eaten, nor can marriage be allowed with them. For whoever considers them as People of the Book, [however], their food and marriage with them are lawful.[103]

Muslim jurists disagreed over whether to conclude an *'aqd al-dhimma* with the Ṣābi'a sect. Abū Yūsuf is in favor of doing so, just as he is with the Zoroastrians, and is ready to accept *jizya* from them.[104] The same opinion was adopted, on the one hand, by the Mālikī as well as Ḥanbali jurists, i.e., that *jizya* can be accepted from them as it can be accepted from the People of the Book.[105] Shāfiʿī jurists, on the other hand, show a reluctance to accept *jizya* from the

Ṣābi'a. On some occasions they are willing to consider them as a sect of Christianity and accept *jizya* from them, while on others they insist that the matter should be looked at carefully. Wherever and whenever the Ṣābi'a are seen to conform to the requirements and qualifications to pay *jizya*, then it is accepted. But should they fail to meet these requirements the *jizya* cannot be accepted and no *'aqd al-dhimma* with them can be concluded or deemed valid. The Ḥanbalī jurists adopt a similar approach.[106] Ibn Qayyim al-Jawziyya for one favors the Ṣābi'a over the Zoroastrians. He claims that, if the *jizya* can be accepted from the Zoroastrians, then this is indirect sign evidence that *jizya* may be accepted from the Ṣābi'a. In his eyes, the Ṣābi'a sect was less polytheistic than the Zoroastrians.[107]

A survey of the legal literature shows that there are the non-Muslim groups with whom the *'aqd al-dhimma* can generally be concluded. The opinions of jurists varied, with some regarding the *'aqd al-dhimma* with different groups as valid, and others being much more restrictive. This leads to the category of non-Muslims with those whom the *'aqd al-dhimma* could not, generally speaking, be concluded. There is some agreement among jurists in the case of with whom the *'aqd al-dhimma* cannot be valid. Some jurists, such as Shaybānī, claim that apostates and Arab polytheists cannot be parties to an *'aqd al-dhimma*. The consensus of jurists regarding apostates was clear on the idea that an *'aqd al-dhimma* with them cannot be concluded and that, consequently, *jizya* cannot be accepted from them. On the other hand, they do disagree over the status of Arab polytheists. The following remarks treat the case of the apostates, followed by that of the Arab polytheists.

6. Apostates (*murtaddūn*):[108]

There are several references to the apostate in the Qur'ān and the Prophetic tradition.[109] The Qur'ān states: "You shall be called to fight against a people given a great warfare, then you shall fight them, or shall surrender." (Q. 48: 16)

This particular verse was revealed in regard to the apostates of the Banū Ḥanīfa, at the time when Abū Bakr, the future first caliph, was by them. He fought against them, sparing only *al-murtadda* (female apostates) and the youth.[110] The *ḥadīth* on the other hand reads: *man baddala dīnahu fa' qtulūh*" ("Who ever changes his religion shall be killed").[111] According to this *ḥadīth*, the apostate shall be killed, and since an *'aqd al-dhimma* forbids killing, the status of the *murtadd* (male apostate) clearly disqualifies him from being party to such an agreement. Therefore, it is prohibited to conclude an *'aqd* with him unless he seeks repentance.[112]

Shaybānī states that, if apostates ask to be allowed to pay *jizya* or *kharāj* and thus become *dhimmī*, their request should not be accepted.[113] If a free or male slave apostate is asked to return to Islam and he refuses, he is to be punished according to the *ḥudūd* law. By contrast, a female, whatever her status, cannot be punished or killed for an act of apostasy.[114] Sarakhsī explains in turn that punishment of the apostate is obligatory, and that punishment should not be commuted in lieu of a sum of money. This is because the point of concluding *'aqd al-dhimma* with the *ahl al-ḥarb* is not to acquire money but to ensure that the Islamic legal statutes are observed in the areas of business and interpersonal relations. Therefore, the Islamic legal statutes must be applied in the case of an apostate, while accepting money in exchange for his release from punishment is unacceptable and illegal.[115]

Therefore, there is a consensus among the jurists that *jizya* cannot be accepted from the apostate, nor can an *'aqd al-dhimma* contracted with them. [116] To enter into such a contract would, after all, contradict the punishment prescribed for them, especially since amnesty is granted to the *dhimmī* at the time of concluding a pact. Therefore, it is illegal to conclude a pact with an apostate.[117]

7. Arab idol worshipers (*wathaniyyūn*):

According to Shaybānī, the *'aqd al-dhimma* is not valid with Arab polytheists either. Furthermore, he indicates that if any Arab polytheist were to request *dhimmī* status and promise to pay *kharāj*, his offer should be rejected.[118] Sarakhsī expresses an opinion regarding the Arab polytheists that calls for absolute rejection of both truce and *jizya* with this group. His opinion was derived from the Qur'ānic verse[119] which refers to the status of Arab polytheists.[120] This was also the opinion of Abū Ḥanīfa, Abū Yūsuf and Shaybāni,[121] and one that Mālikī, Shāfi'ī and Ḥanbalī jurists tended to share.[122]

The consensus of jurists is that *jizya* and the *'aqd al-dhimma* are valid for Jews, Christians, Zoroastrians and non-Arab idol worshipers, but not apostates. However, Abū Ḥanīfa and Shaybānī would treat Arab polytheists in the same way as apostates. Abū Yūsuf goes so far as to say that neither *jizya* nor an *'aqd al-dhimma* can be contracted with Arabs at all, whether they are *Kitābī* (People of the Book) or polytheist. Shāfi'ī indicates that *jizya* is offered on the basis of religion, not of kinship; therefore, it can be accepted from the Ahl al-Kitāb whether they be Arabs or non-Arabs. Awzā'ī and Mālik hold that it can be accepted from all polytheists, except the apostate.

Ibn Taymiyya, Ibn al-Qayyim, Shawkānī, and Muqbilī all favor the opinion of Awzā'ī and Mālik, which is that the *'aqd al-dhimma* extends to all polytheists except the apostate. Their opinions were derived from the Qur'ān in the case of the Ahl al-Kitāb and the Zoroastrians, and from the Prophet's Sunna. Since the *jizya* was accepted from the Zoroastrians, who were polytheists, then it may be accepted from all polytheists. There is no particular Qur'ānic injunction or specific ruling in the Sunna denying Arab polytheists the opportunity to make an agreement to pay *jizya* or conclude an *'aqd al-dhimma* with Muslims.[123]

So far the discussion has focused on relations between the *ahl al-dhimma* and Muslims based on contractual relations. This is an example of how Islamic legal rulings are essentially based on contractual foundations. Indeed, the Imam, who is the representative of the Islamic state and party to such contracts, himself owes his status to a contract of sorts, the *'aqd al-bay'a* (pledge of allegiance), which is governed by and subject to the rulings on contract law. Thus, Islamic jurisprudence is fundamentally dependent on contracts in the areas of both domestic and foreign relations. For this reason, usage of the *'aqd al-dhimma* is widespread and prevailing.[124] If the institution of *dhimma* is seen as a contract, then it is subject to the overall rules concerning contracts in general, though with its own special features.[125] The following section discusses the contractual aspects of the *'aqd al-dhimma*.

E. The *'aqd al-dhimma* as a contract

Shaybānī explains that, in the case of the *'aqd al-dhimma*, should a people belonging to the *ahl al-ḥarb* request of the Imam that they be allowed *dhimmi* status, the Imam must accept their request, because the acceptance of *dhimma* under prescribed conditions is obligatory for Muslims.[126] Ṭabarī, in his treatise entitled *Ikhtilāf al-Fuqahā'*, mentions the consensus among Muslim scholars that it is permissible to accept *jizya* and in return grant *dhimmī* status, without resorting to force of any kind. The Imam duty is to conclude the *'aqd al-dhimma* for non-Muslims.[127] After concluding an *'aqd al-dhimma*, it is forbidden for Muslims to declare war on its signatories: this is because the *'aqd al-dhimma* is meant to put an end to the fighting among the parties involved.[128]

We have seen how verse 9: 29 of the Qur'ān emphasizes that *jizya* is obligatory, and how it limits the potential of fighting.[129] The Prophet's tradition and the practice of the rightly guided caliphs regarding the *jizya* were also commonly known,[130] as was the consensus among jurists from all schools regarding the conditions for *jizya* and the *'aqd al-dhimma*.[131] The purpose of the *'aqd al-dhimma* thus goes beyond the acceptance of *jizya*. It is meant above all to end fighting between Muslims and non-Muslims. *Jizya* is merely accepted in return for full protection granted to the *dhimma* by Muslims for their well-being, wealth, and honor. This, however, does not change the most significant element of the *'aqd al-dhimma*, which, as we shall argue in the following pages, is meant to put a stop to fighting.[132]

The *'aqd al-dhimma* furthermore is an everlasting *'aqd*, one that Muslims cannot terminate, since it is incumbent upon them to honor it.[133] Among the basic obligations imposed by Islamic law is faithfulness to and respect for *'uqūd* (pacts) and *'uhūd* (treaties). The provisions of the *'aqd al-dhimma* are a right accorded to *dhimmīs*, not a privilege. The consensus of scholars regarding the *'aqd al-dhimma* is that if the *dhimmī* fulfills what he is obligated to do, then it is forbidden to abrogate this covenant. Furthermore, he should not be bound by any additional obligations outside the concluded covenant.[134]

1. The conditions (*shurūṭ*) of *'aqd al-dhimma*.

According to Shaybānī, in order for an *'aqd al-dhimma* to be valid, certain essential conditions must be taken into consideration. Later jurists generally voice the same opinion as Shaybānī. The *shurūṭ* (conditions) of an *'aqd* of any kind may be divided into *ja'liyya* (negotiated, settled imposed) and *shar'iyya* (legal) conditions, on which its legal validity depends. The legal conditions consist in what the Islamic law itself specifies or demands, while the negotiation conditions are those that are imposed on each other by the parties themselves. The following discussion briefly examines the legal conditions in light of the jurists' interpretations.[135] Some of these conditions are mentioned above, while others are discussed below in a great detail under the heading of the legal rulings of the *'aqd al-dhimma*.

First, the *'aqd al-dhimma* has no time limit. If any period of time is stipulated, then the *'aqd al-dhimma* will not be valid, according to Ḥanafī jurists.[136] Jurists from the Malikī, Shāfi'ī, and Ḥanbalī schools view it is debatable issue whether to conclude such an *'aqd* on a temporary basis, because it is similar to *'aqd al-Islam*. However, according to these jurists it is permissible to decide on a specific time period in which the *'aqd al-dhimma* will be in effect. As long as the time period is clearly specified, then it is permissible, since there is no eternal *'aqd* according to them.[137]

Secondly, the contract/pact must be concluded with people from whom *jizya* may legally be accepted, such as the Ahl al-Kitāb (the People of the Book), i.e., both Arab and non-Arab, Jews and Christians, Zoroastrians, non-Arab idol worshipers, Ṣābi'a, and so on. The pact is valid only insofar as it is concluded with people from the above-mentioned categories, the exceptions being apostates and Arab polytheists.[138]

Thirdly, among the conditions that a pact requires achieving validity is for the person in charge of concluding it to be either the Imam or his deputy. The Imam or his deputy is obliged to guarantee all rights and full protection to the *dhimmīs*.[139] Lastly, the *dhimmī* is obligated to pay the tribute that was agreed upon at the time of concluding the *'aqd*. By paying *jizya*, the *dhimmī* is granted full protection, with the rights provided for under the Sharī'a.[140] In return, *dhimmīs* are exempted from military service on behalf of the Islamic state.

2. *Aḥkām 'aqd al-dhimma*: The rights and obligations of dhimmīs

It is essential before going into any discussion of the *aḥkām* that apply to *dhimmīs* to clarify in the first place the meaning of *ḥukm*. Linguistically, a *ḥukm* (rule, verdict) is the product of *qaḍā'* (judgment), and its intention is the prevention or prohibition of specific acts. According to Muslims jurists, *aḥkām* means here either 1) legal rulings or 2) specific 'rules' 'regulations' or stipulations' that apply to *dhimmīs*. These regulations or stipulations shape the status of *dhimmīs* within the Islamic state, covering both the rights of *dhimmīs* and the obligations of the Islamic state towards them.[141]

3. Status of *dhimmīs*

a. The general maxim or norm:

The general norm respecting the status of *dhimmīs* within the Islamic state is that they are considered as part of the state. Where Islamic law is applicable to them is in the area of worldly affairs; hence they are bound by Islamic rulings in relation to conduct and punishments in terms of business dealings, and so on, because they are among *ahl dār al-Islām* (part of the Islamic state). However, in terms of their religious rituals and practices, such as marriage and divorce, and other things they believe permissible (such as eating pork or drinking alcohol, etc.), they are entitled to engage in these practices in private and are free to act upon them. Muslims must not interfere in their internal affairs.[142] The general rule was best described by the Caliph 'Alī who said: "whoever is among our *dhimma* (in our protection) his blood is the same as ours and his blood money is equal to ours."[143] Based on this, the jurists established a general maxim in dealing with *ahl al-dhimma* in terms of their status and rights, which has been expressed thus: "They (*ahl al-dhimma*) have what we have and whatever is obligatory upon us is equally obligatory upon them as well."[144] The obligations that Muslims have are different from the obligations imposed on the *dhimmīs*; indeed, the responsibilities and obligations vary considerably between the two. Nevertheless, but the interpretation of that general rule stipulates that there is no distinction between the two parties in terms of the understanding of or the content of the *'aqd al-dhimma*. According to Sarakhsī, if they (*dhimmīs*) accept the *'aqd al-dhimma*, then their wealth is secure and their rights are the same as those of Muslims.[145]

Some modern jurists understand/claim that the status of the *dhimmīs* as meaning that they are to treated on an equal footing with the Muslims before the law, but not granted equality within the law. This is because the obligations and rights of Muslims are to some extent specific to them; not all are applicable to the *dhimmīs*.[146] According to Sarakhsī these definitions emerged and originated because the *dhimmīs* are considered among the people of *dār al-Islām* but not entirely so.[147] They are nationals of the Muslim state, but not a component of the Islamic nation, because the "Islamic nation" is based on religious ideals. Although in the constitution of Medina the Prophet described the Jews and Muslims as one nation, some scholars argue that this was intended only in a political sense.[148] For example, Ibn Ḥanbal too refuted the claim that the Jews and Christians are part of the nation of the Prophet, indicating that it is impossible to include since they do not believe in the Prophet.[149]

Disagreement over this issue was not limited to the classical jurists alone; it has continued to be a point of disagreement among modern scholars too. The following discussion examine the differences of opinion between the two camps regarding the status of *dhimmīs*. One camp considers them to be foreign nationals despite their status as part of the national entity of *dār al-Islām*, even though they have rights and obligations imposed on them. The second camp considers them as residents who are Islamic citizens.

b. Dhimmīs as foreign nationals

Prior to the appearance of Islam, the concept of citizenship or nationality was unknown to jurisprudence. With the coming of Islam, the concept of a spiritual brotherhood was introduced under the Islamic creed. There was a spiritual and social correlation in this development. The Islamic nation is composed of Muslims as well as indigenous non-Muslim residents of the state. Muslims are naturally entitled to all of the political rights that the state can offer. Non-Muslims within the state are considered foreigners since they are not members of the Islamic nation. This "nation" is a religiously inspired construct and is not the same as a modern nation state. The connection of non-Muslims to the Islamic state is therefore based on treaty or '*aqd al-dhimma* which entitles them to exercise their rights without any discrimination, deficiency, injustice, tyranny or oppression. This is because the *dhimmī* retains the status of *dhimma*, i.e., someone under the protection of the Prophet, ensuring the preservation of his life, wealth, and honor. None of the above, however, excludes the *dhimmīs* from enjoying Islamic citizenship. Their rights are to some extent equal to any ordinary Muslim. In that they do not need any permission to live or stay for a time period, such as the modern state demands. The person who applies for citizenship must simply meet specific demands to stay and live within that state for a specific time in order to be qualified to obtain citizenship. The only right that the *dhimmī* cannot enjoy, according to the scholars of the first camp, is that of being appointed to the highest ranks of state, such as the leadership of the Islamic community.[150]

c. Dhimmīs *as full members of the Islamic state*

The second group or camp of scholars claims that the *dhimmīs* are given citizenship in the Islamic state because they are considered part of the people of *dār al-Islām.* They are merely obliged to observe Islamic legal rulings in relation to business transactions and can enjoy an unlimited stay in *dār al-Islām.* These scholars claim that the "citizenship" of the *dhimmī* in *dār al-Islām* is granted through the '*aqd al-dhimma* and the desire of the state that *dhimmī* should become a *dhimmī* through *taba'iyya* (dependence or nationality) or *fatḥ* (conquest).[151]

Medieval Muslim jurists did not discuss the question of citizenship per se, since it is really a modern concept. The early Islamic system was rather based on the religious beliefs of its members. Therefore, there is no harm in considering *dhimmīs* as citizens equipped with the rights they exercised in earlier periods of Islamic history. A similar situation may even be seen in some modern states, for example, in that of Argentina, where one of the candidates for the presidency who was originally a Muslim - - Carlos Menem Saul - - converted to Catholicism to be eligible to run for office, as the constitution of Argentina specifies.[152]

The ensuing discussion looks at the rights and obligations of *dhimmīs* within *dār al-Islām.*

4. The rights of *dhimmīs*

The '*aqd al-dhimma* sets out the rights that a *dhimmī* can expect to exercise in the Islamic state, the first of them being the guarantee of the pact and the fulfillment and honoring of the stipulations and conditions agreed upon at the time of its conclusion.

The prophet pact with the people of Najrān represented by 'Amr Ibn Ḥazm, is taken as a model.[153] The assurance of the fulfillment and guardianship of the pact was granted to the people of Najrān throughout the rule of the four rightly guided caliphs.[154] According to Shaybānī, because the Prophet concluded the pact with the people of Najran in this fashion, Muslims ought to fulfill and honor similar pacts in the same way. Whoever violates or neglects such a pact will be committing a sin and an act of injustice.[155] Muslims should fulfill all of the rights and obligations expected of them and provide all necessary assistance and protection, taking care never to omit any article within that truce.

F. The implementation of the *'aqd al-dhimma*:

Shaybānī indicates that the highest rank of loyalty and honor is accorded to pacts toward *ahl al-dhimma*, and that this is evident in the fact that the pacts must be enforced and implemented even should the *dhimmīs* fail to fulfill what they have agreed to. This is the kind of respect for the principles of the *'ahd* held by the Prophet as well as the four rightly guided caliphs.

During the reign of Hārūn al-Rashīd, Shaybānī was asked by the caliph to express his opinion regarding the case of the Christians of Banū Taghlib. The caliph asked Shaybānī to issue a *fatwā* (legal opinion) on the case of the pact that had been concluded between 'Umar ibn al-Khaṭṭāb and the Christians of Banū Taghlib. The pact had stipulated that they not be immersed or baptized, in return for double the alms that they would normally receive as well as the promise to drop the *jizya* imposed on them.[156]The Banū Taghlib, however, violated the pact by choosing to baptize their children. This case was put to Shaybānī, whose *fatwā* concluded that 'Umar had established the pact with them on the basis of a certain condition that they had violated, rendering it null and void. Hārūn al-Rashīd, however, decided to maintain the practice of the early caliphs towards the Banū Taghlib all the same.[157]

Moreover, in 636 during the rule of the second caliph, 'Umar, Abū 'Ubayda (d. 18/639) sought his advice regarding the pact setting out conditions for the people of Syria.[158] 'Umar advised him to ask them for *jizya* and the release of Muslim prisoners, and in turn to prevent Muslim forces from committing any excesses against them, maintain fair conduct and fulfill all of non-Muslims of Syria requests and obligations. Furthermore, he told Abu 'Ubayda to grant the Christians their request to hoist crosses during public festivals.[159] Abū Yūsuf, in his book *Kitāb al-Kharāj*, writes that the Caliph 'Umar ibn al-Khaṭṭāb also recommended to his successors that they look after the interests of the *ahl al-dhimma*, to fulfill and honor their pacts, to protect them, and not to impose heavy burdens on them or demand things that they were unable to provide.[160]

From the above examples of Muslim traditions and practices in the formative period of Islam, it appears that the pacts or contract with the *ahl al-dhimma* was greatly respected and honored. Furthermore, the Qur'ānic verses and the Prophetic traditions in conjunction with the early practice of the caliphs provide a sound theoretical framework for treatment of the *ahl al-dhimma* that lays out their rights and obligations in great detail and prevents their persecution at the hands of the Muslims.[161]

1. Religious freedom and practice:

Shaybānī clearly states that *dhimmīs* are allowed to practice their own faith without any interference from Muslims. There are ample scripture proof texts from the Qur'ān on which Shaybānī has based his judgment: "There is no compulsion in religion. Verily, the right path has become distinct from the wrong path." (Q. 2: 256)

This verse was revealed in conjunction with the rights of Jews in particular and the Ahl al-Kitāb and the Arab polytheists in general.[162] In any event, the *ahl al-dhimma* may never be forced to convert to Islam.[163]

According to classical Muslim jurists, had it been lawful to compel the Ahl al-Kitāb to accept Islam, then the *jizya* would never have been allowed. Since infidelity is one of the most serious offences, it is between the individual and his God.[164] The Prophet sent his envoy to the people of Yemen to inform them that if they adhered to Judaism or Christianity, they would not be asked to change their faith.[165] In the truce concluded with the Christians of Najrān, as mentioned earlier, the Prophet did not demand that its signatories change their religion; rather, he asked them to persevere in it.[166] The four rightly guided caliphs observed the same policy, as we saw earlier, and especially in the case of 'Umar and his Christian slave Asbaq. Asbaq refused to accept Islam, and 'Umar, despite being caliph, never forced him to convert to Islam. In fact, he set him free before his death.[167]

The prohibition against compulsion in religion seems to have been respected to a remarkable degree over the course of time. According to a number of European scholars, the history of the relations of Muslims with the *ahl al-dhimma* testifies that there was no single instance of Muslims systematically forcing non-Muslims to convert to Islam or intervening in their religious practices. Thomas Arnold states that there were never any systematic attempts by the Muslims to impose restrictions upon the *ahl al-dhimma* to force them to change their religion or any organized attempts at some kind of oppression. The present existence of many churches and synagogues the Muslim world, is a testament to general religious tolerance there.[168]

Similarly, Islamic law does not allow Muslims to prevent *dhimmīs* from freely practicing their own religion in their own places of worship, which are considered sacred and inviolable. [169]

The *ahl al-dhimma* are forbidden to sell alcohol and pork publicly, since these products are prohibited by the Islamic religion. However, they are allowed to consume both in their homes and communal gathering-places. Furthermore, they are prevented from committing adultery. According to Shaybānī, relationships with non-Muslims are based on the acts of truce established with them, and these acknowledge mutual respect and agreement for both parties.[170]

During the Holy Week leading up to Easter, Christian *dhimmīs* are allowed to carry crosses in their own neighborhood areas and churches. They are permitted to practice what their religion allows them to. Muslims should not intervene in their personal affairs and conduct, such as in matters of marriage and divorce. *Dhimmīs* are to follow their own religion and Muslims have no right to intervene, since the *ahl al-dhimma* are allowed their own judicial system and are under no obligation to take their cases to Muslim courts.[171] Furthermore, if the wife of a Muslim is a *dhimmī*, he cannot prevent her from drinking alcohol, because it is permissible in her own religion. However he can prevent her from drinking alcohol in the house.[172]

There is disagreement among Muslim jurists over some of the practices of *dhimmīs*. Mālikī scholars say that if the *ahl al-dhimma* openly practice what is permissible to them according to their religion, e.g., consumption of alcohol and pork, and a Muslim complains when they do so, then that Muslim is liable to pay a penalty. [173] This is because Muslims are forbidden to intervene in *dhimmī* affairs such as this, or in business matters, even if these extend to *ribā* (usury).[174]

Shāfiʿī jurists claim that the *ahl al-dhimma* should not produce in public "signs of abomination and infidelity," such as the cross, alcohol, etc., whether or not this condition was imposed upon them at the time of concluding the pact. If they commit these acts, they should be punished and the infraction automatically invalidates the pact. However, Muslims should not intervene in truly private conduct or deny what it is permissible to them. If any Muslim intervenes in the affairs of *dhimmīs*, he should be punished for violating the pact, but he is not liable for any damages, a position that the Malikī school rejects.[175]

Ḥanbalī scholars insist that the *ahl al-dhimma* should be prevented from selling or consuming alcohol and pork in public. If they do so, then any attempt at spilling the alcohol by Muslims is not an offense deserving punishment.[176] Furthermore, the Imam is allowed to apply the *ḥadd* punishment to a *dhimmī* if he commits any act prohibited in his own religion, such as theft or adultery. On the other hand, the Imam is not allowed to prescribe punishments for any action allowed by his faith, such as drinking alcohol or eating pork, as long as it is conducted in private.[177] Furthermore, a Muslim may not prevent his *dhimmī* wife from drinking alcohol or wearing the cross. Furthermore, he may not prevent her from going to church. Awzāʿī too would permit her to go to church if she obtains her husband's permission.[178] The Muslim husband should not force his *dhimmī* wife to perform ritual ablutions either.[179]

2. The right of *dhimmīs* to build ritual places of worship:

According to Shaybānī there are four divergent opinions regarding the right to build structures for *dhimmī* ritual practice. The first opinion insists that it is prohibited in the Arabian Peninsula [180] and the territories that are overwhelmingly Muslim to build any *kanīsa* (church), *bay'a* (synagogue) or *bayt al-nār* (fire temple).[181] The second opinion maintains that in places conquered by Muslims any ritual places existing that predate the conquest should be preserved. According to the third opinion, in places conquered under an *'aqd al-ṣulḥ* (pact of truce), places of worship may or may not be built depending on the content of the conditions concluded by both parties. The fourth and final opinion is that in places where the majority population is *ahl al-dhimma*, the inhabitants should not be prevented from building new places of worship or renovating old ones.[182]

When the Abbasid caliph Hārūn al-Rashīd consulted Abu Yūsuf regarding the ritual places of worship of *ahl al-dhimma*, he asked why they had resumed their function after the Islamic conquest and had not been demolished, and whether *dhimmīs* are permitted to bring out their crosses during their feasts. Abū Yūsuf replied that if the (truce) pact of peace concluded between Muslims and the *ahl al-dhimma* stipulating payment of the *jizya* prevented the demolishing of any places of worship in the conquered lands and allowed the Christians to bring out their crosses during their feasts, then the agreed upon conditions could not be violated, which explained why these structures must not be demolished.[183] Furthermore, Abū Yūsuf indicated that any new attempt to construct churches outside the conditions of the original pact, should not be forbidden either.

Dhimmī places of worship were kept protected under the rule of the first four caliphs, and this practice established the theoretical framework.[184] The consensus of jurists on the building of places of worship in Muslim territory was that the *ahl al-dhimma* should not build any new such structures in territories freshly conquered by Muslims, or in the Arabian Peninsula.[185] Furthermore, the consensus of jurists was not to prevent the *ahl al-dhimma* from building new places of worship in areas under Muslim control or authority.[186]Mālik, on the one hand indicates that Christians are not permitted to build their churches in Islamic territory unless they have been given permission to do so. Once they are permitted by the government, then Muslims cannot demolish their new churches. For Mālik, as long as there is a written agreement between the *ahl al-dhimma* and Muslims, the latter should treat the *ahl al-dhimma* according to the content of the agreement and its conditions.[187]Shāfi'ī, on the other hand insists that the *ahl al-dhimma* should not build new places of worship within Muslim territories, although any such structures built prior to the Islamic conquest should be left alone and not demolished. In lands conquered by Muslims by force, they should respect whatever conditions were agreed upon in the pact of peace (*'aqd al-ṣulh*).[188] Ibn Ḥanbal too asserts that the *ahl al-dhimma* are not permitted to build new places of worship in any Muslim territory unless there is a condition within the truce of peace that stipulates otherwise. If they are permitted to do so, then they are allowed to build their churches according to the pact.[189]

3. The protection and defense of the *ahl al-dhimma*

The *'aqd al-dhimma* is itself an absolute restraint upon violence against *dhimmīs*. Muslims are not only prevented from intervening in their internal affairs, but, are also obligated to protect them and to defend them from enemies.[190] According to Shaybānī, the Imam is under obligation to defend the *ahl al-dhimma* from any attack, and should they become prisoners of war, the Imam must use all his powers to secure their release.[191]

Furthermore, if Muslims have concluded a pact with the *ahl al-ḥarb* and the latter launch an attack on the *ahl al-dhimma*, the Muslims must break their pact with the *ahl al-ḥarb* in order to protect and defend the *ahl al-dhimma*, since they are part of the *ahl dār al-Islām*. In this specific instance the pact with the *ahl al-dhimma* takes precedence over the pact with the *ahl dār al-ḥarb*.[192] In the event that the *ahl al-ḥarb* propose to renew their pact with Muslims while they have prisoners from among the *ahl al-dhimma*, the Muslims cannot conclude that pact unless they secure the release of all the *ahl al-dhimma* prisoners. This is because the *ahl al-ḥarb*, according to Shaybānī, tend to treat their prisoners harshly. Muslims should not therefore conclude a safe conduct or a pledge with any party that treats their prisoners in this fashion.[193] The practices of the Prophet and the four Rightly Guided Caliphs regarding the protection of the *ahl al-dhimma* are well known, and the truce/peace agreement with the people of Najrān is prime evidence of these practices.[194]

Abū Yūsuf states that if the Muslims are not capable of defending the *ahl al-dhimma* they have to return the entire amount of the *jizya* collected from them, since the purpose of *jizya* is to protect the *dhimmīs* from any foreign attack. An illustration of this can be seen in the practice of Abū 'Ubayda in Syria, who asked all of his deputies to return to the *ahl al-dhimma* what they had collected from them as *jizya* when he had to stage a tactical retreat. Therefore, there exists a consensus among jurists regarding the fulfillment of the condition of protecting and defending *dhimmīs* as long as they have the capability.[195]

Shāfi'ī indicates that the Imam has an obligation to protect fully the *ahl al-dhimma* from any attack, wherever they are. The Imam should prevent the enemies from taking members of the *ahl al-dhimma* prisoner, whether they have written this condition into the *'aqd* or not. In the event that the Imam is not capable of defending them from their enemies, he has to return the *jizya* that was collected from them.[196] Ḥanbali scholars express a similar opinion.[197]

4. The preservation of individual life, honor and wealth

The Qur'ān forbids Muslims to commit any act of aggression against the *ahl al-Kitāb* once they pay the *jizya*.[198] In fact, because fighting against the *ahl al-dhimma* is forbidden in the Qur'ān, it then follows that their preservation is equally important.[199] Among the requirements of the *'aqd al-dhimma* is respect for *dhimmīs* and the prevention of any harassment. According to Shaybānī, if a Muslim kills a *dhimmī* intentionally, then the Muslim will be punished as if he had killed a Muslim.[200] In fact, it is the consensus of Muslim jurists on this issue that the punishment is applicable on an equal basis, i.e., as if a Muslim had killed another Muslim. The family of the person killed should be given the right to demand blood money, and there should be no amnesty without it.[201] However, Shāfi'ī, Mālikī and Ḥanbalī scholars differ from their Ḥanāfī counterparts on this specific issue. They agree that punishment should apply, but not on equal terms, i.e., where the killer must be killed. They agree however, that a sum of blood money must be granted to the murdered person's relatives. The sum varies according to the various groups of *ahl al-dhimma*.[202]

The preservation of an individual is connected with the preservation of his or her honor; therefore, Muslims have no right to assault the honor of the *ahl al-dhimma*. In the case, for instance, that a Muslim commits adultery with a *dhimmī* female within *dār al-Islām*, the full *ḥadd* (punishment) should be inflicted on him.[203] In the event that a Muslim commits adultery outside the realm of *dār al-*

Islām, some scholars are of the opinion that the punishment of adultery is not applicable, since by definition the *ḥudūd* cannot be applied within *dār al-ḥarb*.[204]

Al-Qarāfī explains that the *'aqd al-dhimma* is a contract guaranteeing the rights of *dhimmīs* and obligating Muslims to fulfill these rights. Whoever commits any type of assault on another, whether physical or verbal, or assists in an assault, commits a punishable sin.[205]

The preservation of wealth is also connected with the preservation of an individual and his honor. Islamic legal rulings regarding the preservation of the wealth of the *ahl al-dhimma* are the same as those protecting the wealth of Muslims within *dār al-Islām*.[206] Muslims are prohibited from taking the wealth of *dhimmīs* unjustly or by force.[207] If a Muslim commits such acts and causes any damage or harm to a *dhimmī*'s wealth, he is liable for damages.[208]

The consensus of jurists regarding the preservation of *dhimmī* wealth is that Muslims have an obligation to provide every protection against wrongdoing, harm or damage. Muslims should only earn or benefit from the wealth of the *dhimmī* in a fair and just way. Moreover, Muslims not only should refrain from stealing their wealth, but also protect it from highway robbers and other thieves. Should a Muslim steal from a *dhimmī*, the *ḥadd* punishments must apply, including amputation of the thief's hand and restitution of the property stolen.[209]

In the event that alcohol or pork is stolen, the punishment inflicted on a Muslim will not be amputation of the hand, but simply repayment of the value of what was stolen.[210] The same opinion is expressed by Shāfi'ī and Sufyān al-Thawrī.[211]

5. The protections of *dhimmī* and their rights in social matters

As mentioned above, the *ahl al-dhimma* are seen as part of the *ahl dār al-Islām*[212] and a national sub-category within the greater nation of Islam. The obligation of the Muslim state is to provide to all of its citizens certain basic needs, including a social environment that makes life easier for all. The *ahl al-dhimma* enjoy these advantages as well. According to Muslim jurists, Muslims are obligated to make social contact with *dhimmīs*. The Prophet and his companions were, in practice, open to socializing with non-Muslims, whether they were of the *ahl al-ḥarb* or *dhimmīs*. There is an account of how the Prophet sent five hundred *dinārs* to the people of Mecca at a time of drought, asking that the money to be given to Abū Sufyān and distributed among the poor of the people of Mecca. In most law books as well, there is a special chapter dealing with contacts with non-Muslims.[213]

Abū Yūsuf reports how 'Umar ibn al-Khaṭṭāb, when he noticed an elderly man begging for money, spoke to him and learned that he was a Jew. 'Umar then asked him how he had come to fall so low in life, and was told that he had no choice but to pay *jizya* despite being old and unable to work. 'Umar was very disturbed by the story of the elderly man: he took him to his house, gave him some money and asked the deputy of the *bayt al-māl* (public treasury) to look after the man and other needy people like him. 'Umar stated that, while *jizya* should be collected from the able- bodied young, it was wrong to do so from those of advanced years. This became standard practice with the *ahl al-dhimma*.[214]

Similar decisions were made by the successors of the four Rightly Guided Caliphs. To mention but one example, 'Umar Ibn 'Abd al-'Azīz wrote to his deputy in Baṣra (Irāq), 'Uday ibn Arṭā, and "advised him to look after the *ahl al-dhimma* there, to ascertain the elderly people, the weak and the poor and to give them what they needed from the *bayt al-māl* (public treasury) to enable them to survive and overcome their hardships".[215]

Some scholars saw it as permissible to pay out *zakāh* (alms tax) to *dhimmīs*. This is an extraordinary indication of the extent to which Muslim looked after the needs of the *ahl al-dhimma*. In addition, the Muslims' duty was seen as more than just collecting *jizya*: their prime responsibility in this regard was to look after the *dhimmīs* in times of need. This was the opinion of Zufar, the disciple of Abu Ḥanīfa, and of others as well.[216]

Good will toward *dhimmīs* is a significant aspect of the *'aqd ahl al-dhimma*. Muslims granted the *ahl al-dhimma* privileges and rights such as protection of their wealth, honor and lives. Muslims felt obliged to treat them with fairness and to be kind to them in both social and material aspects, despite their dissent from the Islamic religion.[217]

6. The rights of *ahl al-dhimma* to reside in and move freely within *dār al-Islām*

Since the *dhimmī* is considered an integral member of the *ahl dār al-Islām*, he is therefore permitted to reside anywhere he wants and to move freely within its borders. Ibn Ḥazm indicates that there was a consensus on the part of jurists that the *ahl al-dhimma* were free to reside and move as they pleased within *dār al-Islām*, the sole exception being the sacred places of Mecca.[218] There were some disagreements among jurists, however, regarding the places they can and cannot enter. According to Shaybānī, the *ahl al-dhimma* are not permitted to enter and reside in Muslim sacred places, such as the sacred mosque in Mecca.[219] Shaybānī reached his opinion on the basis of the Qur'ānic verse, "Verily the *Mushrikūn* (polytheists) are impure. So let them not come near al-Masjid al-Ḥarām". (Q. 9: 28)

Nor are they allowed to reside in the Muslim cities built by Muslims such as Kufa, Baghdad, Basra and Wāsiṭ.[220] According to Shaybānī, the Prophet evacuated them from Medina, while 'Alī evacuated them from Kūfa. However they are fully permitted to reside in any other places except those specifically off limits.[221] According to a Prophetic *ḥadīth* recorded in the *Muwaṭṭa'* of Mālik, "There cannot be two religions within the Arabian peninsula."[222]

Abū Ḥanīfa and Abū Yūsuf differ from Shaybānī and maintain that it is up to the *dhimmī* to decide for himself where to live and stay. According to both Abū Ḥanīfa and Abū Yūsuf, the *dhimmī* is allowed and permitted to reside in any place of the *dār al-Islam*. The *dhimmī* is also allowed to enter any mosque. The only reason for not permitting the *dhimmī* to enter the sacred mosque in Mecca is because the polytheists used to perform pilgrimage there in the nude prior to the coming of Islam. They are therefore banned forever afterward from visiting the site out of fear that they will repeat that performance.[223]

Mālik indicates that the *ahl al-dhimma* are permitted to reside in all Islamic territories except for certain places in the Arabian peninsula, i.e., Mecca, Medina and Yamāma.[224] They are permitted to pass through as travelers and to stay temporarily, but no longer than three days. This is what the Prophet permitted with respect to the Jews and Zoroastrians, allowing them to stay three nights for marketing and meeting their needs.[225] A similar opinion was adopted by al-Shāfiʿī.[226] Ibn Ḥanbal held that they are allowed to enter the sacred places for trade purposes. However they are not permitted to stay longer than three days. Should a *dhimmī* fall ill, he is allowed to stay until his recovery, or should they not be able to sell their merchandise within three days, they may be allowed to stay longer with the permission of the Imam. Whatever happens, they are not permitted to enter the sacred mosque of Mecca, but they are allowed to enter the sacred mosque of Medina.[227]

Muḥammad Rashīd Riḍā denies in his *Tafsīr al-Manār* of the right of the *ahl al-dhimma* to stay within the limits of the Arabian Peninsula. In his view, Islam clearly sees the peninsula as the birthplace of the faith, and rightfully forbids any non-Muslims from entering the place, just as it is the right of any state to protect its borders from foreign presence. For him, this provision does not contradict any principle of human rights; rather, it reinforces them.[228]

The previous pages have focused on the rights of *dhimmīs* within *dār al-Islām*. The following pages examine instead the obligations of *dhimmīs* towards *dār al-Islām*. Here the discussion will cover specific elements such as the obligation of the *dhimmī* towards the Islamic judicial system, his responsibilities with regard to payment of *jizya* and his position with respect to the *kharāj*.

7. The submission of *dhimmīs* to the Islamic judicial system

The consensus of jurists regarding the mistreatment of a *dhimmī* by a Muslim is that it constitutes a violation of the *'aqd al-dhimma*. Since *dhimmīs* pay *jizya*, they are entitled to just treatment and fair dealing on the basis of the *'aqd* concluded with them. In the case that a *dhimmī* feels that he has been mistreated, he can take his case before an Muslim judge, and the same applies in the case of a Muslim complainant against a *dhimmī*. The judge must look into this case and issue a verdict according to Islamic law.[229]

However, there are some cases of disagreement on the part of jurists regarding the submission of the *ahl al-dhimma* to the Islamic judicial system. The areas where a *dhimmī* is generally seen as subject to Islamic law are *mu'āmalāt* (business transactions), inheritance, and *'uqūd* (contracts). In such instances the *dhimmī* is under an obligation to submit his case before the Islamic judiciary, unless the case involves the selling of alcohol or pork, since this is permitted only to them.[230]

The Prophet prevented the people of Najrān from engaging in *ribā* (usury) with Muslims.[231] In matters of mutual trade or business transactions, Muslims and the *ahl al-dhimma* must comply with the Islamic law as is clearly stated in the Qur'ān: "O you believe, eat not up your property among yourselves unjustly except it be a trade amongst you, by mutual consent."[232]

Regarding the *ḥudūd* (criminal punishments), the Imam must judge *dhimmīs* in accordance with Islamic law, except insofar as the case deals with what is permissible to *dhimmīs* according to their own religion, such as the drinking of alcohol. In such a case the *ḥadd* would apply to a Muslim but not to a *dhimmī*, because it is permitted for him to drink alcohol according to his own religion. The Islamic laws on adultery are applicable to both Muslims and *ahl al-dhimma*, whenever they report such a case to the Imam. This was the practice during the time of the Prophet and the four Rightly Guided Caliphs. With regard to the *ḥudūd*, all those belonging to *dār al-Islām* are treated according to Islamic law without distinction as to the religion to which they belong.[233]

Mālik is of the opinion that, while the *ahl al-dhimma* must appeal to the Islamic judiciary in the case of business transactions, there are cases where it is not an obligatory but a voluntary decision to present their case to a Muslim judge. The judge may then accept or turn down the case. Should he accept to hear it, his verdict must be in accordance with Islamic law. In a case of theft for instance, the *dhimmī*, if found guilty, will have his hand cut off. He is likewise subject to the Islamic legal penalties for murder. However, if he is convicted of adultery, he will not be judged according to Islamic law but rather according to the provisions of his own religion. In cases of inheritance, *dhimmīs* must first seek redress in their own community's court, but in the event that they do not reach a fair settlement, they may prefer to present it before a Muslim judge, who will make then his decision according to Islamic law. Likewise in divorce cases: if a *dhimmī* divorces his wife three times and decides to seek an Islamic ruling, the judge will likewise make his decision based on Islamic law. Again, in any matter not related to the Islamic judicial system, the *dhimmī* is free to pursue the case in a *dhimmī* court; it is a voluntary decision on his part and on the part of the other party involved to seek a decision from a Muslim judge.[234]

Shāfiʿī, on the other hand, indicates that the *ahl al-dhimma* should present their cases before their own courts or judges. For those cases, which they decide to bring before the Muslim judge, it is entirely up to the latter whether or not to accept the case. Should he accept to try it, he must make it clear at the outset that the ruling will be based on Islamic law and that the testimony of the witnesses will be handled in the same way as in a Muslim court. Furthermore, regarding the *ḥudūd*, the ruling must be applicable to both parties and accepted by them.[235]

Ḥanbalī jurists indicate that anu case involving dispute between a Muslim and a *dhimmī* must be presented before the Muslim judge, because it is the obligation of the Muslim state to protect the *dhimmī* from judge injustice or unfairness of treatment by Muslims and vice-versa. In a case involving a dispute among *dhimmīs* that they decide to present before the Muslim judge, the judge is free to accept or reject their case, and the verdict will be derived from Islamic law in all matters, just as though he were arbitrating in a case between Muslims.[236]

G. *Jizya* (poll tax)

The *jizya*, or the concept behind it, is not an invention of Muslim civilization; it has been the practice of countless other nations to collect a similar tax. With the advent of Islam, the Muslims began to impose *jizya* upon the *ahl al-dhimma*, but for a specific purpose. Moreover, it was collected from those people capable of paying it, and redistributed among the incapable such as the elderly, poor and ill, in accordance with the standards of Islam. This is the type of consideration which overrides the material aspect of collecting the *jizya*, because the incapable were given a share of assistance from the public treasury (*bayt al-māl*).[237]

1. The definition of *Jizya*

Linguistically, *jizya* is the plural of *jazā'*, meaning rewards or recompense for an act.[238] *Jizya*, according to Shaybānī, refers to the *kharāj* of individuals, although *kharāj* can apply to both land and individuals. The common usage of *kharāj* however is in reference to land tax. It is not used for *jizya* unless it is modified limited by as in the term *kharāj al-ra's* (per capita tax).[239]The Ḥanafī jurists define *jizya* as the levy imposed on the *dhimmī*.[240] Moreover, it is the name of whatever is taken from the *ahl al-dhimma* in exchange for the rights and privileges they enjoy under Islam. Its purpose, according to revelation, is to prevent and put an end to fighting.[241] Mālikī jurists define *jizya* as the share of the unbeliever's income that he is obligated to pay for his protection as long as he is living under Islamic law.[242] Shāfi'ī jurists define *jizya* with reference to *'aqd al-dhimma*, and the money payable as determined by the pact. Furthermore, it is used to denote the pact of insurance and compensation granted by the Imam or his deputy in a fixed amount that is collected from the unbelievers every year, with their consent, in return for continuing their residence within *dār al-Islām*.[243] It is the amount of money taken with the consent of the *dhimmīs* residing in *dār al-Islām* in return for protection of their lives, wealth and honors, with the ultimate purpose of putting an end to fighting.[244] The Ḥanbalī jurists define *jizya* as that which is taken from the polytheists for their protection while they reside in *dār al-Islām*.[245]

2. The reason for the obligation of paying *jizya*

The legal basis for *jizya* is the *'aqd al-dhimma*, which makes it possible for non-Muslims to reside within *dār al-Islām* and maintain relations with their hosts. It does not, however, constitute ratification or acceptance of the beliefs of *dhimmīs*. According to Sarakhsī, if the *dhimmī* wants to reside within *dār al-Islām* and insists on keeping his faith, he cannot escape paying the *jizya*. There is an implicit acknowledgment here of the distinction in status between the *dhimmī* and the Muslim in terms of the prestige or esteem enjoyed by the believer. Moreover, the *jizya* is taken in exchange for the aid afforded to *dhimmīs* in maintaining their beliefs. Indeed, whoever belongs to the *ahl dār al-Islām* is obligated to assist and contribute to the protection of the territory. As the *dhimmī* himself cannot fight on behalf of the *dār al-Islām* since he may favor the enemies, particularly if they are his coreligionists, to the detriment of Muslim rule, *jizya* is taken from him as an aid to Muslim soldiers in their efforts to defend the *ahl dār al-Islam* from foreign attack and other enemies.[246]

The amount of *jizya* taken depends on the financial status of the *dhimmī*.[247] Some scholars claim that the collection of *jizya* from the *ahl al-dhimma* is necessary because it is sort of a worldly punishment for being polytheist, which lies at the heart of the dispute with the Muslims. Therefore, *jizya* is given to the Muslim by the *dhimmī* in recognition of the latter's decline in force or power.[248]

3. The conditions necessary for the imposition of *jizya*.

As mentioned above the *jizya* is only collected or taken from capable individuals. It is not taken from the women of the *ahl al-dhimma*, the young, the blind, the handicapped, the insane, the chronically ill, the elderly, the enslaved or the poor. It is taken from their priests, monks, craftsmen, and so on, if they can afford to pay it.[249]

Kāsānī divides the conditions for the necessary imposition of *jizya* into different types. Among these conditions are maturity and manhood, both mentioned the Qur'ān. Individuals capable of paying must also be of good health, since *jizya* is not accepted from ill individuals. Moreover, he states that *jizya* is not being taken from the blind, the elderly and slaves.[250]

The consensus of jurists regarding the conditions of *jizya* is that it should be taken from sound, mature, healthy males, and them alone. Ibn al-Mundhir al-Naysāburī stated in his *Ijmā'* that the jurists have agreed that the *jizya* cannot be taken from the young, women, slaves and those who cannot afford it.[251]

4. The time of the collection of *Jizya*.

Generally, the time of *jizya* collection is at the beginning or end of the year, or at the time of concluding the *'aqd al-dhimma*. According to the three jurists Abū Ḥanīfā, Abū Yūsuf and Shaybānī, *jizya* can be collected every two months.[252] Māliki, Shāfi'ī and Ḥanbalī jurists all state that the *jizya* can or should be collected once every year, basing their opinions on the tradition of the Prophet, who asked the people of Yemen that each mature male pay the *jizya* once every year.[253]

5. Types and Amounts of *Jizya*.

There are two types of *jizya*. The first of these is imposed with the consent of the *dhimmīs* and according to the original treaty with them. Here the amount cannot exceed that which was agreed upon by the two parties. This was the tradition of the Prophet, who concluded an *'aqd al-ṣulḥ* (pact of truce) with the people of Najrān, and also of the Caliph 'Umar Ibn al-Khaṭṭāb, who came to terms with Banū Taghlib. The second type of *jizya* that is determined by any Imam. It is divided into three levels according to the socio-economic classes of *ahl al-dhimma*: the wealthy (48 *dirhams*), those of middle income (40 *dirhams*) and the poor (12 *dirhams*).[254]

The consensus of jurists regarding the valid amounts of *jizya* collected is that it should be 4 *dīnārs* and up. Mālik states that under the second type of *jizya* (that determined by the *imam*), 4 *dīnārs* should be claimed from the *ahl al-dhahab* or gold (wealthy) class 40 *dirhams* from the *ahl al-fiḍḍā* or silver (middle) class, and the rich and the poor treated according to their abilities. Shāfiʿī favored a flat rate of one *dīnār* per person, rich or poor. Yaḥyā ibn Ādam advises that the amount of imposed *jizya* should be gauged according to the abilities of those obliged to pay without limitation. Ibn Ḥanbal states that it is up to the Imam to determine the amount of *jizya*, and that the *dhimmī* is under obligation to pay whatever amount is decided.[255]

6. The cessation of *jizya*:

Payment of *jizya* ceases if the *dhimmī* becomes Muslim before the end of the taxation year, or when the *jizya* was not collected from him in the previous year, or the part he owes of the remaining *jizya*. The *jizya* ceases the minute he becomes a Muslim.[256] In the event that the *dhimmī* dies and leaves some wealth, the *jizya* will not be collected from his estate. Likewise, should the *dhimmī* become ill or blind, or lose his wealth, *jizya* automatically ceases.[257]The consensus of jurists regarding the cessation of *jizya* is that it will cease upon a person's becoming a Muslim. Moreover, it will cease upon the death of a person, and in the case where he has not consented to pay it before the assigned time, then the *jizya* ceases even if he leaves property, since *jizya is* imposed upon the individual alone.[258]

H. *Kharāj* (land tax)

Kharāj is the second material obligation imposed upon the *ahl al-dhimma* by the Islamic state in exchange for protection and other rights mentioned above. Linguistically, *kharāj* signifies revenue and rental premises that can generate revenue. It is used in the Qur'ān as well as in the traditions of the Prophet.[259] As a legal term, *kharāj* refers to items attached to lands that generate revenue, a portion of which is given to the *bayt al-māl* (public treasury) of the state. In practice, however, it is the land tax that is imposed upon the *ahl al-dhimma*.[260] According to Māwardī, *kharāj* is the obligation to pay taxes on the income from land to the Islamic state.[261] The first implementation of *kharāj* in the form of land tax was imposed by the caliph 'Umar ibn al-Khaṭṭāb. He imposed on each arable property a fixed amount (one *dirham* plus a percentage of the value) and on the produce a fixed amount of 10 *dirhams*, but only five *dirhams* on dates.[262]

When lands were conquered by force, the Imam distributed them among Muslims, leaving the land under their control, then imposed the *jizya* upon the non-Muslims and *kharāj* on the land even that under Muslim ownership. In the cases where the land was left in the hands of the original inhabitants under truce, a fixed amount of *kharāj* was imposed upon them, just as the Prophet did with the people of Najrān. Lastly, any lands given by the Imam to *dhimmīs* in return for services was to be considered *kharājī* land.[263]

If the Imam concludes an *'aqd al-dhimma*, the *kharāj* is payable by the *ahl al-dhimma* according to their capabilities; the *kharāj* should not exceed the limit of what they are able to afford.[264] Furthermore, *kharāj* should not be collected more than once every year, no matter how many months of the year the land can be cultivated. Should the land be cultivable and not used by its owner, he is still obligated to pay *kharāj* on that land. Since the owner has no excuse to lease the land untilled except in order to escape the *kharāj*, the Imam has the right to ask him to pay the *kharāj* anyway. If the land is affected by drought or fire, then the *kharāj* will be lifted that year. Thus, *kharāj* is tied to the capacity of the land to generate revenue. The Imam and his deputies should not impose any undue pressure on the *ahl al-dhimma* and should treat them justly with respect to the *kharāj*.[265]

The consensus of jurists regarding the rulings on *kharāj* is that the deputy of the Imam who is in charge of collecting it every year should be kind and just to the people who are paying it. It should be calculated according to a fair standard, which means the amount should not exceed a reasonable percentage of what the land can produce. Ibn Hubayra indicates that no single jurist supports the imposition of *kharāj* at a rate inconsistent with the capacity of the land to produce. All in fact insist that the amount of *kharāj* should benefit the owner, as it is certainly not intended to harm the *ahl al-dhimma*. He adds furthermore that the revenue of *kharāj* should be directed to the public treasury (*bayt al-māl*).[266]

I. *Al-'Ushūr*[267]

'Ushr, (pl. *a'shār* or *'ushūr*), is the tenth or the tithe in Islamic law. It is either a tax levied on lands held in absolute ownership or a tax on commercial goods to be paid by Muslim, *dhimmī*, or *ḥarbī* merchants from non-Muslim countries (*dār al-ḥarb*). It has been regarded as kind of *zakāt* (alms, wealth tax), one of the categories of Islamic worship (*'ibāda*). It is important to note that *zakāt* is not the same thing as charity, *ṣadaqa*, which should be dispensed spontaneously and continually, though *zakāt* is frequently used also in the sense of *ṣadaqa*.[268]

The *'ushr* is the third material obligation imposed upon the *ahl al-dhimma* after *jizya* and *kharāj*. It is calculated at one tenth of the market value of the goods subject to taxation and it is not imposed upon Muslims or *ahl al-dhimma*. It is however imposed on merchants and travelers who fall outside these categories. It is levied by the Imam on the avenues or roads between the territories of Muslims and polytheists, in return for the protection of these latter and their merchandise from robbery.[269]

Two types of *'ushr* are identified by jurists. The first is the *'ushūr al-zakāt* (almsgiving), which amount is taken from Muslims as an alms from their income derived from produce and crops. The second type is the *'ushūr* described above, imposed on polytheist merchants whenever they travel between their own territory and *dār al-Islām*.[270]

'Ushūr was not imposed during the time of the Prophet or that of Caliph Abū Bakr. It was first began to be imposed by the caliph 'Umar ibn al-Khaṭṭāb on foreign merchants when they entered *dār al-Islām*, in response to the taxes imposed by non-Muslims on Muslim merchants, *al-mithl bi 'l-mithl* (quid pro quo). He also took the step of imposing half of the *'ushūr* on the *ahl al-dhimma*.[271]

The *'ushūr* collected from Muslims is used for *zakāt* (almsgiving), to be distributed among the poor and the needy. The *'ushūr* collected from the *ahl al-dhimma* and *ahl al-ḥarb* is treated as *kharāj* and reserved in the public treasury for purposes of defense.[272] Sarakhsī states that Muslims pay a quarter of the *'ushūr*, *dhimmīs* half the amount, and the *ḥarbīs* the full *'ushūr*. We can find no dispute over this issue, which became a subject of consensus.[273]

'Ushūr is imposed upon merchants who enter *dār al-Islām* for trade purposes, and is calculated on the balance of his receipts exceeding a fixed number. The *'ushūr* is taken from free merchants only; slaves and employees need not pay it.[274] The *'ushūr* is furthermore taken from the sales of alcohol but not pork. According to Sarakhsī, this is because alcohol was formerly juice and money derived from the sale of juice is not forbidden, especially at the beginning of the process. Pork, however, is never lawful, from beginning to end. The Imam is responsible for the protection of the sources of alcohol but not those of pork.[275] There is disagreement among jurists regarding what can be taken as *'ushūr*: for instance, Zufar insists that the *'ushūr* can be taken neither from alcohol nor pork.[276] Abū Yūsuf indicates that if the merchant deals in pork alone, *'ushūr* does not apply, but if he sells both alcohol and pork, *'ushūr* is taken from the profits on both.[277]

There are various rules regarding the *'ushūr al-dhimmī*. If the *dhimmī* obtains money and passes through *dār al-Islām* and is asked to pay the *'ushūr* and yet declares that this money does not belong to him or that he has to pay a debt with it, then the *'ushūr* will not apply in his case. Furthermore, if the *dhimmī* enters *dār al-ḥarb* for trade and tells the Imam or his deputy, "I made this money a few months ago" and within the limit of one year, the *'ushūr* does not apply to him. Should the *dhimmī* enter *dār al-ḥarb* and use the money for trade and spend one year there before re-entering *dār al-Islām*, the *'ushūr* is not applied.[278] In case the *dhimmī* engages in trade for three years and is not asked to pay the *'ushūr* and reports this fact in the third year, only the *'ushūr* of the third year will be counted, while that of other two years will be waived.[279] In case the *dhimmī* refuses to report the number of years that he did not pay the *'ushūr*, then he will have to pay the total of all the years that he did not pay it.[280]

Abū Yūsuf, in advising Hārūn al-Rashīd, told him to look after the *ahl al-'ushūr* and to be kind to them, and to ask his deputies to treat them fairly and not to take more than what is needed. In the event that a deputies mistreats *dhimmīs*/tax payers or takes more than he is supposed to, he must be punished and dismissed from his post. Nor should he be too aggressive with his deputies, for if they perform their duties in full, they deserve the generosity of the caliph.[281]

The consensus of jurists regarding the guardianship of *ahl al-'ushūr* makes it clear that *'ushūr* was regarded an obligation of the *ahl al-dhimma*. Mālik for example, states that if a Christian makes a trade in his own territory he is not obligated to pay *'ushūr*. If he should enter *dār al-Islām* as a merchant, he will still not pay *'ushūr* on what he brings with him unless he sells his merchandise. If he cannot sell his merchandise, he will not pay *'ushūr*. Shāfi'ī indicates furthermore that *'ushūr* is to be taken only if the merchants in question have been informed in advance that *'ushūr* will be taken with their consent, but only once a year. Awzā'ī indicates that if the Christian merchant does not manage to sell his merchandise, *'ushūr* will not apply; he will only be obliged to pay the *jizya*. Ibn Ḥanbal, for his part, insists that only half the *'ushūr* should be taken from the *ahl al-dhimma*, including on profits from alcohol and pork sales even if these products are not approved of in Islam.[282]

II.

Muslim *Musta'min* Relations

As we saw above, Islamic law does not limit itself to Muslim - *dhimmī* relations but also regulates the status of foreign nationals who enter *dār al-Islām* under an *amān* (safe conduct) as a *must'amin* (one who has be granted). Before discuss the relationship between the Muslims and the *musta'min*, we must define the term *amān*.

A. The definition of *amān*

There are two kinds of *amān*: one temporary, and the other permanent. The latter is embodied in the *'aqd al-dhimma*, discussed above. The discussion here is devoted to the contract of safe conduct, which in turn is of several kinds. One *'aqd al-amān*, for instance, is the *amān* given to the *ḥarbi* (enemy alien). Another is the *muwāda'a* or *mu'āhada* or *ṣulḥ* meant to end fighting between nations. These two kinds of *amān* will be dealt with at length in the discussion of *mu'āhadāt al-dawliyya* (international treaties). The third kind of *'aqd al-amān* is the pact or contract that is concluded with two or more individuals for the purpose of individual pursuits, such as trade. These individuals are subsequently known as the *musta'minūn*.[283] We attempt in the following pages to define the term *musta'minūn*.

Amān is an Arabic term that has two interrelated senses, the first being *taṣdīq* (attestation, approval) and the second *amāna* (reliability, honesty), as opposed to *khiyāna* (treason, betrayal). Both *taṣdīq* and *amāna* lead to *sukūn al-qalb* (tranquility or calm), and hence both terms refer to the assurance of tranquility or peacefulness. The term *amān* therefore describes the state of the person who is granted the assurance of tranquility as opposed to fear, while *isti'mān* is the act of seeking *amān* and the *musta'min* the person who becomes *mu'amman* (protected).[284]

In their legal definition of the phenomenon, jurists offer a variety of explanations of *amān* and *musta'min* that differ only in the conditions set. For example, according to Ḥanafī jurists, the *musta'min* is the person who enters a territory other than his own under the protection of *amān*, whether he be a Muslim or a *ḥarbī*. This definition of course is not specific as to the homeland or territory, and can apply to both Muslims in foreign territory and foreigners in Muslims territory.[285] The Mālikī jurists defined *amān* as the "removal" or "proscription" of the slavery of the *ḥarbī* at the time of fighting, or at the inception of fighting, when he comes under the Islamic rule/jurisdiction *ḥukm* for a period of time. The *isti'mān* or request for *amān* is the assurance given to the *ḥarbī* that he will be allowed to conduct business.[286] Shāfi'ī jurists defined *amān* as the abandonment of fighting and especially of fighting with the polytheists.[287]The *musta'min*, according to them, is the individual who makes peace through an *'aqd al-jizya, hudna* or *amān*.[288] Lastly, Ḥanbalī jurists define the *musta'min* as the polytheist who is given permission to stay in *dār al-Islām* without the obligation of paying *jizya*.[289]One can conclude that the *musta'minūn* are non-Muslims from the *ḥarbiyyūn* who enter *dār al-Islām* temporarily under safe conduct (*amān*) for the purpose of a specific matter and without being obliged to observe the *aḥkām* al-Islam or the impositions placed on *dhimmīs* in general.

1. The legitimacy of the *'aqd al-amān*:

The legitimacy of the *'aqd al-amān* as a device enabling the *ḥarbī* to move unmolested in *dār al-Islām* is founded on the Qur'ān, the traditions of the Prophet and the deeds and practices of the Companions of the Prophet. It was on the of basis these sources that legal consensus was reached. In the Qur'ān, the sixth verse in chapter nine reads,

And if anyone of the *Mushrikūn* (polytheists, idolaters, pagans, disbeliever's in the Oneness of Allah) seeks your protection, so that may hear the Word of Allah (the Qur'ān), and then escort him to where he can be secure, that is because they are men who know not.[290]

It is interesting to note that the verse preceding this one[291] commands Muslims to fight whoever denies the Oneness of God, yet the verse cited here cautions the Muslim not to do so. The message is that, should polytheists be neighbors of Muslims and request protection, security and safety to hear the Word of God, the Qur'ān, then a Muslim's obligation is to grant him this protection and provide him with the message of Islam. If he should accept this, then well and good; but if even if he does not, the Muslim must ensure his safety until he returns to his own region.[292]

Abū Bakr al-Jaṣṣāṣ's commentary on this verse states that countenances extension of the *amān al-ḥarbī*. The word *istajāraka* (asks to be a neighbor to you) is interpreted by him to mean *ista'manaka* (asks or seeks your pledge of safety). It is prohibited to fight the *ḥarbī* because he might be seeking knowledge of the Islamic religion. In this case, the duty of a Muslim is to educate him and answer his questions and not to pass judgment on him.[293] According to Ibn 'Arabī, in his *Aḥkām al-Qur'ān*, the purpose of this verse is to grant the *ḥarbī amān*, for two reasons: first, to acquire knowledge about the Islamic religion, and second, to put a stop to fighting with him. The word *ajirhu* (grant him safety) places an obligation upon Muslims to grant the *amān*.[294] The verse orders Muslims to convey the Word of God to the polytheists, then to grant them *amān*. According to certain Ḥanafī jurists, it is not necessary that the polytheist should wish to hear the Word of God; rather, the verse is mainly a justification for granting him protection for the purpose of trading and selling merchandise in Muslim markets, and to stay there at least temporarily. Therefore, the duty of the Muslims is to ease the way for him and not prevent him from conducting his business.[295]

According to Ibn Kathīr, the intention behind granting *amān* in the above mentioned verse is to convey the Word of God, but this does not invalidate employing *amān* for another purpose. For him the intent of the verse is to allow *ḥarbī* individuals who are willing to enter *dār al-Islām* for the purpose of trading, negotiating a *ṣulḥ* (truce) or *muhādana* (ceasing of hostilities for a temporary period of time or fixed time), or the like, to do so in all safety if they request *amān* from the Imam or his deputy, they should be granted it until such time as they leave *dār al-Islām* for their own territory.[296]

2. The traditions of the Prophet:

Many traditions refer specifically to protecting the *ḥarbī*. The Companions of the Prophet came to seek answers regarding the status of the *ḥarbī*, asking whether it is permissible to grant him *amān* while he is already in *dār al-Islām* . The Prophet, in reply, encouraged his Companions to grant the *ḥarbī* the *amān*.[297] In the event that one Muslim grants the *ḥarbī* an *amān*, the Prophet indicated that all other Muslims should do so also. This amounts to granting permission to every Muslim to grant *amān*–whether temporary or everlasting.[298]

The consensus of jurists regarding the *amān* for the *ḥarbī* is that, if the *musta'min* requests the *amān* to hear the Word of God, he should be granted that *amān* fully until he returns to his own territory. If a mature, Muslim grants the *amān* to a *ḥarbī* so as to protect him and his wealth and family while he is conducting his affairs within *dār al-Islām*, then the entire community must respect that safe-conduct while being obligated to provide a safe environment to complete his mission.[299]

B. The basis of *amān*:

1. Explicit, or verbal expression:

The *lafẓ* (utterance or declaration) of *amān* consists in a phrase implying the granting of *amān*, although it is not necessary that the *musta'min* should hear the declaration in his own language. Similarly, according to Shaybānī, if Muslims call upon the *ahl al-ḥarb* to grant them *amān*, then they are all musta'mins no matter what the language of the declaration. This is derived from the practice of 'Umar ibn al-Khaṭṭāb, who wrote to the Muslim soldiers in Iraq instructing them to say to their conquered opponents "do not fear or *matarsi*,"[300] and to assure them that they had thus come under *amān*, since God knows all languages.[301] According to 'Izz b. 'Abd al-Salām, the only contract that absolutely requires a set verbal expression that of marriage.[302]

2. Implicit, or non-Verbal expression:

If the Muslim uses a sign of *amān* to the polytheist and the latter does not understand that sign, the *ḥarbī* is still under his protection.[303] Since the sign was made by a Muslim to indicate *amān*, the purpose or consequence of that sign is the *amān*. Muslims, moreover, are prohibited from deceiving the polytheists under *'aqd al-amān*. However, in the event that polytheists try to deceive Muslims under the *'aqd al-amān*, the contract will be void.[304] It was reported that a person came to 'Umar ibn al-Khaṭṭāb and 'Umar asked him to speak. He said "should I speak the speech of the living or the dead? 'Umar chose the former, then ordered that the man be punished. The man asked 'Umar "did your Prophet instruct you to persecute prisoners to whom you have granted *amān*?" 'Umar replied, "when did I grand you the *amān* ?" The man said "the moment you asked me to speak as one living, for the fearful person who is afraid for his life is not alive." Then 'Umar said that he had granted the *amān* and was not aware of it.[305]

3. The writing of the *'aqd al-amān*:

The writing of the contract is the process that reflects its acceptance by the polytheist or *ḥarbī* on the one hand and the Muslim on the other.[306] The writing of the contract must be authentic and original since any fabricated document render the *amān* void.[307] The consensus of scholars regarding the basis for granting the *amān* is agreed that the *'aqd* must contain a declaration of protections such as the words mentioned earlier, i.e., *ajartuka* (I accept you as my neighbor, and *jiwār* also a technical term for a type of protection, it does not simply mean being a neighbor here), *amantuka* (I take you under my protection), *lā takhaf* (do not fear), etc. It should be pointed out that the *'aqd al-amān* can be devised by the individual concerned or by his representatives.[308]

C. The conditions of *'aqd al-amān*:

The conditions on which the *'aqd al-amān* rests include the stipulation that it must be a fully authorized person who issues the contract and that he be a Muslim who has freely chosen to issue that contract for a given period of time. These three conditions - - Islam, free choice and time - -are essential to the validity of an *'aqd al-amān*.

First, Islam is a condition because every Muslim is responsible for upholding the Islamic religion and by extension the Islamic community. This means that any mature Muslim, male or female, free or slave is capable of granting *amān* to a non-Muslim.[309] In the case of the free male Muslim, this may seem obvious, but it is interesting to note that the right extended beyond this class, as demonstrated in the case of free Muslim woman such as Umm Hānī, who granted the *amān* to Ibn Hubayra, in which act the Prophet supported her,[310] and in that of a slave as well. Indeed, it is clear that the primary condition of granting *amān* is that one must be a member of the Islamic community.[311] By contrast, a *dhimmī* is not qualified to grant the *amān* to a *ḥarbī*, because of the condition of being Muslim.[312]

Secondly, it must be voluntary, or given of one's free will and not under duress. For example, if a Muslim prisoner in *dār al-ḥarb* is forced to grant *amān* to a *ḥarbī*, his *amān* is not acceptable because his circumstances do not authorize him to grant the *amān*, in view of the fact that he is under pressure or oppression. If he were to grant *amān* to the *ḥarbī*, it could be that he has done so to avoid ill-treatment at the hands of the *ḥarbī*. This type of *amān* need not be accepted by the Muslim community, although he himself is liable to respect that *amān* personally.[313]

Lastly, there is the time limit of the *'aqd al-amān*. As mentioned above, the *'aqd al-amān* is concluded for a fixed period of time. The *musta'min* is, according to Shaybānī, given up to a year of safe conduct in *dār al-Islām*. This gives the *ḥarbī* enough time to transact his business, whether it is for selling, or buying or trade of merchandise. If he exceeds the one year, the Imam will ask him to leave; otherwise, if he decides to stay, he will have to pay *jizya* and be treated as a *dhimmī*.[314]

Under some circumstances the Imam may forbid Muslims to grant the *amān* to *ḥarbīs*, e.g., in the case of a battle. Since Muslims are obliged to obey the Imam, they must not grant the *ḥarbī* an *amān* without his permission. However, in the event that a Muslim grants the *ḥarbī* an *amān* in spite of the imām's order, the *amān* is still valid, and it becomes the obligation of the Muslim community to respect this *amān*.[315]

The consensus of jurists regarding the conditions for concluding an *'aqd al-amān*, is that any Muslim male, female or slave is authorized to conclude one. They agreed that the insane, minors and *dhimmīs* may not grant *amān*; the *amān* accorded by a prisoner or captive is also invalid.[316]

D. The rights and obligation of the *musta'min*.

The *musta'min* must operate in *dār al-Islām* where he is foreigner and not a resident. Since he is neither encouraged to stay permanently in *dār al-Islām* nor prevented from returning to *dār al-ḥarb* as soon as he complete his mission, he is not obliged to obey the Islamic rulings, since he enters the foreign territory for a specific purpose and will return to his own territory. For example, if he commits any wrongdoing, e.g., adultery, he will not be subject to the Islamic *ḥudūd*. However, he is obliged to respect the legal ruling on transaction and the laws of contract. Upon his request for the *amān* from a Muslim, the latter is expected to provide a safe environment for him. Hence, under *'aqd al-amān* he is authorized to enter *dār al-Islām*, be treated as a *dhimmī* in terms of rights and privileges, including protection and safety of himself, his merchandise and wealth, and observe certain obligations of the *dhimmī*, though not all.[317] In the following, the rights and obligations of the *musta'min* are outlined, but without reference to the differences between individual and group relations.

1. The rights of the *musta'min*

In the first place, a *musta'min* has the right to practice his/her own religion and belief without any compulsion to later on adopt a new religion. The *musta'min* is like the *dhimmī*, as mentioned above, but with an important exception: the *musta'min* did not enter *dār al-Islām* to become a member of the *dhimmī* community, and so he is not obliged to observe Islamic legal rulings as the *dhimmīs* and Muslims are.[318]

Second, the granting of *amān* to *musta'mins* and the obligation of Muslims to protect them is indicated in the *lafẓ* (verbal declaration). Thus, the establishment of *'aqd al-amān* forbids fighting with a *musta'min*, taking him as prisoner or to seizing his wealth.[319] Shaybānī indicates that if a *musta'min* wishes to enter *dār al-Islām* for trade purposes, he should be granted *amān*, because his trade is of benefit to the Muslims.[320]

The Imam is under an obligation to provide a safe environment for the *musta'min* as long as he is within *dār al-Islām*, and he must punish whoever causes any harm to him while under his authority. However, *qiṣāṣ* (punishment or penalty) is applied neither to the *dhimmī* should he kill a *musta'min*, nor to the Muslim. This is because of their inequality in terms of blood value. However, if the *musta'min* kills a *musta'min* while they are in *dār al-Islām*, *qiṣāṣ* does apply and the heir of the persecuted will be compensated. Likewise, if he exceeds his rights in dealing with other *musta'mins*, the *qiṣāṣ* will apply, since they are equal in the eyes of the law.[321]

Certain restrictions are imposed upon both *amān* and the protection afforded to the *musta'min*. The first affects the provisions that he cannot be arrested or punished except for a short time, and the second affects his right to protection. For example, if the *musta'min* enters *dār al-Islām* for the purpose of trade, he is treated with full protection; however, if he enters *dār al-Islām* for the purpose of promoting or creating innovations among Muslims, then the Imam has the right to arrest him until he fixes what he has damaged. The Imam should neither harass nor persecute him, since he is under the *'aqd al-amān*. The purpose of arresting him is to prevent him from continuing to commit such an act and to prevent him from returning to his own territory in order to cause further damage to *dār al-Islām*. At the time of his release, the Imam will compensate him, should he need any help upon his departure to his territory.[322] The agreement is so binding that, should a group of *ḥarbīs* enter *dār al-Islām* under an *'aqd al-amān* and wish to leave *dār al-Islām* to enter another region of *dār al-ḥarb* for the purpose of fighting Muslims, their Muslim hosts cannot prevent them from doing so.[323]

However, the protection normally granted to the *musta'min*, i.e., protection of his life, does not operate when the latter case applies. Thus, if enemies become aware of their purpose and wage a war against them while they are in *dār al-Islām*, the Muslims are not under any obligation to protect him even if they are capable of doing so. The contrast here with the *ahl al-dhimma* is striking: because the *ahl al-dhimma* are considered among *ahl dār al-Islām*, the Imam is obligated to protect them as he protects the Muslims. However, the *musta'min* belongs to *dār al-ḥarb*, and is only present in *dār al-Islām* because of the *'aqd al-amān*. The obligation of the Muslim to prevent any injustice or mistreatment of the *musta'min* is restricted to the *dār al-Islām*.[324]

In event that the *musta'mins* present in *dār al-Islām* under an *'aqd al-amān* for the purpose of trade are subjected to attack from a foreign enemy, Muslims should protect them. Should the *musta'mins* become prisoners of the enemy, then Muslims should try to secure their release, because they were taken prisoners from *dār al-Islām* and under Islamic authority.[325] Similarly if *musta'mins* are granted *amān* by one Muslim and other Muslims arrange an attack on the *musta'mins* and kill them or take their wealth to divide among themselves, the Muslims who committed the attack are obliged to pay the blood money and compensation for the loss and damage.[326]

The consensus of scholars regarding the matter of restricting the obligations of *amān* is that, if the *musta'min* enters *dār al-Islām* under *'aqd al-amān*, he is entitled to all protection and rights, while Muslims are obliged to prevent any harassment or attack on them as well as on their family and wealth. If the *musta'min* decides to leave *dār al-Islām*, the Imam is obligated to escort him and protect him on his way out.[327]

With respect to the preservation of the wealth and honor of the holder of *amān*, the verdict or ruling (*ḥukm*) of the *amān* applies generally; guarding of wealth is the responsibility of the Muslim.[328] If a *ḥarbī* requests the *amān* to cover his return to his territory and a later return to trade, as long as it is within the *'aqd*, the *amān* will be granted to him accordingly.[329] The merchandise being traded should not, however, include any kind of weapon that might be used against Muslims, in case the *ḥarbī* wishes to take it with him to his own territory.[330]

Should any accident befall the *musta'min* within *dār al-Islām*, such as sudden, natural death, the Muslim Imam is under obligation to send an envoy to his family in the *dār al-ḥarb* to come and receive their inheritance.[331]

Another element of the protection of the *musta'min*'s wealth is that if the *ḥarbī* enters *dār al-Islām* for trade purposes through *amān*, the Imam is expected to protect his wealth as well as prevent any robbery or damages occurring to his merchandise. In that case the *musta'min* is treated on an equal footing with the *dhimmī*. Should the *ḥarbī* indicate in the contract that his wealth should remain in *dār al-Islām* while he leaves for his own territory, his personal *amān* will be terminated, but his wealth will remain under the protection of the Imam.[332]

The consensus of jurists is that it is prohibited to sell the *musta'min* any bad merchandise.[333] The *ḥarbī* is free to purchase commodities that cause no threat to Muslims and take them with him to *dār al-ḥarb*. Similarly, as we have seen, his wealth in case of sudden accident belongs to his heirs in *dār al-ḥarb*.[334]

2. The obligations of the *musta'min*:

First, the *musta'min* must show obedience to the Islamic judicial system in relation to matters of trade intercourse and material transactions. For example, the *musta'min* is prohibited from dealing in *ribā* (usury) within *dār al-Islām*. All of his merchandise and transactions are under the supervision of the Islamic system while he is dealing with Muslims. In the event that the *musta'min* requests from the judge that he look into any dispute between him and another *musta'min*, while both are in *dār al-Islām* under an *'aqd amān*, the judge is no under obligation to settle their dispute because the dispute took place while they were in *dār al-ḥarb*, over which he, the judge, has no jurisdiction.[335]

In the case of a dispute between one *ḥarbī* and another, between a *ḥarbī* and a *dhimmī* or between a *ḥarbī* and a Muslim which takes place within *dār al-Islām* under an *'aqd al-amān*, should they take their case or dispute before the judge, the latter will look at their case under the terms of Islamic law. Since the dispute took place within *dār al-Islām*, then they are under the Islamic jurisdiction and Islamic law applies to all.[336]

The consensus of jurists regarding the *ḥarbī*'s obedience to the Islamic judicial system is that, in the event that a dispute takes place between the *ḥarbī* and his own merchants or with Muslim residents, the judge is under obligation to settle their dispute and apply the Islamic legal rulings if and as necessary.[337] The *ḥudūd* punishments will be inflicted on the guilty, though not that prescribed for adultery, (from which the *ḥarbī* is exempt). However, the punishment applies to him for theft, though he is not liable to have his hand chopped off. This is because the *ḥarbī* is not a *dhimmī*, and any *'aqd al-amān* concluded with the *ḥarbī* is not subject to Islamic legal rulings.[338] In the event that a *ḥarbī* kills a Muslim, he will be prosecuted under Islamic law. Should a Muslim oppress a *ḥarbī* or abuse his wealth or honor, he will only be punished by having to compensate the *ḥarbī*. Similarly, if a Muslim commits adultery with a *ḥarbī* woman, the Muslim will be punished, while if a Muslim should steal from a *ḥarbī*, he must compensate the *ḥarbī* and return what he stole from him, although he will not suffer the loss of a hand.[339]

Disagreement among jurists results in some saying that the *ḥudūd* apply in the cases above. Thus, for Abū Ḥanīfa, should a *ḥarbī* commit adultery with a Muslim or *dhimmī* women, the *ḥadd* will not apply to him but to the women alone. Abū Yūsuf contends that the *ḥadd* is not applicable to either, but he states that both should be punished, whereas Shaybāni insists that neither be punished. Abū Yūsuf goes on to say, however, that if the *musta'min* has agreed to obey Islamic legal rulings in terms of mutual trade interactions and the like for the fixed period of the contract, then the *dhimmī*'s obligations towards Islamic legal rulings will apply to him as well. Therefore, the *ḥarbī* is subject, if he commits adultery, murder or theft, to punishment according to the Islamic law. The *ḥarbī* is furthermore prevented from purchasing copies of the Qur'ān or Muslim slaves. However, in terms of drinking alcohol, he is not bound by the Islamic prohibition since it is not forbidden in his own faith. Abū Ḥanīfa and Shaybānī disagree with Abū Yūsuf regarding the punishment of the *ḥarbī*; generally speaking, however, they are in agreement regarding the drinking of alcohol, insisting also that the *ḥarbī* not be punished.[340]

Shāfiʿī agrees with Shaybānī's opinion that if a *ḥarbī* enters *dār al-Islām* under an *'aqd al-amān* and commits a crime, the punishment that applies to him may be either of two kinds. The first is exclusively the domain of the Almighty Creator on the Day of Judgment; nothing can be done there by the Muslim imam. Amnesty may be granted to him; however, he will be warned that if he commits the same act again, termination of the *'aqd al-amān* may result. The second type of punishment is applied in case of murder: if the *ḥarbī* kills someone within *dār al-Islām*, he should be killed in return.[341]

As regards the tax system, i.e., *'ushūr*, the *musta'min* is under obligation to pay this levy on his income from trade in return for protection of his life and wealth while he is within *dār al-Islām*. This is the same treatment that a Muslim can expect upon entering *dār al-ḥarb*, where taxes may be imposed in return for the protection of themselves and their wealth.[342] Thus the imposition of *'ushūr* is regarded as mutual treatment, *al-mithl bi-l-mithl* (quid pro quo). As mentioned above, the payment of *'ushūr*, charged once a year, is not imposed upon women, slaves or children if they enter *dār al-Islām* for trade purposes.[343]

The *musta'min* is obligated to pay *'ushūr* out of revenue from the trade he engaged in while in *dār al-Islām*. It is stated moreover that, even if Muslim merchants enter *dār al-ḥarb* and are charged an amount that is more than the *'ushūr*, Muslims should not treat the *ḥarbī* merchants in the same way, since this is known as (*ghadr al-amān*) betrayal of the contract.[344] Betrayal in Islam is prohibited, just as is failure to respect treaties drawn up according to Islamic principles.[345]

Among the various rulings on the *'ushūr* paid by the *musta'min* is one that states that if a *musta'min* claims that the wealth that he has earned or is carrying is not for trade purposes, or it that is used to pay his debts or belongs to someone else, or pays the *'ushūr* to another Muslim deputy, or claims that the period of time has been less than one year, the *'ushūr* is taken from him all the same. If his claim in the first case is true, then the contract would not have been concluded with him in the first place, since it is for trade purposes. If he is in debt, it is not the *imām*'s responsibility; his debt derives from the *dār al-ḥarb*, and stays there. As for the period of time being less than a year, the *'aqd al-amān* itself states that he cannot stay in *dār al-Islām* for a whole year, otherwise he would be obligated to pay the *jizya*.[346]

In the event that the *ḥarbī* should spend less time in *dār al-Islām* than was specified in the *'aqd al-amān*, and while within *dār al-Islām* he has paid the *'ushūr* and returned to *dār al-ḥarb* and then enters the *dār al-Islām* again, the *'ushūr* is imposed on him again. For with his departure from *dār al-Islām* to his own *dār*, the *'aqd al-amān* is terminated.[347]

The consensus of jurists' opinions regarding the details of payment of the *'ushūr* by the *musta'min* differ slightly between the different schools. Mālikī jurists hold that the *'ushūr* of the *musta'min* is taken but reduced by half, unless there are Muslims in special need, and that it is taken each time a *ḥarbī* enters *dār al-Islām* for trade purposes. Shāfi'ī jurists explain that the *'ushūr* is taken from the *musta'min* as specified in the *'aqd al-amān*, and that it is imposed just as a Muslim merchant entering *dār al-ḥarb* for trade purposes would be obligated to pay according to the conditions of a contract. Ḥanbalī jurists insist that the *'ushūr* should be taken but not out of consideration of mutual treatment, since Islamic principles obligate Muslims to treat others according to scriptural injunctions, not according to the way they have been treated. The *'ushūr* is collected once a year, but should the *musta'min* bring goods that Muslims greatly need, the tax will not be applied.[348]

E. The termination of the *'aqd al-amān*:

Since a major distinction of the *'aqd al-amān* from the *'aqd al-dhimma* is the fact that the former has a time limit and the latter is permanent, the *'aqd al-amān* is naturally void at the end of its period of application. The person who grants an *amān* to the *ḥarbī* should inform him of the time when his departure from *dār al-Islām* is required. If the *ḥarbī* decides to stay longer than the time limit, then he will no longer be treated as a *ḥarbī*, but rather as a *dhimmī*, and will be obligated to pay the *jizya*.[349]

Should the *ḥarbī* not have been informed of the time due for his departure, the imam is obliged to inform him of this date and it is the imam's responsibility to terminate the contract for him with his consent.[350] The *musta'min* is free to terminate his contract in the event he decides to become a Muslim, at which moment he will be treated as a member of the Islamic community, or in the event he decides to become a *dhimmī* and agrees to pay the *jizya* and reside in *dār al-Islām*. In these cases he will be a member of the *dār al-Islām* community with all the pertinent rights and obligations. If, however, the *'aqd al-amān* is violated in one of its conditions, then the contract is void. Also, if the *ḥarbī* declares war upon Muslims and the imam while he is within *dār al-Islām*, then his *'aqd al-amān* will be terminated.[351]

According to Shaybānī there are some deeds that do not terminate *'aqd al-amān*, such as if the *ḥarbī* murders a Muslim mistakenly: in this case the contract will not be subject to termination, but a punishment will certainly apply. Even if the *musta'min* commits espionage for the enemy, or adultery or theft, these acts do not terminate the *'aqd al-amān*, though they may entail punishment.[352]

As soon as the expiration of the contract is due, the imam should not force the *musta'min* to depart from *dār al-Islām* on short notice. He should give him enough time so as not to cause any hardship for the *musta'min*. Should he need extra time to finish his business, the imam is to assign a fixed time for the *must'amin* in order to complete his business.[353]

The imam is under obligation to escort the *musta'min* to his own territory with every protection needed to protect him from highway robbery.[354] As long as he is within the borders of *dār al-Islām*, the imām should provide all necessary protection. Should the *musta'min* need extra money to return to his own territory, due to some offense that he caused while in *dār al-Islām* and for which he suffered imprisonment, the imam is obligated to give him an amount sufficient to cover his expenses until he return there. The money given to the *musta'min* under these circumstances will be taken from the public treasury.[355]

When one compares how previous civilizations acted with regard to the status of the foreigner within the territory, Islam can be seen as quite advanced in its official treatment of aliens. For example, Greeks regarded foreigners as barbarians and slaves, while the Romans maintained a private law governing the relations between Romans and another that governed relations between the indigenous and the foreigners. Those laws did not protect the foreigners; indeed, any foreigner entering Rome could have his wealth seized by any indigenous Roman that caught him first.[356]

Conclusion

The *'aqd al-dhimma*, as well as the definition of the *dhimmī* himself, demonstrates that the Islamic principle of peaceful relations between peoples begins at the heart of the Muslim *umma* itself. Functioning almost like an internal treaty, the contract regulates relations between communities living side by side within *dār al-Islām*, making co-existence possible in spite of fundamentally different legal and social codes. The similarities between the *'aqd al-dhimma* and the international Islamic treaty are striking: both are negotiated by representatives of the respective communities/nations; both are formal agreements setting out conditions to be met on either side; and both are intended to create a peaceful environment that favors development and prosperity.

The over-arching concern to prevent hostilities is shown in the ease with which the *'aqd al-dhimma* could be concluded, both in theory and in practice. To ensure peace during the expansion of Islam, the offer of protected status in exchange for payment of the *jizya* seems almost to have been the preferred approach to non-Muslim communities. While this seems to have been counterproductive to the spread of Islam as a faith, it must be remembered that, while designed to safeguard the religious rights of minorities, the relationship that the *'aqd al-dhimma* entailed served to ensure the spread of Islam by providing an atmosphere of trust and mutual contact.

Yet the contract is far from a casual arrangement: it is a serious undertaking entered into on a permanent basis, and it binds both parties to responsibilities that are far-reaching in their implications. In this respect it was an even more conclusive agreement than an international treaty, which is fixed in duration and assumed to be temporary. By contrast, the contract aims at an ideal, and the strange thing is that this ideal was as often as not achieved in Islamic history.

Although it resembles in many ways the *'aqd al-dhimma* – with which it shares its origin – the *'aqd al-amān* has a different and very practical purpose in that it facilitates contacts between Muslims and non-Muslims lacking *dhimmī* status. It provides for individual non-Muslims from the *dār al-Islām* freely and without prejudice to their lives or property. In this sense it occupies a median position between *'aqd al-dhimma* and the Islamic international treaty. It anticipates some of the elements of the treaty, while at same time it operates at a very personal level: witness the fact that binding *musta'min* status can even be extended, in most cases, by an individual Muslim to an individual non-Muslim. Again, Islamic international law sets forth strict guidelines for the agreement, assigning rights and obligations on both sides. These guidelines are extremely fair, however, and realistic as well. They are designed to facilitate movement and, especially, trade between Muslims and alien non-Muslims. To make such relations possible, the protections offered are considerable and legally binding – in theory at least, Muslims were obliged in some circumstances to wage war against other Muslims should the lives of *musta'min* be endangered. As some scholars have pointed out, Islamic law is unique in the protections offered to aliens.

---

1 al-Azharī, *al-Ẓāhir fī Gharīb Alfāẓ al-Shāfi'ī*. 257; *Mu'jam Maqāyīs al-Lugha*, 2: 345-356; Jawharī, *al-Ṣiḥāḥ*, .5: 1926; Ibn Manẓūr, *Lisān al-'Arab*, 12: 220-223; Fayrūzābādī, *al-Qāmūs al-Muḥīṭ*, 2: 267-268; Jurjānī, *al-Ta'rīfāt*, 143; Kaffawī, *al-Kulliyāt*, 2: 346-347; Munāwī, *al-Tawqīf 'alā Muhimmāt al-Ta'ārīf*, 350; al-Muṭrrizī, *al-Mughrib fī Tartīb al-Mu'rib*, 1: 307-310.

2 See *Tafsīr al-Ṭabarī*, 14: 148; *Tafsīr al-Baghawī*, 4:15, Zamakhsharī, *Tafsīr al-Kashshāf*, 2: 241; Raghib al-Iṣfahānī, *Mufradāt al-Qur'ān*, 262 and Firūzābādī, *Baṣā'ir dhawī al-Tamyīz*, 3: 18.

3 Sarakhsī, *Mabsūṭ*, 10:8; and idem, *Sharḥ al-Siyar al-Kabīr*, 1: 39.

4 Shaybānī, *Aṣl*, 100; Abū Yūsuf, *al-Radd 'alā Siyar al-Awzā'ī*, 59-60; Abū 'Ubayd, *Amwāl*, 215. This same *ḥadīth* states that if a member of a Muslim army grants an enemy *amān*, this *amān* must be respected by all Muslims; no one can violate this pledge of protection.

5 *Kashf al-Asrār 'an Uṣūl al-Bazdawī*, 4: 237- 238. For further reference to the meaning of these terminology please see Sarakhsī, *Uṣūl al-Sarakhsī*, 2: 332-334; Samarqandī, *Mīzān al-Uṣūl*, 742; Nawawī, *Tahdhīb al-Asmā' wa 'l-Lughāt*, 3: 112; Ibn Nujaym, *Fatḥ al-Ghaffār bi-Sharḥ al-Manār*, 3: 80; Qarāfī, *al-Furūq*, 3: 33 and 226-236; Kaffawī, *al-Kulliyāt*, 2: 346-347; Mutarrizī, *al-Mughrib*, 1: 307-310; Thānawī, *Kashshāf Iṣṭilāḥāt al-Funūn*, 2: 324; Jurjānī, *Ta'rifāt*, 143.

6 Sarakhsī, *Sharḥ al-Siyar al-Kabīr*, 1: 252; Kasānī, *Badā'i' al-Ṣanā'i'*, 9: 4318 and 4327.

7 Ibn Qayyim al-Jawziyya, *Aḥkām Ahl al-Dhimma*, 2: 475-476.

8 Tahānawī, *Kashshāf Iṣṭlāḥāṭ al-Funūn*, 2: 953-954; Jaṣṣāṣ, *Aḥkām al-Qur'ān*, 2: 294; *al-Nihāya 'alā al-Hidāya*, 5: 74; Ibn Taymiyya, *Naẓariyyat al-'Aqd*, 18-22.

9 Shaybānī, *Siyar al-Kabīr*, 1: 191.

10 Kāsānī, *Badā'i' al-Ṣanā'i'*, 9: 4311 and 4327.

11 Ghazālī, *Wajīz*, 2: 197; Dusūqī, *Ḥāshiyat al-Dusūqī alā al-Sharḥ al-Kabīr*, 2: 200-201; Ibn Shās, *'Iqd al-Jawāhir al-Thamīnā fī Madhhab A'lām al-Madīna*, 1: 485; Muḥammad 'Alīsh, *Minaḥ al-Jalīl 'alā Mukhtaṣar Khalīl*, 1: 756.

12 Ibn Mufliḥ, *al-Mubdi' Sharḥ al-Muqni'*, 3: 404; Bahūtī, *Kashshāf al-Qinā'*, 3: 103; Raḥibānī, *Maṭālib ūlī al-Nuhā fī Sharḥ Ghāyat al-Muntahā*,, 2: 591.

13 'Abdallāh Muṣṭafā al-Marāghī, *al-Tashrī' al-Islāmī li ghayr al-Muslimīn*, 30.

14 The *Ahl al-Kitāb*, or "People of the Book", are those non-Muslims who possess a recognized scripture (Christians, Jews, etc.) See the following sections for more in depth definitions of their legal identity.

15 Ṣubḥī Maḥmaṣānī, *al-Qānūn wa al-'Alāqāt' al-Dawliyya fī al-Islām*, 101-102.

16 See Muḥammad Ṭal'āt al-Ghunaymī, *Qānūn al-Salām fī al-Islām*, 405, 421, 426-427, 431-432.

17 al-'Aynī, *'Umdat al-Qārī'*, 15: 86.

18 Abū Yūsuf, *al-Kharāj*, 72 and 77; Abu 'Ubayd, *al-Amwāl*, 27; Shaybānī, *Aṣl*, 267, Sarakhsī, *Sharḥ al-Siyar al-Kabīr*, 5: 1783; Muḥammad Ḥamidallāh, *Majmū' al-Wathā'iq al-Siyāsiyya*, 60, 120-121 and 172.

19 al-Azharī, *al-Zāhir fī Gharīb Alfaẓ al-Shāfi'ī*, 375.

20 Ghazalī, *al-Wajīz*, 2: 198.

21 Ibn 'Abd al-Hādī, *al-Durr al-Najī fī Sharḥ Alfāẓ al-Kharqī*, 1: 290.

22 Abū Zahra, *al-'Alāqāt al-Dawliyya fī al-Islām*, 61.

23 Muḥammad Ḥāfiẓ Ghānim, *Mabādi' al-Qānūn al-Dawalī al-'Āmm*, 52.

24 Ḥāmid Sulṭān, *Aḥkām al-Qānūn al-Dawalī fī al-Sharī'a al-Islāmiyya*, 224.

25 Sayyid Quṭb, *Fī Ẓilāl al-Qur'ān*, 3: 1566.

26 Suyūṭī, *al-Durr al-Manthūr*, 4: 119; Scholars agree that this chapter was revealed in the ninth year of *hijras*, but there is disagreement whether it was revealed as a whole or in stages. For example, Sayyid Quṭb indicates that the chapter was revealed in three stages, the first stage before the battle of Tabūk, the second during the preparation for that battle, and the third after the battle. See Sayyid Quṭb, *Fī Ẓilāl al-Qur'ān*, 3: 1564-1565.

27 The Tabūk battle was the last battle in which the Prophet participated. See Suyūṭī, *al-Durr al-Manthūr*, 4: 117; Abu 'Ubayd, *Amwāl*, 29; *Sīrat Ibn Hishām*, 2: 515; Ibn 'Abd al-Barr, *al-Durar fī Ikhtiṣār al-Maghāzī wa 'l-Siyar*, 238.

28 Ibn Qayyim al-Jawziyya, *Zād al-Ma'ād*, 5: 90-91

29 Ibid.; Ibn Ḥazm, *al-Muḥallā*, 7: 349; Abū 'Ubayd, *Amwāl*, 36; Shāfi'ī, *Umm*, 4: 94-95; Bulādhurī, *Futūḥ al-Buldān*, 1: 81.

30 This *ḥadīth* can be found in *Ṣaḥīḥ Muslim* in the chapter on *jihād* and *siyar*, 3: 1357-1368; Shaybāni. *Aṣl*, 93; Sarakhsī, *Sharḥ al-Siyar al-Kabīr*, 1: 38-39; Abū Yūsuf, *Kharāj*, 209-210.

31 Mālik, *Muwaṭṭa'*, 1: 278; Abū 'Ubayd, *Amwāl*, 30-31,36- 37; Abū Yūsuf, *Kharāj*, 140; Balādhurī, *Futūḥ al-Buldān*, 1: 78, 86; Jaṣṣāṣ, *Aḥkām al-Qur'ān*, 3: 93-94;Yaḥyā ibn Ādam, *Kharāj*, 68; Shāfi'ī, *Musnad al-Shāfi'ī*, 2: 129.

32 Baghawī, *Maṣābīḥ al-Sunna*, 3: 115-117; *Ṣaḥīḥ Muslim*, 3: 1387; Ibn Qayyim al-Jawziyya, *Zād al-Ma'ād*, 3: 151-152.

33 Jaṣṣāṣ, *Aḥkām al-Qur'ān*, 1: 142.

34 Ibn Qayyim al-Jawziyya, *Aḥkām Ahl al-Dhimma*, 1: 6-7.

35 Shaybānī, *Siyar*, 268; Abū Yūsuf, *Kharāj*, 85-89; Balādhurī, *Futūḥ al-Buldān*, 1: 77-78.

36 Abū Yūsuf, *Kharāj*, 155-156; Abū 'Ubayd, *Amwāl*, 38 and 43; Muḥammad Ḥamīdallāh, *Majmū'at al-Wathā'iq*, 379-381.

37 Abū Yūsuf, *Kharāj*, 42-45; Balādhurī, *Futūḥ al-Buldān*, 1: 28; Muḥammad Ḥamīdullah, *Majmū'at al-Wathā'iq*, 418, 474 and 487-488.

38 Muḥammad Ḥamīdallāh, *Majmū'at al-Wathā'iq*, 441-446; Balādhurī, *Futūḥ al-Buldān*, 2: 383; Abū 'Ubayd, *Amwāl*, 97-98.

39 Abū Yūsuf, *Kharāj*, 209-210.

40 Ibn Qayyim al-Jawziyya, *Aḥkām Ahl al-Dhimma*, 1: 1-6; Khaṭīb al-Baghdādī, *Mughnī al-Muḥtāj*, 4: 242; Ibn Qudāma, *Mughnī*, 10: 588 Ibn Mufliḥ, *al-Mubdi'*, 3: 405; Ibn Ḥazm, *Marātib al-Ijmā'*, 114; Ṭabarī, *Ikhtilāf al-Fuqahā'*, 199.

41 'Alā' al-Dīn al-Samarqandī, *Tuḥfat al-Fuqahā'*, 3: 500-501; Mawṣilī, *al-Ikhtiyār li-Ta'līl al-Mukhtār*, 4: 187; Simnānī, *Rawḍat al-Quḍāt*, 3: 1237.

42 Abū Yūsuf, *Kharāj*, 134-136; Abū 'Ubayd, *Amwāl*, 53-58; Jaṣṣāṣ, *Aḥkām al-Qur'ān*, 3: 84.

43 Sarakhsī, *Mabsūṭ*, 10: 7 and 77-78; Kāsānī, *Badā'i' al-Ṣanā'i'*, 9: 4229 and 4232; Qarāfī, *Furūq*, 3: 9-11; Khaṭīb al-Baghdādī, *Mughnī al-Muḥtāj*, 4: 233; Subkī, *Fatāwā al-Subkī*, 2: 404.

44 Sarakhsī, *Sharḥ al-Siyar al-Kabīr*, 4: 1529-1530.

45 Jaṣṣāṣ, *Aḥkām al-Qur'ān*, 3: 103.

46 Jurjānī, *Ta'rīfāt*, 149; *al-Kulliyyāt*, 2: 395; *al-Miṣbāḥ al-Munīr*, 1: 237; Nawāwī, *Tahdhīb al-Asmā' wa al-Lughāt*, 3: 126; *'Iqd al-Jawāhir al-Thamīna*, 1: 485.

47 Kāsānī, *Badā'i' al-Ṣanā'i'*, 9: 4327; Bahūtī, *Kashshāf al-Qinā'*, 3: 108; *Mughnī al-Muḥtāj*, 4: 442-443; *Rawḍat al-Ṭālibīn*, 1: 297.

48 Ṭaḥāwī, *Mukhtaṣar al-Ṭaḥāwī*, 283.

49 Kāsānī, *Badā'i' al-Ṣanā'i'*, 4: 814; Ibn Nujaym, *al-Ashbāh wa 'l-Naẓā'ir*, 3343-346; Zarkashī, *al-Manthūr fī al-Qawā'id*, 1: 164-168; Suyūṭī, *al-Ashbāh wa 'l-Naẓā'ir*, 308-316.

50 *al-Siyar al-Kabīr*, 4: 1429-1430.

51 Kasānī, *Badā'i' al-Ṣanā'i'*, 9: 4327.

52 Ṭaḥāwī, *Mukhtaṣar al-Ṭaḥāwī*, 291; *al-Fatāwā al-Hindiyya*, 3: 234-235.

53 *al-Siyar al-Kabīr*, 5: 1867 and 2246-2247; *al-Jāmi' al-Ṣaghīr*, 263.

54 *al-Siyar al-Kabīr*, 5: 2062.

55 Ibid., 5: 1876.

56 Shaybānī, *al-Siyar al-Kabīr*, 5: 2263; Abū Yūsuf, *Kharāj*, 205; Jaṣṣāṣ, *Aḥkām al-Qur'ān*, 3: 84; Sarakhsī, *Mabsūṭ*, 10: 84; Karābīsī, *Furūq*, 1: 336-337; Kāsānī, *Badā'i' al-Ṣanā'i'*, 9: 4328-4329; Ibn Humām, *Fatḥ al-Qadīr*, 4: 351; Zayla'ī, *Tabyīn al-Ḥaqā'iq*, 3: 268; Ibn 'Ābidīn, *Ḥāshiyat Ibn 'Ābidīn*, 4: 168-169.

57 Ibn Jamā'a, *Taḥrīr al-Aḥkām*, 238; *Mughnī al-Muḥtāj*, 4: 243; Māwardī, *Aḥkām al-Sulṭāniyya*, 146; Abū Ya'lā, *Aḥkām al-Sulṭaniyya*, 145; Ibn Qayyim al-Jawziyya, *Aḥkām Ahl al-Dhimma*, 2: 476.

58 Sarakhsī, *Mabsūṭ*, 10: 84; and idem, *Sharḥ al-Siyar al-Kabīr*, 5: 1869 and 2244-2245; *al-Jāmi' al-Ṣaghīr*, 263; *Kitāb al-Siyar*, 159; Ṭabarī, *Ikhtilāf al-Fuqahā'*, 131 and 227; Zayla'ī, *Tabyīn al-Ḥaqā'iq*, 3: 269; Ṭaḥāwī, *Mukhtaṣar al-Ṭaḥāwī*, 291; Kāsānī, *Badā'i' al-Ṣanā'i'*, 9: 4328. *Kharāj* is merely taxation levied on the land at the time of its cultivation.

59 *Mukhtaṣar al-Ṭaḥāwī*, 291; *al-Mabsūṭ*, 10: 84; Kāsānī, *Badā'i' al-Ṣanā'i'*, 9: 4328-4329; Ibn Humām, *Fatḥ al-Qadīr*, 4: 353; Zaylaʿī, *Tabyīn al-Ḥaqā'iq*, 3: 269; *al-Fatāwā al-Hindiyya*, 2: 235

60 Sarakhsī, *Sharḥ al-Siyar al-Kabīr*, 5: 1533-1434 and 1865-1865.

61 Ṭaḥāwī, *Mukhtaṣar Ikhtilāf al-'Ulamā'*, 3: 452.

62 Sarakhsī, *Sharḥ al-Siyar al-Kabīr*, 5: 1533-1434 and 1865-1865.

63 Shaybāni, *Kitāb al-Siyar*, 159; Sarakhsī, *Mabsūṭ*, 10: 84; and idem, *Sharḥ al-Siyar al-Kabir*, 5: 1533-1534 and 1864-1865; Ṭaḥāwī, *Mukhtaṣar al-Ṭaḥāwī*, 291; Kasānī, *Badā'i' al-Ṣanā'i'*, 9: 4328; Zaylaʿī, *Tabyīn al-Ḥaqā'iq*, 3: 269; Ibn Humām, *Fatḥ al-Qadīr*, 4: 353; *al-Fatāwā al-Hindiyya*, 2: 235.

64 Shaybānī, *al-Siyar al-Kabīr*, 5: 1869-1871; Ibn Shās, *'Iqd al-Jawāhir al-Thamīna*, 1: 486; *Mughnī al-Muḥtāj*, 4: 245

65 The *laqīṭ* is an infant found abandoned or one without known parents or guardians. See Jurjānī, *Ta'rīfāt*, 248.

66 See Maydānī, *al-Lubāb Sharḥ al-Kitāb*, 2: 206; Sarakhsī, *Mabsūṭ*, 10: 214-215 and 17: 128-130; Ibn Humām, *Fatḥ al-Qadīr*, 4: 420.

67 Ibn Mundhir al-Naysābūrī, *al-Ijmā'*, 131; Ibn Qudāma, *Mughnī*, 6: 403; Mardāwī, *al-Inṣāf*, 6: 434-435; *Mughnī al-Muḥtāj*, 2: 422-423.

68 Abū Yūsuf, *Kharāj*, 30-34; Abu 'Ubayd, *Amwāl*, 25 and 73; Yaḥya, Ibn Ādam, *Kharāj*, 27

69 Sarakhsī, *Sharḥ al-Siyar al-Kabīr*, 3: 1039, 1536, and 5: 1143; Bukhārī, *Ṣaḥīḥ*, 5: 10 and 15 and 6: 496.

70 Shaybānī, *al-Jāmi' al-Ṣaghīr*, 254; Abū Yūsuf, *Kharāj*, 30-34; Sarakhsī, *Mabsūṭ*, 10: 15 and 23; Ibn Humām, *Fatḥ al-Qadīr*, 4: 303-304 Kasānī, *Badā'i' al-Ṣanā'i'*, 9: 4329. Ibn Qayyim al-Jawziyya, *Aḥkām Ahl al-Dhimma*, 1: 105; Yaḥyā ibn Ādam, *Kharāj*, 45.

71 Yaḥyā ibn Ādam, *Kharāj*, 45; Ibn Qayyim al-Jawziyya, *Aḥkām Ahl al-Dhimma*, 1: 105.

72 Sarakhsī, *Sharḥ al-Siyar al-Kabīr*, 1: 189 and 5: 1955.

73 Ibn Khaldūn, *Muqaddima*, 1: 338; Māwardī, *al-Aḥkām al-Sulṭāniyya*, 5; Juwaynī, *Ghiyāth al-Umam*, 22.

74 Ibn Nujaym, *al-Ashbāh wa 'l-Naẓā'ir*, 123-124; Suyūṭī, *al-Manthūr fī al-Qawā'id*, 121-122; Zarkashī, *Durar al-Ḥukkām Sharḥ Majallat al-Aḥkām*, 1: 51-52; Zarqā, *Sharḥ al-Qawā'id al-Fiqhiyya*, 247-251.

75 Shīrāzī, *al-Muhadhdhab*, 18: 190; Bahūtī, *Kashshāf al-Qinā'*, 3: 108; Maqdisī, *Sharḥ al-Kabīr*, 10: 575; Raḥbānī, *Maṭālib ūlī al-Nuhā*, 2: 592; Ṣubḥī Maḥmaṣanī, *al-Qānūn wa al-'Alāqāt al-Dawliyya fī al-Islām*, 102.

76 Shaybānī, *al-Siyar al-Kabīr*, 5: 1867, *al-Jāmi' al-Ṣaghīr*, 263; Sarakhsī, *Mabsūṭ*, 10:84; Ibn Humām, *Fatḥ al-Qadīr*, 4: 351; *Mukhtaṣar al-Ṭaḥāwī*, 291; *al-Fatāwā al-Hindiyya*, 3: 234-235; Zayalʿī, *Tabyīn al-Ḥaqā'iq*, 2: 276.

77 Sarakhsī, *Sharḥ al-Siyar al-Kabīr*, 5: 2252.

78 Shaybānī, *al-Siyar al-Kabīr*, 5: 2179-2180.

79 Ṭabarī, *Ikhtilāf al-Fuqahā'*, 199 and 208.

80 See Ibn Shāsh, *'Iqd al-Jawāhir al-Thamīna*, 6: 486; *Ḥāshiyat al-Dasūqī 'alā al-Sharḥ al-Kabīr*, 2: 201; Shīrāzī, *al-Muhadhdhab*, 18: 190; Qarāfī, *Furūq*, 3: 23; Ibn al-Murtaḍā, *al-Baḥr al-Zakhkhār*, 6: 447; *al-'Azīz Sharḥ al-Wajīz*, 13: 496-497; *Mughnī al-Muḥtāj*, 4: 234

81 Shaybānī, *Sharḥ al-Siyar al-Kabīr*, 3: 1035-1036.

82 Shāfi'ī, *al-Umm*, 1: 90-92; Ibn Jamā'a, *Taḥrīr al-Aḥkām fī Tadbīr Ahl al-Islām*, 249; Abū Yūsuf, *al-Kharāj*, 122-124; Ibn Qayyim al-Jawziyya, *Aḥkām Ahl al-Dhimma*, 1: 90-92.

83 See for example, Ibn Humām, *Fatḥ al-Qadīr*, 4: 370; Kasānī, *Badā'i' al-Ṣanā'i'*, 9: 4329; *al-Fatāwī al-Hindiyya*, 2: 244-245; *Ḥāshiyat Ibn 'Ābidīn*, 4: 198; Ibn Shāsh, *'Iqd al-Jawāhir al-Thamīna*, 1: 486; Ibn Rushd, *al-Muqaddimāt al-Mumahhidāt*, 1: 375-376; Shāfi'ī, *al-Umm*, 4: 304; Ibn Qudāma, *al-Mughnī*, 10: 558-559; Ibn Mufliḥ, *al-Mubdi'*, 3: 404; *Majmū'at Fatāwā Shaykh al-Islām Ibn Taymiyya*, 28: 356, and 29: 218; Bahūtī, *Kashshāf al-Qinā'*, 3: 108; Ibn Hubayrā, *al-Ifṣāḥ 'an Ma'ānī al-Ṣiḥāḥ*, 1: 292; Sha'rānī, *al-Mīzān al-Kubrā*, 2: 184; Ibn Qayyim al-Jawziyya, *Aḥkām Ahl al-Dhimma*, 1: 1; Ibn Ḥazm, *al-Muḥallā*, 7: 345; Abū Manṣūr al-Baghdādī, *Uṣūl al-Dīn*, 318.

84 Ibn 'Ābidīn, *Durr al-Muntaqā Sharḥ al-Multaqā*, 10: 670; Nawawī, *al-Muhadhdhab*, 18: 170; and idem, *Rawḍat al-Ṭālibīn*, 10: 304; *Mughnī al-Muḥtāj*, 4: 244; Ibn Qudāma, *al-Mughnī*, 10: 559, 564-565; Mirdāwī, *al-Inṣāf*, 4: 217; *Majmū'at Fatāwā Shaykh al-Islām Ibn Taymiyya*, 35: 223-233 and 7: 50 and 56.

85 According to medieval Islamic sources, Zoroastrians worshipped the sun, moon and fire, and believed in two gods, one representing the good and the other the bad, or light and dark. Furthermore, they believe in two principles, the first the intermixture of the light with the dark and the second the salvation of light from the dark. They are many sects such as the Zardoshtiyya, Zarwaiyya and Kiyomorthiyya. For more details see Shahrastānī, *al-Milal wa al-Niḥal*, 245-263; Ibn Ḥazm, *al-Fiṣal fī al-Milal wa 'l-Niḥal*, 1: 86-90; Rāzī, *I'tiqādāt Firaq al-Muslimīn wa al-Mushrikīn*, 86-87; Aḥmad 'Abd al-Ghāfūr 'Aṭṭār, *al-Diyānāt wa 'l-'Aqā'id fī Mukhtalif al-'Uṣūr*, 1: 240.

86 Ibn Humām, *Fatḥ al-Qadīr*, 4: 370-371; Kāsānī, *Badā'i' al-Ṣanā'i'*, 9: 4329; Zayla'ī, *Tabyīn al-Ḥaqā'iq*, 3: 377; Ibn Shāsh, *'Iqd al-Jawāhir*, 1: 486; Ibn Rushd, *al-Muqaddimāt al-Mumahhidāt*, 1: 376; Māwardī, *al-Aḥkām al-Sulṭāniyya*, 143; Nawawī, *Rawḍat al-Ṭālibīn*, 10: 304; Ibn Qudāma, *al-Mughnī*, 10: 599; Ibn Qayyim al-Jawziyya, *Aḥkām Ahl al-Dhimma*, 1:1-2; Mardāwī, *al-Inṣāf*, 4: 217; Bahūtī, *Kashshāf al-Qinā'*, 3: 109; Ibn al-Mundhir, *al-Ijmā'*, 17; Sha'rānī, *al-Mīzān al-Kubrā*, 2: 184; Jaṣṣāṣ, *Aḥkām al-Qur'ān*, 3: 92-93; Ibn Ḥazm, *al-Muḥallā*, 7: 354; Baghdādī, *Uṣūl al-Dīn*, 319.

87 Ibid.

88 Ibn 'Arabī, *Aḥkām al-Qur'ān*, 2: 921; *Tafsīr al-Qurṭubī*, 8: 110; Baghawī, *Sharḥ al-Sunna*, 11: 170.

89 Ṭabarī, *Ikhtilāf al-Fuqahā'*, 203; Khallāl, *Aḥkām Ahl al-Milal*, 298; Ibn Qayyim al-Jawziyya, *Aḥkām Ahl al-Dhimma*, 1: 10; Ibn Qudāma, *al-Mughnī*, 10:559; Abū Yūsuf, *Kharāj*, 140; Shāfi'ī, *Umm*, 4: 96.

---

90 Jaṣṣāṣ, *Aḥkām al-Qur'ān*, 3: 91 and 93; Ibn Qayyim al-Jawziyya, *Aḥkām Ahl al-Dhimma*, 1: 6.

91 Mālik, *Muwaṭṭa'*, 1: 278; Shāfiʿī, *Risāla*, 430; Ṭaḥāwī, *Ikhtilāf al-'Ulamā'*, 3: 485; Shawkānī, *Nayl al-Awṭār*, 8: 64; Ibn 'Abd al-Barr, *al-Tamhīd*, 2: 116; Baghawī, *Tafsīr*, 4: 35.

92 Shaybānī, *al-Jāmi' al-Ṣaghīr*, 248; also see Sarakhsī, *Mabsūṭ*, 10: 118-119; Ibn Humām, *Fatḥ al-Qadīr*, 4: 95-96; Zaylaʿī, *Tabyīn al-Ḥaqā'iq*, 3: 277.

93 Abū 'Ubayd, *Amwāl*, 36; Shāfiʿī, *Umm*, 4: 95-96; Ibn Rushd, *al-Muqaddimāt al-Mumahhidāt*, 1: 375; *al-Mubdi'*, 2: 404; Ibn Qayyim al-Jawziyya, *Aḥkām Ahl al-Dhimma*, 1:3; and idem, *Zād al-Ma'ād*, 3: 155-157; Ibn al-Mundhir, *Mukhtaṣar Ikhtilāf al-'Ulamā'*, 3: 484.

94 According to Ṭaḥāwī that Shāfiʿī was the only jurist to narrate this opinion from Abu Yūsuf. See Ṭabarī, *Ikhtilāf al-Fuqahā'*, 203; Ṭaḥāwī, *Mukhtaṣar Ikhtilāf al-'Ulamā'*, 3: 486; Shāfiʿī, *Umm*, 4: 196; Abū Yūsuf, *Kharāj*, 131.

95 See Ibn Qudāma, *al-Mughnī*, 10: 561-562; Ibn Qayyim al-Jawziyya, *Aḥkām Ahl al-Dhimma*, 1:2-7; Abū 'Ubayd, *Amwāl*, 36-40; Siyāghī, *al-Rawḍ al-Naḍīr*, 4: 641-642.

96 Shaybānī, *Siyar al-Kabīr*, 1: 38-39. *Ṣaḥīḥ Muslim*, "Jihād," 3: 1357.

97 Jaṣṣāṣ, *Aḥkām al-Qur'ān*, 3: 93.

98 Sarakhsī, *Mabsūṭ*, 10: 119; Ibn Humām, *Fatḥ al-Qadīr*, 4: 371; Abū Yūsuf, *Kharāj*, 139; Zaylaʿī, *Tabyīn al-Ḥaqā'iq*, 3: 277; Dāmād Afandī, *Majma' al-Anhur*, 1: 670; Jaṣṣāṣ. *Aḥkām al-Qur'ān*, 3: 91 and 93; Mālik, *Mudawwana*, 3: 46; Abū 'Ubayd, *Amwāl*, 40-41; Ṭabarī, *Ikhtilāf al-Fuqahā'*, 200-203; Ṭaḥāwī, *Mukhtaṣar Ikhtilāf al-'Ulamā'*, 3: 484-485; Sha'rānī, *al-Mīzān al-Kubrā*, 2: 184; Ibn Shāsh, *'Iqd al-Jawāhir al-Thamīna*, 1: 486.

99 Shāfiʿī, *al-Umm*, 4: 95 and 96; Ibn Jamā'a, *Taḥrīr al-Aḥkām*, 249; Ibn Shāsh, *'Iqd al-Jawāhir al-Thamīna*, 1: 486; Ibn 'Arabī, *Aḥkām al-Qur'ān*, 2: 919; Jaṣṣāṣ, *Aḥkām al-Qur'ān*, 3: 91-92; Ṭabarī, *Ikhtilāf al-Fuqahā'*, 203; Sha'rānī, *al-Mīzān al-Kubrā*, 2: 182; Baghdādī, *Uṣūl al-Dīn*, 319.

100 The Ṣābi'a group claim to be the descendants of Yaḥyā (John the Baptist) and they have their own scripture. See T. Fahd, "Ṣābi'a" in the *Encyclopaedia of Islam*, new edition, vol. 8, (Leiden: E. J. Brill, 1994) 675-678; Albert Riḥānī, *al-Mawsū'ā al-'Arabiyya*, 458-459; 'Abd al-Karīm Zaydān, *Aḥkām al-Dhimmīyyīn wa 'l-Musta'minīn fī Dār al-Islām*, 14-15.

101 Sarakhsī,, *Sharḥ al-Siyar al-Kabīr*, 1: 149; the various types of Ṣābi'a can be found as described in Baghdādī, *Uṣūl al-Dīn*, 324-327.

102 See Ibn Qayyim al-Jawziyya, *Aḥkām Ahl al-Dhimma*, 1: 92, 99; Ibn Qudāma, *al-Mughnī*, 10: 558-559; *Tafsīr al-Qurṭubī*, 1: 434-435.

103 Jaṣṣāṣ, *Aḥkām al-Qur'ān*, 2: 328 and 3: 91

104 Abū Yūsuf, *Kharāj*, 131.

105 Ibn al-Rushd, *Bidāyat al-Mujtahid*, 1: 389 and 404; *Tafsīr al-Qurṭubī*, 1: 435; Ibn Qudāma, *al-Mughnī*, 10: 559; Ibn Qayyim al-Jawziyya, *Aḥkām Ahl al-Dhimma*, 1: 92-93; Ibn Mufliḥ, *al-Mubdi'*, 4: 405; Mardāwī, *al-Inṣāf*, 4: 218.

106 Nawawī, *Rawḍat al-Ṭālibīn*, 10: 305-306; *Mughnī al-Muḥtāj*, 4:244; Māwardī, *al-Aḥkām al-Sulṭāniyya*, 143-144; Nawawī, *al-Muhadhdhab*, 18: 170.

107 Ibn Qayyim al-Jawziyya, *Aḥkām Ahl al-Dhimma*, 1: 98-99.

108 Apostates (*murtaddūn*), the plural of *murtadd*, are those who have abandoned their religious faith or a cause to which they were once loyal. In legal terms it refers to those who withdraw from the true religion and who adopt another faith, such as in the case of Muslim apostates from Islam, either intentionally or inadvertently or through performing the action of an infidel. See Jawharī, *al-Ṣiḥaḥ*, 2: 473; *al-Qāmūs al-Muḥiṭ*, 2: 323; Kafūwī, *al-Kulliyāt*, 2: 387; Rāghib al-Iṣbahānī, *Mufradāt al-Qur'ān*, 280; Qūnawī, *Anīs al-Fuqahā'*, 186-187.

109 Ibn al-'Arabī, *Aḥkām al-Qur'ān*, 4: 1693; Jaṣṣāṣ, *Aḥkām al-Qur'ān*, 3: 393; *Tafsīr al-Qurṭubī*, 26: 83; *Tafsīr al-Baghawī*, 7: 303.

110 Wāqidī, *Kitāb al-Ridda*, 3: 450-451.

111 Bukhārī, *Bāb Ḥukm al-Murtadd*, 12: 267.

112 Sarakhsī, *Mabsūṭ*, 10: 7, 77; Kāsānī, *Badā'i' al-Ṣanā'i'*, 9: 4330; *Tafsīr al-Qurṭubī*, 8: 110 and 16: 272; Shawkānī, *Nayl al-Awṭār*, 7: 219; Sa'dī Abū Ḥabīb, *Mawsū'at al-Ijmā'*, 1: 263.

113 Shaybānī, *al-Siyar al-Kabīr*, 1: 76-77 and 189, 5: 2016; Abū Yūsuf, *Kharāj*, 139.

114 Sarakhsī, *Mabsūṭ*, 10: 117-118.

115 Sarakhsī, *Sharḥ al-Siyar al-Kabīr*, 5: 2016.

116 Ibn Humām, *Fatḥ al-Qadīr*, 4: 372; Kāsānī, *Badā'i' al-Ṣanā'i'*, 9: 4385-4386; al-'Aynī, *'Umdat al-Qārī'*, 14: 264; 'Abd al-Qādir 'Awdah, *al-Tashrī' al-Jinā'ī al-Islāmī*, 2: 721-722.

117 Sarakhsī, *Mabsūṭ*, 10: 7, 77; Kasānī, *Badā'i' al-Ṣanā'i'*, 9: 4330; Ibn Humām, *Fatḥ al-Qadīr*, 4: 371; Zayla'ī, *Tabyīn al-Ḥaqā'iq*, 3: 277-278; *Ḥāshiyat Ibn 'Ābidīn*, 4: 198; Ibn al-Rushd, *al-Muqaddimāt al-Mumahhidāt*, 1: 376; *Kashshāf al-Qinā'*, 3: 109; *Majmū'at Fatāwā Ibn Taymiyya*, 28: 414; *Tafsīr al-Qurṭubī*, 8: 110, 16: 272; Shawkānī,*Nayl al-Awṭār*, 7: 219; Sa'dī Abū Ḥabīb, *Mawsū'at al-Ijmā'*, 1: 263.

118 Shaybānī, *al-Jāmi' al-Ṣaghīr*, 348-349; Sarakhsī, *Mabsūṭ*, 10: 117.

119 Q: 48: 16, reads,

Say to the Bedouins who lagged behind: "You shall be called to fight against a people given to great warfare, then you shall fight them, or they shall surrender..."

120 *Mabsūṭ*, 10: 117-118;

121 Abū Yūsuf, *Kharāj*, 139; idem, *al-Radd 'alā Siyar al-Awzā'ī*, 131; Majid Khadduri, *Shaybānī Kitāb al-Siyar*, 222;

122 Kasānī, *Badā'i' al-Ṣanā'i'*, 9: 4329; Ibn Humām, *Fatḥ al-Qadīr*, 4: 173; Zayla'ī, *Tabyīn al-Ḥaqā'iq*, 3: 277; *Ḥāshiyat Ibn 'Ābidīn*, 4: 198; Shāfi'ī, *al-Umm*, 4: 95-96 and 158-160; Nawawī, *Rawḍat al-Ṭālibīn*, 10: 305; Ibn Rushd, *al-Muqaddimāt al-Mumahhidāt*, 1: 376-377; Ibn Shāsh, *'Iqd al-Jawāhir al-Thamīna*, 1: 486; Ibn Mufliḥ, *al-Mubdi'*, 3: 405; Mardāwī, *al-Inṣāf*, 4: 217; Abū 'Ubayd, *Amwāl*, 40; Jaṣṣāṣ, *Aḥkām al-*

Qur'ān, 3: 91; *Tafsīr al-Qurṭubī*, 8: 110; Ṭabarī, *Ikhtilāf al-Fuqahā'*, 200-203; *Majmū 'at Fatāwā Ibn Taymiyya*, 19: 18-30.

123 Shawkānī, *al-Sayl al-Jarrār*, 4: 571; Ibn al-'Arabī, *Aḥkām al-Qur'ān*, 2; 922; *Majmū'at Fatāwā Ibn Taymiyya*, 19: 18-30; Ibn Qayyim al-Jawziyya, *Zād al-Ma'ād*, 5: 91-92 and idem, *Aḥkām Ahl al-Dhimma*, 1: 6-12; *al-Rawḍ al-Naḍīr*, 4: 642; 'Abdallāh al-Jabūrī, *Fiqh al-Imām al-Awzā'ī*, 2: 530.

124 Sarakhsī, *Sharḥ al-Siyar al-Kabīr*, 4: 1530, 1537; Kasānī, *Badā'i' al-Ṣanā'i'*, 9: 4327; Ibn Shāsh, *'Iqd al-Jawāhir al-Thamīna*, 1: 485; Bahūtī, *Kashshāf al-Qinā'*, 3: 108; Ibn Qayyim al-Jawziyya, *Zād al-Ma'ād*, 3: 136-137, 151-152; Nawawī, *Rawḍat al-Ṭālibīn*, 10: 289, 303, and 320; Ibn Jamā'a, *Taḥrīr al-Aḥkām*, 248; Ibn Hubayrā, *al-Ifṣāḥ*, 2: 296.

125 Ṭal'at al-Ghunaymī, *Qānūn al-Salām fī al-Islām*, 407.

126 Shaybānī, *al-Siyar al-Kabīr*, 4: 1529, 5: 2191, 2198-2199.

127 Ṭabarī, *Ikhtilāf al-Fuqahā'*, 208.

128 Shāfi'ī, *al-Umm*, 4: 97; Ibn Shāsh, *'Iqd al-Jawāhir al-Thamīna*, 1: 486; Ghazālī, *Wajīz*, 2: 198; Nawawī, *al-Muhadhdhab*, 18: 190; and idem, *Rawḍat al-Ṭālibīn*; Ibn Jamā'a, *Taḥrīr al-Aḥkām*, 248; 10: 297; *Mughnī al-Muḥtāj*, 4: 234; Ibn Mufliḥ, *al-Mubdi'*, 3: 404.

129 In Q. 9: 29, the verse reads,

Fight against who believe not in Allāh, nor in the Last Day, nor forbid that which has been forbidden by Allāh and His Messenger and those who acknowledge not the religion of truth among the people of the Scripture, until they pay *jizya* with willing submission, and feel themselves subdued

130 The Prophet advised his generals never to begin fighting until they had first given the enemy two options. First, they were to invite the enemy to accept Islam, and if they did, war would be avoided. Should they refuse, however, the second option was to ask the enemy to pay *jizya*. In the event this was rejected, the generals could proceed to battle with the blessing of Allah. See *al-Siyar al-Kabīr*, 1: 38-39; Abū Yūsuf, *Kharāj*, 209-210.

131 *'Iqd al-Jawāhir al-Thamīna*, 1: 486; Ghazālī, *Wajīz*, 2: 198; *al-Muhadhdab*, 18: 190; *Rawḍat al-Ṭālibīn*, 10: 297; *Mughnī al-Muḥtāj*, 4: 234; *Kashshāf al-Qinā'*, 3: 108.

132 Kāsānī, *Badā'i' al-Ṣanā'i'*, 10: 4330; Ibn Shāsh, *'Iqd al-Jawāhir al-Thamīna*, 1; 491; Ghazālī, *Wajīz*, 2: 201; Nawawī, *Rawḍat al-Ṭālibīn*, 10: 303; Ibn Jamā'a, *Taḥrīr al-Aḥkām*, 252.

133 Zarkashī, *al-Manthūr fī al-Qawā'id*, 2: 398-402; Ibn Nujaym, *al-Ashbāh wa 'l-Naẓā'ir*, 336-338; Muḥammad Yūsuf Mūsā, *al-Amwāl wa-Naẓariyyat al-'Aqd*, 447, Sarakhsī, *Sharḥ al-Siyar al-Kabīr*, 4: 1614 and 1616; Kāsānī, *Badā'i' al-Ṣanā'i'*, 10: 4330.

134 Qarāfī, *Furūq*, 3: 13; Shāfi'ī, *al-Umm*, 4: 188; Ghazālī, *Wajīz*, 2: 197; *Mughnī al-Muḥtāj*, 4: 285; Ibn Qudāma, *al-Mughnī*, 1: 563.

135 *Sharṭ* is an Arabic term meaning "sign" (plural, *shurūṭ*). As a legal term, *sharṭ* mean what the abidance of *ḥukm* stands for the source of determination according the person or party desire, to make *'aqd* based or connected to him., If the condition exists then the *'aqd* is valid. If the *sharṭ* fails to address the demanded matter then the *'aqd* will not be accomplished. However, the *shar'ī sharṭ* is the obligatory fulfillment of what the *shar'* demands and it is beyond the parties limit. Because the *shar'* condition derived from the Texts. See: *Mu'jam Maqāyīs al-Lugha*, 3: 260; Kaffawī, *al-Kulliyyāt*, 3: 64; Jurjānī, *Ta'rīfāt*, 166; Samarqandī, *Mīzān al-Uṣūl*, 616-617; Nazīh Ḥammād, *Mu'jam al-Muṣṭalaḥāt al-Iqtiṣādiyya fī Lughat al-Fuqahā'*, 163-164.

136 This point was discussed earlier, for more discussion see Kāsānī, *Badā'i' al-Ṣanā'i'*, 9: 4330; Sarakhsī, *Sharḥ Ziyādāt al-Ziyādāt*, 144.

137 *Mughnī al-Muḥtāj*, 2: 234; Ghazālī, *Wajīz*, 2: 197; Ibn Jamā'a, *Taḥrīr al-Aḥkām*, 248; Qarāfī, *Furūq*, 3: 23; Bahūtī, *Kashshāf al-Qinā'*, 3: 108; Ibn Qayyim al-Jawziyya, *Aḥkām Ahl al-Dhimma*, 1: 475 and 477; Maqdisī, *al-Sharḥ al-Kabīr*, 10: 575; Ibn Qudāma, *al-Mughnī*, 10: 563.

138 This was discussed earlier under the subheading "The contractee (*al-ma'qūd lahu*) or *al-dhimmī*"; see also the following: Shawkānī, *al-Sayl al-Jarrār*, 4: 571; Ibn al-'Arabī, *Aḥkām al-Qur'ān*, 2; 922; *Majmū'at Fatāwā Ibn Taymiyya*, 19: 18-30; Ibn Qayyim al-Jawziyya, *Zād al-Ma'ād*, 5: 91-92 and idem, *Aḥkām Ahl al-Dhimma*, 1: 6-12; Siyāghī, *al-Rawḍ al-Naḍīr*, 4: 642; 'Abdallāh al-Jabūrī, *Fiqh al-Imām al-Awzā'ī*, 2: 530.

139 Shaybānī, *al-Siyar al-Kabīr*, 4: 1529; Ibn Qudāma, *al-Mughnī*, 10: 563; Ramlī, *Nihāyat al-Muḥtāj*, 8: 86.

140 Kasānī, *Badā'i' al-Ṣanā'i'*, 9: 4330; Ibn Qudāma, *al-Mughnī*, 10: 563 and 608; Bahūtī, *Kashshāf al-Qinā'*, 3: 108; *Majmū'at Fatāwā Ibn Taymiyya*, 18: 190.

141 Samarqandī, *Mīzān al-Uṣūl*, 17-23; *al-Talwīḥ 'alā al-Tawḍīḥ*, 1: 12-15; Āmadī, *al-Aḥkām*, 1: 90-91; *Sharḥ al-Kawkab al-Munīr*, 1: 333-340; Jurjānī, *Ta'rīfāt*, 123; Tahānawī, *Kashshāf Iṣṭilāḥāt al-Funūn*, 1: 134-142; Ibn al-Ghars, *al-Fawākih al-Badriyya fī al-Aqḍiya al-Ḥukmiyya*, 5-7, *Mu'jam Maqāyīs al-Lugha*, 2: 91-92; *al-Qāmūs al-Muḥīṭ*, 1: 685-686; Ibn Manẓūr, *Lisān al-'Arab*, 14: 145, Rāghib, *Mufradāt al-Qur'ān*, 126-128; Fayrūzābādī, *Baṣā'ir Dhawī al-Tamyīz*, 2: 487-490.

142 Sanhūrī, *Fiqh al-Khilāfa*, 132; Tal'at al-Ghunaymī, *Qānūn al-Salām fī al-Islām*, 423; 'Abd al-Karīm Zaydān, *Aḥkām al-Dhimmiyyīn wa al-Musta'minīn*, 70; Ḥāzim al-Ṣa'īdī, *al-Naẓariyya al-Islāmiyya fī al-Dawla*, 197.

143 Shāfi'ī, *Musnad*, 2: 105-106; Shaybānī, *al-Ḥujja 'alā Ahl al-Madīna*, 4: 352-354; Jaṣṣāṣ, *Aḥkām al-Qur'ān*, 1: 141.

144 See, *al-Hidāya*, 3: 286; *Ḥāshiyat Ibn 'Ābidīn*, 4: 128.

145 Sarakhsī, *Sharḥ al-Siyar al-Kabīr*, 4: 1530.

146 Ṭal'at al-Ghunaymi, *Qānūn al-Salām fī al-Islām*, 423-428.

147 Sarakhsī, *Sharḥ al-Siyar al-Kabīr*, 2: 688, 5: 1703, 1832 and 2245; idem, *Mabsūṭ*, 10: 84.

148 Muḥammad Ḥamīdallāh, *Majmū'at al-Wathā'iq al-Siyāsiyya*, 59-61. For further details see *al-Islamī wa 'Alāqatuhu bi al-Sharā i' al-Ukhrā*, 51-92

149 Khallāl, *Aḥkām Ahl al-Milal*, edited by Sayyid Kasūri Ḥusayn, 5-8. According to the translation of the constitution of Medina by Muḥammad Ḥamīdallāh specifically in reference to the question of *umma*, article number two reads: "Verily they constitute a political unit (*umma*) as distinct from all the people". The Jews were thus mentioned in the constitution as a distinct *umma* rather than part of the Muslim *umma*. See Muḥammad Ḥamidullāh, *The First Written Constitution in the World*, third revised edition, 1975: 35. For further details regarding the meaning of *umma* see the following: *Sharḥ al-Nawawī 'alā Muslim*, 1: 369; 'Arāqī, *Ṭarḥ al-Tathrīb*, 7: 16.

150 Ḥāmid Sulṭān, *Aḥkām al-Qānūn al-Dawlī fī al-Sharī'a al-Islāmiyya*, 17-218, 220-223; *Aḥkām Ahl al-Dhimma*, 1: 89-90; Aḥmad Ṭāhā al-Sanūsī, *Fikrat al-Jinsiyya fī al-Tashrī' al-Islāmī*, 44, 57-63; 'Abd al-Karīm Zaydān, *Aḥkām al-Dhimmīyyīn wa'l-Musta'minīn*, 64; Majid Khadduri, *al-Ḥarb wa 'l-Silm fī Shar' al-Islām*, 219.

151 Ṣubḥī Maḥmaṣānī, *al-Qānūn wa al-'Alāqāt' al-Dawliyya fī al-Islām*, 122-123; 'Abd al-Karīm Zaydān, *Aḥkām al-Dhimmīyyin wa al-Musta'minīn*, 65-66; Ṭal'at al-Ghunaymī, *Qānūn al-Salām fī al-Islām*, 323-324; Sanhūrī, *Fiqh al-Khilāfā*, 32.

152 Barbara A. Tenenbauum, ed., *Encyclopaedia of Latin American History and Culture* (New York: Simon and Schster Macmillan, 1996) 1, 113, 3. 300, and 4, 46; John Coggins and D. .S. Lewis, *Political Parties of the Americas and the Caribbean*, (London: Longman Group, 1992) 16-17.

153 The text of that *ṣulḥ* can be found in the following writings: Shaybānī, *Kitāb al-Siyar*, 267; Ibn Hishām, *Sīra*, 2: 594-595; Balādhurī, *Futūḥ al-Buldān*, 1: 77-78; *Ṭabaqāt Ibn Sa'd*, 1: 358; Abū 'Ubayd, *Amwāl*, 218-220; Ibn Zanjawīh, *Amwāl*, 2: 499; Abū Yūsuf, *Kharāj*, 77-78; Ṭabarī, *Tārīkh*, 3: 128-129; Ibn Qayyim al-Jawziyya, *Zād al-Ma'ād*, 3: 636; Maqrīzī, *Imtā' al-Asmā'*, 1: 502; Ibn Kathīr, *al-Bidāya wa 'l-Nihāya*, 5: 77, 99; Muḥammad Ḥamīdallāh, *Majmū'at al-Wathā'iq al-Siyāsiyya*, 175-179.

154 Abū Yūsuf, *Kharāj*, 77-81; Bulādhurī, *Futūḥ al-Buldān*, 1: 76-81; *Ṭabaqāt Ibn Sa'd*, 1: 358; Ibn Zanjwayh, *Amwāl*, 2:450; Muḥammad Ḥamidallāh, *Majmū'at al-Wathā'iq al-Siyāsiyya*, 191-193.

155 Shaybānī, *Aṣl*, 269; Ibn Humām, *Fatḥ al-Qadīr*, 4: 382-383.

156 Abū Yūsuf, *Kharāj*, 129-130; Yaḥyā ibn Ādam, *Kharāj*, 62-63; Abū 'Ubayd, *Amwāl*, 38; Ṭabarī, *Tārīkh*, 4: 55-56; Muḥammad Ḥamīdallāh, *Majmū'at al-Wathā'iq al-Siyāsiyya*, 523-525.

157 Khaṭīb al-Baghdādī, *Tārīkh Baghdād*, 2: 174; Ṣaymarī, *Akhbār Abī Ḥanīfa*, 121; Kardarī, *Manāqib Abī Ḥanīfa*, 434; Jaṣṣāṣ, *Aḥkām al-Qur'ān*, 3: 95; Sarakhsī, *Sharḥ Ziyādāt al-Ziyādāt*, 140. This case will be discussed in detail bellow in the section on international treaty in chapter three.

158 Abū 'Ubayda ibn al-Jarāḥ, among the closet and favored Companions to the Prophet, gained a great repitation during the Prophet time and from the first two rightly guided caliphs. Abū 'Ubayda was given a prestigas tilte by the Prophet "*Amīn al-Umma*" (upright of the community) and was among the first recommended candidate for the caliphship after the death of the Prophet, but he declined and recommended Abū Bakr, In 634 under the leadership of Khālid ibn al-Walīd the Muslim army defeated the Byzantine army at the battle of *Ajnadayn* near the city of Ramla in Palestine. In the wake of the battle the Arab moved against the Byzantine province of Syria and they

took Damascus in 636. During that time the Caliph 'Umar sent a letter to Abū 'Ubayda ibn al-Jarāḥ (asking him to replace Khālid and lead the Muslim army. Abū 'Ubayda reserved the news until they reached Syria, in order to avoid dividion within the Muslim army, and acted as a unified army rather than separate raiding parties. The decision of Abu 'Ubayda contributed to the Muslim success and after their victory Khālid realized that Abū 'Ubayda was a brave soldier of the Muslim army under his leadership, and after the battle Khālid assigned 'Abu 'Ubayda the leadership of the Muslim army in Syria, where Abū 'Ubyada sign a pact of turce with the people of Syria, which was agreed upon by Khālid. See 'Abd al-Barr, *al-Istī'āb fī Ma'rifat al-Aṣḥāb*, ed. 'Alī Muḥammad al-Bajāwī (Beirut: Dār al-Jīl, 1992); Ibn al-Athīr, *Asad al-Gābā fī Ma'rifat al-Ṣaḥābā*, ed. Muḥammad Ibrāhīm al-Banā (Cairo: Dār al-Sha'b, n.d.); al-Dhahabī, *Siyar 'Alām al-Nubalā'* (Beirut: Mu'asassat al-Risālā, 1992).

159 Abū Yūsuf, *Kharāj*, 152.

160 Ibid., 136. Examples of the extent to which Muslims went in honoring the *'uhūd* will be discussed in detail in a later section of this study.

161 Q. 9: 7 "So long, as they are true to you, stand you true to them"; The Prophet's tradition reads: "*wafā'un bil-'ahd khayrun min ghadrin bi ghadr*" (Standing by and honoring the treaty supersedes treachery by perfidy). See Abū 'Ubayd, *Amwāl*, 190; Balādhurī, *Futūḥ al-Buldān*, 1: 188; Māwardī, *al-Aḥkām al-Sulṭāniyya*, 51.

162 Wāḥidī, *Asbāb al-Nuzūl*, 78; *Tafsīr al-Qurṭubī*, 5: 409-410; *Tafsīr al-Baghawī*, 1: 314; Suyūṭī, *al-Durr al-Manthūr*, 2: 20; Ibn Humām, *Fatḥ al-Qadīr*, 1: 275; Jaṣṣāṣ, *Aḥkām al-Qur'ān*, 1: 452-453; see also the *Muṣannaf* of Ibn Abī Shayba, 10: 318-319, where he discusses matters dealing with the *ḥukm* on the *mushrik* (polytheist) changing his religion to another one.

163 Ibn 'Arabī, *Aḥkām al-Qur'ān*, 1: 233-234; *Tafsīr al-Ṭabarī*, 5: 409; Fakhr al-Dīn al-Rāzī, *Tafsīr*, 4: 15-16; Ibn Kathīr, *Tafsīr*, 1: 311-312; Ibn 'Aṭiyya, *al-Muḥarrar al-Wajīz*, 2: 388-391.

164 Abū 'Ubayd, *Amwāl*, 37.

165 Muḥammad Ḥamīdallāh, *Majmū'at al-Wathā'iq al-Siyāsiyya*, 209.

166 Abū 'Ubayd, *Amwāl*, 37. The actions of the Prophet in preventing Muslims from interfering in the practice of non-Muslim faith provided an example. When a group of the people from Najrān approached him in his mosque, he was still performing the *'aṣr* (afternoon) prayer with his companions, and as this was the time for the Christians to do the same, they too began praying. Some Muslims objected and tried to prevent them from praying in the mosque, but the Prophet asked the Muslims not to interrupt or intervene. He said to let them pray, and they did. See Ibn Isḥāq, *Sīra*, 1: 574; Ibn Sa'd, *Ṭabaqāt*, 1: 357; Ṭabarī, *Tafsīr*, 6: 151-153; Baghawī, *Tafsīr*, 2: 5; Suyūṭī, *al-Durr al-Manthūr*, 2: 141-142; Ibn Qayyim al-Jawziyya, *Zād al-Ma'ād*, 3: 629; Ibn Kathīr, *Tafsīr*, 1: 369-371; and idem, *al-Bidāya wa 'l-Nihāya*, 5: 56.

167 Ibn Sa'd, *Ṭabaqāt*. 6: 158; Abū 'Ubayd, *Amwāl*, 44; Suyūṭī, *al-Durr al-Manthūr*, 2: 22; Ibn Qayyim al-Jawziyya, *Sīrat 'Umar Ibn al-Khaṭṭāb*, 82-83.

168 See Thomas Arnold, *Preaching of Islam*, translated into Arabic as "Da'wat al-Islām" by Ḥasan Ibrahim, 98-99; Edmond Rabbāṭ, *Min Ajl Naẓariyya fī al-Qānūn al-*

Dawlī al-Islāmī, translated into Arabic by Ibrahim 'Awaḍ, 40; Gustave LeBon, *Ḥaḍārat al-'Arab*, translated to Arabic by 'Ādil Zu'aytar, 128-129; Najīb Armazānī, *al-Shar' al-Dawlī fī al-Islām*, 132; S. D. Goitein, *Jews and Arabs* (New York: Schoken Books, 1964):7. Goitein, asserts,

There can be no doubt that the legal status of the Jewish religion under Islam, particularly during its early period when the Arabs still predominant, was very much better than their situation in the Byzantine Empire, which ruled over many countries occupied later on by Arabs.

169 *Sharḥ al-Siyar al-Kabīr*, 14: 1531; Ibn Humām, *Fatḥ al-Qadīr*, 4: 378; Shāfi'ī, *al-Umm*, 4: 125-126; *Mukhtaṣar al-Muzanī*, on the margins of Shāfi'ī's *al-Umm*, 5: 203; Ṭabarī, *Ikhtilāf al-Fuqahā'*, 239.

170 See Sarakhsī, *Sharḥ al-Siyar al-Kabīr*, 4: 1531-1536 and 1546-1547; Kāsānī, *Badā'i' al-Ṣanā'i'*, 9: 4335-4336; Khaṣṣāf, *Adab al-Qāḍī*, 596-597 along with Jaṣṣāṣ's commentary; Ibn Humām, *Fatḥ al-Qadīr*, 4: 379-380; *Mukhtaṣar Ikhtilāf al-'Ulamā'*, 3: 497; *al-Fatāwā al-Hindiyya*, 2: 348, 350-351.

171 Jaṣṣāṣ, *Adab al-Qāḍī*, 596-600; Ibn Humām, *Fatḥ al-Qadīr*, 2: 483; Ṭabarī, *Ikhtilāf al-Fuqahā'*, 233.

172 *Al-Fatāwā al-Hindiyya*, 2: 252; *al-Fatāwā al-Khāniyya*, 3: 591. The consensus of Muslim scholars regarding what the *dhimmī* rights and obligation as was mentioned above, see Ibn Ḥazm, *Marātib al-Ijmā'*, 115-116; Ṭabarī, *Ikhtilāf al-Fuqahā'*, 199, 208, 233 and 236

173 The term *ḍamān* in Arabic means liability i.e., the obligation of person who has caused some damage or loss to another, he is obligated to pay an amount of money or compensation for the damage or loss he caused. See Nazīh Ḥammād, *Mu'jam al-Muṣṭalāḥāt al-Iqtiṣādiyya fī Lughat al-Fuqahā'*, 182; 'Alī al-Khafīf, *al-Ḍamān fī al-Fiqh al-Islāmī*, 5.

174 Ibn 'Abd al-Barr, *al-Kāfī*, 1: 418; Ibn Juzay', *al-Qawānīn al-Fiqhiyya*, 164-165; Ibn Shāsh, *'Iqd al-Jawāhir al-Thamīna*, 1: 491; *Tafsīr al-Qurṭubī*, 8: 113.

175 Shāfi'ī, *al-Umm*, 4: 126-127; Ghazālī, *Wajīz*, 2: 201-202; *Mughnī al-Muḥtāj*, 4: 255, 257; *Nihāyat al-Muḥtāj*, 8: 98, 103-104; Ibn Jamā'a, *Taḥrīr al-Aḥkām fī Tadbīr Ahl al-Islām*, 253; Nawawī, *Rawḍat al-Ṭālibīn*, 10-321; *Fatāwā al-Ramlī*, 4: 59-60; Māwardī, *al-Aḥkām al-Sulṭāniyya*, 145.

176 *Aḥkām Ahl al-Milal*, from *al-Jāmi' li-Masā'il al-Imām Aḥmad*, 287-288.

177 Bahūtī, *Kashshaf al-Qinā'*, 3: 117; Ibn Qayyim al-Jawziyya, *Aḥkām Ahl al-Dhimma*, 1: 61, 672, 727; and idem, *Zād al-Ma'ād*, 3: 638; Mirdāwī, *Inṣāf*, 4: 238; Ibn Qudāma, *Mughnī*, 10: 608-609; *Majmū'at Fatāwā Ibn Taymiyya*, 28: 642-643 and 677; Ibn Mufliḥ, *al-Mubdi'*, 3: 416; Raḥbānī, *Maṭālib Ūlī Nuhā*, 2: 603.

178 Khalāl, *Aḥkām Ahl al-Milal*, 355-356; Ibn Qudāma, *Mughnī*, 8: 130.

179 Ibn Qudāma, *Mughnī*, 8: 129.

180 The Arabian Peninsula. Mālik the jurist defined the limit of the Arabian Peninsula as Madina, Ḥijāz, Yemen and Yamāma. Bukhārī considered it to include only the territories of Mecca and Medina. See, Ibn Ḥajar al-'Asqalānī, *Hadiyya al-Sārī*, 98 and 102; Ibn Humām, *Fatḥ al-Qadīr*, 4: 379-380. In regard to the territories gained by

Muslims, according to Ibn 'Abbās, this was Arab territory, or the territory that was taken from the polytheists. See, 'Abd al-Razzāq, *al-Muṣannaf*, 6: 90.

181 *Kanīsa*, not originally an Arabic word, refers to a Christian church, the *Bi'a* to a Jewish synagogue, and *bayt al-nār* house of fire to a Zoroastrian temple. See, Ibn Humām, *Fatḥ al-Qadīr*, 4: 377; Ṭabarī, *Ikhtilāf al-Fuqahā'*, 238.

182 Shaybānī, *Aṣl*, 265; and idem, *al-Siyar al-Kabīr*, 4:1528; Ṭabarī, *Ikhtilāf al-Fuqahā'*, 238;; *Mukhtaṣar Ikhtilāf al-'Ulamā'*, 3: 497; see also in detail the following: Sarakhsī, *Mabsūṭ*, 16: 39; Ibn Humām, *Fatḥ al-Qadīr*, along with *al-'Ināya 'alā al-Hidāya*, 4: 377-379; *Ḥāshiyat Ibn 'Ābidīn*, 4: 202; Zayla'ī, *Tabyīn al-Ḥaqā'iq*, 3: 279-280; *al-Fatāwā al-Hindiyya*, 2: 247-248; Ramlī, *Fatāwā al-Khāyriyya li-Naf' al-Bariya*, 1: 92-93; Kāsānī, *Badā'i' al-Ṣanā'i'*, 9: 4336.

183 Abū Yūsuf, *Kharāj*, 149.

184 Ibid., 159.

185 Ṭabarī, *Ikhtilāf al-Fuqahā'*, 236.

186 Jaṣṣāṣ, *Mukhtaṣar Ikhtilāf al-'Ulamā'*, 3: 497.

187 Mālik, *Mudawwana*, 4: 424; *al-Qawānīn al-Fiqhiyya*, 164; *al-Sharḥ al-Ṣaghīr 'alā Aqrab al-Masālik*, 2: 60-61; *Mawāhib al-Jalīl*, 2: 335-336; *'Iqd al-Jawāhir al-Thamīna*, 1: 492-493; Ibn 'Abd al-Barr, *Kāfī*, 1: 464; Ṭabarī, *Ikhtilāf al-Fuqahā'*, 234; *Mukhtaṣar Ikhtilāf al-'Ulamā'*, 3: 497; *Tafsīr al-Qurṭubī*, 11: 70-71.

188 Shāfi'ī, *Umm*, 4: 126; *Mukhtaṣar al-Muzanī* on the margins of Shāfi'ī, *al-Umm*, 5: 198; *Rawḍat al-Ṭālibīn*, 10: 323; *Mughnī al-Muḥtāj*, 4: 254; Ramlī,*Nihāyat al-Muḥtāj*, 8: 92-94; Māwardī, *Aḥkām al-Sulṭāniyya*, 146; *Fatāwā al-Subkī*, 2: 369; Ibn Ḥajar al-Haythamī, *al-Fatāwā al-Fiqhiyya al-Kubrā*, 4: 248; *Fatāwā al-Ramlī*, 56.

189 Khallal, *Aḥkām Ahl al-Milal*, 345-350; *Majmū'at Fatāwā Shaykh al-Islām Ibn Taymiyya*, 18: 632; Ibn Qayyim al-Jawziyya, *Aḥkām Ahl al-Dhimma*, 2: 662; Ibn Miflih, *al-Mubdi'*, 3: 420-421; Mardāwī, *al-Inṣāf*, 4: 236-239; Bahūtī, *Kashshāf al-Qinā'*, 3: 123-124; Ibn Qudāma, *al-Mughnī*, 10: 599-602.

190 *al-Siyar al-Kabīr* with Sarakhsī's commentary, 1: 208-209, 2: 688, 4: 1299; *al-Fatāwā al-Hindiyya*, 2: 190-191; Sarakhsī, *Mabsūṭ*, 10: 89; Jaṣṣāṣ, *Aḥkām al-Qur'ān*, 3: 84.

191 Shaybānī, *al-Siyar al-Kabīr*, 4: 1854-1855.

192 Ibid., 4: 1856.

193 Ibid., 5: 1892.

194 Shaybānī, *Aṣl*, 268.

195 Abū Yūsuf, *Kharāj*, 149-150; Bulādhurī, *Futūḥ al-Buldān*, 1: 162; Muḥammad Ḥamīdullāh, *Majmū'at al-Wathā'iq al-Siyāsiyya*, 470; Ṭabarī, *Ikhtilāf al-Fuqahā'*, 240; Ibn Ḥazm, *Marātib al-Ijmā'*, 116, 138.

196 Shāfi'ī, *al-Umm*, 4: 127; Bayḍāwī, *al-Ghāya al-Quṣwā fī Dirāyat al-Fatwā*, 2: 158; Nawawī, *al-Muhadhdhab*, 18: 196; and idem, *Rawḍat al-Ṭālibīn*, 10: 321-322; Ramlī, *Mughnī al-Muḥtāj*, 4: 253; *Taḥrīr al-Aḥkām*, 253; Māwardī, *al-Aḥkām al-Sulṭāniyya*, 143; Ṭabarī, *Ikhtilāf al-Fuqahā'*, 240-241.

197 Khallāl, *Aḥkām Ahl al-Milal*, 336-337; Ibn Taymiyya, *al-Muḥarrar fī al-Fiqh*, 2: 187; Ibn Mufliḥ, *al-Mubdi'*, 3: 428; Ibn Qudāma, *al-Mughnī*, 10: 613; Bahūtī, *Kashshāf al-Qinā'*, 3: 129; Mardāwī, *al-Inṣāf*, 4: 247; *Majmū' Fatāwā Ibn Taymiyya*, 28: 617-618.

198 Q. 9: 29,

And those who acknowledge not the religion of truth (i.e. Islam) among the people of the Scripture (Jews and Christians), until they pay the *Jizyah* with willing submission, and feel themselves subdued.

199 Kāsānī, *Badā'i' al-Ṣanā'i'*, 9: 4330.

200 Shaybānī, *al-Ḥujja 'alā Ahl al-Madina*, 4: 341; *Aṣl*, 4: 488; *Kitāb al-Āthār*, 128. Jaṣṣāṣ, *Aḥkām al-Qur'ān*, 1: 140-144; Sarakhsī, *Mabsūṭ*, 26: 132-136; Ibn Humām, *Fatḥ al-Qadīr*, 6: 44; Kāsānī, *Badā'i' al-Ṣanā'i'*, 10: 4625-4626; *Mukhtaṣar Ikhtilāf al-'Ulamā'*, 5: 157-159;

201 Ibn Ḥazm, *Marātib al-Ijmā'*, 116, 138-139; and idem, *al-Muḥallā*, 10: 348; Ṭabarī, *Ikhtilāf al-Fuqahā'*, 240.

202 Mālik, *Mudawwana*, 6: 427-428; Ibn al-Rushd, *al-Muqaddamāt al-Mumahhidāt*, 3: 281; Ibn Juzay', *al-Qawānīn al-Fiqhiyya*, 362; Shāfi'ī, *al-Umm*, 6: 32-34; Nawawī, *al-Muhadhdhab*, 18: 197-202; and idem, *Rawḍat al-Ṭālibīn*, 9: 148; Ramlī, *Mughnī al-Muḥtāj*, 4: 14; Ibn Qudāma, *al-Mughnī*, 9: 334; Ibn Taymiyya, *al-Muḥarrar fī al-Fiqh*, 2: 125; Mardāwī, *al-Inṣāf*, 9: 462; *Aḥkām Ahl al-Milal*, 318-323; Ibn Ḥazm, *al-Muḥallā*, 10: 347-355; Ibn 'Arabī, *Aḥkām al-Qur'ān*, 2: 626; *Tafsīr, al-Qurṭubī*, 2: 248; Shawkānī, *Nayl al-Awṭār*, 7: 10-14; 'Abd al-Karīm Zaydān, *Aḥkām al-Dhimmīyyīn wa 'l-Musta'minīn*, 254.

203 Sarakhsī, *Mabsūṭ*, 9: 57; Ibn Humām, *Fatḥ al-Qadīr*, 4: 213; Kasānī, *Badā'i' al-Ṣanā'i'*, 9: 4125.

204 Abū Yūsuf, *al-Radd 'alā Siyar al-Awzā'ī*, 80-83; Shāfi'ī, *al-Umm*, 7: 323; Ibn Humām, *Fatḥ al-Qadīr*, 4: 152-154, 6: 30; Sarakhsī, *Mabsūṭ*, 9: 99-100; and idem, *Sharḥ al-Siyar al-Kabīr*, 5: 1851-1852; Kasānī, *Badā'i' al-Ṣanā'i'*, 9: 4152-4153; Ibn Qudāma, *al-Mughnī*, 10: 528.

205 Qarāfī, *Furūq*, 3: 14.

206 Shaybānī, *al-Siyar al-Kabīr*, 4: 1299, 1324; Sarakhsī, *Sharḥ al-Siyar al-Kabīr*, 4: 1530; Wāqidī, *Maghāzī*, 2: 691.

207 'Abd al-Razzāq, *al-Muṣannaf*, 6: 91-96.

208 Shaybānī, *al-Siyar al-Kabīr*, 4: 1544-1545; *al-Fatāwā al-Hindiyya*, 2: 251-252; Sarakhsī, *Mabsūṭ*, 11: 53, 102-104; Kasānī, *Badā'i' al-Ṣanā'i'*, 9: 4413-4414; Ṭabarī, *Ikhtilāf al-Fuqahā'*, 160.

209 Ṭabarī, *Ikhtilāf al-Fuqahā'*, 146; Ibn Rushd, *Bidāyat al-Mujtahid*, 2: 446; Ibn Qudāma, *al-Mughnī*, 10: 271; Ibn Taymiyya, *al-Muharrar fī al-Fiqh*, 2: 158; Ramlī, *Mughnī al-Muḥtāj*, 4: 453; *Mawsū'at al-Ijmā' fī al-Fiqh al-Islāmī*, 1; 342.

210 Khallāl, *Aḥkām Ahl al-Milal*, 289-291; Ibn Qudāma, *al-Mughnī*, 10: 278-279; Ibn Rushd, *al-Muqaddamāt al-Mumahhidāt*, 3: 220.

211 Mālik, *Mudawwana*, 5: 365; Ibn Shāsh, *'Iqd al-Jawāhir al-Thamīna*, 2: 743; Khallāl, *Aḥkām Ahl al-Milal*, 290; Ibn Qudāma, *al-Mughnī*, 10: 442-443; Bahūtī, *Kashshāf al-Qinā'*, 4: 84; 'Alī al-Khafīf, *al-Ḍamān fī al-Fiqh al-Islāmī*, 49-51.

212 Sarakhsī, *Sharḥ al-Siyar al-Kabīr*, 2: 688, 5: 1703, 2245.

213 See for example. Abū 'Ubayd, *Amwāl*, p. 643; Ibn Zanjawayh, *Amwāl*, 3: 1212.; *Sharḥ al-Siyar al-Kabīr*, 1: 96; *Ṭabaqāt Ibn Sa'd*, 2: 90; *Sīrat Ibn Hishām*, 2: 617.

214 The Qur'ān makes two allusions to this matter, the first in regard to the description of charity (*ṣadaqa*) to the poor and needy, and the second to occasions when a fellow Muslim asks for money, in which case one should not repulse him. Q. 94: 10; see Abu Yūsuf. *Kharāj*, 136. A similar event is that reported by Abū Yūsuf regarding the *ṣulḥ* concluded with the people of Ḥīra under the rule of Abū Bakr. The *'aqd* contained articles making provisions for elderly people who could not find work and feed their families, who were sick, or were wealthy and then became poor. In such cases, their own charity, *jizya* will be lifted, and the Muslims will look after their needs from Bayt al-Māl (public treasury) as long as they reside within *dār al-Islām*. See Abū Yūsuf, *Kharāj*, 155-156.; Abū 'Ubayd, *Amwāl*, 56-57.

215 Abū 'Ubayd, *Amwāl*, 56-57; Ibn Zanjawayh, *Amwāl*, 1: 163.

216 Sarakhsī, *Mabsūṭ*, 2: 202, 3: 3: 19 and Shaybānī, *Aṣl*, 2: 183.

217 Q. 60: 8, reads:

Allah does not forbid you to deal justly and kindly with those who fought not against you on account of religion and did not drive you out of your home. Verily, Allah loves those who deal with equity. See al-Qarāfī, *Furūq*, 3: 14-16.

218 Ibn Ḥazm, *Marātib al-Ijmā'*, 122; Ṭabarī, *Ikhtilāf al-Fuqahā'*, 233; *Mawsū'at al-Ijmā' fī al-Fiqh al-Islāmī*, 1: 444.

219 The word *jānib* (near) used in this verse does not necessarily mean permit them not, it meant staying within the mosque. See *Sharḥ al-Siyar al-Kabīr*, 1: 134-135; *Ikhtilāf al-Fuqahā'*, 226; *Ḥāshiyat Ibn 'Ābidīn*, 4: 208-208; Ibn Nujaym, *al-Ashbāh wa 'l-Naẓā'ir*, 325; Jaṣṣāṣ, *Aḥkām al-Qur'ān*, 3: 88-89; 'Aynī, *'Umdat al-Qāri'*, 14: 299-300; Ṭaḥāwī, *Mushkil al-Āthār*, 7: 183

220 *Ḥāshiyat Ibn 'Ābdīn*, 4: 203.

221 Ṭabarī, *Ikhtilāf al-Fuqahā'*, 236.

222 See, *al-Muwaṭṭā'* with Sharḥ al-Zarqānī, 4: 233-243; *Ṣaḥīḥ al-Bukhārī*, 6: 170, 270; 'Umar the caliph evacuated the Jews and Christians from the Arabian Peninsula and it is surroundings, i.e., Mecca and Medina, see, al-Tamarāshī, *al-Durr al-Mukhtār*, 4: 208, along with *Ḥāshiyat Ibn 'Ābidīn*

223 Sarakhsī, *Sharḥ al-Siyar al-Kabīr*, 1: 134-135; Ṭabarī, *Ikhtilāf al-Fuqahā'*, 226; *Ḥāshiyyat Ibn 'Ābidīn*, 4: 208-208; Ibn Nujaym, *al-Ashbāh wa al-Naẓā'ir*, 325; Jaṣṣāṣ, *Aḥkām al-Qur'ān*, 3: 88-89; 'Aynī, *'Umdat al-Qāri'*, 14: 299-300; Ṭaḥāwī, *Mushkhal al-Āthār*, 7: 183

223 *Ḥāshiyat Ibn 'Ābidīn*, 4: 203.

224 Ibn Shāsh, *'Iqd al-Jawāhir al-Thamīna*, 1: 487; Ibn Qayyim al-Jawziyya, *Aḥkām Ahl al-Dhimma*, 1: 187-188; *al-Muntaqā Sharḥ al-Muwaṭṭa'*, 7: 195-196; *Tafsīr al-Qurṭubī*, 8: 104; 'Aynī, *'Amdat al-Qārī'*, 14: 299.

225 Shaybānī, *Muwaṭṭā' Malik.*, 3: 378; *Muṣannaf 'Abd al-Razzāq*, 6: 51 and Ibn Zanjaweyh, *Amwāl*, 1: 276.

226 See, Shāfi'ī, *al-Umm*, 4: 99-101; Ramlī, *Mughnī al-Muḥtāj*, 4: 246-247; Nawawī, *Rawḍat al-Ṭālibīn*, 10: 308-309; and idem, *Takmilat al-Majmū'*, 18: 311; Māwardī, *Aḥkām al-Sulṭāniyya*, 51; Nawawī, *Sharḥ Ṣaḥīḥ Muslim*, 11: 393-394; Ibn Ḥajar, *Fatḥ al-Bārī*, 6: 171, 272.

227 Ibn Qayyim al-Jawziyya, *Aḥkām Ahl al-Dhimma*, 1: 185-187; Khallāl, *Aḥkām Ahl al-Milal*, 54-56; Ibn Qudāma, *al-Mughnī*, 10: 428; Ibn Mufliḥ, *al-Mubdi'*, 2: 424-425; Mardāwī, *al-Inṣāf*, 4: 239-241; Bahūtī, *Kashshāf al-Qinā'*, 3: 101; *Majmū'at Fatāwā Ibn Taymiyya*, 22: 194.

228 Muḥammad Rashīd Riḍā, *Tafsīr al-Manār*, 10: 373-374.

229 Ibn al-Qāṣṣ al-Ṭabarī, *Adab al-Qāḍī*, 1: 141; Ibn Ḥazm, *Marātib al-Ijmā'*, 50; Ibn Farḥūn, *Tabṣirat al-Ḥukkām*, 1: 96; *Mawsū'at al-Ijmā' fī al-Fiqh al-Islamī*, 2: 909.

230 Q. 5: 48,

And so judge between them by what Allah has revealed and follow not their vain desires.

231 Q. 4: 161,

And they're taking of usury though they were forbidden from taking it and they are devouring of men's substance wrongfully (bribery, etc.).

232 Q. 4: 29.

233 Shaybānī, *Aṣl*, 5: 221; Jaṣṣāṣ, *Aḥkām al-Qur'ān*, 2: 436; Ṭaḥāwī, *Sharḥ Ma'ānī al-Āthār*, 4: 141-144; Sarakhsī, *Sharḥ al-Siyar al-Kabīr*, 1: 306; and idem, *Mabsūṭ*, 5: 38; Kāsānī, *Badā'i' al-Ṣanā'i'*, 3: 1503; Khaṣṣāf, *Adab al-Qāḍī*, 596-601; *Mukhtaṣar Ikhtilāf al-'Ulamā'*, 3: 390; Ramlī, *al-Fatāwā al-Khayriyya li-Naf' al-Bariyya*, 1: 93; Ibn Nujaym, *al-Baḥr al-Rā'iq*, 6: 188; Ibn Humām, *Fatḥ al-Qadīr*, 2: 483-485, 7: 399; Ṭarābulsī, *Mu'īn al-Ḥukkām fīmā Yataraddadu bayna al-Khaṣmayn min al-Aḥkām*, 36.

234 Jaṣṣāṣ, *Mukhtaṣar Ikhtilāf al-'Ulamā'*, 3: 391; Ibn Rushd, *al-Bayān wa al-Taḥṣīl*, 4: 181-186; and idem, *al-Muqaddimāt al-Mumahhidāt*, 2: 156; Ibn Farḥūn, *Tabṣirat al-Ḥukkām*, 1: 96; Ibn Juzayy, *al-Qawānīn al-Fiqhiyya*, 307; Ibn 'Abd al-Barr, *al-Kāfī*, 1: 418 and *al-Tamhīd*, 14: 385; Ibn 'Arabī, *Aḥkām al-Qur'ān*, 2: 620-623; *Tafsīr al-Qurṭubī*, 6: 179, 184-186; Sarakhsī, *Sharḥ al-Siyar al-Kabīr*, 1: 306, in which he make some reference to the opinion of the *ahl al-Madīna* regarding the cases of *ahl al-Dhimma* and whether these can be presented before a Muslim *qāḍī*, such the *ḥudūd* cases of adultery, theft, etc.

235 Shāfi'ī, *al-Umm*, 7: 38-39, 4: 183, 6: 124; Ibn al-Qaṣṣ al-Ṭabarī, *Adab al-Qāḍī*, 1: 142-144; Nawawī, *al-Muhadhdhab with the Majmū'*, 18: 201; and idem, *Rawḍat al-Ṭālibīn*, 10: 327; Ramlī, *Mughnī al-Muḥtāj*, 4: 127-128; Jaṣṣāṣ, *Mukhtaṣar Ikhtilāf al-'Ulamā'*, 3: 392.

236 Ibn Qudāma, *al-Mughnī.*, 10: 613-614; Ibn Qayyim al-Jawziyya, *Aḥkām Ahl al-Dhimma*, 1: 391; Khallāl, *Aḥkām Ahl al-Milal*, 122; Ibn Mufliḥ, *al-Mubdi'*, 3: 429-430; Bahūtī, *Kashshāf al-Qinā'*, 3: 117, 130-131.

237 Najīb Armazānī, *al-Shar' al-Duwalī fī al-Islam*, 126. Daniel C. Dennett in his *Conversion and Poll Tax in Early Islam* states that the collection or imposition of *jizya* on non-Muslims lacks classical evidence, but he attributes it to deliberate falsification by Muslim jurists and historians. Demmett echoes the opinions of Western scholars such as Jullius Wellhausen, L. Caetani, and others who raised doubts regarding the imposition of *jizya* on no-Muslims and relevant literature. Western scholars do not, however, universally share this opinion. For example, Goitein challenge this claims in his work *Jews and Arabs: Their Contacts through the Ages*. Space does not allow for a full of the authenticity of the classical literature, but it does have certain consistency: witness the recent work of Bat Ye'or, *Islam and Dhimmitude: Wherer* Civilization Collide (New Jersey: Fairleigh Dikston University Press, 2002), 65-66 and 74-75. She writes on the status of the *dhimmī* under Islam, specifically referring to the status of the Jews and Christians. Her research indicates that the *dhimmī* under Islam was not treated fairly, citing in illustration a few examples from the legal domain, such as the fact that the *dhimmī* cannot testify against a Muslim in an Islamic court. This, however, was clearly indicated and pointed out by early jurists and cannot be denied. Her definitions of *kharāj* and *jizya* , are almost in agreement with our information, but her analysis, is different. She nevertheless indicates in her recent book, in theory the status of the *dhimmī* under Islam in terms of treatment is fair, which is similar to what this study seeks to illustrate.

238 Jawharī, *al-Ṣiḥāḥ*, 6: 2302-2303; *Tartīb al-Qāmūs al-Muḥīṭ*, 1: 490; Fayyūmī, *al-Miṣbāḥ al-Munīr*, 1: 100; Ibn Manẓūr, *Lisān al-'Arab*, 14: 143; Ibn Athīr, *al-Nihāyya fī Gharīb al-Ḥadīth*, 1: 270-271; *Majma' Biḥār al-Anwār*, 1: 358-359.

239 Shaybānī, *Aṣl*, 152, 263; Sarakhsī, *Mabsūṭ*, 10: 77; Ibn Humām, *Fatḥ al-Qadīr*, 4: 367.

240 Tahānawī, *Kashshāf Iṣṭilāḥāt al-Funūn*, 1: 383; Muṭarrizī, *al-Mughrib*, 1: 143.

241 *al-Fatāwā al-Hindiyya*, 2: 244; Ibn Humām, *Fatḥ al-Qadīr*, 4: 367; *al-Ikhtiyār li-Ta'līl al-Mukhtār*, 4: 215; Ibn Nujaym, *al-Baḥr al-Rā'iq*, 5: 119; Dāmād Afandī, *Majma' al-Anhur*, 1: 667; *Anīs al-Fuqahā'*, 182.

242 *Ḥudūd Ibn 'Arafa*, with the commentary of Raṣā', 1: 227; *Jawāhir al-Iklīl*, 1: 266; *Mawāhib al-Jalīl*, 2: 332; Dasūqī, *Ḥāshiyat al-Dasūqi 'alā al-Sharḥ al-Kabīr*, 2: 201; *al-Sharḥ al-Ṣaghīr 'ala Aqrab al-Masālik*, 3: 52-53.

243 *Mughnī al-Muḥtāj*, 4: 242; Ramlī, *Nihāyat al-Muḥtāj*, 8: 85; *Mawāhib al-Ṣamad fī Alfāẓ al-Zubad*, 2: 629; *al-Tawqīf 'alā Muhimmāt al-Ta'ārīf*, 242; *Ḥāshiyat al-Sharqāwī 'alā al-Taḥrīr*, 2: 456-457; Māwardī, *al-Aḥkām al-Sulṭāniyya*, 142.

244 Ḥiṣnī, *Kifāyat al-Akhyār fī Ghāyat al-Ikhtiṣār*, 2: 407.

245 *al-Durr al-Naqī fī Sharḥ Alfāẓ al-Khiraqī*, 3: 777; Ibn Mufliḥ, *al-Mubdi'*, 3: 404; Bahūtī, *Kashshāf al-Qinā'*, 3: 108;

246 Sarakhsī, *Mabsūṭ*, 10: 78.

247 Ibid.

248 Ibn Humām, *Fatḥ al-Qadīr*, 4: 370, 375; Kāsānī, *Badā'i' al-Ṣanā'ī'*, 9: 4332-4333; Ibn Qayyim al-Jawziyya, *Aḥkām Ahl al-Dhimma*, 1: 17-22.

249 Shaybānī, *Aṣl*, 152, 263-264; *Mukhtaṣar al-Ṭaḥāwī*, 294; Sarakhsī, *Mabsūṭ*, 10: 79-80; Jaṣṣās, *Aḥkām al-Qur'ān*, 3: 96.

250 Kāsānī, *Badā'i' al-Ṣanā'i'*, 9: 4330-4331; Abū Yūsuf, *Kharāj*, 131-132; *Tuḥfat al-Fuqahā'*, 3: 527-528; Ibn Humām, *Fatḥ al-Qadīr*, 4: 372-374; *al-Ikhtiyār li-Ta'līl al-Mukhtār*, 4: 217-218; *Mukhtaṣar al-Qudūrī* with the *Lubāb*, 4: 145; Dāmād Afandī, *Majma' al-Anhur*, 1: 671-672; Zayla'ī, *Tabyīn al-Ḥaqā'iq*, 3: 218-219; *Ḥāshiyat Ibn 'Ābidīn*, 4: 199-201; *al-Fatāwā al-Hindiyya*, 2: 245-246; Jaṣṣāṣ, *Aḥkām al-Qur'ān*, 3: 93; Abū 'Ubayd, *Amwāl*, 47.

251 Ibn al-Mundhir Naysābūri, *Ijmā'*, 71; Ṭabarī, *Ikhtilāf al-Fuqahā'*, 203-208; Ibn Ḥazm, *Marātib al-Ijmā'*, 114-115; Sha'rānī, *al-Mīzān al-Kubra*, 2: 184; *al-Kāfī fī Fiqh Ahl al-Medina*, 1: 413; Ibn Juzayy, *al-Qawānīn al-Fiqhiyya*, 264; Shāfi'ī, *al-Umm*, 4: 98; Nawawī, *Rawḍat al-Ṭālibīn*, 10: 299-302; *Mughnī al-Muḥtāj*, 4: 245-246; Ibn Qudāma, *al-Mughnī*, 10: 572-577; *Majmū' Fatāwā Ibn Taymiyya*, 28: 659-663; Ibn Qayyim al-Jawziyya, *Aḥkām Ahl al-Dhimma*, 1: 42-50; Ibn Jamā'a, *Taḥrīr al-Aḥkām*, 252-253; *Tafsīr al-Qurṭubī*, 8: 110-112; *Mawsū'at al-Ijmā' fī al-Fiqh al-Islami*, 1: 262-263.

252 Shaybānī, *Aṣl.* 263-264; Sarakhsī, *Mabsūṭ*, 10: 82; Kāsānī, *Badā'i' al-Ṣanā'i'*, 9: 4331; Ibn Humām, *Fatḥ al-Qadīr*, 4: 368; *al-Fatāwā al-Hindiyya*, 2: 244; *Ḥāshiyat Ibn 'Ābidīn*, 4: 197-198; Jaṣṣās, *Aḥkām al-Qur'ān*, 3: 100-103.

253 Ibn 'Abd al-Barr, *al-Kāfī*, 1: 413; Dardīr, *al-Sharḥ al-Ṣaghīr*, 3: 56; *al-Muhadhdhab* with the *Majmū'*, 18: 177; *Mughnī al-Muḥtāj*, 4: 246; Ibn Qudāma, *al-Mughnī*, 10: 568; Bahūtī, *Kashshāf al-Qinā'*, 3: 112; Ibn Hubayra, *al-Ifṣāḥ*, 2: 294; Ibn Jamā'a, *Taḥrīr al-Aḥkām*, 250; Ibn Qayyim al-Jawziyya, *Aḥkām Ahl al-Dhimma*, 1: 39-42; *Mawsū'at al-Ijmā' fī al-Fiqh al-Islami*, 1: 264.

254 Shaybānī, *Aṣl*, 2: 184; *Siyar*, 152; Abū Yūsuf, *Kharāj*, 39; Abū 'Ubayd, *Amwāl*, 50; Ibn Abī Shayaba, 14: 574; Ibn Sa'd, *Ṭabaqāt*, 3: 283; *Naṣb al-Rāya*, 3: 447-448.

255 Ṭabarī, *Ikhtilāf al-Fuqahā'*, 208-211; *Mukhtaṣar Ikhtilāf al-'Ulamā'*, 3: 486-487; Ibn Hubayra, *al-Ifṣāḥ*, 2: 292-293; Shāfi'ī, *al-Umm*, 4: 101-102; Nawawī, *Rawḍat al-Ṭālibīn*, 10: 311-314; Ibn Jamā'a, *Taḥrīr al-Aḥkām*, 250; Mālik, *al-Mudawwana*, 3: 46; Ibn 'Abd al-Barr, *al-Kāfī*, 1: 413-414; Ibn Shāsh, *'Iqd al-Jawāhir al-Thamīna*, 1: 488; Dardīr, *al-Sharḥ al-Ṣaghīr*, 3: 56; Ibn Qudāma, *Mughnī*, 10: 566; Khallāl, *Aḥkām Ahl al-Milal*, 64; Jaṣṣāṣ, *Aḥkām al-Qur'ān*, 3: 96-97; *Tafsīr al-Qurṭubī*, 8: 111-112. Ibn Qayyim al-Jawziyya, *Zād al-Ma'ād fī Hudā Khayr al-'Ibād*, 3: 155-158; and idem, *Aḥkām Ahl al-Dhimma*, 1: 26; *Majmū'at Fatāwā Ibn Taymiyya*,19: 253, 35: 350; Yaḥyā Ibn Ādam, *Kharāj*, 66; Abū 'Ubayd, *Amwāl*, 49-53.

256 As mentioned above, the *jizya* was imposed upon the *dhimmī* for a reason. The moment he becomes a Muslim, however, there is no reason to impose the *jizya*, for the *jizya* is only applicable or collected from non-Muslims. See Abū 'Ubayd, *Amwāl*, 58.

257 Shaybānī, *Aṣl*, 153, 263; and idem, *al-Siyar al-Kabīr*, 5: 2137-2138; Sarakhsī, *Mabsūṭ*, 10: 72-79; Abū Yūsuf, *Kharāj*, 132; Kasānī, *Badā'i' al-Ṣanā'i'*, 9: 4332-4334; Ibn Humām, *Fatḥ al-Qadīr*, 4: 374; Zaylā'ī, *Tabyīn al-Ḥaqā'iq*, 3: 278-279; *al-Fatāwā al-Hindiyya*, 2: 246; Jaṣṣāṣ, *Aḥkām al-Qur'ān*, 3: 100-101; *Rawḍat al-Quḍāt*, 2: 2253; *Mukhtaṣar Ikhtilāf al-'Ulamā'*, 3: 487-488.

258 Mālik, *al-Mudawwana*, 1: 282; Shāfiʿī, *al-Umm*, 4: 123; Ibn Qayyim al-Jawziyya, *Aḥkām Ahl al-Dhimma*, 1: 39, 57-60; Ibn Ḥazm, *Marātib al-Ijmā'*, 120; Ṭabarī, *Ikhtilāf al-Fuqahā'*, 211-213; *Mukhtaṣar Ikhtilāf al-'Ulamā'*, 3: 487-488; Abū 'Ubayd, *Amwāl*, 58-63.

259 See Jawharī, *al-Ṣiḥāḥ*, 1: 309; Ibn Manẓūr, *Lisān al-'Arab*, 2: 215-252; *Tartīb al-Qāmūs al-Muḥīṭ*, 2: 32; Azharī, *al-Zāhir*, 208, 356; Rāghib, *Mufradāt Gharīb al-Qur'ān*, 145.

260 Ibn Humām, *Fatḥ al-Qadīr*, 4: 283, 358; Wansharīshī, *al-Mughrib*, 1: 249-250; Tahānāwī, *Kashshāf Iṣṭilāḥāt al-Funūn*, 2: 183; *Mu'jam al-Iṣṭilāḥat al-Fiqhiyya*, 125; *al-Kharāj wa al-Nuẓum al-Māliyya*, 116; *Aḥkām al-Kharāj fī al-Fiqh al-Islami*, 13; Hossein Modarressi Tabataba'i, *Kharāj in Islamic law*, 27; Karābisī, *al-Furūq*, 1: 344.

261 Māwardī, *Aḥkām al-Ṣulṭaniyya*, 146, Abū Ya'lā, *al-Aḥkām al-Sulṭāniyya*, 163.

262 See for example regarding the measurement and the amount of money that was divided with reference to the type of land and its product, Ibn Rifʿa, *al-Īdhāḥ wa 'l-Tibyān*, 72, and 81. In addition with reference to 'Umar ibn al-Khaṭṭāb's practice see *Muṣannaf 'Abd al-Razzāq*, 10: 333.

263 *al-Jāmi' al-Ṣaghīr*, 104; Shaybānī, *al-Aṣl*, 257-258; Kāsānī, *Badā'i' al-Ṣanā'i'*, 2: 935-936; Ibn Humām, *Fatḥ al-Qadīr*, 4: 358-360; Abū Yūsuf, *Kharāj*, 30, 75; *Ḥāshiyat Ibn 'Ābidīn*, 4: 177.

264 There is the case of 'Umar ibn al-Khaṭṭāb, who fixed the amount *kharāj*'s on land at varying amounts, depending on the circumstances of the owner. Hossein Modarressi Tabataba'i, *Kharāj in Islamic Law*, *Kharāj in Islamic law*, 33.

265 Shaybānī, *Aṣl*, 152, 257-258, 279; *al-Jāmi' al-Ṣaghīr*, 104-104; Sarakhsī, *al-Mabsūṭ*, 10: 79; Abū Yūsuf, *Kharāj*, 38-42 and 134-135; Kāsānī, *Badā'i' al-Ṣanā'i'*, 2: 945-946; Ibn Humām, *Fatḥ al-Qadīr*, 4: 362-367; *Ḥāshiyat Ibn 'Ābidīn*, 4: 177; Zaylaʿī, *Tabyīn al-Ḥaqā'iq*, 3: 271-274; Dāmād Afandī, *Majma' al-Anhur*, 1: 666-668; *al-Fatāwā al-Hindiyya*, 2: 238; Hossein Modarressi Tabataba'i, *Kharāj in Islamic law*, 27-30.

266 Ibn Hubayra, *Ifṣāḥ*, 2: 283-285; Ṭabarī, *Ikhtilāf al-Fuqahā'*, 218-225; Māwardī, *Aḥkām al-Sulṭāniyya*, 152; Shāfiʿī, *al-Umm*, 4: 192-193; *Jawāhir al-'Uqūd*, 1: 482-483; Ibn Qudāma, *al-Mughnī*, 2: 575-581, 725; Abū 'Ubayd, *Amwāl*, 81; Ibn Ādam, *Kharāj*, 50-58, 160-168; Muḥammad 'Uthmān Shabīr, *Aḥkām al-Kharāj fī al-Fiqh al-Islāmi*, 79; for further details on *Kharāj* see the work of Hossein Modarressi Tabātaba'i, *Kharāj in Islamic Law*,

267 T. Sato, "'Ushūr," in the *Encyclopaedia of Islam*, new edition (Leiden: Brill, 2000), 10: 917

268 Ibid.

269 Ibid.

270 *al-Qāmūs al-Muḥīṭ*, 3: 230; Fayyūmī, *al-Miṣbāḥ al-Munīr*, 1: 166; Muṭarrizī, *al-Mughrib*, 2: 62; Tahānāwī, *Kashshāf Iṣṭilāḥāt al-Funūn*, 2: 960; Sarakhsī, *al-Mabsūṭ*, 10: 199; Ibn Humām, *Fatḥ al-Qadīr*, 1: 531; *al-Fatāwā al-Hindiyya*, 1: 183; Zaylaʿī, *Tabyīn al-Ḥaqā'iq*, 1: 282; Nazīh Ḥammadd, *Mu'jam al-Muṣṭalaḥāt al-Iqtiṣādiyya fī Lughat al-Fuqahā'*, 198; *Aḥkām al-Kharāj fī al-Fiqh al-Islami*, 11-15.

271 Aḥmad Ibn Ḥanbal, *Faḍā'il al-Ṣaḥāba*, 1: 329; Abū 'Ubayd, *Amwāl*, 566; 'Abd al-Razzāq, *Muṣannaf*, 6: 97; Abū Yūsuf, *Kharāj*, 145; Khawārizmī, *Jāmi' al-Masānīd*, 1: 465; Sarakhsī, *Sharḥ al-Siyar al-Kabīr*, 5: 2136; Akram 'Umarī, *'Aṣr al-Ṣaḥāba*, 198.

272 Shaybānī, *Kitāb al-Āthār*, 63.

273 Sarakhsī, *Mabsūṭ*, 2: 199; and idem, *Sharḥ al-Siyar al-Kabīr*, 5: 2133-2134; Kāsānī, *Badā'i' al-Ṣanā'i'*, 2: 891; Ṭaḥāwī, *Sharḥ Ma'ānī al-Āthār*, 2: 32; Shawkānī, *Nayl al-Awṭār*, 8: 71. See Abū Yūsuf in reference to the 'Umar ibn 'Abd al-'Azīz imposing the *'ushūr*, in his *Kharāj*, 147.

274 Sarakhsī, *Sharḥ al-Siyar al-Kabīr*, 5: 2136; and idem, *Mabsūṭ*, 2: 199, 10: 80; Shaybānī, *Aṣl*, 2: 102-103; *Jāmi' al-Ṣaghīr*, 100-101; Abū Yūsuf, *Kharāj*, 143-144; *Sharḥ al-Hidāya*, 1: 533-544; Kasānī, *Badā'i' al-Ṣanā'i'*, 2: 899-890; Zayla'ī, *Tabyīn al-Ḥaqā'iq*, 1: 286; Jaṣṣāṣ, *Mukhtaṣar Ikhtilāf al-'Ulamā'*, 1: 462; *Ḥāshiyat Ibn 'Ābidīn*, 2: 314.

275 Shaybānī, *al-Siyar al-Kabīr*, 5: 2142-2143; *al-Jāmi' al-Ṣaghīr*, 102; Sarakhsī, *Mabsūṭ*, 2: 205; Kāsānī, *Badā'i' al-Ṣanā'i'*, 2: 890; Zayla'ī, *Tabyīn al-Ḥaqā'iq*, 1: 286; *al-Fatāwā al-Hindiyya*, 1: 184; *Ḥāshiyat Ibn 'Ābidīn*, 2: 315; Dāmād Afandī, *Majma' al-Anhur*, 1: 211.

276 Laknāwī, *al-Nāfi' al-Kabīr Sharḥ al-Jāmi' al-Ṣaghīr*, 102.

277 Sarakhsī, *Mabsūṭ*, 2: 205, *al-Nāfi' al-Kabīr*, 102; Kāsānī, *Badā'i' al-Ṣanā'i'*, 2: 840; Zayla'ī, *Tabyīn al-Ḥaqā'iq*, 1: 286.

278 Shaybānī, *al-Siyar al-Kabīr*, 5: 2147-2148; *al-Jāmi' al-Ṣaghīr*, 100; Ibn Humām, *Fatḥ al-Qadīr*, 1: 531.

279 Shaybānī, *al-Siyar al-Kabīr*, 5: 2149-2150.

280 Ibid., 5: 2148-2149; Kāsānī, *Badā'i' al-Ṣanā'i'*, 2: 889; *al-Fatāwā al-Hindiyya*, 1: 184.

281 Abu Yūsuf, *Kharāj*, 142-143.

282 Mālik, *Mudawwana*, 1: 280- 281; *al-Kāfī fī Fiqh Ahl al-Madina*, 1: 414; Shāfi'ī, *al-Umm*, 4: 193-194; Khallāl, *Aḥkām Ahl al-Milal*, 62-67; Abū 'Ubayd, *Amwāl*, 566-571; Jaṣṣāṣ, *Mukhtaṣar Ikhtilāf al-'Ulamā'*, 1: 462-466; Ibn Hubayrā, *Ifṣāḥ*, 2: 297; Dimashqī, *Raḥmat al-Umma fī Ikhtilāf al-Umma*, 399; Sha'rānī, *al-Mīzān al-Kubra*, 2: 185-186; Ibn Qayyim al-Jawziyya, *Aḥkām Ahl al-Dhimma*, 1: 61-64.

283 Kāsānī, *Badā'i' al-Ṣanā'i'*, 9: 4318.

284 See, Jawharī, *al-Ṣiḥāḥ*, 5: 2072; *Mu'jam Maqāyīs al-Lugha*, 1: 133-134; Fayrūzabādī, *Tartīb al-Qāmūs al-Muḥīṭ*, 1: 181; Ibn Manẓūr, *Lisān al-'Arab*, 13: 21; Fayyūmī, *al-Miṣbāḥ al-Munīr*, 1: 24-25; Kaffawī, *al-Kulliyyāt*, 1: 170; *al-Mu'jam, al-Wasīṭ*, 1: 28

285 Ḥaṣkafī, *al-Durr al-Mukhtār*, 4: 166; *Majma' al-Anhur*, 1: 655.

286 See *Ḥudūd Ibn 'Arafa* with *Sharḥ al-Raṣā'*, 1: 224-226,

287 Ramlī, *Mughnī al-Muḥtāj*, 4: 236.

288 *Ḥāshiyat al-Sharqāwī 'alā al-Taḥrīr*, 4: 236.

289 Bahūtī, *Kashshāf al-Qinā'*, 3: 100; Rahībānī, *Maṭālib ūlī al-Nuhā*, 2: 577.

290 Q. 9: 6.

291 Q. 9: 5,

Then when the Sacred months (the 1st, 7th, 11th and the 12th months of the Islamic calendar) have passed, then kill the *Mushrikūn* wherever you find them, and capture them besiege them, and prepare for them each and every ambush. But if they repent and perform *al-Ṣalāt* (*Iqāmat al-Ṣalāt*), and give *Zakāt*, then leave their way free. Verily, Allāh is Oft-Forgiving, Most Merciful.

292 See the following works of Qur'ān commentary with reference to this particular verse, *Tafsīr al-Ṭabarī*, 14: 138; *Tafsīr al-Baghawī*, 4: 14; Zamakhsharī, *Kashshāf*, 2: 140; Ibn Ḥayān, *al-Baḥr al-Muḥīṭ*, 5: 11; Fakhr al-Dīn al-Rāzī, *al-Tafsīr al-Kabīr*, 15: 237; Suyūṭī, *al-Durr al-Manthūr*, 4: 133; *Tafsīr al-Qurṭubī*, 8: 77; Ibn Humām, *al-Fatḥ al-Qadīr*, 2: 338.

293 Jaṣṣāṣ, *Aḥkām al-Qur'ān*, 3: 83-84.

294 Ibn 'Arabī, *Aḥkām al-Qur'ān*, 2: 903.

295 'Imād al-Dīn al-Ṭabarī al-Harās, *Aḥkām al-Qur'ān*, 4: 25-27; *Tafsīr Abū Su'ūd*, 2: 385.

296 *Tafsīr Ibn Kathīr*, 2: 338; Zamakhsharī, *Kashshāf*, 2: 140; Ālūsī, *Rūḥ al-Ma'ānī*, 10: 52; Rashīd Riḍā, *Tafsīr al-Manār*, 10: 214.

297 Abū Yūsuf, *Kharāj*, 223.

298 Shaybānī, *al-Siyar al-Kabīr*, 1: 252-253.

299 Ibn al-Mundhir al-Naysābūrī, *Ijmā'*, 73-74; Ibn Ḥazm, *Marātib al-Ijmā'*, 121; Ṭabarī, *Ikhtilāf al-Fuqahā'*, 25; Ibn Qudāma, *al-Mughnī*, 10: 428; *Mawsū'at al-Ijmā' fī al-Fiqh al-Islāmi*, 1: 142-143.

300 *Matarsī* is a Persian word that means: "do not fear". See Ibn Ḥajar, *Fatḥ al-Bārī*, 6: 275.

301 Shaybānī, *al-Siyar al-Kabīr*, 1: 283; Abū Yūsuf, *Kharāj*, 222; Malik, *Muwaṭṭa'*, 2: 448-449;

302 'Izz ibn 'Abd al-Salam, *Qawā'id al-Aḥkām fī Maṣāliḥ al-Anām*, 2: 91.

303 Shaybānī, *al-Siyar al-Kabīr*, 2: 263-264; Balādhurī, *Futūḥ al-Buldān*, 2: 469; Abū 'Ubayd, *Amwāl*, 133-134; Ibn Hajar, *Fatḥ al-Bārī*, 6: 275.

304 Sarakhsī, *Sharḥ al-Siyar al-Kabīr*, 1: 266.

305 Ibid.

306 Sarakhsī, *Sharḥ al-Siyar al-Kabīr*, 1: 359-360; and idem, *Mabsūṭ*, 10: 71.

307 Sarakhsī, *Mabsūṭ*, 10: 71

308 *Mudawwana*, 2: 42; Dardīr, *Sharḥ al-Ṣaghīr*, 3: 28; Ibn Juzayy, *al-Qawānīn al-Fiqhiyya*, 116; Nawawī, *Rawḍat al-Ṭalibīn*, 10: 278-280; *Mughnī al-Muḥtāj*, 4: 237; Ramlī, *Nihāyat al-Muḥtāj*, 8: 80-81; Ibn Qudāma, *Mughnī*, 10: 548-550; Bahūtī, *Kashshāf al-Qinā'*, 3: 98; Ibn Taymiyya, *al-Muḥarrar fī al-Fiqh*, 2: 180; Ibn Miflih, *al-Mubdi' Sharḥ al-Muqni'*, 3: 390-391; Sarakhsī, *Sharḥ al-Siyar al-Kabīr*, 1: 253.

309 Srakhsī, *Sharḥ al-Siyar al-Kabīr*, 1: 253.

310 Malik, *Mudawwana*, 2: 41.

311 Abū Yūsuf, *Kharāj*, 222; and idem, *al-Radd 'alā Siyar al-Awzā'ī*, 69.

312 Shaybānī, *al-Siyar al-Kabīr*, 1: 253.

313 Sarakhsī, *Mabsūṭ*, 10: 69-71; Abū Yūsuf, *al-Radd 'alā Siyar al-Awzā'ī*, 68-70; and idem, *Kharāj*, 222-223; *Mukhtaṣar al-Ṭaḥāwī*, 292; Ibn Humām, *Fatḥ al-Qadīr*, 4: 298; Kāsānī, *Badā'i' al-Ṣanā'i'*, 9: 4319-4320; Ṭabarī, *Ikhtilāf al-Fuqahā'*, 27-30; Simnānī, *Rawḍat al-Quḍā*, 2: 1240-1241; *Mukhtaṣar Ikhtilāf al-'Ulamā'*, 3: 499; *al-Fatāwā al-Hindiyya*, 2: 198-199; *Ḥāshiyat Ibn 'Ābidīn*, 4: 136-137.

314 This matter was discussed earlier in reference to the bases of the *'aqd al-dhimma*.

315 Shaybānī, *al-Siyar al-Kabīr*, 2: 576-577; Kāsānī, *Badā'i' al-Ṣanā'i'*, 9: 4318; Mālik, *Mudawwana*, 2: 41-42; Shāfi'ī, *al-Umm*, 4: 110-112; Bahūtī, *Kashshāf al-Qinā'*, 3: 98.

316 Ibn al-Mundhir al-Naysābūrī, *Ijmā'*, 73-74; Ṭabarī, *Ikhtilāf al-Fuqahā'*, 25-30; Sha'rānī, *al-Mīzān al-Kubrā*, 2: 176; Khaṭṭābī, *Ma'ālim al-Sunan*, 4: 66-67; *Fatḥ al-Bārī*, 6: 273-274; Khallāl, *Aḥkām Ahl al-Milal*, 235; Ibn Rushd, *al-Bayān wa 'l-Taḥṣīl*, 2: 592.

317 Shaybānī, *al-Siyar al-Kabīr*, 1: 306, 5: 1790; Sarakhsī, *Mabsūṭ*, 9: 55-56; Kasānī, *Badā'i' al-Ṣanā'i'*, 9: 4152; Ibn Humām, *Fatḥ al-Qadīr*, 4: 154-156; Karābīsī, *Furūq*, 1: 326.

318 Sarakhsī, *Sharḥ al-Siyar al-Kabīr*, 4; 1531; Kāsānī, *Badā'i' al-Ṣanā'i'*, 9: 4335-4337.

319 Kasānī, *Badā' i' a l-Ṣanā'i'*, 9: 4320-4321.

320 Shaybānī, *al-Siyar al-Kabīr*, 2: 515.

321 Ibid, 2: 1853.

322 Sarakhsī, *Sharḥ al-Siyar al-Kabīr*, 2: 515-517.

323 Ibid., 2: 1873.

324 Shaybānī, *al-Siyar al-Kabīr*, 5: 1854-1856.

325 Ibid., 5: 1891, 1858-1859.

326 Sarakhsī, *Sharḥ al-Siyar al-Kabīr*, 1: 258-260.

327 Ṭabarī, *Ikhtilāf al-Fuqahā'*, 34; Ibn Ḥazm, *Marātib al-Ijmā'*, 121; *Mawsū'at al-Ijmā' fī al-Fiqh al-Islāmī*, 1: 141, 144; *Mukhtaṣar Ikhtilāf al-Fuqahā'*, 3: 447; Mālik, *Mudawwana*, 2: 9-11; Shāfi'ī, *al-Umm*, 4: 201; Nawawī, *Rawḍat al-Ṭālibīn*, 10: 244; and idem, *Takmilat al-Majmū'*, 18: 78; Ghazālī, *Wajīz*, 2: 196; Ibn Jamā'a, *Taḥrīr al-Aḥkām*, 237; Bahūtī, *Kashshāf al-Qinā'*, 3: 100; Mardāwī, *al-Inṣāf*, 4: 209; Ibn Miflịḥ, *al-Mubdi'*, 3: 394.

328 Shaybānī, *al-Siyar al-Kabīr*, 5: 1895; Kāsānī, *Badā'i' al-Ṣanā'i'*, 9: 4316, 4321, 4330.

329 Shaybānī, *al-Siyar al-Kabīr*, 2: 453.

330 Ibid., 4: 1242-1243, 5: 1873.

331 Sarakhsī, *Mabsūṭ*, 10: 91; Ibn Humām, *Fatḥ al-Qadīr*, 4: 352; *al-Fatāwā al-Hindiyya*, 2: 235; Ṭabarī, *Ikhtilāf al-Fuqahā'*, 52-53.

332 Nawawī, *al-Muhadhdhab* with *Takmilat al-Majmū'*, 18: 234; and idem, *Rawḍat al-Ṭālibīn*, 10: 280 and 289; Ibn Jamā'a, *Taḥrīr al-Aḥkām*, 236 and 238; Ibn Qudāma, *al-Mughnī*, 10: 429; Khallāl, *Aḥkām Ahl al-Milal*, 290-291; *al-Furū'*, 6: 250; Mardāwī, *al-Inṣāf*, 4: 208; Ṭabarī, *Ikhtilāf al-Fuqahā'*, 146.

333 Ṭabarī, *Ikhtilāf al-Fuqahā'*, 144.

334 Ibid., 48, 50, 52-53.

335 Sarakhsī, *Mabsūṭ*, 10: 93; Kāsānī, *Badā'i' al-Ṣanā'i'*, 9: 4379; Ṭabarī, *Ikhtilāf al-Fuqahā'*, 56-57, 59-60.

336 Ṭabarī, *Ikhtilāf al-Fuqahā'*, 56-57, 59-60. As regards to the extent to which non-Muslims are subject to the Islamic judiciary system see the following: *Tafsīr al-Baghawī*, 3: 59; *Tafsīr, Qurṭubī*, 6: 184-186; Jaṣṣāṣ, *Aḥkām al-Qur'ān*, 2: 434-438; Ibn 'Arabī, *Aḥkām al-Qur'ān*, 2: 632-633.

337 Ṭabarī, *Ikhtilāf al-Fuqahā'*, 56; Karābīsī, *Furūq*, 1: 326.

338 Abū Yūsuf, *Kharāj*, 204-205; and idem, *al-Radd 'alā Siyar al-Awzā'ī*, 94; Ṭabarī, *Ikhtilāf al-Fuqahā'*, 56-57; *Mukhtaṣar Ikhtilāf al-'Ulamā'*, 3: 450.

339 Abū Yūsuf, *Kharāj*, 204-205; Ṭabarī, *Ikhtilāf al-Fuqahā'*, 56-57.

340 For further details regarding the opinions of Abū Ḥanīfa, Abū Yūsuf and Shaybānī see the following: Ibn al-Humām, *Fatḥ al-Qadīr*, 4: 154-156; Sarakhsī, *Sharḥ al-Siyar al-Kabīr*, 5: 1852; Zayla'ī, *Tabyīn al-Ḥaqā'iq*, 3: 182-183; Ibn Nujaym, *al-Baḥr al-Rā'iq*, 5: 19; Jaṣṣāṣ, *Mukhtaṣar Ikhtilāf al-'Ulamā'*, 3: 450.

341 Shāfi'ī, *al-Umm*, 7: 324; Ṭabarī, *Ikhtilāf al-Fuqahā'*, 55; Jaṣṣāṣ, *Mukhtaṣar Ikhtilāf al'Ulamā'*, 3: 450.

342 Abū Yūsuf, *Kharāj*, 146; Yaḥyā Ibn Ādam, *Kharāj*, 169; Sarakhsī, *Sharḥ al-Siyar al-Kabīr*, 5: 2135; and idem, *Mabsūṭ*, 2: 199-200.

343 Abū Yūsuf, *Kharāj*, 143-146; Kāsānī, *Badā'i' al-Ṣanā'i'*, 2: 891; Ibn Humām, *Fatḥ al-Qadīr*, 1: 534; *al-Fatāwā al-Hindiyya*, 1: 84; Zayla'ī, *Tabyīn al-Ḥaqā'iq*, 1: 286; Jaṣṣāṣ, *Mukhtaṣar Ikhtilāf al-'Ulamā'*, 1: 462.

344 Sarakhsī, *Mabsūṭ*, 2: 200.

345 *Sharḥ al-Hidāya*, 1: 534; *Ḥāshiyat Ibn 'Ābidīn*, 2: 314-315; *al-Fatāwā al-Hindiyya*, 1:184; Damād Afandī, *Majma' al-Anhur*, 1: 290.

346 Shaybānī, *Kitāb al-Siyar*, edited by Majid Khadduri, 182; *Kitāb al-Aṣl*, edited by al-Afghānī, 2: 102-103; *al-Jāmi' al-Ṣaghīr*, 101; Sarakhsī, *Mabsūṭ*, 2: 200; Abū Yūsuf, *Kharāj*, 144; Kāsānī, *Badā'i' al-Ṣanā'i'*, 2: 887; Ibn Humām, *Fatḥ al-Qadīr*, 1: 534; *al-Fatāwā al-Hindiyya*, 1: 184; Dāmād Afandī, *Majma' al-Anhur*, 1: 209; *Ḥāshiyat Ibn 'Ābidīn*, 2: 314.

347 Abū Yūsuf, *Kharāj*, 147; Abū 'Ubayd, *Amwāl*, 570; Shaybānī, *al-Siyar al-Kabīr*, 5: 2141.

348 Jaṣṣāṣ, *Mukhtaṣar Ikhtilāf al-'Ulamā'*, 1: 462; Sha'rānī, *al-Mīzān al-Kubrā*, 2: 185-186; Mālik, *al-Mudawwana*, 1: 280-281; Shāfi'ī, *al-Umm*, 4: 281; Ibn Qudāma, *al-Mughnī*, 10: 597-604; Khallāl, *Aḥkām Ahl al-Milal*, 62-63.

---

349 Kāsānī, *Badā'i' al-Ṣanā'i'*, 9: 4321; Sarakhsī, *Sharḥ al-Siyar al-Kabīr*, 5: 1710; *Tafsīr Abī Su'ūd*, 2: 386.

350 Ibid,

351 Sarakhsī, *Sharḥ al-Siyar al-Kabīr*, 5: 1873; and idem, *Mabsūṭ*, 10: 85-86; Kāsānī, *Badā'i' al-Ṣanā'i'*, 9: 4334; Ibn Humām, *Fatḥ al-Qadīr*, 4: 381; Jaṣṣāṣ, *Mukhtaṣar Ikhtilāf al-'Ulamā'*, 3: 451; Ibn Nujaym, *al-Baḥr al-Rā'iq*, 5: 111.

352 Shaybānī, *al-Siyar al-Kabīr*, 1: 305, 5: 1690, 2040-2042; Sarakhsī, *Mabsūṭ*, 10: 89; Ibn Humām, *Fatḥ al-Qadīr*, 4: 381-382.

353 Sarakhsī, *al-Siyar al-Kabīr*, 5: 1867 and 2246; *al-Jāmi' al-Ṣaghīr*, 263; Ibn Humām, *Fatḥ al-Qadīr*, 4: 352; Ḥaṣkafī, *al-Durr al-Mukhtār*, 4: 168.

354 Sarakhsī, *Sharḥ al-Siyar al-Kabīr*, 1: 514.

355 Ibid.

356 Ḥāmid Ṣulṭān, *al-Qānūn al-Dawlī al-'Āmm*, 24-25; also see Goitein, *Jews and Arabs: Their Contacts Through the Ages*, 7.

Chapter Three

International Treaties *Mu'āhadāt*

Treaties have been among the most important instruments of international relations both in ancient and modern times. They have provided the framework for peaceful relations in the spheres of both internal and external relations between Muslims and non-Muslims. International treaties were of particular interest to classical Muslim jurists, chief among them Shaybānī. These jurists constructed a system of drawing up such instruments that covered all aspects of the process, such as the establishment, conclusion, effects and termination of international treaties. Classical Muslim scholars focused on specific aspects of these treaties, in particular the fulfillment of the contract and the ramifications of acts of treachery and violation. A discussion and analysis of international treaties follows here, examining the philological roots of the term treaties/*mu'āhadāt* and its basis for legitimization in Islamic law.

I. Definition of Treaties *Mu'āhadāt*

A. Linguistic

The root of *mu'āhada* is *'ahd*, which means a promise or commitment. *Mu'āhada* is the verbal noun of the verb *'āhada*, denoting the conclusion of a covenant between two parties. *'Ahd* is a covenant, pact, treaty or agreement that requires commitment and fulfillment whenever it is concluded and enforced.[1] *'Ahd* also signifies a firm commitment to observe an agreed-upon contract. The Qur'ānic verses that deal explicitly with the concept of *'ahd* laid the foundations for later interpretation:

> And fulfill the Covenant of Allāh (*Bai'a*: pledge for Islam) when you have covenanted. (Q. 16: 91)

> But if they seek your help in religion, it is your duty to help them except against a people with whom you have a treaty of mutual alliance. (Q. 8: 72)
>
> O you who believe! Fulfill your obligations. (Q. 5: 1)

'Ahd also encompasses the concepts of *amān* and *dhimma*, two terms discussed earlier. The *ahl al-'ahd* are the people or the parties who are involved in concluding a covenant (*'ahd*). *Mu'āhada* is both the act of conclusion of a contract between parties and the resulting covenant itself.[2] On an international level a *mu'āhada* is a contract between two or more states designed to normalize relations among them.

Shaybāni uses the term *mu'āhada* interchangeably with *muwāda'a* (truce), *'ahd* (contract or pact), *murāwaḍa*, *hudna*, *muṣālaḥa* (external peace), *mutāraka* and *musālama* (external peace) in his writings,[3] but he writes *muwāda'a* and *mu'āhada* more frequently than other terms. For Shaybānī, a *mu'āhada* is a *muwāda'a* between Muslims and non-Muslims for a fixed period of time.[4] Many Ḥanafi jurists adopted this definition, including the eminent Samarqandī, who defines a *muwāda'a* as a *ṣulḥ* (reconciliation) designed to end physical conflict for a fixed time period, involving the paying of tribute or other conditions.[5] Kāsānī agrees with Samarqandī and defines *muwāda'a* as a *ṣulḥ* that puts an end to physical conflict for a temporary period.[6] Other Ḥanafi jurists likewise use different expressions for *mu'āhada*, such as *muwāda'a* and *muqāḍāt*;[7] moreover, jurists sometimes define it as *amān* or *isti'mān*,[8] and some refer to it by the term *muhāwada*.[9] Ḥanbalī jurists adopt the same definition as the Ḥanafi jurists do, and use terms such as *muhādana*, *muwāda'a*, *mu'āhada*, *musālama*, *isti'mān* and *ṣulḥ* interchangeably.[10]

It is essential to explain the meanings of certain Islamic legal terms that lie at the heart of our discussion. Firstly, *muwāda'a* (reconciliation) refers to the achievement of *ṣulḥ* (peace or truce); it is a verbal noun designating the cessation of fighting, usually for a specific period of time. *Mutāraka* (suspension of hostilities) is also commonly used, and, where present, the parties involved (in particular *ahl al-ḥarb*) are bestowed with the attribute of *musta'min* by virtue of being granted the *amān*. That is why some Ḥanafi jurists describe it as the "appeal for *amān* and abstention from fighting."[11]

The majority of jurists define *mu'āhada* as a *muhādana* (conclusion of a truce). If a peaceful state is reached between the two parties engaged in a battle or dispute under the condition of reconciliation for a period of time to reduce tension and aggression, it is called a *muhādana*.[12] Mālikī jurists define *mu'āhada* as a truce between Muslims and *ḥarbīs* concluded to end physical conflict for a fixed period of time under Islamic law,[13] while Shāfi'ī jurists define it as a contract concluded for the sake of ending fighting for a fixed time period with or without compensation.[14] Ḥanbalī jurists define it as an abstention from fighting for a fixed time period with or without compensation.[15] *Muṣālaḥa* (the making of peace), refers to the initiative taken by two parties involved in a dispute to reach a peaceful agreement.[16] *Muqāḍāt*, or taking legal action, is the recourse by which parties seek a *ḥukm* (verdict) in a disputed case.[17] *Mutāraka*, or the suspension of hostilities, is similar in concept to *muṣālaḥa* (to make peace) or *musālama* (to demand a peaceful agreement).[18]

Some scholars try to define further the distinctions between these terms: for example, Abū Hilāl al-'Askari indicates that there is a difference between *'aqd* and *'ahd*. According to al-'Askari, an *'aqd* is more elastic than an *'ahd*, for when a person or a party reaches an *'ahd* with another person or party, it means that each is bound to that particular agreement with the other, while in the case of an *'aqd*, the person or party is bound by conditions that can be waived under certain circumstances. The difference between an *'ahd* and a *mīthāq* "covenant" is that a *mīthāq* is only a confirmation of an *'ahd*.[19]

In modern international law, the *mu'āhada* (treaty or international treaty) is restricted to significant political agreements such as peace treaties or affiliations or alliances between nations or supranational agencies. In the case of economic international treaties, the term *'ahd* or *mīthāq* is normally used in the case of agreements with world organizations such as the International Monetary Fund, the World Bank, the Asian Development Bank, etc.

B. The basis of mu'āhadāt:

According to Shaybānī there are two sets of circumstances in which Muslims might conclude *mu'āhadāt* with non-Muslims, both of which must consider the best interests of Muslims and maintain their honor, prestige and dignity.

The first situation obtains where the Muslims are in a position of power; in such an instance they should not seek a *muwāda'a* with non-Muslims, especially if it is not in the best interests of the greater Muslim community. This condition is made explicitly in the following Qur'ānic verses:

So do not become weak (against your enemy), nor sad, and you will be superior (in victory) if you are indeed (true) believers.[20]

Then "So be not weak and ask not for peace (from the enemy of Islam), while you are having the upper hand. Allah is with you, and will never decrease the reward of your good deeds.[21]

The second situation obtains when Muslims are not in a position of advantage over non-Muslims, at which time it is permissible to seek a *muwāda'a*, since in these circumstances it may serve the interests of Muslims to do so.[22] Further justification of *muwāda'a* is found in the Qur'ān: " But if they incline to peace, you also incline to it, and (put your) trust in Allah. Verily, He is the All-Hearer, the All-Knower." (Q. 8: 61)

This verse validates *muwāda'a* in circumstances where non-Muslims are inclined to propose peace; however, jurists argue that if a *muwāda'a* serves the interests of Muslims, it is permissible for them to take the initiative in cases where it is required or advantageous.[23] The other Qur'ānic verse that pertains to this situation is the following: "If he belonged to a people with whom you have a treaty of mutual alliance, compensation must be paid to his family." (Q. 4: 92).

This verse addresses cases in which a Muslim has killed a person with whom a pre-existing treaty or alliance had been established. It encourages the parties to seek redress within the confines of that particular treaty or understanding. The verse also indicates and encourages the concept of *muwāda'a* or *mu'āhada*, referring to it as a *mīthāq* (covenant), i.e., a confirmed contract.[24]

When the Qur'ān exhorts Muslims to fight, it also stipulates that Muslims not take up arms against those who have established a treaty with them: "Except those who join a group, between you and whom there is a treaty (of peace), or those who approach you with their breasts restraining from fighting you as well as fighting their own people." (Q. 4: 90).

It is clear from this verse that the Qur'ān places a restriction upon fighting those with whom a *muwāda'a* has been concluded or with their affiliated parties. This also validates and legitimizes the standing of affiliated parties to the *muwāda'a* as members covered by the agreement.[25]

Another source for the institution of *mu'āhada* with non-Muslims arises from the conduct of the Prophet as spelled out in the traditions. When the Prophet Muhammad entered Medina, for instance, he concluded a treaty (strictly speaking, a *muwāda'a*) with the various Jewish tribes living there.[26] This agreement drawn up by the Prophet illustrates the validity of *mu'āhada* with non-Muslims at a time of weakness on the part of Muslims.[27] The conduct of the Prophet in this instance became a source for validating a *muwāda'a* under special circumstances.

The Battle of the Trench (5/627) marked another aspect of *muwāda'a*, in that on that occasion the Prophet received an envoy from the non-Muslims, 'Uyayna ibn Ḥiṣn, who requested that the Prophet hand over all of the produce of Medina for one year and in return for the Meccans' renouncing hostilities. The Prophet consulted two community leaders from the Aws and Khazraj, Sa'd ibn Mu'ādh and Sa'd ibn 'Ubāda, regarding the offer. The Prophet and his two consultants agreed to give half of the produce, and a *ṣulḥ* was concluded.[28] However, a *muwāda'a* was not established in this circumstance; rather, only a *murāwaḍa* (to restore relations between parties to a normal condition) was agreed to, since Sa'd ibn Mu'ādh and Sa'd ibn 'Ubāda asked the Prophet whether his action had been revealed to him and he replied no. They questioned the grounds of the agreement to hand over half of the produce of Medina, since their opponents had never demanded this from them before, but had always purchased the produce. At their urging, the Prophet realized the possible effect of the treaty and decided not to change the norms or deny the will of the inhabitants of Medina.[29]

Another event that provided a precedent for future *muwāda'as* was the *ṣulḥ* of al-Ḥudaybiya concluded between the Prophet and the Meccan chiefs. The *ṣulḥ* came with conditions stipulating a fixed duration. In the case of Ḥudaybiya, the time period was set at ten years, and imposed a further condition in proscribing theft or betrayal by either party. Whoever left for or escaped to Medina from Mecca after the *ṣulḥ* was concluded would be handed back, even if he or she were a Muslim, whereas whoever left Medina for Mecca would not be returned to the

Prophet. The Prophet and the Meccan representatives agreed upon these conditions.[30]

Al-Jaṣṣāṣ summarizes the opinions of Ḥanafī jurists with regard to the validity of a *mu'āhada* being concluded under such circumstances. The jurists pointed out that the Prophet concluded several *ṣulḥ* contracts with non-Muslim tribes such as the Naḍīr, Qaynuqā', and Qurayẓa, as well as the *ṣulḥ* of Ḥudaybiya, upon his arrival in Medina. All of these *ṣulḥs* were concluded at a time when the Muslims were weak and reduced in number, a fact mentioned also in treatises on *maghāzī* and *siyar*. When the Muslims became stronger and Islam and the Prophet's authority in Medina were recognized, however, agreements with Ahl al-Kitāb were more likely to include a demand for *jizya*. The revelation of two *sūras* (chapters)–the eighth and ninth–dealing with fighting and concluding *mu'āhadāt* with non-Muslims is an evident of encouragements to conclude agreement in order to eliminate and avoid further fighting. However, the apparent difference in the legal effect in these chapters depends on the political status of Muslims. In the first, we see encouragement to conclude a *musālama* or *muhādana* with the non-Muslims at a time of weakness for Muslims. In the second is the assumption that fighting should resume whenever the Muslims are in a position of power.[31]

The opinions of Ḥanafī jurists were largely mirrored in consensus among the Mālikī, Shāfi'ī and Ḥanbalī jurists. For example Mālikī jurists hold that, if *jihād* is obligatory upon all, then the *muwāda'a* is not permissible, in case the *jihād* was a collective duty with an intention to conclude truce/*ṣulḥ* for what is seen as public interest is for Muslim as it is seen by the Imam. Shāfi'ī jurists gave their opinion that if the Imam is in a position of strength and the outcome of the truce/*ṣulḥ* does not serve the interests of the Muslim, then it is not permissible to conclude it. Similarly, Ḥanbalī jurists believed that as long as the truce/*ṣulḥ* favors the interests of Muslims, it can be of use in cases where the Muslims are weak or there is some other necessity; otherwise, it is not permissible.[32]

Thus, treaties vary according to their status, requirements and conditions. They can be permanent as in the case of an *'aqd al-dhimma*, or temporary, as in the case of *amān*, *hudna* or *muwāda'a*, and they can contain a condition limiting their duration to a fixed period of time. Moreover, in the eyes of Muslims scholars, the *mu'āhada* can be concluded with all types of people regardless of their faith or nationality; for example, it can be a treaty to end a battle or hostilities (such as the *hudna*) or it can relate to matters of trade. It can be a simple bilateral treaty, or a multilateral one with several different signatories affiliated with either of the two main contracting parties, as occurred in the case of the *ṣulḥ* of al-Ḥudaybiya.[33] As far as these *mu'āhadāt* are concerned, each one has its own regulations *aḥkām* that depend upon the circumstances of Muslims stipulated in the document itself, as we shall see when dealing with selected treaties concluded between Muslims and non-Muslims in the final chapter, below.

However, the validity of such treaties depends to a large measure on how they are concluded. A valid treaty should fulfill basic elements and conditions that take place in the process leading up to it. Each party might impose conditions that conform to its interests and that would have to be agreed upon by both parties involved in order for the treaty to be ratified. These elements and conditions fall into four main categories: basic elements, conditions, the process of its establishment and reservations.

C. Basic elements of the treaty/*mu'āhada*

The first necessary element of the treaty is the *ṣīgha* (form), which reflects the acceptance and consent of both parties involved as in any other legal contract in Islamic law. The *ṣīgha* can be made known either by expression or by indication, and expression can be either explicit or implicit. Explicit expression include, for example, use of the terms *muwāda'a*, *mu'āhada*, *musālama* or *muṣālaḥa*.[34] Shaybānī gives as an example of an explicit expression a hypothetical case where a non-Muslim army lays siege to Muslim territory. If the Muslims fear that the siege could lead to the loss of their lives and families, then they can offer the enemy a tribute of ten thousand *dinars* in return for withdrawing from their territory. If the enemy accepts, this agreement is an explicit expression of truce/*ṣulḥ*. Another example that he offers is where non-Muslims theoretically impose a condition for their withdrawal from Islamic territory, such as the payment of a tribute of ten thousand dinars, and the Muslims accept this. If the Muslims realize that the non-Muslims have broken the treaty prior to their withdrawal, they cannot retaliate until the non-Muslims reach their own territory, for the Muslims' acceptance of paying tribute to the non-Muslims is based on a truce containing an explicit expression. Should a Muslim retaliate while the truce is in effect, it would be considered as perfidy, an act forbidden in Islam.[35]

On the other hand, an implicit expression is reflected in the case where Muslims do not specify the amount or type of tribute offered to non-Muslims in exchange for their withdrawal from Muslim territory. This is an indication of *muṣālaḥa* (conciliation, settlement or peace) and *muwāda'a* (truce) alike, since the impetus to fight may stem from both sides. The implicit expression of truce/*ṣulḥ* has, as one of its conditions, the termination of fighting on the part of both sides. This imposes an obligation for a *muwāda'a* to be established, binding on both parties.[36] However, where the expression does not indicate any explicit form of safe conduct, the contract of truce is not accomplished and neither party is obligated to terminate the fighting, since non-explicit expression does not impose any type of explicit safe conduct.[37]

If any Muslim should give any sign or gesture that might be taken as a sign of *amān* by non-Muslims, then it is a valid *amān* and restricts any Muslim from committing any kind of attack upon them. According to Ḥanafī jurists, even on the battlefield, if any Muslim makes any sign to non-Muslims that they understand as an indication of *amān*, whether the intention was known or unknown to them, it is still considered a valid safe conduct (*amān*).[38]

Ibn Taymiyya summarizes the opinions of scholars on the validity of three general modes of concluding contracts. First, the contract cannot be valid unless the condition of the consent of both parties is met, and this must be made known as an explicit expression. The second is that the contract is made valid by actions taken by both parties according to the interpretations and details of both parties involved in concluding the contract. And third, the contract is concluded in all of its indications by expression or action that is known to the people or customary practice among the people. The third mode is not limited by language or code of law, but varies according to the people involved and their customary practices.[39]

D. The conditions of treaty/*mu'āhadāt*

In order for the treaty to be genuine and sound it should impose effective conditions that are incumbent upon the signatories or agreeing parties. If any one of the conditions is violated, omitted or disputed by any party, it will terminate the treaty.[40] The conditions may be related to the parties, or to the treaty itself and the motives that lead to its conclusion. In the following pages, we examine the conditions of a genuine and sound treaty.

1. Signatories of the treaty/*mu'āhada*

The Imam (Muslim ruler or Caliph) or his deputy must conclude the *mu'āhada* on behalf of the Muslim community, on the condition that the *mu'āhada* is in the interest of Muslims, for only then is it permissible to pursue it.[41] According to Shaybānī, if the caliph may appoints a deputy, such as the chief of the army, and he may invite a group of non-Muslims to Islam. If they accept it, then they are free as Muslims and the obligation to pay *jizya* will be dropped. If they reject this offer, the deputy can propose that they become *dhimma*, and then they will be treated according to the rules regulating *ahl al-dhimma* as indicated earlier. The actions of the chief of the army or deputy here represent the caliph's or the Imam's wishes.[42] Anyone else from the Muslim community who wishes to offer *amān* to non-Muslims must consult the Imām first, since it is obligatory for all Muslims to obey him.[43] However there are exceptions to limit the right to conclude a treaty to the Imam and his deputy. In some circumstances, according to Shaybānī, it is permissible for an ordinary Muslim to conclude *muwāda'a* without the permission of the Imam, since no Muslim would conclude any *muwāda'a* without first considering the interests of Muslims. As long as the treaty favors the Muslims at large, it is permissible to conclude it.[44]

The opinion of the majority of jurists is at variance with the opinions of Ḥanafi jurists on the question of who is entitled to conclude a *mu'āhada* with non-Muslims. The jurists agree that the only individual who is allowed to negotiate and conclude a *mu'āhada* with the non-Muslims is the Imam or his deputy. It is unacceptable for anyone besides those vested with authority to conclude a treaty. Hence, in the case where a Muslim has concluded a *hudna* (truce) with a group of people and subsequently they enter *dār al-Islām* based upon that *hudna*, it is not acceptable. Therefore, the Muslim's obligation under these circumstances is limited to securing their departure, because they had entered the *dār al-Islām* under the assumption that they enjoyed full protection of safe conduct (*amān*). However it is permissible for an ordinary individual Muslim to conclude an *'aqd al-amān* (contract of safe conduct) with an individual non-Muslim.[45]

2. Consent

For the *mu'āhada* to be valid, the consent of the two parties involved must be expressed, as indicated by the Qur'ānic verse which reads: "O you who believe! Eat not up your property among yourselves unjustly except it be a trade amongst you, by mutual consent." (Q. 4: 29)

This verse is the basis for the principle of the mutual consent of both parties. This applies to all contracts or agreements, such as those dealing with trade or reciprocal arrangements.[46] The Prophet's tradition shows that there is no sale without mutual consent, as illustrated by the following *ḥadīth*, "Transfer of the wealth of the Muslim is not lawful unless with his consent."[47] This is extended to include the consent of both parties, translated into action by obligation and acceptance, in the concluding of a *mu'āhada*.[48]

If consent is necessary with reference to trade and other related contracts, then it is *a fortiori* much more necessary in international treaties that are primarily connected with the Islamic state.[49] Furthermore, if consent is one of the basic conditions of concluding contracts, including treaties, absence of consent because of shortcomings (such as compulsion or blunder) does not preclude the motive to conclude a treaty, but it does have a negative impact upon the contract, or contractual aspect of the treaty. To Ḥanafī jurists this degrades the contract so that, if the contract is accepted, it will be immediately void in the eyes of the law.[50] The consent here is not one of the treaty's optional conditions; rather, it is a condition of its soundness as a whole. The contract that deals with money is a compulsory contract, despite its conclusion; it is degraded since it lacks consent. The condition for soundness of these contracts is consent. If the compulsion is removed and the party that had suffered compulsion turned around and consented, the contract would become sound and genuine.[51]

3. Public interest

According to Muslim jurists, one of the conditions for concluding a *mu'āhada* is that it perpetuates the interests of Muslims, and it is never more necessary to do so than in cases where the Muslims are weak and unable to confront the enemy. This also applies, when they fear a legitimate threat to their security, or when the Imam wishes to pursue peace with non-Muslims in order to bring them under the category of *dhimmīs* or acquire some other benefit or aid to the Muslim state.[52]

Shaybānī observes:

The condition of interest for the Muslims in concluding a *muwāda'a* with the non-Muslims. For example, if the Imam is engaged in making peace with non-Muslims in return for the payment of tribute that would benefit the Muslims it is permissible as long as it serves the interests of the Muslims. The Imam should not forget about the duty of Muslims to spread and preach Islam while he is accepting the tribute of others.[53]

The Qur'ānic verse that encourages Muslims to make peace with others, is as follows: "But if they incline to peace, you also incline to it, and (put your) trust in God. Verily, He is the (All)-Hearer, the (All-) Knower." (Q. 8: 61)

For Muslims to preserve the status of the Islamic state in cases where they are the weaker party, it is important to consider their own interests in pursuing a *muwāda'a*.[54] Similarly, if the non-Muslims ask to conclude a *muwāda'a* with the Muslims for a fixed period of time without paying *jizya*, the Imam should take this offer into consideration, especially if the Muslims are in a position of weakness and it is in the interests of Muslims to conclude the *muwāda'a* and accept the offer.[55]

If the above-mentioned interests are dropped from the treaty, which then is no longer in the interest of Muslims, then it is not valid. In the case where Muslims realize that the treaty is going to cause or lead to further threats to them, the Imam should oppose this suspected threat since it will render the treaty.[56] If it appears to the Imam that the outcome of a *mu'āhada* will be different from what was agreed upon, he can terminate it by informing the other parties of his decision prior to its termination.[57]

Based on the verses cited above, the consensus of jurists is that if the situation or conditions are not in the interest of Muslims who are about to conclude a treaty, then it is not permissible to conclude it.[58] Among the conditions of interest for a *muwāda'a* is the spread of Islam, its protection and the prevention of any foreign attack.[59] The obligation of Muslims to address this common interest of Islam has a spiritual dimension, and must be addressed whenever there is a prospect of concluding a *muwāda'a*.[60]

4. The status of treaty/*mu'āhada* in the Qur'ān and Sunna

In order for the *mu'āhada* to be valid it must not contradict the legal rulings of the scriptural texts, i.e., the Qur'ān and the Sunna. It should fall within the realm of Islamic law, preventing wrongdoing and encouraging good deeds.[61]However, it is permissible to pursue any obligation that is not imposed or mentioned in the Qur'ān that is directly related to the outcome of a treaty or the purpose of the treaties, or does not contradict the Qur'ān and the teachings of the Prophet.[62]

One of the Prophet's traditions that refers to this obligation to conform to the Qur'ānic text at the time of concluding a treaty, reads, "Every condition that has no root in the Qur'ān is void".[63]This *ḥadīth* is interpreted by Shaybāni thus:

If any member of the *ahl al-ḥarb* requests to make *ṣulḥ* with the Muslims under the condition that if the Muslims conquer a part of their territory they should not prevent the non-Muslims from selling alcohol or pork. Since alcohol, pork and *ribā* (unlawful interest) are prohibited in the Islamic legal statutes the Imam should not conclude a truce (*ṣulḥ*) that is based on these condition because it is a violation of Islamic law and jurisdiction.[64]

The Prophet's conduct at Ḥudaybiya, moreover, gives a practical dimension of what is permissible and what is not. For example, one of the conditions that the *ṣulḥ* established was that, whenever a member of the Meccan community escaped to Medina, the Prophet was obliged to return that person to Mecca. The verse that was revealed regarding the matter reads: "If you ascertain that they are true believers, send them not back to the disbeliever."[65]

This verse imposed a restriction upon Muslims, whereby some of the conditions required of the Muslims were to be fulfilled and honored, while others were declared void and were not to be fulfilled. Therefore, among the duties of the Imam is the task of looking into what is permissible and what is prohibited and acting upon this knowledge.[66]

Shaybānī also indicates that it is not permissible to violate justice and encourage oppression, just as it is prohibited to conclude a contract with parties who practice oppression on their people, because it is a violation of Islamic rulings. It is also forbidden to conclude a contract that justifies the acceptance of oppression because this is a type of validation of oppression, and it is not lawful to fulfill that condition in the event of concluding a truce.[67] Shaybānī illustrates this point further by giving an example:

If the monarch of *ahl al-ḥarb* rules over a broad territory where people residing under his realm are treated like slaves and he exercises oppressive means on them, if he has suggested to the Muslims to become *dhimmī* and to pay *kharāj* in return for letting him maintained his oppressive treatment of his own people, it is not acceptable accord to the principle of *dār al-Islām*. The Muslims should not conclude a truce with a party who imposes oppressive acts.[68]

According to Sarakhsī, the perpetuation of oppression is unlawful. Since a *dhimmī* is bound to respect the Islamic legal transactions, any violation of this can lead to the termination of the contract. Even if the king became a Muslim under the condition of resuming his oppressive practices against his own people, it is considered a violation of the principles of the contract.[69]

The same Islamic legal rulings applies to prisoners, as in cases where a representative of a party approaches the Imam holding Muslim prisoners and seeks to conclude a truce with the Muslims on the condition that the Muslim prisoners not be released. Under such circumstances the Muslims should not accept this condition. The Imam should proclaim that no truce is possible without the release of the Muslim prisoners, or he can impose conditions whereby an exchange of prisoners occurs. The Muslim is therefore not obligated to fulfill the conditions that are contradictory to Islam.[70]

The consensus of jurists regarding the legal aspects of the *mu'āhada* maintains that any *mu'āhada* that includes conditions contradictory to the Islamic legal rulings is automatically void. Muslims should look into the scriptural texts (i.e., Qur'ān and Sunna) prior to the conclusion of any treaty, and that treaty should be free of any such conditions that contravene Islamic principles.[71]

II. Time limits

Among the conditions of the *mu'āhada* is its designated time.[72] It can be short or long, in order to allow for reflection upon the situation of the *mu'āhada* and its obligations. This condition is founded on the understanding that both parties are aware of the exact duration.[73]The *mu'āhada* can either be temporary, limited to a specific time period, or it can be a permanent treaty that is not restricted to any time period. This condition is explored at greater length in the following section.

A. The permanent *mu'āhada*

According to the consensus of jurists, the permanent treaty (*mu'āhada*) is one that is concluded with non-Muslims, with the exception of idol worshipers and the (*muṣālaḥat*) conciliation with the People of the Book (Ahl al-Kitāb). Islamic legal rulings stipulate that a treaty cannot be forever,[74] since it must be immediately void should the Muslims become capable of fighting them.[75]

Shaybānī indicate that a *muwāda'a* can be permanent and not subject to annulment by Muslims on the occasion of a renewed capacity to fight, even if they are able to redeem all the pledges or obtain the consent of the other party.[76]

B. Temporary *mu'āhada* that is restricted to a fixed time period

It is in the nature of any *mu'āhada* that it contain explicit reference to its duration, for the prevention of fighting demands that the period of suspension of hostilities be specified.[77] A typical, temporary *mu'āhada* is thus effective for one to three years or less even for a few months.[78] The classical jurists derived their opinion from the conduct of the Prophet, again demonstrated in the treaty of Ḥudaybiya, where the two parties fixed the specification of the time period, i.e., the Prophet and the Meccan representative. They consented to terminating fighting between the two parties for a period of ten years.[79]

However, the time period specified in the case of Ḥudaybiya is not, according to Abū Ḥanifa, Abū Yūsuf and Shaybānī, a precedent that must be followed in all treaties (*mu'āhadāt*); rather, it is left to the Imam to determine the time period, based on the interests and needs of Muslims. Furthermore, the specified time limit should stand to benefit Muslims in the event it is exceeded, or is deemed subject to extension. If it does not serve the interests of Muslim it is not permissible for the Imam to renew the treaty or extend its duration.[80]

Since the Qur'ān does not specify the time period, and even permits and encourages Muslims to seek *muwāda'a* and *mu'āhada* with others without imposing a specific duration,[81] the Prophet's decision to agree to a ten year treaty in the case of Ḥudaybiya was made on the understanding that the *'illa* (cause or reason) determining the necessary duration must be sought in each case whenever other treaties or temporary truce are being negotiated.[82] For the truce terminating fighting and putting an end to all hostilities can often serve the interests of the Muslim.

For example, Māliki jurists state that the period of effectiveness of a treaty is not restricted, but is left to the Imam to determine according to the community's needs. However, it is suggested that it not exceed four months, unless there is an unexpected shortfall in the Muslim ability to perform *jihād*. Here we see Muslim interests equated with the time period, which is determined by what serves the greater public interest.[83]

This was also the opinion of Khaṭṭābī and Ibn Ḥajar of the Shāfiʿī school, as well as of al-'Aynī of the Ḥanafī school and Shawkānī, who all insist that there is no restriction on the time limit, in the event that a *muhādana* is concluded. This will be based on the needs of Muslims and will be left to the Imam to decide along with the learned jurists. However, the time period must be specified, however long or short it may be.[84]

The Shāfiʿī scholars distinguished between two cases, the first being one where the Imam retains full authority, and where he can see that some interests can be served through agreeing to a truce or cessation (*hudna*). He may in this case conclude that truce or *hudna* for four months or less. The time limit is derived from both the Qur'ān[85] and the Prophetic tradition.[86] Here the Imam is not allowed to agree to a truce of more than four months' duration because, according to these scholars, any period chosen requires the *jizya* to be imposed at its termination, and Muslims should not be under any obligation to do so. According to al-Māwardī, the time may be extended to between more than four months and under one year, but there are two opinions on this, one of which insists that it is not permissible.[87]

The second case, according to the Shāfiʿī, school is where the Imam or the Islamic state is weak or developing strength, only slowly. To strengthen his authority, it is permissible for the Imam to conclude a truce in order to fend off any outside attacks in the meantime. The truce (*hudna*) is to be limited to ten years, as we saw in the case of Ḥudaybiya, and it should not exceed that time period. If the imām needs to extend the ten year period in line with Muslim interests, then he may conclude or renew the previous truce for a time period that should not itself exceed ten years; otherwise, according to the Shāfiʿī jurists, it would be null and void.[88]

For Ḥanbalī and Zaydī jurists, a truce (*hudna*) is not permissible unless the time period is determined, by the Imam in consideration of the interests of the Muslim community. The maximum permissible term for a truce (*hudna*) is theoretically ten years, the maximum length of a lease contract, it being understood that they are too parallel reflect the interests of the two parties. The welfare of the Muslim state may indeed be answered through truce (*ṣulḥ*) more than by war. As long as the community's interest is served better by peace it is permissible to conclude a *mu'āhada* for a ten year period and extend it as necessary.[89]

C. The *mu'āhada* that is not limited by time

According to Shaybānī, this particular *mu'āhada* is permissible in certain circumstances, though it is neither permanent nor temporary. It is a type of treaty (*mu'āhada*) in which the condition of time is not a factor, and in this sense it is better termed a *muwāda'a* (temporary truce). For example, in a situation where non-Muslims are willing to surrender to one of the Muslim territories, and the Muslims fear their continued threat, they can make an offer of truce with the enemy offering them, for example, ten thousand *dīnars*, in order to persuade them to withdraw from their territory and return to their own.[90] Sarakhsī describes this temporary truce (*muwāda'a*) as conditional on withdrawal. Here withdrawal means an enemy leaving a territory formerly under their control and returning to their original territory, which in the case of the non-Muslims is *dār al-ḥarb* and in the case of the Muslims is *dār al-Islām*.[91] This is what Ḥanafī, some Mālikī, and some Ḥanbali jurists declare to be their opinion.[92]

However, various Shāfi'ī and other Ḥanbalī, Mālikī and Zaydī jurists advance the opinion that a temporary truce (*muwāda'a*) is not permissible without being conditioned by a definite period of time. In the case where a *muwāda'a* is concluded without a definite time limit, it may be considered null and void.[93] Should the temporary truce (*muwāda'a*) have been concluded according to some trustworthy Muslim or a group of scholars, it is permissible for him or them to terminate it on the grounds that, by concluding the *muwāda'a* according to the wishes of a non-Muslim party, it would give the latter authority over Muslims.[94] That such an outcome is regarded as anathema is reflected in the Prophetic tradition, which reads, "Islam is superior but nothing rises over it."[95]

Some jurists acknowledged the validity of the *'aqd al-muwāda'a* and *hudna* without a definite time period, among them Ibn Taymiyya and Ibn Qayyim al-Jawziyya. These two scholars state that whatever is consistent with the Qur'ānic text, such as the obligation to fulfill and honor the contact, or conforms to the practice of the Prophet, is allowable. The Muslim should under no circumstances fight against those with whom they have concluded a temporary truce (*muwāda'a*) or cessation, truce (*hudna*) unless the non-Muslims are the ones who first violate that contract. As long as the contract that was concluded between the two parties is respected, and irregardless of whether the condition of a time limit is indicated or not, it is a permissible and valid contract.[96]

Some modern scholars favor the opinion of concluding a *mu'āhada* without indication of the time period. Some go so far even as to approve the concept of such a treaty, which in a sense is an extension the concept of *'aqd al-dhimma*, in order to establish goodwill and friendly relationships and a peaceful environment in which to spread the teachings of Islam. According to them, a permanent or ever-lasting truce with non-Muslims has its origin in the basic principle of Islam, i.e., that the external affairs of Muslims consist in peace, not war. They realize that the rulings or opinions of classical scholars were based on their own personal *ijtihād* (or discretion) and that it is permissible for the rulers to override them.[97]

This opinion, voiced mainly by modern scholars, is not however accepted by Ghunaymī. He insists that to follow the example of others instead of that of the Prophet, who concluded the truce of (*ṣulḥ*) al-Ḥudaybiya makes no sense, because the Prophet concluded that truce under political circumstances to accomplish specific needs.[98] Ja'far Abd al-Salām states that the emphasis on concluding a contract such as a *muwāda'a* or a *hudna* should be conditional on a fixed time period, since the permanent treaty or everlasting contract with non-Muslims contradicts the reality of a world that has never seen a *mu'āhada* that lasted for a long period of time.[99]

D. The *mu'āhada* should be free of unsound conditions

According to the majority of jurists from the Mālikī and Shāfi'ī schools, one the conditions of the treaty or conclusion of truce is that it should be imposed free of unsound conditions. What they mean by unsound conditions is that it is not permissible to conclude agree to the return of Muslims who escaped from *dār al-ḥarb* to *dār al-Islām*, whether they be male or female.[100] This is a legally established verdict and cannot be made subject to a condition, just as it is not permitted to conclude a *mu'āhada* with the condition of ransoming Muslim prisoners, leaving empty territory to the non-Muslims, arbitration between Muslim and non-Muslims on the basis of non-Muslims rulings, permitting non-Muslims to reside in the Arab peninsula, drink alcohol within *dār al-Islām* publicly or to build a place of worship within the Arab peninsula.[101]

According to Shaybānī, should the other party make it a condition to return to it a Muslim who had escaped to *dār al-Islām*, the condition is automatically void, and there is no need or obligation to fulfill that particular condition.[102] In case the representative of the other party brings up the ransom of prisoners and imposes a condition upon the Muslims to which, they cannot agree, they should not accept this condition. Shaybānī says that this is because the *ahl al-ḥarb* torture their Muslim prisoners, and there is no point in returning them to that *dār* once their release has been secured. Since they cannot accept this condition, or still less honor it, it is prohibited to give promise of fulfillment. In the event that the negotiations fail, this is not a violation of any contract. It is more important to keep Muslim prisoners safe in *dār al-Islām*, even if this might cause or lead to further dispute.[103]

The majority of scholars are in agreement with the termination of a treaty in the event that one of the conditions is defective or is no longer applicable.[104] If the treaty was concluded on the condition of paying money to enemies, this is not permissible except in cases of dire necessity, for example, fear of threat or attack which might lead to the killing of Muslims; therefore, paying money in that specific instance in order to survive is permissible.[105]This opinion constituted a consensus among most scholars. They countenanced the conclusion of a truce that calls for paying money to ensure their safety and survival only under the most severe of circumstances.[106] Ḥasan Ibn Ziyād, a Ḥanafī jurist, does not agree with the policy of agreeing to a temporary truce with non-Muslims that stipulates giving the latter money every year, because this amounts to a form of *jizya*. Therefore, they should neither accept this condition nor conclude a temporary truce (*muwāda'a*) in these circumstances.[107]

On the other hand, should the non-Muslim suggest a condition stipulating that money be paid to Muslims, it is permissible to conclude the treaty. The amount of money that is to be paid by the non-Muslim under the treaty is subject to the same rules as *kharāj* and *jizya*.[108] According to the majority of scholars it is permissible to conclude a treaty with non-Muslims by accepting an amount of money every year from them.[109]

III. The Process of drafting *mu'āhadāt* and their conclusion

The entire treaty has to go through a specific process that cannot be avoided, for it is crucial to the validity of the document. A certain measure of caution must be taken and careful calculations made by the parties involved prior to the conclusion of the treaty. In the following section an attempt is made to analyze the process that is involved when the prospective treaty is taking shape. This includes the negotiation process, the writing down of the draft, verification or consent, the exchange of verifications and the implementation of what was agreed upon by the parties.

A. Negotiation Process

Some scholars describe the negotiation elements as *murāwaḍa* (to habituate or accustom).[110] It is the first and one of the most essential steps in establishing the grounds on which to conclude the *mu'āhada*. It is at this stage that a willingness to interact and express opinions vis-a-vis the subject of the *mu'āhada* and its conditions is most evident. It can help the parties reach agreement on all pre-requisites, whether the negotiation takes a long or a short period of time, or whether it is an easy or a hard task to undertake.

Some jurists devote an entire chapter of their treatises to the subject of *murāwaḍa 'alā al-amān* (to habituate of the safe conduct) and does Shaybāni in his *al-Siyar al-Kabīr*, where he describes the negotiations between the Muslim army and the *ahl al-ḥarb* in the case of one conquering the other's territory, leading to an agreement to negotiate an *amān* under consent to certain conditions.[111] Shaybānī lists in his *Siyar* the conditions for temporary truce (*muwāda'a*), where he refers to the negotiation that took place during the *ṣulḥ* of Ḥudaybiya.[112]The process of negotiation undertaken at the Battle of the Trench (5/627) in the wake of Ḥudaybiya was conducted very carefully. They followed a procedure that incorporated delays and carefully avoided any elements of the contract that might delay the process or favor one party over another. The Prophet tolerated many issues such giving more privileges and recognition to the Meccan for the sake of peace, at the time of concluding the contract with the Meccans. However, the Prophet's indulgence gave him an advantage in the long run. By concluding the *ṣulḥ* al-Ḥudaybiya, the Prophet was officially recognized as leader of the Muslim community by his opponents. This eased the way for Muslim adherents to preach the message of Islam without the interruptions and persecution that had hindered them before.[113]

Shaybānī indicates that at the time of negotiating a treaty, the Muslim must take into account what compromises may be offered at the beginning in order to reach the goal of a completed treaty. This is to say, he must demand more in order to obtain less than what he expects to get.[114] The writer of the *mu'āhada* should begin by identifying the most significant and most important demands by the other party in case they disagree on a condition, which may be subject to omission. This is because it is much easier to omit something at the time of negotiation than to add some element. Should the *ahl al-ḥarb* not be prepared to accept any but the most drastic conditions, the writer should be aware of this. If they readily accept the conditions offered, the Muslims can drop whatever conditions they wish.[115] This process of negotiation is derived from the time of the Prophet and his conduct in the Ḥudaybiya treaty and during the battle of the Trench and the negotiations that took place between the Prophet and 'Uyayna ibn Ḥiṣn al-Fazārī, where 'Uyaynā demanded all of the produce of Medina that year. The Prophet negotiated a reduction in that demand by offering one third, before they eventually agreed to half of the produce only.[116]

B. The writing and editing of the *mu'āhada*

The process of writing the treaty is counted as an important element in its construction, since this amounts to certifying its authenticity. Although the writing of a treaty is not one of the conditions for making a valid contract in Islamic law, nor it is obligatory, it is a valuable attestation, reference, evidence and assertion of the dispute in which the parties are involved.[117]

Shaybānī emphasizes that it is important to write down the treaty along with its conditions. Should the Muslims conclude a treaty with the non-Muslims for a fixed time, they have to write it down, since some conditions of the contract may be subject to continuity or renewal.[118] Indeed, this recording conditions of a fixed-term of treaty is ordained by the Qur'ān. The verse reads, " O you who believe! When you contract a debt for fixed period, write it down." (Q. 2: 282) [actually it was used by later jurists to apply to any contract]

The writing of the treaty is also acknowledged to be useful, especially in view of the fallibility of memory. The verse goes on to say:

You should not become weary to write it (your contract), whether it be small or big, for a fixed term, that is more just with Allah; more solid as evidence, and more convenient to prevent doubts among yourselves, save when it is a present trade which you carry out on the spot among yourselves, then there is no sin on you if you do not write. (Q. 2: 282)

The implication of this verse is that anything that is subject to continuity or renewal must be written down.[119]

Sarakhsī indicates that the Prophet instructed Muslims to conduct their affairs at the time of dealing with non-Muslims in writing, since there was a benefit to having the facts set down on paper. It was in the best interest of one's wealth and rights, whether matters went for or against them, since it is a record of the dispute should any misunderstanding or conflict arise. The written document would help in any attempt to judge and arbitrate between the people in order to prevent misinterpretation. It helps provide justice to all, and guards against the infraction of the contract, whatever its nature, since some may not understand the causes that can make a contract null. It will also eliminate the fears of the parties in the short or long term in that it spells out the obligations along with the rights that each has to honor and fulfill, even in the case of sudden death or inheritance. As soon as one refers to the written text of the contract, all anxieties will disappear.[120]

The majority of overstates jurists agrees regarding the significance of writing down the treaty. Nawawī explains that it is obligatory upon the Imam, at the time of concluding *'aqd al-hudna* (contract of truce), to write it down and to have it witnessed so that his successor will understand what the contract requires of him.[121]

The language used in writing the *mu'āhada* is instrumental in indicating the purpose and validity of the contract. It is not however obligatory that the treaty to be written in any specific language. For example, the safe conduct is valid no matter what language it is expressed in; Arabic is not a requisite. Nor is there any specification of the language of the written text in the Qur'ān. However, Muslims prefer Arabic as a vehicle for addressing people or dealing with matters of mutual concern, since it has such prestige with them. Any community that has prestige, this in turn is reflected upon their own language.[122] Most probably the original draft of a treaty always, was written in Arabic, and the copy given to the non-Muslim party was translated into the tongue of that party as well as certified by a notary public (*kātib 'adl*).[123] According to Shaybānī, should the Muslims call to the *ahl al-ḥarb* and grant them safe conduct they will be all under the safe conduct whatever the language they heard it in, whether Arabic, Persian, Greek or Coptic, to name only a few.[124]

Accuracy and circumspection in writing the treaty and its editing has a significant impact upon its outcome and implementation. For instance, Shāfi'ī emphasizes that the accuracy of the writing of the document is as important as its conditions.[125] The importance of the accuracy of writing down the treaty is reflected in the notaries' concerns to prevent any contamination by either of the parties involved. This is derived from the Qur'ānic verse that reads,

Let a scribe write it down in justice between you. Let not the scribe refuse to write as Allah has taught him, so let him write. Let him who incurs the liability dictate, and he must fear Allah, his Lord, and dimish not anything of what he owes. But if the debtor is poor understanding, or weak, or is unable himself to dictate in justice.[126]

The scribe should write the treaty down in terms that cannot cause injustice to anyone.[127] Al-Jaṣṣāṣ stresses that the purpose of writing down the treaty in a completely accurate manner is to avoid any misconception; justice is achieved when all of the conditions are listed and applied according to Islamic law (*shar'*). Furthermore, the treaty must be written in a language that expresses all of the obligations and rights in a way that is understandable to both parties. The language of the treaty should be precise so as to prevent jurists from questioning its content. The writer or the scribe should be a trustworthy and learned individual, while his version of the treaty should indicate the consent of both the parties listed to what was dictated to him. In the event he leaves out any one of the conditions, the treaty is void. Therefore, he must write down all of the conditions in a clear and sound manner that contributes to the validity of the treaty.[128] The treaty should include all of the conditions and their clarifications as discussed and negotiated and consented to by the parties.[129]

The specification of the time period must be included, and the effectiveness of the treaty indicated by beginning and end dates. Therefore, according to Shaybānī, the parties who have concluded the treaty must indicate the dates by year and month - - the start date by month and then year, and the end date by month, followed by the year.[130] The dates written in the treaty must follow the calendar established by 'Umar ibn al-Khaṭṭāb and agreed to by the Companions, i.e., the Ḥijrī calendar, which begins with the year of the Prophet's *hijra* (migration) to Medina and whose first month is the month of *Muḥarram*.[131] The treaty will be dated at the bottom according to the time of its signing, and will indicate the time period by its beginning and end date. The signatures of witnesses guarantee that this is known to all of the parties, and this helped to avoid any dispute regarding the length of the treaty effectiveness.[132]

The treaty includes several parts and divisions. The body of the treaty is headed by the name of the Imam or Caliph, who is listed as the one responsible for the conclusion of treaty and truce *mu'āhada*, *muwāda'a* or *hudna* along with the individuals with whom he is affiliated, along with the names of any others party accompanying him.[133] The Prophet, at the time of the truce of Ḥudaybiya, appointed 'Alī to write down "in the Name of God the Merciful" what had been agreed on, but then the Meccan representative Suhayl ibn 'Amr voiced objections and the Prophet had again to assign 'Alī to write what had been agreed to between Muḥammad and Suhayl regarding the people of Mecca, etc. Then he wrote the year and the month in which the agreement would come into effect, and that each party had to fulfill its obligations and honor what they had sworn to.[134] Finally he listed the names of the witnesses, as the Prophet did with all of his truce agreements. In this case the Prophet asked Abū Bakr, 'Umar ibn al-Khaṭṭāb, 'Abd al-Raḥmān ibn 'Awf, 'Abd Allāh ibn Suhayl ibn 'Amr, Sa'd ibn Abī Waqqāṣ, Muḥammad ibn Maslama and Makraz ibn Ḥafṣ to witness the agreement.[135] He also followed this procedure in his agreement with the people of Najrān.[136]

C. Verification or endorsement and the exchange of copies of the treaty/*mu'āhada*

Endorsement represents the final step in the treaty process, where the obligation of each party to fulfill and apply the content of the treaty is made official. Since this is final, neither party is allowed to back out of the treaty at this stage.[137] The Imam and his deputy are in charge of this process.[138] At the time of concluding the Ḥudaybiya the Prophet ordered that two copies be drawn up, one for himself and the other for the people of Mecca.[139] This was a common practice, because each party had to have its own copy to prevent misunderstanding.[140] The exchange of the treaties became a common practice where each party received its own copy.[141]

Finally, the implementation of the treaty is obligatory, and each party is held responsible by the other for enforcing and honoring each condition or article agreed upon. Once the *mu'āhada* becomes binding, no violation can be tolerated. Indeed, if either party breaks one of the conditions of the treaty, it will automatically be terminated, and if there were any hostilities prior to the conclusion of the treaty, these may resume failing any explanation or compensation for the violation by the offending party.[142]

D. Reservation (*taḥaffuẓ*) of *mu'āhadāt*

The reservation of *mu'āhadāt*, i.e., a precautionary measure against making errors while the *mu'āhada* is in progress so as to prevent its failure, was usually dealt with by jurists under a separate heading in the chapter on the conditions of the contract as we saw earlier in the case of the *'aqd al-dhimma*.[143] There the concept of reservation is applied to the *shurūṭ al-ja'liyya*, i.e., the negotiated conditions.[144] The subjects discussed under these conditions are the legally valid conditions determining what is acceptable into the contract and what is not. In the *Siyar al-Kabīr* of Shaybānī, and especially in his long chapter on the conditions of the treaty and other treaties,[145] he outlines the significance of conditions imposed on the treaty and the obligation to fulfill these obligations, as well as the conditions that are not suitable for the covenant or the contract of treaty (*'aqd al-mu'āhada*) as imposed by the participants. This is very similar to what is known as the reservation of treaty in modern international law.[146]

The conditions imposed on the contracts generally speaking are known as valid (*sharṭ ṣaḥīḥ*), irregular (*sharṭ fāsid*) and void (*sharṭ bāṭil*). According to the Ḥanafi jurists Abū Yūsuf and Shaybānī, valid conditions are essential conditions that are required to make the contract certain and that contribute to its validity. As long as these described conditions conform with the contract they valid. Void conditions on the other hand are those not connected or related to the *'aqd*, and are not customary. An example of such a condition is one that might benefit one party but harm the other. If such a condition is included in an contract of compensation, it can render the contract void, while if it forms part of a contract that does not deal with compensation, the contract may still be valid despite the condition being void, since this does not have any negative impact upon the contract itself. The irregular condition (*sharṭ fāsid*) is a condition that is neither required nor necessary to the final shape of the contract. Furthermore, an irregular condition entails no benefits for any party. For example, if someone were to sell his camel and impose a condition upon the buyer not to use it, this condition would be an irregular one, and it has no effects on the contract or its validity.[147]

The disagreement of jurists from various schools regarding the liberty of contracts and specifically the imposing of conditions on the contract in terms of their validity or irregularity is wide ranging. The Ḥanbalīs were more tolerant and open than others, whereas Ẓāhirī jurists were among the most strict and firmly opposed to the conditions of contracts.[148]

According to Shaybānī, the compensational contract is not among the contracts that deal with compensation; therefore, if it incorporates any irregular conditions it will not have any effect on the validity of the treaty. Similarly, Shāfi'ī jurists indicate that contract that does not deal with material aspects from the point of view of the participants is an *'aqd al-hudna* (contract of cessation or truce), as long as both parties agree to honor the principle of what they have agreed upon.[149] Should the contract come under the heading of an *'aqd al-mu'āwaḍa* (compensational contract), then it be affected by any irregular condition, possibly leading to its termination.[150] The bottom line is that the conditions must be directly related to the contract in order for it to be effective.[151] Where an irregular condition was proposed prior to the conclusion of the contract and the contract was established not- withstanding the presence of this irregular condition, it will definitely affect its outcome.[152]

The valid conditions must be honored and fulfilled by all of the participants. This is what the *muwāda'a* stands for. Thus, in the event that a Muslim offers safe conduct to a *ḥarbī* upon his entrance into *dār al-Islām*, and the *ḥarbī* requests from the Muslim that he be made exempt from tithes in return for the same treatment being extended to the Muslim on his entrance to *dār al-ḥarb*,[153] and as long as this condition was agreed upon by the parties prior to the conclusion of the contract, it must be honored and fulfilled. For example, the signatories may agree to a release of prisoners of both parties; they have to respect this condition and release them. It cannot be a valid condition if one party requests the release of its prisoners and keeps the prisoners of the other parties. The condition should be reciprocal in order to make the treaty effective and sound.[154]

IV. *Āthār*[155] (effects) of *mu'āhadāt* (treaties)

The effects of treaties upon the participants, in terms of their having to honor and fulfill their obligations toward one another, may be divided into five categories.

A. The fulfillment and honoring of the contractual obligation and the precautions against treachery or faithlessness

The concept of honoring and fulfilling the contractual obligation (*'ahd*) [156] is derived from the Qur'ān, where it is explicitly ordained that the Muslims honor their covenants: "O you who believe! Fulfill [your] obligations."[157]

The term obligation here applies, among other things, to the contract and what has been agreed upon in the contract. This obviously includes all types of contracts, such as those of partnership, sale, and purchase and leasing, as well as the *'aqd al-dhimma* and *al-amān*.[158]

In addition to the particular obligations imposed by the treaty, the Qur'ān insists that the contractual obligation must be respected to the fullest and warns of the consequence of any violation of this principle:

Except those of the *Mushrikūn* (polytheists or idolaters) with whom you have treaty, who have not subsequently failed you in ought, nor have supported anyone against you. So fulfill their treaty to them to the end of their term. Surely God loves the pious (*Muttaqīn*).[159]

Despite the hardships with which Muslims were confronted during the early period of Islam, the Qur'ān urges and motivates them to obey its commandments with regard to the fulfilling of the contractual obligations; as we have seen in Q. 16: 91-92 and Q. 17: 34.[160] These verses coincide precisely on the subject the fulfillment of contractual obligations and with the spirit and principles of Islamic teaching on how to conduct oneself in a society and in the world, as well as in such matters of interpersonal dealings as trade and business transaction. The Qur'ān's verses indicate this by a variety of approaches, including explicit commands, reports on ideal behavior, or by warning of the consequences of failing to fulfill such obligations. Indeed, it ranks those who fulfill the contractual obligation as demonstrating qualities and attributes that are characteristic of the ideal conduct of believers.[161]

As we stated above, the Qur'ān does not just command Muslims to obey and honor the contractual obligations, it also provides warnings against betrayal of contracts, breaking or violation of contracts, breach of trust and lack of observance. For example, one verse reads:

Verily, the worst of moving (living) creatures before God are those who disbelieve, so they shall not believe. They are those with whom you made covenant every time and they do not fear God. So if you gain the mastery over tem in war, punish them severely in order to disperse those who are behind them, so that they may learn a lesson.162

Along the same lines we find another verse that refers to the consequences for violators of a contractual obligation:

Is it not (the case) that every time they make covenant, some party among them throw it aside? Nay! The truth is most of them believe not.[163] But if they violate their oaths after their covenant, and attack your religion with disapproval and criticism then fight (you) the leaders of disbelief (chief of Quraish-pagans of Mecca) – for surely their oaths are nothing to them – so that they may stop (evil action). Will you not fight a people who have violated their oaths and intended to expel the Messenger, while they did attack you first? Do you fear them? God as more right that you should fear Him, if you are believers.[164]

As for the Prophet's own teaching on these matters, he took a wider perspective in terms of the obligation of fulfillment of contractual obligations and the prohibition of betrayal and or violation of the same. There are many *ḥadīths* dealing specifically with the obligation to fulfill the contractual obligation.[165] Among them is one narrated by Abu Hurayra in which the Prophet is reported to have said: "Carry out the trust with respect to those trusted you and act of treacherously or perfidiously toward those even if they betray you".[166]

Muslims should not demand anything from non-Muslims above and beyond what they agreed to have included in the contract of truce (*'aqd al-ṣulḥ*). Hence it is obligatory for them to fulfill and obey the contractual obligation; otherwise, this will be an act of treachery, which is expressly prohibited by the Qur'ān and the Prophet's teaching.[167]

Abū Yūsuf indicates that, when Abu 'Ubayda ibn al-Jarrāḥ concluded the truce with the people of Syria, each party imposed conditions upon the other. One of the conditions included was that the Syrian Christians be allowed one day of the year to celebrate a feast with the crosses displayed in the street. This condition was honored, and the Muslim fulfillment of this contractual obligation and the respect they gained from the *ahl al-dhimma* as a result paid off for them in the long run in the form of assistance to the Muslims in their battle against Byzantium.[168]

Muslim jurists dwell at length in their treatises on the nobility of fulfilling contractual obligations and the importance of avoiding treachery. Among these jurists is Shaybānī, who in his *Siyar al-Kabīr* insists that Muslim are obligated to fulfill the contractual obligation (*'ahd*) or covenant (*mīthāq*) with non-Muslims in all situations. Should there be a contractual obligation between Muslims and non-Muslims, the Muslims should honor it to the fullest, and as long as it is in effect.[169] As stated in the Qur'ān: "But if they seek your help in religion, it is your duty to help them except against a people with whom you have a treaty of mutual alliance, and Allah is the Seer of what you do."[170]

The Muslim is therefore obligated to fulfill all of the conditions imposed in the contractual obligation. Thus, for example, if the *ahl al-ḥarb* impose a condition upon the Muslims such as not to drink from their river, the Muslims must respect this condition.[171] Moreover, whether the conditions are among the articles within the contractual obligation or only related to them, they must be fulfilled. For instance, Shaybānī holds that if the non-Muslims impose a condition upon the Muslims such as not to eat from their crops or not to have access to their fodder, the Muslims by extension are prohibited from burning or ruining their cultivated land. Similarly, if they impose a condition that Muslims not take prisoners from them, Muslims should neither violate that condition nor kill any non-Muslims, since killing people is more severe than taking prisoners.[172]

The consensus of jurists is that all the conditions imposed within the treaty must be fulfilled as long as it is in force.[173] Ibn Ḥazm indicates that jurists were in agreement on the fulfillment of contractual obligations that respected what the Qur'ān defines as permissible and obligatory. They agreed also on the fact that it is incumbent upon Muslims to fulfill the conditions of the treaty and to respect these as long as they are in effect.[174]

B. The basic protection of the rights of the *mu'āhidūn* (covenanters)

The signatory of a *mu'āhada* is automatically granted *amān*, and this entails guaranteed protection of the wealth, families and personal well-being of the *musta'min*, and protection of their holy practices and sacred places as well.[175] Should a Muslim kill one of the people to whom *amān* has been granted, the

Muslim is under obligation to pay the blood money or wergild. This is explicitly indicated by the Qur'ānic verse which reads:

If the deceased belonged to a people at war with you and he was a believer; the freeing of a believing slave (is prescribed), and if he belonged to a people with whom you have a treaty of mutual alliance, compensation (blood money –*Diyya*) must be paid to his family, and a believing slave must be freed.[176]

It is among the duties of the Imam to provide protection and safety to them and to prevent any kind of injustice from being inflicted upon them. The Imam should prevent and protect them from oppression as long as they reside within *dār al-Islām*, much in the same way that protection is provided to the *ahl al-dhimma*.[177]

The treaty must continue to function despite changes in status on the part of either side. For example, if the Muslims give *amān* to detachment of the *ahl al-ḥarb* in return for payment of five hundred *dinars*, and then another detachment joins the first detachment, the Muslims cannot do battle with them unless they return the money they took from them. Since there was a safe conduct granted to them for a specific time and under certain specific conditions, the Muslims are obligated to fulfill this safe conduct (*amān*).[178]

Furthermore, should the Imam or his deputy be replaced by someone else for any of a variety of reasons, the successors are obliged to fulfill any agreement that was concluded by the former Imam. Thus a treaty will continue to function in spite of changes in leadership.[179] This was the practice of the four Rightly Guided Caliphs and that of successive Islamic dynasties as well. The case of the caliph Hārūn al-Rashīd, when he consulted Shaybānī on a similar question regarding the Christians of Taghlib, provides a good example. Since the Rightly Guided Caliphs had concluded a truce *ṣulḥ* with them, Hārūn al-Rashīd took over and maintained the same policy as his predecessors.[180] The opinions of other jurists on how the agreements in a treaty are affected by incidents such as the death of a caliph coincide in holding that his successor must not terminate the treaty but rather carry on with it and fulfill it accordingly.[181] A question that might be asked is how the liabilities and obligations of treaties were overseen.[182] The Qur'ān, as we have seen, is explicit as to the necessity of attestation and registration of contracts and treaties. In reality, as we saw earlier, the process consisted of four components: the writing, the testimony of witnesses, the *rahn* (pledge) and the *amānah* (trust or deposit). The first two have been discussed above, and so in the following we discuss the remaining two components:

a. *Amāna* (trust or religious sanction)

Islam ordains that Muslims be bound by the Qur'ān and the Prophet's teachings; thus, because according to the texts Muslims are obliged to honor their commitments, Islamic doctrine expects Muslims to respect treaties of every kind.[183] We have seen the Qur'ānic verses that command Muslims to fulfill the contractual obligations, and not to breach the trust. Khadduri indicates in his book *War and Peace in Islamic Law* that, in the past, Islamic authorities considered the conduct of treaties as part of their religious obligation; therefore, it was not an option to do otherwise. As long as the *mu'āhada* stands, it must be honored and implemented, at least until the end of its term.[184] To symbolize this commitment, the participants make a promise to fulfill what they have agreed upon, using such oaths as *'ahd Allāh*, *mīthāqihi*, *dhimmat Allāh wa Rasūlih* and *dhimmat al-Masīḥ* (Jesus) Ibn Maryam. What these oaths represent is confirmation of a *muwāda'a* by different expressions of commitment.[185]

2. *Rahā'in* (pledging and hostage)

It was a custom for the *rahīna*[186] (pledge, hostage) to be offered by both parties or by only one of them. This practice was known to ancient civilizations prior to Islam. As the *mu'āhada* in the past may well have required various hostages for the purpose of fulfilling the conditions of the treaty by both participants, this custom was respected in Islamic law, while honor dictated that each party to a treaty be obligated to return the *rahā'in* without their having suffered harm.[187]

After all, the concept of *rahn* was not among the Islamic legal rulings, though because it was a custom of the early and surrounding environment, Islam had to deal with it as an existing practice as well as a principle of mutual treatment. Modern international law on the other hand forbids the practice of taking hostages.[188] Since the *rahn* is not among the original Islamic legal rulings, it may be of interest how it became a practice under Islam and how Muslim scholars dealt with this subject.

Shaybānī explains that it is prohibited for Muslims to give *rahn* to the polytheists, because it violates the principle of the protection of Muslims and invites harm or humiliations to their persons. For example, if the non-Muslims party to a treaty were to require that Muslim men be given as hostage in exchange for some of their own men, this is not permissible, and Muslims should not accept their request unless there is a necessity.[189] Sarakhsī furnishes a justification in his analysis, explaining that this is because polytheists do not preserve the rights and obligations of Muslims.[190] The prohibition derives from the fear of killing–unless there is a necessity.[191] It does become permissible, however, as long as the non-Muslims guarantee to treat the Muslims as Muslims would treat them, and that whoever shows disloyalty to the condition will be punished. The Imam must provide for the protection of Muslims wherever they are; therefore, he should emphasize and discuss this matter with the non-Muslims at the time of concluding the treaty.[192] The only case where the Imam is permitted to accept the condition of giving Muslim men as hostage is if it can benefit the Muslim community or if the Imam has no choice but to conclude the truce to prevent further threat to Muslims. This is permitted on the idea that it is lesser evil to the sacrifice the hostage safety.[193]

In case non-Muslims betray the Muslims by killing the hostage, the Muslims are prevented from doing the same to their hostages. Despite the condition of mutual treatment, the Muslims should not treat their hostages in the same way, jurists used the Qur'ānic verse to justify specific rulings and practices, which reads: "And no bearer of burdens shall another's burden, and if heavily laden calls another to (bear) his load, nothing of it will be lifted even though he be near of kin."[194]

Also, the condition that contradicts or violates the Islamic judgment is a void condition.[195] The Imam should not take revenge and he should treat his prisoner with dignity and respect. He should keep them within *dār al-Islām* as *musta'minūn*, although he must prevent them from returning to their own territory. Furthermore, they can become *ahl al-dhimma* and, should they agree to this condition, they are subject to *jizya*.[196]

Even if a condition is emphasized in the treaty to the effect that, if one side violates the treaty conditions, their pledge should be killed and vice versa, and even if the non-Muslims should kill their Muslim hostages in accordance with the condition, the Muslims are not permitted to kill theirs; indeed, they are even prohibited to do so.[197] This was the ruling that emerged from an event that took place during the time of 'Abbasid caliph Abū Ja'far al-Manṣūr (r. 137-159/754-775, who consulted legal scholars on the matter.[198] When the Byzantines violated the truce with Mu'āwiya and another truce was concluded, in accordance with which the Byzantines were given money in exchange for hostages, the Byzantines violated the second truce, Mu'āwiya nevertheless refused to kill their prisoners, and instead released them, telling Muslims to be loyal and fulfill their obligation rather than to return disloyalty for disloyalty (*wafā' bi 'l-'ahd khayr min ghadr bi ghadr*).[199] There was also a ruling that, should a Muslim kill anyone of the hostages, the Muslims would have to pay blood money out of the public treasury, and that it should be reserved as an endowment until the non-Muslims pay the blood money of the Muslim killed in exchange.[200] This was the opinion of Awzā'ī, Malik, Shāfi'ī and Ibn Ḥanbal.[201] They agreed that the Muslims should not kill the hostage in response to betrayal by the polytheists. Furthermore, they refer to the principle of fulfilling and honoring the contracts and of preserving the trust and the example of Mu'āwiya.[202]

However, in the event that non-Muslims propose to give the blood money to the Imam, he should accept it; this is an act of fairness on their behalf. The Imam should choose what is best for the interests of the Muslim community.[203] Should both the non-Muslims and the Muslims agree to give the hostages, and they do not provide for their expenses, the Muslims are nonetheless obligated to cover their expenses from the public treasury as long as they remain hostages.[204]

The Imam should look after the hostage's interest as long as they are still under his authority. Whenever the period of treaty is officially over, he is obligated to return the hostages to the other party.[205] In the event that a war breaks out between Muslims and polytheists, the Muslims should release the hostages first and return them to their territory, even if the other party refuses to release the Muslim hostages and proceeds to war.[206] In some cases the Muslims are under no obligation to return the hostages. These cases include the situation where a hostage becomes Muslim and a part of the Muslim community, but then asks to be returned as a non-Muslim to *dār al-ḥarb*, in such an instance the Imam should not permit him to go back. Even if the non-Muslims announce that, if he refuses to return the hostages, they will kill the Imam's Muslim hostages in revenge, he should not return them.[207] In some cases the hostages may prefer to stay within *dār al-Islām*, becoming *dhimmīs*; then the imām is not permitted to return them unless they request this. If the non-Muslims demand that the hostages who would like to stay in *dār al-Islām* be returned, and the non-Muslims announce that, if they are accepted as *dhimmīs*, the Muslim hostages will be killed or made slaves; then the Imam must not accept the hostages as *dhimma* and return them to their own territory in exchange for releasing the Muslim hostages and their safe return. From the Muslim perspective, as the Imam had not concluded an *'aqd al-dhimma* with them, this was valid. Should he have concluded an *'aqd al-dhimma* with them, however, he would be committing a violation of the *'aqd al-dhimma* in returning them, which is forbidden according to Islamic law.[208]

In case the non-Muslims refuse to return the Muslim hostages after the time period of the treaty is expired, then the Imam will not return their hostages until they return his. The Imam should write to them and express his demand and in case they refuse, he is permitted to keep the hostages and offer them the chance to become a *dhimmī*, and if they refuse to become a *dhimmī*, return them to their territory with their consent.[209]

V. The Termination of *mu'āhadāt*

A. By consent

As mentioned above, consent of the participants will make this treaty an official agreement, binding each party to fulfill and apply the conditions accordingly. In the following pages, an attempt is made to discuss the sorts of the reasons that may lead to the termination of the treaty. The termination of the treaty in this discussion does not refer to the expiry date that was agreed upon by the parties,[210] since this is not a termination that needs much discussion. Furthermore, the termination of the treaty does not refer to whether the treaty is valid or not, since if it is not valid and based on Islamic law, it cannot have been concluded in the first place.[211]

Kāsānī explains the reasons for terminating the treaty, and points out that it can be terminated for two reasons: first, due to the expiry of the period of effectiveness of the treaty, and second, for a reason that is not limited to time periods. The latter includes for two subsidiary reasons, the *naṣṣ* (explicit text) or *dalāla* (intended meaning). Termination on the basis of the text usually involves the (*naqḍ*) violation of any of the conditions agreed upon by both parties, although the violation must be evident to both parties. The *dalāla* (intended meaning) which accommodates the clarification of the parties decision relates to the termination of the treaty with respect to both parties consent without offence. Should the treaty be concluded for a fixed time period, it will terminate on the expiry date without the need of any excuse for its termination.[212] If members of an *ahl al-'ahd*, however, enter *dār al-Islām* through a temporary treaty and the period of effectiveness of the treaty expires while they are still in *dār al-Islām*, their safety is automatically guaranteed under a safe conduct until they return to their territory. This is because the act of interference with him may be perceived as treachery. Therefore, the Muslims should be very careful about measuring the length of a treaty's effectiveness and should also avoid any violation of the truce while it is in progress;[213] therefore, as long as the contract remains in effect, mutual respect should apply.[214]

Abū Su'ūd reminds the reader of the command to the contractual party to be true to the provisions of a treaty is contained in the Qur'ānic verse which reads, "Except those with whom you made covenant near al-Masjid al-Ḥarām (at Mecca)? So long, as they are true to you, stand you true to them. Verily, God loves the pious."[215]

Compliance with the rights granted by the contractual obligation *'ahd* is obligatory as long as the time period specified has not expired. According to another verse, "Except those of the polytheists with whom you have a treaty, and who have not subsequently failed you in aught, not have supported anyone against you. So fulfill their treaty to them to the end of their terms."[216]

The above verses make it clear that there is an obligation to respect the time period that is imposed by the treaty, without any restriction.[217]

b. The termination of the treaty with the consent of both parties

The *mu'āhada* that is not associated with a time period is subject to termination with the consent of both sides, as stated by Kāsānī. The text must indicate the reason for termination of the treaty,[218] such as the *iqāla*[219] (dismissal) of a contractual agreement. Scholars distinguish between the acts of *faskh* and *mufāsakha* (both meaning cancellation): *faskh* is cancellation by one party without the other,[220] while *mufāsakha* is cancellation that occurs by the choice of both parties.[221]

Shaybānī indicates that, if one of the two parties proposes to the other party that they should make truce and the other party gives up arms in exchange for a thousand *dīnars* and leaves the theatre of war, the Muslim party cannot go back to fighting until it has fulfilled its part of the bargain. This is facilitated by an exchange of safe conduct. Should one party want to change its commitment to the safe conduct, it cannot do so until the other party receives the money it paid or the weapons it surrendered. As long as they agree to return what they took from each other, then the termination is valid, although should the non-Muslims refuse to give back what they took, it is permissible to terminate the truce without any obligation to return what was taken from the non-Muslims.[222]

B. Termination of the treaty/*mu'āhada* when it is violated by the other party

The treaty can be terminated should one of the parties violate its content by committing a deed that is against the treaty, or perhaps by violating the conditions of the treaty or by failing to fulfill a condition. Should the non-Muslims break the contractual obligation it is permissible for the Muslims to resume fighting without breaking the contractual obligation or giving previous notification. Since dismissing or renouncing the contractual obligation may be interpreted to mean violating it, it has to be made clear what the differences are. When the non-Muslims violate contractual obligation by committing treachery, it cannot be violated after that.[223] In fact the Muslim is commanded by the Qur'ān to terminate the contractual obligation after its having been violated by the non-Muslims: "How can there be a covenant with Allah and with His Messenger for the *Mushrikūn* (polytheists, idolaters, pagans, disbeliever in the Oneness of God)."[224]

Shaybānī explains that the non-Muslims can violate the contractual obligation either by sending soldiers to fight Muslims, or by sending a messenger to convey the termination of the contractual obligation to the Imam.[225] The reaction of the Muslims at a violation of the Ḥudaybiya treaty provided a pattern: the people of Mecca, having agreed not to help the enemies of the Muslims or their allies, chose to assist the tribe of Bakr over Khuzā'a, which tribe had formed an alliance with the Prophet. The Prophet retaliated without giving any notification.[226]

The consensus of the jurists is based on similar instances. Shāfi'ī explains that the Prophet retaliated against the raid of Banū Qurayẓa when the latter violated the truce that had been concluded with them.[227] The same opinion is voiced by both al-Layth ibn Sa'd and Sufyān ibn 'Uyayna with regard to the violation of the contractual obligation by the people of Cyprus.[228]

Muslims can terminate the treaty by their own initiative from fear of treachery, as ordained by the Qur'ānic verse, "If you (Muḥammad) fear treachery from any people throw back (their covenant) to them (so as to be) on equal terms (that there will be no more covenant between you and them). Certainly Allah likes not the treacherous."[229]

According to al-Jaṣṣāṣ, Muslims can break or terminate the *'ahd* prior to the expiry date as long as they first notify the other parties of the forthcoming termination of the contractual obligation. This is permissible in the case of fear of treachery or betrayal, in case the non-Muslims plan their treachery secretly. In such cases, Muslims should retaliate openly, or, if there is a condition in the contractual obligation to this effect, then it is up to the Muslims to break the contractual obligations if they feel there is a need to do so. This is not an act of treachery or a failure to meet an obligation on the part of Muslims, since it is not a violation of loyalty to or failure to fulfill the contractual obligations. Only if the Muslims terminate the contractual obligation without previous notification, may it be considered treachery.[230]

Muslims may terminate the treaty for two reasons. The first is due to the impracticability of fulfilling it or certain of the treaty's conditions, while the second is due to a change in circumstances, such as when the interests that originally favoured the conclusion of the treaty change.

C. The termination of the treaty because of the impracticability of the condition under the Islamic law

The treaty cannot be concluded with the presence or occurrence of conditions that constitute a violation of the Islamic legal rulings. Should the treaty be concluded it is necessary for the Muslims to terminate it. Shaybānī offers the following illustration: should the representative or messengers of the non-Muslims have Muslim prisoners and offer to hand them over in exchange for a concession, but try to impose a condition that, should the concession not be met fully, the prisoners would have to be returned to them, then the Muslims cannot conclude the treaty even if they agree to this condition. This is because non-Muslims were supposedly cruel in their treatment of prisoners and there was no point in returning prisoners once they had been released. This explanation derived from the Prophet's Sunna which reads, "Any condition that has no bases in the Kitāb Allah[231] (Qur'ān) is invalid".[232]

D. The termination of the treaty/*mu'āhada* due to changes of circumstance

As mentioned above, one of the basic elements to determining the validity of a treaty is that it suits the interest of Muslims. The consensus of the scholars was that, in order for the treaty to be valid, it had to meet this basic condition. Some jurists explained that at the time of concluding the treaty the Muslims' interest must be met. Other jurists, such as the Ḥanafīs, indicated that Muslim interests must be respected for the duration of the treaty.[233]

The contract, is not a necessary element of a treaty, it can be potentially revoked. If the contract is revoked, the Imam might break the treaty out of fear from treachery or breach of trust.[234] As was stated earlier regarding the Qur'ānic verse,[235] Shaybānī illustrates that if the treaty does not suit the interests of the Muslims it is not valid. He bases this opinion on the following Qur'ānic verse: "So be not weak and ask not for peace (from the enemies of Islam), while you are having the upper hand." (Q. 47: 35)

Unless the treaty reflects a good deed and an outcome that will benefit the Muslims, it has the potential to lead to injustice. It is permissible, then, to break it. If the injustice appears towards the end of the period covered by the treaty, the obvious result would be its termination.[236] It is not permissible for the Muslims to retaliate unless the non-Muslim inform them of the treaty's termination in advance. If this is not done, it would be considered an act of treachery, and this is prohibited by both the Qur'ān and Sunna.[237]

E. The significance of termination of the treaty/*mu'āhada* by the Muslim side

Muslims should not terminate or break a treaty unless this intention is made known to the entire people with whom they concluded the treaty in the first place. After breaking the treaty, the Muslims are prohibited from fighting against or raiding the non-Muslims until giving them a period of time to spread the termination of the *mu'āhada*. Even if some of them were out of their territory, the Muslim should wait until all of them have returned, and give them extra time to establish themselves as they were before. This conduct of the Muslims is in order to avoid treachery, especially in the case of those whom they were granted safe conduct within *dār al-Islām*. The Muslims should not exhaust them with their effort to be secured, they should ease their way and be certain of their safe departure and arrival in their own territory. In case the treaty was concluded in exchange for compensation, the Muslim should return that amount in full at the time of termination. The termination of the treaty should achieve the interests of the Muslims and should be conducted openly. Finally, the breaking of the treaty by the Imamm should not consider as an act of permissible not obligatory and that is determined in accordance with what is a suitable and necessary act.[238] This illustration is not limited to the Ḥanafī jurists but is shared by Mālikī jurists such as Ibn Mājishūn, Ibn Abī Zayd al-Qayrawānī, Abū Bakr Ibn 'Arabī and some of the Shāfi'ī jurist such as al-Khaṭṭābī and Suyūṭī.[239]

Scholarly consensus regarding the conclusion of a treaty depicts it as a necessary act. The obligation for fulfilling the terms of treaty, as ordained by the Qur'ānic verses and the Prophetic *ḥadīth*, are important, but in certain situation, as previously mentioned, this cannot always take place. It is up to the Imam to make known the breaking of the treaty by notification. In the case of a proven act of treachery, notification is not obligatory, since the other party started the treachery.[240]

Conclusion

The model Islamic treaty—as outlined in the foregoing–possesses the legal validity assigned to any contract and agreement in Islamic law. Essentially a contract, its conclusion demands all the preconditions and insists on the same formalities found in other forms of legal undertaking. In the eyes of the law, it is for this reason surrounded by obligations and sanctions that guarantee its status. Strict adherence to the treaty is thus ensured, from the Muslim side, not by vague notions of international convention or ethical considerations, but by the full force of Islamic law itself. Violating any of the conditions or even the spirit of a treaty is tantamount to violating the law as set down in the Qur'ān and Sunna. The jurists surveyed in this chapter are in agreement on this, and make an exception only in the case where the non-Muslim party violates a treaty's conditions. In such an instance, Muslims are entitled to break the legal accord, but even here strict legal provisions demand that formal notice be given to the other side – yet another indication that the Islamic treaty is no document of political convenience.

1 Jurjānī, *Ta'rīfāt*, 204.
2 *Mu'jam Maqāyīs al-Lugha*, 4: 167-170; Jawharī, *al-Ṣiḥāḥ*, : 515-516; Fayrūzabādī, *Tartīb al-Qāmūs al-Muḥīṭ*, 3: 335-336; *Lisān al-'Arab*, 3: 311-315; Fayūmī, *al-Miṣbāḥ al-Munīr*, 2: 435; Kaffawī, *al-Kulliyyāt*, 3: 255; Rakbī, *al-Naẓm al-Musta'dhab*, 1: 156, 2: 340; Muṭarrizī, *al-Mughrib fī Tartīb al-Mu'rib*, 2: 91-92; Jurjānī, *al-Ta'rīfāt*, 204; Ibn al-Athīr, *al-Nihāyah fī Gharīb al-Ḥadhīth*, 3: 325; Rāghib al-Iṣfahānī, *Mufradāt al-Qur'ān*, 350-351; Nāṣr Sulaymān al-'Umar, *al-'Ahd wa 'l-Mīthāq fī al-Qur'ān al-Karīm*, 17-19; *al-Mu'jam al-Wasīṭ*, 2: 134.
Sarakhsī, *Sharḥ al-Siyar al-Kabīr*, 2: 409-419, 461, 5: 1689-1697; and idem, *Mabṣūṭ*, 10: 85; Kāsānī, *Badā'i' al-Ṣanā'i'*, 9: 4324; Ibn Humām, *Fatḥ al-Qadīr*, 4: 292; Ḥaṣkafī, *Durr al-Muntaqā*, 1: 638.
4 Shaybānī, *al-Siyar al-Kabīr*, 5: 1780.
5 Samarqandī, *Tuḥfat al-Fuqahā'*, 3: 507.
6 Kāsānī, *Badā'i' al-Ṣanā'i'*, 9: 4324.
7 Mutarrizī, *al-Mughrib fī Tartīb al-Mu'rib*, 2: 184.
8 Raṣṣāḥ al-Mālikī, *Sharḥ Ḥudūd Ibn 'Arafa*, 1: 226.
9 Azharī, *al-Zāhir fī Gharīb Alfāẓ al-Shāfi'ī*, 398.
10 For more details see, Raṣṣāḥ al-Mālikī, *Sharḥ Ḥudūd Ibn 'Arafa*, 1: 226; Mordāwī, *al-Inṣāf*, 4: 211; Bahūtī, *Kashāf al-Qinā'*, 3: 103
11 See, Kāsānī, *Badā'i' al-Ṣanā'i'*, 9: 4324; *al-Mughrib*, 2: 346; *al-Nuẓum al-Musta'dhab*, 2: 8; Fayūmī, *al-Miṣbāḥ al-Munīr*, 2: 653; *Ḥāshiyat al-Sharqāwī 'alā al-Taḥrīr*, 2: 466; *Ḥāshiyat al-Shalabī 'alā Tabyīn al-Ḥaqā'iq*, 3: 245.
12 Bahūtī, *Kashshāf al-Qinā'*, 3: 103; Muṭarrizī, *al-Mughrab*, 2: 381; *al-Nuẓum al-Musta'dhab*, 2: 381; *al-Zāhir*, 397-398; *al-Miṣbāḥ al-Munīr*, 2: 636.
13 Ibn 'Arafa, *Ḥudūd Ibn 'Arafa*, 1: 226; Dardīr, *al-Sharḥ al-Kabīr*, 2: 206; Wansharīsī, *al-Mi'yār al-Mu'arib*, 2: 209.
14 See, Zakariyyā al-Anṣārī, *Sharḥ al-Taḥrīr*, 2: 465-466; *Fatḥ al-Wahhāb and Ḥāshiyat al-Bajīrmī*, 4: 285; Ramlī, *Nihāyat al-Muḥtāj*, 8: 106; *Mughnī al-Muḥtāj*, 4: 260; *Sharḥ al-Maḥallī 'alā al-Minhāj*, 4: 237; Ibn Ḥajar, *Fatḥ al-Bārī*, 6: 259.
15 *Al-Mubdi'*, 3: 398; *al-Mughnī*, 9: 509; *Ghāyat al-Muntahā* with *Maṭālib ūlī al-Nahī*, 2: 585-586.
16 Muṭarrizī, *al-Mughrab*, 1: 479.
17 Ibn Manẓūr, *Lisān al-'Arab*, 15: 186.
18 Muṭarrizī, *al-Mughrab*, 1: 104; Fayūmī, *Muṣbāḥ al-Munīr*, 1: 287.
19 Abu Hilāl al-'Askarī, *al-Furūq al-Lughawiyya*, 42-43; Ibn al-'Arabī, *Aḥkām al-Qur'ān*, 2: 525; Nāṣir Sulaymān al-'Umar, *al-'Ahd wa al-Mīthāq fī al-Qur'ān al-Karīm*, 44-47; Muḥammad Ṭal'at al-Ghunaymī, *Aḥkām al-Mu'āhadāt fī al-Sharī'a al-Islāmiyya*, 49-50.
20 Q. 3: 139.
21 Q. 47: 35.
22 Sarakhsī, *Sharḥ al-Siyar al-Kabīr*, 5: 1689; and idem, *Mabsūṭ*, 10: 86; Zayla'ī, *Tabyīn al-Ḥaqā'iq*, 3: 245-246; Jaṣṣāṣ, *Aḥkām al-Qur'ān*, 3: 69-70 and 428-429.
23 *Tafsīr al-Ṭabarī*, 14: 40; *Tafsīr al-Baghawī*, 3: 373; Jaṣṣāṣ, *Aḥkām al-Qur'ān*, 3: 69-70; *Fatḥ al-Bārī*, 6: 275.
24 *Tafsīr al-Baghawī*, 5: 263; *Tafsīr al-Qurṭubī*, 5: 325; Jaṣṣāṣ, *Aḥkām al-Qur'ān* 2: 239; Ibn al-'Arabī, *Aḥkām al-Qur'ān*, 1: 477.

25 *Tafsīr al-Ṭabarī*, 9: 24-25; *Tafsīr al-Baghawī*, 2: 260.
26 Balāduri, *Ansāb al-Ashrāf*, 1: 286; Shāfi'ī, *Umm*, 4: 124; Abū 'Ubayd, *Amwāl*, 232; Ṭabarī, *Tārīkh*, 2: 479; For the text of the treaty in detail see, Muḥammad Ḥamidallāh, *Majmū'at al-Wathā'iq al-Siyāsiyya*, 57-59.
27 *Sharḥ al-Siyar al-Kabīr*, 5: 1690.
28 Ibn Sa'd, *al-Ṭabaqāt al-Kubrā*, 2: 73; Ibn Isḥāq, *Sīra*, 2: 232; Abū Yūsuf, *Kharāj*, 225; Abū 'Ubayd, *Amwāl*, 189-190; Ibn Zanjawayh, *Amwāl*, 1: 399; Wāqidī, *Maghāzī*, 2: 477-479.
29 Ibn Abī Shayba, *al-Muṣannaf*, 14: 420; Haythamī, *Majma' al-Zawā'id*, 6: 132; Wāqidī, *Maghāzī*, 2: 477-479; Maqrīzī, *Imtā' al-Asmā'*, 1: 235.
30 Ibn Isḥāq, *Sīra*, 2: 316-317; Ibn Sa'd, *Ṭabaqāt al-Kubrā*, 2: 97; Ibn Ḥajar, *Fatḥ al-Bārī*, 5: 343; Ibn Qayyim al-Jawziyya, *Zād al-Ma'ād*, 3: 140; Ibn Humām, *Fatḥ al-Qadīr*, 4: 293; Shawkānī, *Nayl al-Awṭār*, 8: 56. Some disagreements evolved among scholars as to the period of effectiveness of the treaty of Ḥudaybīya, with some saying that it was for ten years and others saying four years. Ibn 'Adī in his *al-Kāmil*, Ibn al-Ḥākim in his *Mustadrak*, Ṭabarānī in *al-Awsaṭ* and Abū 'Ubayd in his *Amwāl* indicate the time period of the *ṣulḥ* concluded between the Prophet and the Meccans was four years. However, according to the majority of classical sources, the al-Ḥudaybiya *ṣulḥ* was ten years, as indicated in Ibn Isḥāq, *Sīra*, 2: 316-317 and Ibn Sa'd, *Ṭabaqāt*, 2: 92.
31 Jaṣṣāṣ, *Aḥkām al-Qur'ān*, 3: 69-70.
32 Dardīr, *al-Sharḥ al-Kabīr*, 2: 205-206; Wansharīshī, *al-Mi'yār al-Mu'rib*, 2: 207-208; Shāfi'ī, *Umm*, 4: 108; Nawawī, *al-Muhadhdhab* with *the Majmū'*, 18: 221-222; *al-'Azīz Sharḥ al-Wajīz*, 13: 553; Ibn Qudāma, *al-Mughnī*, 10: 509-510; Abū Ya'lā, *al-Aḥkām al-Sulṭāniyya*, 49; *al-Baḥr al-Zashkhār*, 6: 446; Shawkānī, *al-Sayl al-Jarrār*, 4: 565; Ibn al-Azraq, *Badā'i' al-Sulk fī Ṭabā'i' al-Mulk*, 2: 576-577.
33 Sarakhsī, *Sharḥ al-Siyar al-Kabīr*, 5: 1689, 1706-1707, 2016-2017; Mawṣilī, *al-Ikhtiyār l-Ta'līl al-Mukhtār*, 4: 191.
34 Kāsānī, *Badā'i' al-Ṣanā'i'*, 9: 4324.
35 Sarakhsī, *Sharḥ al-Siyar al-Kabīr*, 5: 1711-1712, 2: 418-419.
36 Shaybānī, *al-Siyar al-Kabīr*, 5: 1713.
37 Ibid.
38 Ibn Humām, *Fatḥ al-Qadīr*, 4: 302. See Abū Yūsuf, *Kharāj*, 232; Malik, *Muwaṭṭa'*, 2: 49 and *Mudawwana*, 2: 42, in reference to the conduct of 'Umar ibn al-Khaṭṭāb, and whether it validates the *amān* or not. See also, Abū 'Ubayd, *Amwāl*, 133-134; Balādhurī, *Futūḥ al-Buldān*, 2: 469; Ṭabarī, *Ikhtilāf al-Fuqahā'*, 25; Nawawī, *Rawḍat al-Ṭālibīn*, 10: 279-280.
39 Ibn Taymiyya, *al-Qawā'id al-Nūwrāniyya al-Fiqhiyya*, 104-114; Malik, *Mudawwana*, 2: 42; Dardīr, *al-Sharḥ al-Ṣaghīr*, 3: 28; Ibn Juzayy', *al-Qawānīn al-Fiqhiyya*, 161; Nawawī, *Rawḍat al-Ṭālibīn*, 10: 279-280; *Mughnī al-Muḥtāj*, 4: 237; *Nihāyat al-Muḥtāj*, 8: 80-81; Ibn Qudāma, *Mughnī*, 10: 548-550; Bahūtī, *Kashshāf al-Qinā'*, 3: 93; *al-Muḥarrar fī al-Fiqh*, 2: 180; *al-Mubdi' Sharḥ al-Muqni'*, 3: 390-391.
40 The genuine *'aqd*, according to the jurists, is that binds its signatories to all of the conditions agreed upon. See for example, Jurjāni, *Ta'rīfāt*, 173; Kaffawī, *al-Kulliyyāt*, 3: 113; Fayyūmī, *al-Maṣbāḥ al-Munīr*, 1: 333; Manāwī, *al-Tawqīf 'alā Muhimmāt al-Ta'ārīf*, 448; Ibn Najjār, *Sharḥ al-Kawkab al-Munīr*, 1: 467; Amīrbādishāh, *Taysīr al-Taḥrīr*, 2: 234-235; Ghazālī, *al-Mustaṣfā*, 1: 94; Nazīh Ḥammād, *Mu'jam al-Muṣṭalaḥāt al-Iqtiṣādiyya fī Lughat al-Fuqahā'*, 172.

41 Samarqandī, *Tuḥfat al-Fuqahā'*, 3: 507; Ibn Humām, *al-Hidāya* with *Fatḥ al-Qadīr*, 4: 293; Qarāfī, *Furūq*, 1: 106-107; and also Qarāfī, *al-Aḥkām fī Tamyīz al-Fatāwā 'an al-Aḥkām wa Taṣarrufāt al-Qāḍī wa al-Imām*, 24-25; *al-Fatāwā al-Hindiyya*, 2: 196.
42 Sarakhsī, *Sharḥ al-Siyar al-Kabīr*, 5: 2179-2181.
43 Shaybānī, *al-Siyar al-Kabīr*, 2: 576.
44Kāsānī, *Badā'i' al-Ṣanā'i'*, 9: 4324-4325; *al-Fatāwā al-Hindiyya*, 2: 196; This was also the opinion of the Maliki jurist Saḥnūn, as reported by al-Dardīr, *Sharḥ al-Kabīr*, 2: 205-206.
45 See, *Ḥāshiyat al- Dasūqī 'alā al-Sharḥ al-Kabīr*, 205-206; Ibn Juzayy, *al-Qawānīn al-Fiqhiyya*, 163; Ibn Shāsh, *'Iqd al-Jawāhir al-Thamīna*, 1: 496; Shāfi'ī, *al-Umm*, 4: 111; *al-'Azīz Sharḥ al-Wajīz*, 13: 554; Nawawī, *Rawḍat al-Ṭālibīn*, 10: 343; and idem, *al-Muhadhdhab* with *Takmilat al-Majmū'*, 18: 221; Ibn Jamā'a, *Taḥrīr al-Aḥkām*, 231; *Mughni al-Muḥtāj*, 4: 260; Ghazālī, *al-Wajīz*, 203; Ibn Qudāma, *al-Mughnī*, 10: 512; Ibn Miflīḥ, *al-Mubdi'*, 3: 398; Bahūtī, *Kashshāf al-Qinā'*, 3: 103; Shawkānī, *al-Sayl al-Jarār*, 4: 564.
46 Sarakhsī, *Sharḥ al-Siyar al-Kabir*, 2: 584-585.
47 This *ḥadīth* can be found in the *Sunan* of Ibn Māja in the trade section under the heading *Bay' al-Khiyār*, 2: 737; Bayhaqī. *Sunan*, 6: 17; Ibn Ḥibbān, *Mawārid al-Ḍamān*, 271. See *Musnad of Aḥmad*, 5: 113; Ṭaḥāwī, *Mushkil al-Āthār*, 7: 251; Haythamī, *Majma'*, 4: 171; Ibn Ḥajar, *Talkhīṣ al-Ḥabīr*, 3: 45-46.
48 *Tabyīn al-Ḥaqā'iq*, 4: 2; Ibn Humām, *Fatḥ al-Qadīr* with *al-'Ināya 'alā Sharḥ al-Hidāya*, 5: 73-74; *Ḥāshiyat al-Dasūqī 'alā al-Sharḥ al-Kabīr*, 3: 2; Nawawī, *al-Majmū' Sharḥ al-Muhadhdhab*, 9: 167; Mardāwī, *Inṣāf*, 4: 265; Jaṣṣāṣ, *Aḥkām al-Qur'ān*, 2: 172-173; Muḥammad Yūsuf Mūsā, *al-Amwāl wa-Naẓariyyat al-'Aqd*, 254-257.
49 Aḥmad Abū al-Wafā, *al-Mu'āhadāt al-Dawliyya fī al-Sharī'a*, 64; Shaltūt, *al-Islam 'Aqīda wa Sharī'a*, 457.
50 Some Ḥanafī jurists reject the option of annulment, since any such objections should have been raised before consent was given. For further details see the following sources, Kāsānī, *Badā'i' al-Ṣanā'i'*, 9: 4492-4501; Sarakhsī, *al-Mabsūṭ*, 24: 40-44 and 85-87; *Mukhtaṣar al-Ṭaḥāwī*, 407-408.
51 Sarakhsī, *Mabsūṭ*, 24: 38-39; Kāsānī, *Badā'i' al-Ṣanā'i'*, 9: 4503-4504; Ibn Humām, *Fatḥ al-Qadīr*, 5: 74; *Takmilat Fatḥ al-Qadīr*, 7: 293-294; Zayla'ī, *Tabyīn al-Ḥaqā'iq*, 5: 192; Bukhārī, *Kashf al-Asrār*, 4: 357; Amīrbādishāh, *Taysīr al-Taḥrīr*, 2: 307; Taftazānī, *al-Talwīḥ wa 'l-Tawḍīḥ*, 2: 197-198; Muḥammad Yūsuf Mūsā, *al-Amwāl wa Naẓariyyat al-'Aqd*, 398-399; 'Alī Muḥyī al-Dīn, *Mabdā' al-Riḍā fī al-Uqūd*, 2: 1002-1005; *Ḥāshiyat al-Dasūqī 'alā al-Sharḥ al-Kabīr*, 3: 2-3; *al-Kurshī 'alā Khalīl* with *Ḥāshiyat al-'Adawī*, 5: 9; Nawawī, *Rawḍat al-Ṭālibīn*, 8: 56-58; Ibn Qudāma, *al-Mughnī*, 8: 260.
52 Majid Khadduri, *Kitāb al-Siyar of Shaybānī*, 165; Sarakhsī, *al-Mabsūṭ*, 10: 86; Kāsānī, *Badā'i' al-Ṣanā'i'*, 9: 4324; Ibn Humām, *Fatḥ al-Qadīr*, 4: 293; Zayla'ī, *Tabyīn al-Ḥaqā'iq*, 3: 245-246; Ibn Nujaym, *al-Baḥr al-Rā'iq*, 5: 85; Abū Yūsuf, *Kharāj*, 224-225; *al-Fatāwā al-Hindiyya*, 2: 196; 'Abd al-Ghanī ibn Ṭālib al-Ghunaymī, *al-Libāb Sharḥ al-Kitāb*, 4: 120; *al-Ikhtiyār li-Ta'līl al-Mukhtār*, 4: 189-190.
53 Shaybānī, *Al-Siyar al-Kabīr*, 2: 498.
54 Sarakhsī, *Sharḥ al-Siyar al-Kabīr*, 5: 1689 and 1: 190-191; and idem, *Mabsūṭ*, 10: 86; Zayla'ī, *Tabyīn al-Ḥaqā'iq*, 3: 246; Jaṣṣāṣ, *Aḥkām al-Qur'ān*, 3: 69; *al-Fatāwā al-Hindiyya*, 2: 196-197; *Ḥāshiyat Ibn 'Ābidīn*, 4: 133; Ibn Nujaym, *al-Baḥr al-Rā'iq*, 5: 85-86.
55 Majid Khadduri, *Kitāb al-Siyar of Shaybānī*, 165.

56 Abū Yūsuf, *Kharāj*, 224; Ibn Humām, *Fatḥ al-Qadīr*, 4: 294; Zaylaʿī, *Tabyīn al-Ḥaqā'iq*, 3: 246; *al-Fatāwā al-Hindiyya*, 2: 197; *Ḥāshiyat Ibn 'Ābidīn*, 4: 133; Maydānī, *al-Lubāb Sharḥ al-Kitāb*, 4: 120.

57 Jaṣṣāṣ, *Aḥkām al-Qur'ān*, 3: 77; Sarakhsī, *Mabsūṭ*, 10: 86-87; and idem, *Sharḥ al-Siyar al-Kabīr*, 2: 499. According to Zuḥaylī and Abū Zahra, the act of terminating the *muwāda'a* in any given event is considered as a violation to the emergence of the Islamic principle of loyalty and fulfillment of *'ahd.* Zuḥaylī, *Āthār al-Ḥarb fī al-Fiqh al-Islāmī*, 671-672; Muḥammad Abū Zahra, *al-'Alāqāt al-Dawliyya fī al-Islām*, 80. The Ḥanafi jurists favor the termination of the *'aqd* due to the suspicion of outcome. However, the termination of an *'aqd* does not necessarily mean a violation of the principle of loyalty and fulfillment that is associated with any given *'aqd.* The Prophet and his Companions was to observe a *mu'āhada* until its conclusion unless it was violated by the other side. For further regarding see: al-Jaṣṣās, *Aḥkām al-Qur'ān*, 3: 77; Muṣṭafā Āmāl Waṣfī, *Muṣannafat al-Nuẓum al-Islāmiyya*, 371-372.

58 Ibn Humām, *Fatḥ al-Qadīr*, 4: 293; Zaylaʿī, *Tabyīn al-Ḥaqā'iq*, 3: 246; *Ḥāshiyat al-Sharqāwī 'alā al-Taḥrīr fī Fiqh al-Shāfiʿīyya*, 2: 266; Ibn Nujaym, *al-Ashbāh wa 'l-Naẓā'ir*, 109; Zarkashī, *al-Manthūr fī al-Qawā'id*, 1: 125; Amīr Bādishāh, *Taysīr al-Taḥrīr*, 3: 144.

59 Qarāfī, *Furūq*, 3: 260.

60 Jaṣṣāṣ, *Aḥkām al-Qur'ān*, 2: 294.

61 Shāṭibī, *Muwāfaqāt*, 2: 227, 244-247; Zarkashī, *al-Manthūr fī al-Qawā'id*, 3: 106; Suyūṭī, *al-Ashbāh wa 'l-Naẓā'ir*, 285.

62 Jaṣṣāṣ, *Aḥkām al-Qur'ān*, 2: 294.

63 This *ḥadīth* distinguishes between Qur'ānic rulings and other rulings such as the *Aḥkām al-Sharī'a* or the Prophet's sayings, as well as other Books that was sent to other people. See the followings, Ibn Qutayba, *Tā'wīl Mukhtalif al-Ḥadīth*, 84; Ibn al-Athīr, *al-Nihāya fī Gharīb al-Ḥadīth*, 4: 147; Rāghib, *al-Mufradāt fī Gharīb al-Qur'ān*, 423; Sarakhsī, *Sharḥ al-Siyar al-Kabīr*, 5: 1788.

64 *Al-Siyar al-Kabir*, 4: 1547-1548.

65 Q. 60: 10.

66 Sarakhsī, *Sharḥ al-Siyar al-Kabīr*, 4: 1548, 1594-1595; Jaṣṣāṣ, *Aḥkām al-Qur'ān*, 3: 437; *Fatḥ al-Qadīr*, 4: 296; Shāfiʿī, *Umm*, 4: 113; Baghawī, *Sharḥ al-Sunna*, 11: 161-162.

67 *Al-Siyar al-Kabīr*, 4: 1595; Shāfiʿī, *Umm*, 4: 113. This was the conduct of the Prophet when he concluded the Ḥudaybiya *ṣulḥ* with the Meccans, for afterwards he did not return the women.

68 Sarakhsī, *Mabsūṭ*, 10: 85; Shaybānī, *Kitāb al-Siyar*, 162.

69 Sarakhsī, *Mabsūṭ*, 10: 85; *Kitāb al-Siyar*, 162.

70 *Sharḥ al-Siyar al-Kabīr*, 5: 1813-1814; Shāfiʿī, *al-Umm*, 4: 114.

71 Shāfiʿī, *al-Umm*, 4: 110-111; Nawāwī, *Rawḍat al-Ṭālibīn*, 10: 334; Ibn Jamā'a, *Taḥrīr al-Aḥkām fī Tadbīr Ahl al-Islam*, 233; Ibn Qudāma, *Mughnī*, 10: 510-511; Ṭabarī, *Ikhtilāf al-Fuqahā'*, 18-19; *Fatāwā al-Shaykh 'Alīsh*, 1: 391; Bayḍāwī, *al-Ghāya al-Quṣwā*, 2: 961.

72 Dāmād, *Majma' al-Anhur Sharḥ Multaqā al-Abḥur*, 1: 637.

73 Sarakhsī, *Sharḥ al-Siyar al-Kabīr*, 5: 1782; an exception is the *'aqd al-dhimma*, which, as we saw earlier, is not limited to time period. It is a permanent *'aqd* as far as

the Muslims are concerned, but it is subject to termination by the *ahl al-dhimma* in the event that they decide to become Muslim.
74 Rāghib al-Iṣfahānī in his *Mufradāt al-Qur'ān*, 8; Jurjānī in his *Ta'rifāt*, 21; Jawharī, in his *Ṣiḥāḥ*, 2: 439.
75 Ṭabarī, *Ikhtilāf al-Fuqahā'*, 14; Shawkānī, *al-Sayl al-Jarrār*, 4: 565; Ibn al-Murtaḍā, *al-Baḥr al-Zakhkhār al-Jāmi' li-Madhāhib 'Ulamā' al-Amṣār*, 6: 448; *Fatāwā al-Shaykh 'Alīsh*, 11: 392; Wansharīshī, *al-Mi'yār al-Mu'rib*, 2: 208; Some modern scholars, such as al-Zuḥaylī in his *Āthār al-Ḥarb fī al-Fiqh al-Islamī*, 675, indicate that the consensus of scholars is that no *muhādana* is valid without the designation of a time period. See, Abu Zahra, *al-'Alāqāt al-Dawliyya fī al-Islām*, 78-79; 'Alī Manṣūr, *al-Sharī'a al-Islāmiyya wa 'l-Qānūn al-Dawlī*, 375-379; Zuḥayli, *Āthār al-Ḥarb*, 359.
76 Shaybānī, *al-Siyar al-Kabīr*, 5: 1758-1759.
77 Sarakhsī, *Sharḥ al-Siyar al-Kabīr*, 2: 486, 5: 1713; Zarkashī, *al-Manthūr fī al-Qawā'id*, 1: 240, Zarkashī indicates that any *'aqd* specifying a time period is a temporary *'aqd*, such as contracts of rent or lease, sharecropping and armistice or truce; Suyūṭī, *al-Ashbāh wa 'l-Naẓā'ir*, 282-283.
78 *Sharḥ al-Siyar al-Kabīr*, 5: 1713-1714, 1780.
79 Ibid.; 5: 1780; Ibn Isḥāq, *Sīra*, 2: 316-317; Ibn Sa'd, *Ṭabaqāt*, 2:97; Ibn Ḥajar, *Fatḥ al-Bārī*, 5: 343; Ibn Qayyim al-Jawziyya, *Zād al-Ma'ād*, 3: 140; Ibn Humām, *Fatḥ al-Qadīr*, 4: 293; Shawkānī, *Nayl al-Awṭār*, 8: 56.
80 Ibid.
81 "But if they incline to peace, you also incline to it." Q. 8: 61,
82 *Uṣūl al-Sarakhsī*, 2: 158-162; *Kashf al-Asrār*, 3: 389-390; *Taysīr al-Taḥrīr*, 4: 5-6; *Mīzān al-Uṣūl*, 630; *Sharḥ al-Kawkab al-Munīr*, 4: 52-53; *al-Mustaṣfā*, 2: 345.
83 See for example, *Jawāhir al-Iklīl*, 1: 269-270; *al-Khurashī 'alā Khalīl*, 3: 151; *Fatāwā al-Shaykh 'Ulish*, 1: 390; Wansharīsī, *al-Mi'yār al-Mu'rib*, 6: 208; *al-Qawānīn al-Fiqhiyya*, 163; *'Iqd al-Jawāhir al-Thamīna*, 1: 497; Dardīr, *al-Sharḥ al-Kabīr*, 2: 206; Ibn 'Abd al-Barr, *al-Kāfī*, 1: 404; Baghawī, *Sharḥ al-Sunna*, 11: 161; Bayḍāwī, *al-Ghāya al-Quṣwā*, 2: 961.
84 Khaṭṭābī, *Ma'ālim al-Sunan*, 4: 80; Ibn Ḥajar, *Fatḥ al-Bārī*, 6: 282; 'Aynī, *'Umdat al-Qārī'*, 15: 105; Baghawī, *Sharḥ al-Sunna*, 11: 161; Shawkānī, *al-Sayl al-Jarrār*, 4: 565.
85 Q. 9: 1 and 2,
"Freedom from (all) obligations (is declared) from Allah and His Messenger to those of the *Mushrikūn* (polytheists, pagans, idolaters, disbeliveers in the Oneness of Allah), with whom you made treaty" "So travel freely (O *Mushrikūn*) for four months (as you will) throughout the land."
86 The Prophet concluded armistice or truce with Ṣafwān Ibn Umayya for four months. References to this may be found in: Malik, *Muwaṭṭa'*, 2: 543-544; Shāfi'ī, *Umm*, 4: 112; Ibn 'Abd al-Barr, *Tamhīd*, 12: 19.
87 Mawārdī, *al-Aḥkām al-Sulṭāniyya*, 151.
88 See for example: Shāfi'ī, *al-Umm*, 4: 110, and *Aḥkām al-Qur'ān*, 2: 62-64; Ṭabarī, *Ikhtilāf al-Fuqahā'*, 15-17; Nawāwī, *Rawḍat al-Ṭālibīn*, 10: 335; and idem, *al-Muhadhdhab* with *Takmilat al-Majmū'*, 18: 221-222; Ghazālī, *al-Wajīz*, 2: 240; *al-'Azīz Sharḥ al-Wajīz*, 13: 556-559; *Mughnī al-Muḥtāj*, 4: 260-261; Ibn Jamā'a, *Taḥrīr al-Aḥkām*, 232; Māwardī, *al-Aḥkām al-Sulṭāniyya*, 151; *Ḥāshiyat al-Bujrimī 'alā al-Manhaj*, 4: 258-259; Baghawī, *Sharḥ al-Sunna*, 11: 161; Ibn Ḥajar, *Fatḥ al-Bārī*, 5: 343; Shawkānī, *Nayl al-Awṭār*, 8: 56.

89 Ibn Qudāma, *al-Mughnī*, 10: 509-510; Ibn Taymiyya, *al-Muḥarrar*, 2: 182; Mardāwī, *al-Inṣāf*, 4: 212; Ibn Mifliḥ, *al-Mubdi'*, 3: 398; Bahūtī, *Kashshāf al-Qinā'*, 3: 104; *Ḥadā'iq al-Azhār* with *Sharḥ al-Sayl al-Jarrār*, 4: 564-565; Ibn al-Murtaḍā, *al-Baḥr al-Zakhār*, 6: 448.

90 Shaybānī, *al-Siyar al-Kabīr*, 5: 1711-1712.

91 Sarakhsī, *Sharḥ al-Siyar al-Kabīr*, 5: 1712.

92 Kāsānī, *Badā'i' al-Ṣanā'i'*, 9: 4327; Ibn 'Arabī, *Aḥkām al-Qur'ān*, 4: 1789; Ibn Hubayrā, *Ifṣāḥ*, 2: 296; *Mukhtaṣar al-Muzanī* in the margin of *al-Umm*, 3: 399-400.

93 Shāfi'ī, *Umm*, 4: 110-111; Nawawī, *al-Muhadhdhab* with *Takmilat al-Majmū'*, 18: 222; and idem, *Rawḍat al-Ṭālibīn*, 10: 335-336; *al-Sharqāwī 'alā al-Taḥrīr*, 3: 467; Ghazālī, *al-Wajīz*, 2: 204; Ibn Qudāma, *al-Mughnī*, 10: 509; Ibn Mifliḥ, *al-Mubdi'*, 3: 399; Mardāwī, *al-Inṣāf*, 4: 212-213; Bahūtī, *Kashshāf al-Qinā'*, 3: 104; Ibn Hubayrā, *al-Ifṣāḥ*, 2: 296; Ibn Murtaḍā, *al-Baḥr al-Zakhkhār*, 6: 449.

94 Nawawī, *al-Muhadhdhab* with *Takmilat al-Majmū'*, 18: 222, Shāfi'ī, *Umm*, 4: 110-111; *Sunan al-Bayhaqī*, 9: 224.

95 Abū 'Ubayd, *Amwāl*, 149; Ṭaḥāwī, *Ma'ānī al-Āthār*, 3: 257; *Fatḥ al-Bārī*, 3: 220; *Irwā' al-Ghalīl*, 5: 106-109.

96 *Majmū' Fatāwā Ibn Taymiyya*, 29: 140; Ibn Qayyim al-Jawziyya, *Aḥkām Ahl al-Dhimma*, 2: 476-490; and idem, *Zād al-Ma'ād*, 3: 146; Ba'lī, *al-Ikhtiyārāt al-Fiqhiyya*, 542; *Mukhtaṣar al-Muzanī* within the margin of *al-Umm*, 3: 399-400.

97 See, for example: Abū Zahra, *al-'Alāqāt al-Dawliyya fī al-Islam*, 78, and his preface to Sarakhsī, *Sharḥ al-Siyar al-Kabīr*, 96; 'Alī Manṣūr, *al-Sharī'a al-Islāmiyya wa al-Qānūn al-Duwalī*, 377-378; Ṣubḥī Maḥmaṣānī, *al-Qānūn wa al-'Alāqāt al-Dawliyya*, 144-145; Wahbī al-Zuḥaylī, *Āthār al-Ḥarb fī al-Fiqh al-Islāmī*, 678-680, and his *'Alāqāt al-Dawliyya fī al-Islām*, 139; Muḥammad Kamāl Imām, *al-Ḥarb wa 'l-Silm fī al-Fiqh al-Islāmī*, 136.

98 *Aḥkām al-Mu'āhadāt fī al-Sharī'a al-Islāmiyya*, 97, *Qānūn al-Salām fī al-Islām*, 511. He labels these scholars as imitators and criticizes the Islamic legal tradition for the same fault, stressing the need to follow logically in the footsteps of the Prophet indicated by the Qur'ānic verse " You have the Prophet as the right example".

99 *Qawā'id al-'Alāqāt al-Dawliyya fī al-Qānūn al-Dawlī wa 'l-Sharī'a al-Islāmiyya*, 393, and *Sharṭ Baqā' al-Shay' 'alā Ḥālih*, 403; It is worth mentioning that a recent Maliki jurist, Muḥammad 'Alīsh, in his *Fatḥ al-'Alī al-Malik fī al-Fatwā 'ala Madhhab al-Imām Mālik*, 1: 190, states a similar opinion. Other modern scholars, such as Muḥammad 'Alī Ḥasan in his book *al-'Alāqāt al-Dawliyya fī al-Qur'ān wa Sunna*, 360, indicate that the early jurists were in no disagreement (*ikhtilāf*) over the fact that a *mu'āhada* not conditioned by time period is impermissible. He insists furthermore that there is no text in either the Qur'ān or the Sunna that approves the *mu'āhada* without fixed duration, but that one can find evidence indicating that such a treaty would be invalid.

100 The majority of scholars are in agreement on not returning female Muslims and disagree over whether to return Muslim males. Ḥanbalī and Malikī jurists allowed the latter under severe circumstances, while Abū Ḥanīfa and some Malikī jurists did not permit it because it was a null condition; thus, should the Muslim not fulfill this condition, the *mu'āhada* would resume and remain accurate and valid. Some Shafi'ī jurists permitted it only should the male Muslim have some family to protect him within *dār al-ḥarb*. See *Sharḥ al-Siyar al-Kabīr*, 4: 1594-1595; Jaṣṣāṣ, *Mukhtaṣar Ikhtilāf al-*

Fuqahā', 3: 45; idem, *Aḥkām al-Qur'ān*, 3: 437; *al-Fatāwā al-Hindiyya*, 2: 197; *al-Bayān wa al-Taḥṣīl*, 3: 46-48; *'Iqd al-Jawāhir al-Thamīna*, 1: 397-398; *Ḥāshiyat al-Dasūqī*, 2: 206; *Ḥāshiyat al-Ṣāwī 'alā al-Sharḥ al-Saghīr*, 2: 64; Nawawī, *al-Muhadhdhab* with the *Majmū'*, 18: 225; Māwardī, *al-Aḥkām al-Sulṭāniyya*, 52; Ibn Ḥajar al-Haythamī, *al-Fatāwā al-Kubrā al-Fiqhiyya*, 4: 249; Ibn Qudāma, *al-Mughnī*, 5: 517; Mardāwī, *al-Inṣāf*, 4: 214; Ibn Qayyim al-Jawziyya, *Zād al-Ma'ād*, 3: 140-141; Shawkānī, *al-Sayl al-Jarrār*, 4: 566-567; Shāfi'ī, *Aḥkām al-Qur'ān*, 2: 66, 68; Ibn 'Arabī, *Aḥkām al-Qur'ān*, 4: 1789; Ibn Ḥajar, *Fatḥ al-Bārī*, 5: 345.

101 Sarakhsī, *Sharḥ al-Siyar al-Kabīr*, 4: 1536, 1594; *al-Dasūqī 'alā al-Sharḥ al-Kabīr*, 2: 206; *al-Qawānīn al-Fiqhiyya*, 163; Shāfi'ī, *al-Umm*, 4: 110-111; *al-'Azīz Sharḥ al-Wajīz*, 13: 555; Nawāwī, *Rawḍat al-Ṭālibīn*, 10: 334-335; Ibn Jamā'a, *Taḥrīr al-Aḥkām*, 233; Mardāwī, *al-Inṣāf*, 4: 213-214; Ibn Taymiyya, *al-Muḥarrar fī al-Fiqh*, 2: 182; Ibn Mifliḥ, *al-Mubdi'*, 3: 400; Ibn Murtaḍā, *al-Baḥr al-Zakhkhār al-Jāmi' li-'Ulamā al-Amṣār*, 6: 448; Ṭabarī, *Ikhtilāf al-Fuqhā'*, 18-19; Ibn Ḥajar, *Fatḥ al-Bārī*, 6: 276; Qalqashandī. *Ṣubḥ al-A'shā*, 14: 7-8.

102 *Al-Fatāwā al-Hindiyya*, 2: 197; Abū Yūsuf, *Kharāj*, 224; Khawārizmī, *Mufīd al-'Ulūm wa Mubīd al-Humūm*, 344.

103 Sarakhsī, *Sharḥ al-Siyar al-Kabīr*, 5: 1788, 1813-1814, 4: 1594-1595; and idem, *al-Mabsūṭ*, 10: 88; *al-Fatāwā al-Hindiyya*, 2: 197; Ibn Nujaym, *al-Baḥr al-Rā'iq*, 5: 86.

104 Ibn Shāsh, *'Iqd al-Jawāhir al-Thamīna*, 1: 497; *al-Sharḥ al-Kabīr* with *Ḥāshiyat al-Dasūqī*, 2: 206; Ghazālī, *al-Wajīz*, 2: 203; Nawāwī, *Rawḍat al-Ṭālibīn*, 10: 334-335; Ibn Qudāma, *al-Mughnī*, 10: 517-519; and idem, *al-Sharḥ al-Kabīr*, 10: 568-569; Ibn Mifliḥ, *al-Mubdi'*, 3: 400-401.

105 *Al-Fatāwā al-Hindiyya*, 2: 196; *Fatḥ al-Qadīr*, 4: 296; *Ḥāshiyat Ibn 'Ābidīn*, 4: 133; Zayla'ī, *Tabyīn al-Ḥaqā'iq*, 3: 246; Dāmād Afandī, *Majm' al-Anhur*, 1: 637; Mawṣilī, *al-Ikhtiyār li-Ta'līl al-Mukhtār*, 4: 191; Ṭabarī, *Ikhtilāf al-Fuqahā'*, 19.

106 *Al-Karshī 'alā Khalīl*, 2: 449; Ibn Rushd, *Bidāyat al-Mujtahid*, 1: 388; and idem, *al-Bayān wa al-Taḥṣīl*, 3: 80; Wansharīsī, *al-Mi'yār al-Mu'rib*, 2: 210-211; Ibn Shāsh, *'Iqd al-Jawāhir al-Thamīna*, 1: 497; Shāfi'ī, *al-Umm*, 4: 110-111; *al-'Azīz Sharḥ al-Wajīz*, 13: 555-556; Nawāwī, *Rawḍat al-Ṭālibīn*, 10: 335; and idem, *al-Muhadhdhab* with *Takmilat al-Majmū'*, 18: 223; Suyūṭī, *al-Ashbāh wa 'l-Naẓā'ir*, 491; Ibn Jamā'a, *Taḥrīr al-Aḥkām fī Tadbīr Ahl al-Islam*, 233; Ibn Qudāma, *al-Mughnī*, 10: 511; Ibn Taymiyya, *al-Muḥarrar fī al-Fiqh*, 2: 182; Mardāwī, *al-Inṣāf*, 4: 211; Bahūtī, *Kashshāf al-Qinā'*, 3: 104; Ibn Murtaḍā, *al-Baḥr al-Zakhkhār al-Jāmi' li Madhāhib 'Ulamā' al-Amṣār*, 6: 447; Ṭabarī, *Ikhtilāf al-Fuqahā'*, 171-172; Ibn 'Arabī, *Aḥkām al-Qur'ān*, 2: 876; Ibn Ḥazm, *Marātib al-Ijmā'*, 122; Ibn Ḥajar, *Fatḥ al-Bārī*, 6: 276.

107 Ṭabarī, *Ikhtilāf al-Fuqahā'*, 19-20; 'Abd al-Sattār Ḥāmid, *al-Ḥasan Ibn Ziyād wa-Fiqhih*, 624-626; the Maliki jurist al-Māzirī adopted a similar opinion, *Badā'i' al-Sulūk*, 2: 577

108 Sarakhsī, *Sharḥ al-Siyar al-Kabīr*, 5: 1690-1691; and idem, *Mabsūṭ*, 10: 87; Ibn Humām, *Fatḥ al-Qadīr*, 4: 295.

109 Ibn Ḥazm, *Marātib al-Ijmā'*, 122; Ṭabarī, *Ikhtilāf al-Fuqahā'*, 20-21; Māwardī, *al-Aḥkām al-Sulṭāniyya*, 51; *Nihāyat al-Muḥtāj*, 8: 108; Ibn Shāsh, *'Iqd al-Jawāhir al-Thamīna*, 1: 497; Nawāwī, *al-Muhadhdhab* with *Takmilat al-Majmū'*, 18: 222-223; Karābīsī, *Furūq*, 1: 334.

110 Murāwaḍa means humoring or complying with someone's moods or willingness to please them and eventually double deal him in terms of trade or negotiation a contract of all kind. For further details see the followings: *al-Mughrib fī al-Tartīb al-Mu'arib*, 1:

353; *al-Nihāya fī Gharīb al-Ḥadīth wa al-Āthār*, 2: 276; Ibn Manẓūr, *Lisān al-'Arab*, 7: 164; *Sharḥ al-Zarqānī 'ala al-Muwaṭṭa'*, 3: 282.
111 *Sarakhsī, Sharḥ al-Siyar al-Kabīr*, 2: 461-463.
112 Ibid., 5: 1780-1881.
113 Najīb Armazānī, *al-Shar' al-Dawlī fī al-Islam*, 146; Ja'far 'Abd al-Salam, *Qawā'id al-'Alāqāt al-Dawliyya*, 386-388.
114 Aḥmad Abū al-Wafā, *al-Mu'āhadāt al-Dawliyya fī al-Sharī'a al-Islamiyya*, 29.
115 Sarakhsī, *Sharḥ al-Siyar al-Kabīr*, 5: 1798.
116 Ibn Sa'd, *Ṭabaqāt al-Kubrā*, 2: 73; Ibn Isḥāq, *Sīra*, 2:223; Abū Yūsuf, *Kharāj*, 225; Abū 'Ubayd, *Amwāl*, 189-190; Wāqidī, *Maghāzī*, 2: 477-478; Shaybānī, *al-Siyar al-Kabīr*, 5: 1693-1694.
117 Jaṣṣāṣ, *Aḥkām al-Qur'ān*, 1: 484.
118 The *'aqd* or contract that is conditioned by a time period, such as in leasing where the gain of benefits established along the time period, the process of implementation is subject to continuity, renewable or rotating. See: Muḥammad Yūsuf Mūsā, *al-Amwāl wa-Naẓarīyat al-'Aqd*, 485; Zarkashī, *al-Manthūr fī al-Qawā'id*, 1: 240; Suyūṭī, *al-Ashbāh wa al-Naẓā'ir*, 282-283.
119 Shaybānī, *al-Siyar al-Kabīr*, 5: 1780.
120 Sarakhsī, *Mabsūṭ*, 30: 167-168.
121 Nawawī, *Rawḍat al-Ṭālibīn*, 10: 337; Shāfi'ī, *Umm*, 4: 103-104, 118; Ibn Qudāma, *al-Mughnī*, 10: 610-611.
122 *Majmū' Fatāwā Ibn Taymiyya*, 29:12; Ibn Qayyim al-Jawziyya, *A'lām al-Muwaqi'īn*, 2: 4; Shams al-Dīn Muḥammad ibn Aḥmad al-Minhājī al-Suyūṭī, *Jawāhir al-'Uqūd wa-Mu'īn al-Quḍāt wa 'l-Muwaqqi'īn wa al-Shuhūd*, 1: 12.
123 Najib Armazānī, *al-Shar' al-Dawlī fī al-Islam*, 148.
124 Sarakhsī, *Sharḥ al-Siyar al-Kabīr*, 1: 283-284; Abū Yūsuf, *Kharāj*, 222-223.
125 Shāfi'ī, *Umm*, 4: 118-119; *Jawāhir al-'Uqūd*, 1: 12; For modern scholars who emphasize on the accuracy of writing of *mu'āhada* see the followings: Maḥmūd Shaltūt, *al-Islam 'Aqīda wa Sharī'a*, 457; Wahbī al-Zuḥaylī, *al-'Alāqāt al-Dawliyya fī al-Islam*, 141-142; Aḥmad Abū al-Wafā, *al-Mu'āhadāt al-Dawliyya*, 39-41.
126 Q. 2: 282.
127 Shaybānī, *al-Siyar al-Kabīr*, 5: 1781, 1785.
128 Jaṣṣāṣ, *Aḥkām al-Qur'ān*, 1: 484.
129 Sarakhsī, *Sharḥ al-Siyar al-Kabīr*, 5: 1782-83, 1798.
130 Ibid., 5: 1784; Ṭabarī, *Tārīkh al-Ṭabarī*, 2: 389-92; Ibn al-Jawzī, *Talqīḥ Fuhūm Ahl al-Āthār*, 7; Qalqashandī, *Ṣubḥ al-A'shā*, 6: 240-242.
131 Ibid.
132 Sarakhsī, *Sharḥ al-Siyar al-Kabīr*, 5: 1782-1784.
133 See for example, "Sulḥ al-Ḥudaybiya" format in appendix (A); Sarakhsī, *Mabsūṭ*, 30-168-179.
134 Sarakhsī, *Sharḥ al-Siyar al-Kabīr*, 5: 1783, 1798; and idem, *Mabsūṭ*, 10: 8.
135 Ibn Sa'd, *Ṭabaqāt al-Kubrā*, 2: 97; Maqrīzī, *Imtā' al-Asmā'*, 1: 298
136 Ibn Humām, *Fatḥ al-Qadīr*, 5: 296; Muḥammad Ḥamidallāh, *Majmū'at al-Wathā'iq al-Siyāsiyya*, 75.
137 Aḥmad Abū al-Wafā, *al-Mu'āhadāt al-Dawliyya*, 44.
138 Sarakhsī, *Sharḥ al-Siyar al-Kabīr*, 5: 2180.

139 Ibn Sa'd in his *Ṭabaqāt*, explains that 'Alī wrote one copy for the Prophet and the other for Suhayl ibn 'Amr. See *Ṭabaqāt al-Kubrā*, 2: 97; Maqrīzī, *Imtā' al-Asmā'*, vol.1: 298.
140 Sarakhsī, *Sharḥ al-Siyar al-Kabīr*, 5: 1780-1781.
141 Najīb Armazānī, *al-Shar' al-Dawlī fī al-Islam*, 148.
142 Sarakhsī, *Mabsūṭ*, 13: 25; and idem, *Uṣūl al-Sarakhsī*, 2: 310; Ghazālī, *Mustaṣfā*, 1: 93-94; Shāṭibī, *Muwāfaqāt*, 1: 143; Bukhārī, *Kashshaf al-Asrār*, 4: 171.
143 Ibn Manẓūr, *Lisān al-'Arab*, 7: 441; Zamakhsharī, *Asās al-Balāgha*, 1: 184.
144 *Mu'jam Maqāyīs al-Lugha*, .3: 260; Kaffawī, *Kulliyyāt*, 3: 64; Jurjānī, *Ta'rīfāt*, 166; Samarqandī, *Mīzān al-Uṣūl*, 616-617.
145 Sarakhsī, *Sharḥ al-Siyar al-Kabīr*, 5: 1780.
146 'Abd al-Ghanī Maḥmūd, *al-Taḥaffuẓ 'alā al-Mu'āhadāt al-Dawliyya*, 17; Ghunaymī, *Qānūn al-Salām fī al-Islām*, 522. 526 and 530; and idem, *Aḥkām al-Mu'āhadāt fī al-Sharī'a al-Islamiyya*, 109, 111-112; Aḥmad Abū al-Wafā, *al-Mu'āhadāt al-Dawliyya*,. 89;'Abd al-Ghanī Maḥmūd, *al-Taḥaffuẓ 'alā al-Mu'āhadāt*, 136-139.
147 Sarakhsī, *Mabsūṭ*, 13: 13; Ibn Humām, *Fatḥ al-Qadīr*, 5: 215-216; Zayla'ī, *Tabyīn al-Ḥaqā'iq*, 4: 57-59 and 131-134; *Ḥāshiyat Ibn 'Ābidīn*, 5: 84-88; Ibn Qāḍī Samāwinā, *Jāmi' al-Fuṣūlayn*, 2: 4; Ibn Nujaym, *al-Baḥr al-Rā'iq*, 6: 194; *al-Fatāwā al-Hindiyya*, 4: 396.
148 See the opinions of the school given in detail in the following: Ibn Shāsh, *'Iqd al-Jawāir al-Thamīna*, 2: 422; Ibn Rushd, *Bidāyat al-Mujtahid*, 2: 116-164; *Ḥāshiyat al-Dasūqī 'alā al-Sharḥ al-Kabīr*, 3: 65; *al-Karashī 'alā Mukhtaṣar Khalīl*, 3: 175; (Māliki) Manjūr, *Sharḥ al-Manhaj al-Muntakhab ilā Qawā'id al-Madhhab*, 313; (Shāfi'ī) Nawawī, *al-Majmū' Sharḥ al-Muhadhdhab*, 9: 404-420; and idem, *Rawḍat al-Ṭālibīn*, 3: 403-410; Ibn Qudāma, *Mughnī al-Muḥtāj*, 2: 33-36; (Ḥanbalī) *al-Mughnī* and the *Sharḥ al-Kabīr*, 4: 309-312, 10: 517-519; Bahūtī, *Kashshāf al-Qinā'*, 3: 177-184; (Ẓāhirī) Ibn Ḥazm, *al-Muḥallā*, 8: 412-420; (modern scholars) Abū Zahra, *al-Milkiya wa Naẓariyyat al-'Aqd*, 272-283; Muḥammad Yūsuf Mūsā, *al-Amwāl wa-Naẓariyyat al-'Aqd*, 410-433; Ḥaṣan al-Shādhilī, *al-Sharṭ fī al-'Aqd*, 177.
149 Zarkashī, *al-Manthūr fī al-'Uqūd*, 2: 402.
150 Sarakhsī, *Sharḥ al-Siyar al-Kabīr*, 2: 584-585.
151 Jaṣṣāṣ, *Aḥkām al-Qur'ān*, 3: 214.
152 Ibn Qāḍī Simāwna, *Jāmi' al-Fuṣūlayn*, 2: 221-222; *Ḥāshiyat Ibn 'Ābidīn*, 5: 84; Nawawī, *al-Majmū'*, 9: 18; and idem, *Rawḍat al-Ṭālibīn*, 10:410-411; Bahūtī, *Kashshāf al-Qinā'*, 3: 177; *al-Furū'*, 4: 56.
153 Shaybānī, *al-Siyar al-Kabīr*, 5: 1790.
154 Sarakhsī, *Sharḥ al-Siyar al-Kabīr.*
155 *Āthār* is the plural of *athar*, which means effect, influence. It refers to something that affects the *mu'āhada* and its sound existence. See Jurjānī, *Ta'rīfāt*, 23; Tahānawī, *Kashshāf Iṣṭlāḥāt al-Funūn*, 1: 95; Rāghib al-Iṣfahānī, *Gharīb al-Qur'ān*, 9.
156 The term used for fulfillment in Arabic is usually *wafā'*, which means to honor fully what has been agreed upon, without any violations. See the following: Ṭabarī, *Tafsīr*, 9: 455; Raghib al-Isfahānī, *al-Mufradāt fī Gharīb al-Qur'ān*, 528; Fayrūzābādī, *Baṣā'ir Dhawī al-Tamyīz*, 5: 244-245.
157 Q. 5: 1.
158 Jaṣṣās, *Aḥkām al-Qur'ān*, 2: 293-294; Ṭabarī, *Tafsīr*, 9: 449-454; *Tafsīr al-Qurṭubī*, 10: 169; *Tafsīr al-Baghawī*, 3: 5-6; *Tafsīr Ibn Kathīr*, 3: 4; *Majmū' Fatāwā Shaykh al-Islām Ibn Taymiyya*, 29: 145-151.

159 Q. 9: 4.
160 See also Jaṣṣās, *Aḥkām al-Qur'ān*, 2: 190.
161 Nāṣir Sulaymān al-'Umar, *al-'Ahd wa 'l-Mīthāq fī al-Qur'ān al-Karīm*, 153; Quṭb, *Fī Ẓilāl al-Qur'ān*, 4: 2190-2193.
162 Q. 8: 55-57.
163 Q. 2: 100.
164 Q. 9: 12-13.
165 See for example the following: Ibn al-Athīr, *Jāmi' al-Uṣūl*, 2: 647-656 and 8: 458-459; al-Mundhirī, *al-Targhīb wa 'l-Tarhīb*, 4: 3-13; Baghawī, *Maṣābīḥ al-Sunna*, 3: 92-94.
166 Ibid.
167 Shawkānī, *Nayl al-Awṭār*, 8: 69; Ibn 'Abd al-Barr, *al-Tamhīd*, 2: 124.
168 Abū Yūsuf, *Kharāj*, 149-151; Balādhurī, *Futūḥ al-Buldān*, 1: 162; Muḥammad Ḥamīdallāh, *Majmū'at al-Wathā'iq al-Siyāsiyya*, 470; Muḥammad Rashīd Riḍa, *Tafsīr al-Manār*, 10: 349; Thomas Arnold, *Preaching of Islam*, 73.
169 Sarakhsī, *Sharḥ al-Siyar al-Kabīr*, 4: 1667; Jaṣṣāṣ, *Aḥkām al-Qur'ān*, 3: 75-76; Ibn 'Arabī, *Aḥkām al-Qur'ān*, 2: 875; *Tafsīr al-Ṭabarī*, 14: 82-83; *Tafsīr Abū Su'ūd*, 2: 377.
170 Q. 8: 72.
171 Sarakhsī, *Sharḥ al-Siyar al-Kabīr*, 1: 299; *al-Fatāwā al-Hindiyya*, 2: 303.
172 Sarakhsī, *Sharḥ al-Siyar al-Kabīr*, 1: 302-304; 2: 499, 582-583, 4: 1520-1521 and 5: 1856-1858; *al-Fatāwā al-Hindiyya*, 2: 203.
173 Ibn Shāsh, *'Iqd al-Jawāhir al-Thamīna*, 1: 498; *al-Dasūqī 'ala Sharḥ al-Kabīr*, 2: 206; Ghazālī, *al-Wajīz*, 2: 204; Bayḍāwī, *al-Ghāya al-Quṣwā*, 2: 962; *Nihāyat al-Muḥtāj*, 8: 108; Nawāwī, *Rawḍat al-Ṭālibīn*, 10: 337; *Taḥrīr al-Aḥkām*, 233; Ibn Qudāma, *al-Mughnī*, 10: 513; Ibn Miflih, *al-Mubdi'*, 3: 401.
174 Ibn Ḥazm, *Marātib al-Ijmā'*, 123.
175 Shaybānī, *al-Siyar al-Kabīr*, 5: 1786; Kāsānī, *Badā'i' al-Ṣanā'i'*, 9: 4325; Sarakhsī, *al-Mabsūṭ*, 10: 89; Abū Yūsuf, *Kharāj*, 42.
176 Q. 4: 92.
177 Sarakhsī, *Sharḥ al-Siyar al-Kabīr*, 5: 1853-1854 and 1856-1857.
178 Shaybānī, *al-Siyar al-Kabīr*, 2: 481-482; *al-Fatāwā al-Hindiyya*, 2: 197; Aḥmad Abū al-Wafā, *al-Mu'āhadāt al-Dawliyya*, 156.
179 Abu Yūsuf, *Kharāj*, 77-81; Balādhurī, *Futūḥ al-Buldān*, 1: 76-81
180 For more details see the following: Khaṭīb al-Baghdādī, *Tārīkh Baghdād*, 2: 174; Jaṣṣāṣ, *Aḥkām al-Qur'ān*, 3: 95.
181 Shāfi'ī, *al-Umm*, 4: 103-104; Nawawī, *al-Muhadhdhab* with the *Takmilat Majmū'*, 18: 226; and idem, *Rawḍat al-Ṭālibīn*, 10: 337; Ibn Qudāma, *al-Mughnī*, 10: 513 and 611; Mardāwī, *al-Inṣāf*, 4: 217; Bahūtī, *Kashshaf al-Qinā'*, 3: 103-104; Qarāfī, *al-Aḥkām fī Tamyīz al-Fatāwā 'an al-Aḥkām*, 18-20.
182 Q. 2: 282.
183 See for example Shāṭibī, *Muwāfaqāt*, 2: 58-62; Ibn Ḥazm, *al-Aḥkām fī Uṣūl al-Aḥkām*, 4: 453; Zarqānī, *Manāhil al-'Irfān fī 'Ulūm al-Qur'ān*, 1: 289-337.
184 Majid Khadduri, *War and Peace in the Law of Islam*, 293-294.
185 Sarakhsī, *Sharḥ al-Siyar al-Kabīr*, 5: 1782-1783.
186 *Rahn* (pl. *rahā'in*), is an Arabic term referring to a valuable that can be deposited as surety for a debt. According to the jurists, *'aqd al-rahn* is the amount of money to be deposited as a guarantee that some task be completed. In discussion above, refers to

rahn a hostage on whom the parties might impose conditions in order for the *mu'āhada* to be respected, such as by giving individuals from both sides for guarantee or surety to fulfill the *mu'āhada* on the understanding that, as soon as the period of time is over the parties will give these *rahā'in* back. See for more details the following: *Tartīb al-Qāmūs al-Muḥīṭ*, 2: 403-404; Ibn Manẓūr, *Lisān al-'Arab*, 13: 188-190; Rāghib, *al-Mufradāt fī Gharīb al-Qur'ān*, 204; Jurjānī, *Ta'rīfāt*, 150; Kaffawī, *Kulliyyāt*, 2: 394;

187 Majīd Khaddūrī, *al-Ḥarb wa 'l-Silm fī Sharī'at al-Islām*, 291; Najib Armazāni, *al-Shar' al-Dawlī*, 141; Muḥammad Ṭal'at al-Ghunaymī, *Qānūn al-Salām fī al-Islām*, 515; Subḥi Maḥmaṣānī, *al-Qānūn wa al-'Alāqāt al-Dawliyya*, 148.

188 Muḥammad Ṭal'at al-Ghunaymī, *Qānūn al-Salām fī al-Islām*, 515

189 Shaybānī, *al-Siyar al-Kabīr*, 5: 1750.

190 Sarakhsī, *Sharḥ al-Siyar al-Kabīr*, 5: 1758. History records, as G. Lubin points out in his *Islamic Civilization*, many instances of the killing of Muslim prisoners, 330-331; Muḥammad 'Abdallāh 'Anān, *Dīwān al-Taḥqīq wa 'l-Muḥākamāt al-Kubrā*, 23. The situation for Muslims in Spain under Ferdinand (1452-1516) and Isabella (1451-1504) was particularly dire in this regard.

191 Sarakhsī, *Sharḥ al-Siyar al-Kabīr*, 4: 1663 and 5: 1750.

192 Ibid., 4: 1663-1664; 5: 1758.

193 Ibn Nujaym, *al-Ashbāh wa 'l-Naẓā'ir*, 87-88; Suyūṭī, *al-Ashbāh wa 'l-Naẓā'ir*, 87; Aḥmad al-Zarqā, *Sharḥ al-Qawā 'id al-Fiqhiyya*, 147 and 149.

194 Q. 35: 18.

195 Sarakhsī, *Sharḥ al-Siyar al-Kabīr*, 4: 1664 and 1753.

196 Ibid., 5: 1769-1770; 4: 1664-1665; *Mabsūṭ*, 10: 129.

197 Shaybānī, *Aṣl* "*Kitāb al-Siyar*", 232.

198 Shaybānī, *al-Siyar al-Kabīr*, 4: 1664-1665; Sarakhsī, *Mabsūṭ*, 10: 129; see also Ibn Jamā'a, *Taḥrīr al-Aḥkām*, 234; Abū Ya' lā, *al-Aḥkām al-Sulṭāniyya*, 48-49; Abū 'Ubayd, *Amwāl*, 190; *Maṭālib ūlū al-Nuhā*, 3: 589.

199 'Abū 'Ubayd, *Amwāl*, 190; Balādhurī, *Futūḥ al-Buldān*, 1: 188; Māwardī, *al-Aḥkām al-Sulṭāniyya*, 51.

200 Ibid.

201 'Abū 'Ubayd, *Amwāl*, 190; *al-Karāshī 'alā Mukhtaṣar Khalīl*, 2: 449; Ibn Jamā'a, *Taḥrīr al-Aḥkām*, 234; Abū Ya'lā, *al-Aḥkām al-Sulṭāniyya*, 48-49.

202 Ibid.

203 Shaybānī, *al-Siyar al-Kabīr*, 4: 1762-1764.

204 Ibid., 5: 1777.

205 Ibid., 5: 1778.

206 Ibid., 4: 1666; Māwardī, *al-Aḥkām al-Sulṭāniyya*, 51-52; Abū Ya'lā, *al-Aḥkām al-Sulṭāniyya*, 49.

207 Shaybānī, *al-Siyar al-Kabīr*, 5: 1753-1754; Ibn Shāsh, *'Iqd al-Jawāhir al-Thamīna*, 1: 498; *Ḥāshiyat al-Dasūqī 'alā al-Sharḥ al-Kabīr*, 2: 206-207; *al-Karashī 'alā Khalīl*, 2: 449; Jaṣṣāṣ, *Mukhtaṣar Ikhtilāf al-'Ulamā'*, 3: 449.

208 Shaybānī, *al-Siyar al-Kabīr*, 5: 1753-1756.

209 Ibid., 5: 1778; 4: 1666-1667.

210 See the meaning of the Arabic word for termination (*ibṭāl or ilghā'*) in the following: *Lisān al-'Arab*, 15: 186; *al-Mu'jam al-Wasīṭ*, 2: 743.

211 Many scholars consider "null" and "void" to mean the same thing whether in *mu'āmalāt* (mutual conduct) or *'ibādāt* (ritual practices). al-Jaṣṣāṣ, *Uṣūl*, 2: 169; Samarqandī, *Mīzān al-Uṣūl*, 39-40 and 223-248; Sarakhsī, *Uṣūl al-Sarakhsī*, 1: 18;

Bukhārī, *Kashshaf al-Asrār,* 1: 258; Bādishāh, *Taysīr al-Taḥrīr,* 2: 376; Ghazālī, *al-Mustaṣfā,* 2: 24; *Sharḥ al-Kawkab al-Munīr,* 3: 84-95; *Takhrīj al-Furū' 'alā al-Uṣūl,* 168-171.
212 Kāsānī, *Badā'i' al-Ṣanā'i',* 9: 4327.
213 *Al-Fatāwā al-Hindiyya,* 2: 197
214 Sarakhsī, *Sharḥ al-Siyar al-Kabīr,* 1: 304.
215 Q. 9: 7.
216 Q. 9: 4.
217 *Tafsīr Abī Su'ūd, Irshād al-'Aql al-Salīm 'alā Mazāyā al-Kitāb al-Ḥakīm,* 2: 386.
218 Kāsānī, *Badā'i' al-Ṣanā'i',* 9: 4327.
219 *Iqāla* is dismissal or discharge, as when one say' to forgive or to reward someone's offense or lapse as undone or to raise someone from a fall. According the jurists or *fuqahā', iqāla* is the dismissal of the contract with the consent of both parties involved. See Kaffawī, *al-Kuliyyāt,* 1: 259; Tahānawī, *Kashshāf Iṣṭilāḥāt al-Funūn,* 3: 1211; *al-Tawqīf 'alā Muhimmāt al-Ta'ārīf,* 81; Nazīh Ḥammād, *Mu'jam al-Muṣṭalaḥāt al-Iqtiṣādiyya fī Lughat al-Fuqahā',* 64.
220 According to Ibn al-Subkī and Ibn Nujaym *faskh* is the breaking of the contract/ *'aqd.* See Zarkashī, *al-Manthūr fī al-Qawā'id,* 3: 42; Ibn Nujaym, *al-Ashbāh wa 'l-Naẓā'ir,* 338.
221 The *mufāsakha* is the agreement of both parties to cancel the contract/ *'aqd.* Some contracts/ *'uqūd* are subject to cancellation with the agreement of both parties. See Fayyūmī, *al-Miṣbāḥ al-Munīr,* 2: 472; Ibn Manẓūr, *Lisān al-'Arab,* 3: 44-45; Nazīh Ḥammād, *Mu'jam al-Muṣṭalaḥāt al-Iqtiṣādiyya fī Lughat al-Fuqahā',* 218.
222 Sarakhsī, *Sharḥ al-Siyar al-Kabir,* 5: 1712 and 1715.
223 Kāsānī, *Badā'i' al-Ṣanā'i',* 9: 4362-4327; Ibn Humām, *Fatḥ al-Qadīr,* 4: 294; Zayla'ī, *Tabyīn al-Ḥaqā'iq,* 3: 246; Ibn Nujaym, *al-Baḥr al-Rā'iq,* 5: 86; *Ḥāshiyat Ibn 'Ābidīn,* 4: 134; *al-Fatāwā al-Hindiyya,* 2: 197; Dāmād Afandī, *Majma' al-Anhur,* 1: 638; Jaṣṣāṣ. *Aḥkām al-Qur'ān,* 3: 85.
224 Q. 9: 7; Ibn 'Arabī, *Aḥkām al-Qur'ān,* 2: 600.
225 Sarakhsī, *Sharḥ al-Siyar al-Kabīr,* 5: 1698 and 1708.
226 Ibn Isḥāq, *Sīra,* 2: 394-395; Ṭabarī, *Tārīkh,* 3: 43-45; Wāqidī, *Maghāzī,* 2: 795-796; Ibn Qayyim al-Jawziyya, *Zād al-Ma'ād,* 3: 394; Maqrīzī, *Imtā' al-Asmā',* 1: 357.
227 Shāfi'ī, *al-Umm,* 4: 107; Kiyā Harāsī al-Ṭabarī, *Aḥkām al-Qur'ān,* 3: 412; Baghawī, *Sharḥ al-Sunna,* 11: 167; *Taḥrīr al-Aḥkām fī Tadbīr Ahl al-Islām,* 233; *Mughnī al-Muḥtāj,* 4: 262; Ibn Qudāma, *al-Mughnī,* 10: 513; Mardāwī, *al-Inṣāf,* 4: 216; Ibn Qayyim al-Jawziyya, *Zād al-Ma'ād,* 3: 136-138; Nawawī, *Rawḍat al-Ṭālibīn,* 10: 337; *Nihāyat al-Muḥtāj,* 8: 109.
228 See the opinion of these scholars in the works of Abū 'Ubayd, *Amwāl,* 200-204; Balādhurī, *Futūḥ al-Buldān,* 1: 184-186.
229 Q. 8: 58; See *Tafsīr al-Ṭabarī,* 14: 25; *Zād al-Masīr fī 'ilm al-Tafsīr,* 3: 373; Jaṣṣāṣ, *Aḥkām al-Qur'ān,* 3: 77; Ibn 'Arabī, *Aḥkām al-Qur'ān,* 2: 871-872; Kiyā Harāsī al-Ṭabarī, *Aḥkām al-Qur'ān,* 3: 412; *Tafsīr al-Qurṭubī,* 8: 31-32.
230 Jaṣṣāṣ, *Aḥkām al-Qur'ān,* 3: 77
231 For further details see the following: Ibn Qutayba, *Ta'wīl Mukhtalif al-Ḥadīth,* 94; Ibn Athīr, *al-Nihāya fī Gharīb al-Ḥadīth,* 4: 147; Rāghib al-Iṣbahānī, *al-Mufradāt fī Gharīb al-Ḥadīth,* 423.
232 Sarakhsī, *Sharḥ al-Siyar al-Kabīr,* 5: 1788; Shāfi'ī, *Umm,* 4: 114.

233 Sarakhsī, *Sharḥ al-Siyar al-Kabīr*, 1: 190-191 and 5: 1689; Ibn Rushd, *Bidāyat al-Mujtahid*, 1: 388; Ibn Juzayy, *al-Qawānīn al-Fiqhiyya*, 163; Ibn Shāsh, *'Iqd al-Jawāhir al-Thamīna*, 1: 496-497; Shāfi'ī, *al-Umm*, 4: 110-112; Ghazālī, *Wajīz*, 2: 203; *al-'Azīz Sharḥ al-Wajīz*, 13: 554; Nawāwī, *Rawḍat al-Ṭālibīn*, 10: 334; Māwardī, *al-Aḥkām al-Sulṭāniyya*, 52; Ibn Jamā'a, *Taḥrīr al-Aḥkām*, 231; Ibn Taymiyya, *al-Muḥarrar fī al-Fiqh*, 2: 182; Ibn Qudāma, *al-Mughnī*, 10: 509; Bahūtī, *Kashshāf al-Qinā'*, 3: 103; Mardāwī, *al-Inṣāf*, 4: 212; *Majmū' Fatāwā Ibn Taymiyya*, 15: 174; *Sharḥ al-Nawāwī 'alā Ṣaḥīḥ Muslim*, 11: 135; Shawkānī, *al-Sayl al-Jarār*, 4: 564; Bayḍāwī, *al-Ghāya al-Quṣwā*, 2: 961; Ibn Murtaḍā, *al-Baḥr al-Zakhkhār*, 6: 446-447.

234 Kāsānī, *Badā'i' al-Ṣanā'i'*, 9: 4326.

235 Q. 9: 58 : "If you (Muh}ammad) fear treachery from any people throw back (their covenant) to them (so as to)on equal terms (that there will be no more covenant between you and them). Certainly Allah likes not the treacherous."

236 Dabūsī, *Ta'sīs al-Naẓar*, 49.

237 Sarakhsī, *al-Mabsūṭ*, 10: 86-87; and idem, *Sharḥ al-Siyar al-Kabīr*, 2: 499; Ibn Humām, *Fatḥ al-Qadīr*, 4: 294; Zayla'ī, *Tabyīn al-Ḥaqā'iq*, 3: 246; *Mirqāt al-Mafātīḥ*, 8: 21.

238 Sarakhsī, *Sharḥ al-Siyar al-Kabīr*, 2: 287 and 499, 5: 1697-1713; and idem, *Mabsūṭ*, 10: 86-87; Abū Yūsuf, *Kharāj*, 224; Ibn Humām, *Fatḥ al-Qadīr*, 4: 294; Zayla'ī, *Tabyīn al-Ḥaqā'iq*, 3: 246; *Ḥāshiyyat Ibn 'Ābidīn*, 4: 133; *al-Fatāwā al-Hindiyya*, 2: 197.

239 See for example, Ibn al-'Arabī, *Aḥkām al-Qur'ān*, 2: 876; Muḥammad 'Alish, *Fatḥ al-'Alī al-Mālik*, 1: 392; Suyūṭī, *al-Ashbāh wa 'l-Naẓā'ir*, 527; Khuṭābī. *Ma'ālim al-Sunan*, 4: 64; Ibn Qayyim al-Jawziyya, *Aḥkām Ahl al-Dhimma*, 2: 478; Khawārizmī, *Mufīd al-'Ulūm wa-Mubīd al-Humūm*, 344.

240 Ibn Shāsh, *'Iqd al-Jawāhir al-Thamīna*, 1: 498; *al-Sharḥ al-Kabīr* by al-Dardīr with *Ḥashiyat al-Dasūqī*, 2: 206; Shāfi'ī, *al-Umm*, 4: 107; Nawawī, *al-Muhadhdhab* with *Takmilat al-Majmū'*, 18: 225-226 and 232; and idem, *Rawḍat al-Ṭālibīn*, 10: 338-339; Ibn Qudāma, *al-Mughnī*, 9: 513-514; Mardāwī, *al-Inṣāf*, 4: 216; Bahūtī, *Kashshāf al-Qinā'*, 3: 103; Ibn Hubayrā, *al-Ifṣāḥ*, 2: 296; Dimashqī, *Raḥmat al-Umma fī Ikhtilāf al-A'imma*, 398; Sha'rānī, *al-Mīzān al-Kubrā*, 2: 185.

Chapter Four

Selected Treaties

This chapter discusses and analyses the five selected treaties mentioned earlier, drawn up between Muslims and non-Muslims at various points in the course of the period of pre-modern Islamic history. These treaties are: the Treaty of Ḥudaybiya, from the lifetime of the Prophet, between the Prophet and Suhail b. 'Amr the representative of Maccan, dated to 6/628; the treaty of 'Abd al-Malik ibn Marwān (r. 65/685-86/705), from the Umayyad period, with Emperor Justinian II of Byzantine, concluded in 70/689; the treaty of Hārūn al-Rashīd (r. 170/786-193/809), from the 'Abbasid era, with Empress Iren, drawn up in 187/802; the treaty of al-Malik al-Kāmil (r. 615/1218-636/1238), from the Ayyūbid era, with Fredrick II, dated 625/1229; and the treaty of Sulṭān Sulaymān the Magnifisant (r. 926/1520-974/1566), from the Ottoman era, with King Francis I, concluded in 942/1535. The basic elements and definitions of their components, as well as the literature directly related to the treaties, has been introduced in earlier chapters. Therefore, the following discussions will concentrate on the practical elements of the selected treaties, which are essential for an understanding of the nature of international treaties in Islam. Furthermore, this chapter attempts to illustrate the practical necessities and the special circumstances and contexts that compelled the Muslim states to negotiate and conclude these treaties with non-Muslims.

Throughout the history of human civilizations, treaties have been drafted in order to organize relations between nations as well as to establish the rights of each party and to enforce the terms and conditions mutually agreed upon. In the process, treaties have became one of the most fundamental elements in organizing the relations of nations at times of peace and war. Treaties have been drawn up in order to stop bloodshed and to crown efforts at achieving peace. Furthermore, under the terms of these treaties, the status of prisoners of war has been determined, booty distributed, and the sovereignty and territory of states established and recognized. The aims behind the treaties concluded between nations can differ widely. A treaty may be concluded, for instance, to achieve economic and trade advantages, to effect exchange of embassies in order to improve political relations, or simply to end hostilities and deal with the issue of prisoners of war. Other treaties deal with educational or other social purposes.

In Islamic civilization, too, treaties have been used as a tool to organize the relations between the Islamic state and its neighboring states. Yet, in Islam, treaties were not limited to the state alone; indeed, they came to be a means of settling matters between tribes, individuals and groups of individuals. The *'aqd al-dhimma* was in fact the first incarnation of such treaties; only later did states expand the use of treaties to seal the end of fighting, armistice agreements, the spread of peace (*amān*), *hudna* (truce of suspension of fighting), *muwāda'a* (temporary/ceasefire cessation of hostilities), etc. Under these treaties, the spread of religious practices and the terms of trade were established. The treaty became a way of honoring these sorts of agreements and organizing and summarizing political relations among nations.[1]

The purpose of the treaties concluded between Muslims and non-Muslims in the pre-modern era were not limited, either; rather, it was left to the Islamic state to determine, evaluate and decide the potential advantages for the Muslims in the short or long terms. Treaties have sometimes been essential to safeguarding Muslims from outside threats to their faith and property. Indeed, if the conclusion of a treaty does no harm or damage to the interests of the Muslim community at large and does not contradict and violate Islamic teachings, Islamic law encourages the Muslim state or its representatives to proceed and make the commitments necessary to conclude it.

It is important to note the circumstances under which Muslim rulers or statesmen resorted to concluding a treaty with non-Muslims. These circumstances may be divided into three categories: The first is from a position of power, and in order to avoid further conflict and bloodshed (sometimes as well as to gain more time for reinforcements and supplies to arrive). The second category is from a position of equilibrium, and in order to settle differences for which a military solution is not desirable. The third category is from a position of weakness, where the object is to make the best of adverse circumstances and perhaps to gain time for planning and readjustments for potential future conflict.[2]

Instances of the first category, in which Muslims negotiated from a position of power, are many and diverse. They include, for example, the talks concerning the capitulation of Jerusalem in 638 A.H.[3] and the surrender of Alexandria in 642.[4] As for the second category, from the position of equilibrium of power, Muslims frequently concluded treaties with the Byzantines in connection with their frontier wars in Asia Minor during both the Umayyad and Abbasid eras.[5] Finally, negotiating from a position of weakness, Muslims often signed treaties with non-Muslims when faced with internal disputes, as we shall see below in the treaties of 'Abd al-Malik ibn Marwān and Malik al-Kāmil.[6]

The practice of concluding Islamic treaties was initiated by the Prophet and continued during the time of the four Rightly Guided Caliphs. The treaties negotiated between these early caliphs or their representatives and their adversaries were limited to establishing peaceful relations or alliances; these agreements took the form of treaties of *hudna* (ceasefire) or *'aqd al-dhimma*. In the negotiations for these treaties, non-Muslims were given the choice of three options: conversion to Islam, becoming *dhimmīs*, or resuming the hostilities. Among the treaties of *dhimma*, known as a continuous truce (*ṣulḥ*), was the one negotiated by 'Umar ibn al-Khaṭṭāb with the people of 'Ilyā' (Jerusalem) in 638 A. D.[7] This treaty granted mutually agreed rights and protection to non-Muslims.[8] It also asserted the right of movement, freedom of practice and beliefs, the choice to stay in or leave the territory, and finally, the protection of (*dhimmīs*' lives and property in return for the payment of the *jizya*.[9] Similarly, in 636 A.H. Khālid ibn al-Walīd concluded a treaty with the people of Damascus, granting them protection of their properties and churches in return for their paying *jizya*.[10] Likewise in early 640 A.D. Abū 'Ubayda ibn al-Jarrāḥ and the people of Syria concluded another treaty along the same lines.[11]

The Muslims continued to conclude treaties of ceasefire (*hudna*) and *dhimma* with non-Muslims after the era of the four Rightly Guided Caliphs, following the conduct of the Prophet and his immediate successors. For example, under the Umayyad dynasty, many treaties were concluded between Muslims and the Byzantines, non-Muslim nations of the *dār al-ḥarb*. According to the *Futūḥ al-Buldān* of Balādhurī, during the time of Mu'āwiya, a great percentage of Byzantine territory was subject to treaties of safe conduct.[12] During the time of hostilities and tensions between Mu'āwiya and 'Alī ibn Abī Ṭālib, Mu'āwiya drafted a treaty of ceasefire (*hudna*) with the Byzantine emperor Constans II (527-565 C. E.), prior to his battle with 'Alī in 658 A.H. Then, when he proclaimed himself caliph in 662, he renewed and signed a treaty on his own authority with the Byzantine emperor in which tribute was paid to the latter.[13] In the same way Caliph 'Abd al-Malik ibn Marwān (685-705) was obliged to conclude a peace treaty with the Byzantines while he was fighting insurgents and rebels in Iraq. At the beginning of his reign he sent money and gifts to the Byzantine emperor Justinian II (685-695), released all Byzantine prisoners, and paid weekly tribute thereafter. In 70/689, he renewed the same ceasefire (*hudna*) again.[14]

During the Abbasid period, the political relationships between Muslims and Byzantines followed the pattern set by their predecessors. In fact this political trend became more marked under the rule of al-Manṣūr, the second 'Abbasid caliph (r. 136/754-158/785), when in 765 the exchange of ambassadors was resumed. These political or diplomatic types of relations were not limited to negotiating treaties but also entailed exchanges of gifts and the release of prisoners. Because of the improvement in the relations between Muslims and Byzantines, mutual interests were more easily accommodated: for example, trade barriers were lifted. This process at work is also clearly seen, as well, in the exchange of gifts, letters, and representatives between Hārūn al-Rashīd and Charlemagne, who in 802 arranged a treaty of friendship and alliance after establishing diplomatic ties.[15]

The Fatimids and the Mamluks followed the lead of the Abbasids by concluding treaties with non-Muslims. Their relations extended to Europe and to Central and East Asia.[16] Furthermore, during the Crusades, political relations between eastern and western ruling powers in general, and in particular between Ṣalāḥ al-Dīn al-Ayyūbī (r. 1169-93) and Richard Lionheart , were further developed. A treaty was concluded between the two leaders in 1192.[17] Toward the end of the Crusades, in 1258, an exchange of embassies between Western and Islamic countries took place in an effort to re-establish and resume political and trade connections.[18] During the Ottoman period, a friendly treaty was concluded between Suleiman the Magnificent (152-1566) and the King of France, Francis I. The treaty was known as the "Treaty of Amity and Commerce: The Ottoman Empire and France, February 1535."[19]

The purpose of the following discussion, therefore, is to examine certain treaties in greater depth so as to illustrate in detail how Muslims dealt with non-Muslims in neighboring countries in the process of concluding treaties. The art of negotiation and the purpose of concluding treaties often led to compromises between Muslims and their enemies, but generally achieved, if only temporarily, the ultimate goal of ending bloodshed and establishing peace. Without these treaties, the balance of power could never have been maintained and hostilities would have continued.

In the following survey, the intention is to highlight the significance and outcome of all five treaties, but especially of the Ḥudaybiya treaty. The Ḥudaybiya treaty has long been considered by classical and modern historians and jurists as a model the most influential document in the Islamic history of treaty – writing. Historians and jurists agree that the validity of later treaties was usually measured according to the standard set by Ḥudaybiya. Although some of the Prophet's Companions were not in favor of the treaty when it was being negotiated, among them 'Umar ibn al-Khaṭṭāb, they eventually realized that the Prophet would not make concessions at the expense of Muslims unless it entailed a major gain in the long term. What became evident in hindsight was that the Muslims gained much more than they lost due to any concessions they were forced to make.

A. The Ḥudaybiya Treaty:[20]

To understand the background that led to the conclusion of Ḥudaybiya, it is essential to note here that the Prophet, before embarking on his mission, had attended the formation of the confederacy of the Fuḍūl in ca. 580, where all of the small and large tribes present made a covenant that, as God was their witness, they would forever stand on the side of the victims of injustice.[21] Through participation in this event, the Prophet gained early experience of negotiation.. The Prophet is supposed to have said, "I uphold the pact concluded in my presence when Ibn Jud'ān gave us a great banquet. Should it ever be invoked, I shall immediately rise to answer the call."[22]

The Arabs in the pre-Islamic era were thus used to concluding peace treaties with neighboring societies, and this tradition of negotiation and treaty-making likewise had an impact on those who later converted to Islam. Their past experience and background, or that of their ancestors, contributed to the formulation of future treaties that took place under Islam.[23]

The treaty of Ḥudaybiya[24] was concluded between the Prophet Muḥammad and Suhayl ibn ʻAmr, a representative of the Quraysh tribe of Mecca. The treaty, as noted before, became in the eyes of Muslim scholars the model for all subsequent Islamic treaties, mainly because of the Prophet's role in negotiating its terms and conditions.[25] Another reason for its fame is the circumstances that faced the Prophet while drafting this agreement: characteristically, his determination and personal qualities allowed him to achieve peace, despite the harsh demands and conditions imposed by the other party.

Another point of consideration is the political status of the Muslim community in Medina and its relations with the neighboring tribe of Quraysh in Mecca prior to the Ḥudaybiya treaty. Within Medina, the Prophet made an alliance in 622 between himself (as the representative of the Muslims) and the non-Muslims (chiefly Jews) of Medina, which rendered the Muslim position or status in Medina secure enough to allow them to turn their attention toward Mecca.[26] Mecca was a very strategic and important city to Muslims, since it is the birthplace of the Prophet and many of the Companions, as well as being a religious, economic and historical center of long standing. Between the years 622 and 628, several skirmishes and three major battles took place between the Muslims of Medina and the Meccans, resulting in a stalemate where neither side could really claim absolute victory over the other. For example, the battle of Badr in 624 was a victory for the Muslims of Medina, the battle of Uḥud in 625 a victory for the Meccans, and the battle of the Trench in 627, where the Meccans broke off their siege of Medina without either reaching victory or admitting defeat, a draw.[27] After the battle of the Trench, the Meccans remained strong and decided to protect their city from any attempt at invasion by the Muslims of Medina.[28]

At this stage, the Muslims knew the strength of their Meccan enemy and there was a general awareness that Muslims could not take Mecca through military invasion. In view of this situation, and considering as well the threat from hostile tribes within Medina itself, invasion of Mecca must have seemed an unwise choice at the time. The outcome would probably have been disastrous to the nascent Muslim community.[29] Therefore, for the best interest of the Muslim community, an alternative course of action was sought. At this point, the Prophet realized that the Islamic cause would be better served by a peaceful settlement with the Meccans. It was also then that the Prophet declared that the Kaʻba (the chief religious shrine in Mecca) was sacred to the Muslims too.[30]

In 628, during the pilgrimage season, the Prophet, with an estimated fourteen hundred Muslims accompanying him, traveled to the Kaʻba to perform the religious duty of *ḥajj* (pilgrimage). As the Prophet approached Mecca, he dispatched several peace emissaries to assure the Meccans of his peaceful intentions and his desire to reach an agreement with them through negotiations.[31] He sent 'Uthmān ibn 'Affān, among others, as a delegate on his behalf to inform the Meccans of his intended pilgrimage. The Meccans acknowledged the efforts and intentions of the Prophet and also dispatched their own delegations to the Prophet to negotiate a settlement.[32]

The negotiation process between the Muslims and the Meccans was at first a failure. However, a final agreement was eventually reached by their representatives - - Suhayl ibn 'Amr on behalf of the polytheist Meccans and the Prophet on behalf of the Islamic community. The treaty was moreover concluded at a time when the Muslims were in a position of power: thus, in the course of negotiating this agreement, they were able to reject conditions that many of the Companions of the Prophet strongly disapproved of, though they remained calm and trusted the Prophet to negotiate on their behalf. Moreover, in the course of the discussions, the Meccan representative insulted the Prophet in the presence of fifteen hundred Muslims.[33] Yet despite the fact that Suhayl was alone, no one harmed him; indeed, the Muslims treated him with respect and in keeping with the Islamic ruling that messengers should not be mistreated or killed.[34] The Prophet in particular tolerated his words patiently in order to proclaim publicly to the Meccans that, indeed, the ultimate objective of Islam is to avoid bloodshed and let peace and understanding prevails.[35]

It would seem as though the Prophet saw an importance in the treaty that went beyond its immediate purpose, for at the time of the negotiation and conclusion of the Ḥudaibiyya treaty there were, in fact, internal disputes within the nascent Muslim community. In some respects, the Prophet concluded the treaty despite their objections in order for it to serve as a lesson to his Companions and oblige them to fulfill the treaty conditions. From this perspective, the events surrounding the Ḥudaibiyya treaty served as an example to his fellow Muslims, and it became the priciple model of a treaty to the following generations of Muslims.[36]

By the sixth year of *hijra*, the Prophet faced two powerful enemies: from the north, the formidable Jewish colony of Khaybar, and from the south, the Quraysh. It seemed it was merely a matter of time before the two forces might join together in an alliance against the Prophet in Medina. The Prophet realized that a possible alliance between the two enemies would pose a major threat to the Muslims in Medina and elsewhere. The treaty of Ḥudaybiya was thus only one aspect of a major political and security initiative undertaken by the Prophet, designed to secure the southern frontier with the Meccans. The situation in the north, however, was another matter. Fifteen days after the Ḥudaybiya treaty was signed, the Muslims took advantage of Khaybar's weakness and defeated this powerful Jewish tribe.[37]

The Prophet's peace initiative, in the context of the diplomatic and political dynamics of the strategic environment of the time-period, permitted the Muslims to eliminate the dangers posed by enemies both more or less powerful than they were. As a result, the Muslims managed to attain a greater degree of security and strength and were able to build on this foundation.[38]

The treaty of Ḥudaybiya of 628 stands in Islamic history as an enduring masterpiece, revealing and telling of the Prophet's political skill and statesmanship. As a result of the agreement, within a period of two years, the Muslim community was able to win over from the ranks of the Meccans more converts to Islam through the peaceful demonstration of their faith than they had during all the preceding years of contention and strife. Within two years, the time was ripe for the Muslims to capture Mecca without a single blow being struck or one drop of blood spilled, thus paving the way for the peaceful Islamaization of the entire Arabian Peninsula.[39] In reality, the treaty of Ḥudaybiya was a genuine victory for the Muslims over the Meccans, which ultimately enabled the Prophet to be recognized as leader of the Muslim community by the neighboring non-Muslim tribes and kings. This was a major accomplishment for the Muslims, for it enabled them to preach Islam beyond the Arabian Peninsula.[40]

In the writings of classical Muslim historians and scholars, the treaty of Ḥudaybiyya is paid very careful attention, and accorded a high degree of prominence, with many details and commentary provided. Most of the details of the actual treaty and the historical background are identical in their presentation, with the exception of a few minor differences, such as the number of Muslims who accompanied the Prophet and the duration of the treaty. Later treaties did not receive the same measure of recognition by the classical Muslim historians as Ḥudaybiyya did. In their case, only scant details are furnished. In this section, we will discuss and bring forward some of the opinions of Muslim scholars regarding these treaties.

B. An Umayyad Period Treaty

The second treaty selected for analysis is the one negotiated by the fifth Umayyad caliph 'Abd al-Malik Ibn Marwān with the Byzantine Empire. 'Abd al-Malik had assumed the caliphate in 685 at a time when revolts against the Umayyads were raging in almost every province of the Islamic Empire, with the exception of Egypt.[41] According to al-Mas'ūdī (d. 346/956), writing in his *Murūj al-Dhahab*, the political situation during the rule of 'Abd al-Malik ibn Marwān was as follows:

While 'Abd al-Malik was leading an army of Syrians, he halted at Ṭanān in order to receive the latest news of Ibn Ziyād (his commander of Iraq). The news came heralding his (Ibn Ziyād's) murder and the murder of those who were with him, as well as the defeat of the army during the night. At the same time, 'Abd al-Malik received the news of the capture of Palestine by Babl ibn Qays, a commander of Ibn al-Zubayr, and the march of Muṣ'ab ibn al-Zubayr from Medina to Palestine. Then he received the news of the king of Byzantine ... and his capture of the town of Miṣṣīṣa on the way to Syria. Then he received the news that the mobs of

Damascus (capital of the Umayyad Empire) had rioted and begun to loot the property of the habitants...[42]

'Abd al-Malik was very disappointed but not troubled by these discouraging reports from all sides. He handled the news with extreme caution and forethought.[43] A very clever politician, he knew very well that the conflicting factions inside Iraq, such as the Shī'ites and the Khārijites, would rise in the meantime against Ibn al-Zubayr.[44] He therefore turned his attention from Iraq to the Byzantine Empire's borders in Asia Minor. His political insights were accurate, for Ibn al-Zubayr's forces in Iraq were weakened by the rebellions, especially in Basra and Kufa, and were as a result unable to resist a fresh attack. 'Abd al-Malik was thus able to restore Palestine and Iraq to Umayyad rule.[45]

'Abd al-Malik's success or victory over the rebels was carefully measured and calculated. In order for him to protect himself against the rebellions and protect his empire, he first sent tribute and gifts to the Byzantine Emperor. He turned the Byzantine Emperor's mind away from war and made a truce with him. Then he marched against Palestine.[46]

In referring to the events of 691 A.H., and especially the truce with the Byzantine emperor, al-Ṭabarī (d. 310/ 923) records the following:

During these years the Byzantines launched an attack against the Muslim inhabitants of Syria. 'Abd al-Malik, therefore, made a peace with the king of Byzantium on the condition that 'Abd al-Malik should pay him one thousand *dīnars* every Friday.[47]

The duration of that truce was set at ten years, beginning in 69/689.[48]

From what we are told by Mas'ūdī and Ṭabarī, it can easily be inferred that 'Abd al-Malik sent emissaries to the Byzantine court with instructions to negotiate a truce on the best possible terms.[49] Apparently out of concern for the best interests of the Muslim community, 'Abd al-Malik agreed not only to negotiate with a non-Muslim head of state, but to pay tribute to him as well.[50] 'Abd al-Malik's conduct also reflects some aspects of the Ḥudaybiya treaty. In the first place, 'Abd al-Malik realized the dangers of confronting directly the rebellions in Iraq, just as the Prophet perceived the disasters that might befall the Muslims in Medina. Secondly, 'Abd al-Malik saw that he needed a free hand to rescue the Umayyad Empire from the rebellion. He therefore shifted his attention to the Byzantines and concluded a truce with them, before trying to reclaim the territory captured by Ibn al-Zubayr's commanders. The Prophet similarly waited for a limited period of time to restore order and gain local support, making alliances with the non-Muslims of Medina, prior to his march toward Mecca. Through diplomatic efforts and negotiations, therefore, 'Abd al-Malik regained power and accomplished his mission, saving the Empire from both local rebellion as well as an outside attack by the Byzantines, just as the Prophet did with the Meccans. The main differences between the Ḥudaibiyya treaty and 'Abd al-Malik's conduct lay in his decision to pay tribute to the Byzantines. Yet, there is no record to indicate that Muslim jurists or theologians ever held this precedent against 'Abd al-Malik. On the contrary, Shaybānī and many other leading jurists are in agreement with the action of 'Abd al-Malik, which they say was done for the sake of public interest and thus permissible according to the Sharī'a.[51]

Needless to say, when 'Abd al-Malik sabdued the rebellious regions of the Empire to Umayyad rule in 72/692, he stopped paying tribute to the Byzantine Emperor and instead resumed the annual border attacks against Asia Minor. Thus he proved himself not only a capable administrator, but also a far-sighted statesman. It is no wonder that while Mu'āwiya is considered in Islamic history as the founder of the Umayyad dynasty, 'Abd al-Malik is credited with consolidating the regime and placing it on a firm foundation. The last years of his reign were, on the whole, years of prosperity and peaceful unity.[52]

'Abd al-Malik ibn Marwān's treaty with the Byzantine Emperor proved to fit the Islamic criteria for concluding a treaty with non-Muslims. According to Muslim jurists, its provisions, far from causing any harm to the Muslim community, actually worked in its best interest. 'Abd al-Malik's treaty met all of the requirements and conditions that Muslim rulers had to observe in negotiating terms with non-Muslims.

C. An Abbasid Period Treaty

The next treaty that we shall examine was drawn up in the Abbasid period during the reign of Hārūn al-Rashīd (764-809), one of the most powerful caliphs of that dynasty. For the purposes of this analysis, we shall attempt neither to study the reign of Hārūn al-Rashīd in terms of its political or social aspects nor to compare him with other 'Abbasid or Umayyad caliphs, but to focus on a specific period of time during his caliphate that led him to conclude truces with the neighboring non-Muslim states: the Byzantine Empire under the Empress Irene (r. 797-802) (known in the Muslim sources as Ughusta or *Augusta*) and the Emperor Nicephorus I (r. 802-811) (known in the Muslim sources as Niqfūr), and the holy Roman Empire under Charlemagne (r. 768-814).[53]

Again, there is no record of the details of the treaty drawn up between al-Rashīd and the Byzantine emperors. However, there are a few references in the classical literature dealing with this particular event. The information presented below is derived from the works of the historians Ṭabarī, Ya'qūbī, Ibn Kathīr, Balādhurī, Mas'ūdī and others, as well as the works of classical jurists who lived under his reign and commented upon his actions.

It is useful to recall what al-Dhahabī says about Hārūn al-Rashīd in his *Siyar A'lām al-Nubalā'*: "The account of al-Rashīd are too long, his good deeds many, yet in spite of his good actions he has a bad reputation because of [his predilection for] music and enjoyment as well as pleasurable times, God forgive him."[54]

Indeed, the general prosperity that persisted during his reign earned him this reputation. With the prices of commodities so low, economic well-being prevailed as well as a tendency to enjoy its advantages. The personal indulgence of the caliph was also commented upon. Many attributed the eruption of disobedience and heresy during this age to his lifestyle.[55] As a direct response to these disturbances, and in reply to a request from the caliph himself, Abū Yūsuf wrote his work entitled *Kitāb al-Kharāj*, in which he calls for reforms in the Muslim community, including enforcement of the payment of *kharāj* (land tax) and *'ushūr*.[56] On the other hand, Suyūṭī describes the reign of Hārūn al-Rashīd as one of great achievement, prosperity and development. Trade came from all regions, the public treasury was full and its resources were distributed to all. Suyūṭī goes so far as to say: "The days of al-Rashīd were full of great deeds, they seemed like a wedding because they were full of enjoyment".[57]

The first period (132/750-232/844) of the 'Abbasid dynasty was a golden one, especially Hārūn al-Rashīd's reign. Though some historians have accused him of being a drunkard and alcoholic, Ibn Khaldūn rejects this claim:

This accusation has no evidence. If his critics assumed this, then how was he able to run his caliphate justly and according to the Sharī'a? He associated himself with the scholars and jurists and engaged in debate with them … al-Ṭabarī and al-Mas'ūdī's works defend al-Rashīd agains his critics …[58]

Albert Hourani indicates moreover that the stories which make up the *Thousand and One Nights* (or *Arabian Nights*) have no relation to Hārūn al-Rashīd. The stories were written between the tenth and twelfth centuries C. E. and most likely expanded upon further in Cairo during the Mamlūk period. They were then attributed to Baghdad during the time of the Abbasid caliph Hārūn al-Rashīd.[59]

If these stories and accusations made against Hārūn al-Rahīd are reliable, then how come classical scholars, such as Abū Yūsuf, Ṭabarī, al-Mas'ūdī, Suyūṭī, Ibn Khaldūn and many modern scholars alike questioned their authenticity, as may be seen in such works as *al-Aghānī*, *al-'Iqd al-Farīd*, and *al-Tāj fī Akhlāq al-Mulūk*? One might also ask, if it is true that the caliph was so corrupt, how come the first period of the Abbasid caliphs witnessed such a surge in knowledge and the emergence of so many scholars during that time? The Abbasid caliphs in the first period favored knowledge over enjoyment, not otherwise.[60] Indeed, the majority of the prominent scholars cited above admired the early Abbasid period and claimed the early caliphs were free of all the accusations attributed to them. This position is summarized by Suyūṭī as follows:

I have not seen or known a King who has valued knowledge or the search for knowledge as al-Rashīd; he took his two sons al-Amīn and al-Ma'mūn to study Mālik's *Muwāṭṭa'*. Al-Rashīd, Manṣūr and al-Mahdī narrated many *ḥadīths* from the Prophet's traditions.[61]

The above account is meant only to clarify a misconceptions regarding the early Abbasid caliphs, and especially Hārūn al-Rashīd, who, like his predecessors and successors, developed a basis for international relations with neighboring empires, such as Byzantium and Persia. Drawing on his considerable knowledge and skills as a statesman, he took the initiative to represent the

Muslim community during his reign and concluded several treaties with Byzantine emperors.[62]

The treaty that was concluded between Hārūn al-Rashīd and Empress Irene was a very significant one. This is because Irene demanded a peace treaty with the Muslims out of consideration for the best interests of her own empire. During her reign (181/797-186/802), Irene was faced with internal problems, and especially the conflict with the Bulgarians. At the same time, the Byzantines were fending off attacks by Hārūn al-Rashīd against their frontier.[63] Classical Muslim historians all agree that the caliph was thereby fulfilling one of his most important duties: attacks and counter attacks occurred regularly, almost annually.[64]

The content of the treaty that was agreed to by Hārūn al-Rashīd and Empress Irene can be found in al-Ṭabarī's *Tārīkh*:

In the year 195/812, after al-Rashīd's triumph in the battle against the Byzantine forces ... al-Rashīd's forces reached Constantinople. The Byzantine Emperor at that time was Auqusta (Irene), the wife of Leon (Alyūn); her son was young and his father had lost his life while he was with her. Negotiations took place between herself and Hārūn ibn al-Mahdī, an exchange of envoys and messengers was made for the demand of a truce and treaty and ransom of prisoners. Hārūn accepted those offers from her. Hārun also imposed a condition of fulfillment and honoring what they had agreed upon, in addition to opening the avenues of her markets and trade. In case he [Hārūn] was confronted with threats [i.e., civil war or outside attacks] by [other] Muslims, she should cooperate with him. They agreed to conclude the truce (ṣulh) for the payment of tribute of ninety or seventy thousand dīnārs for the beginning of April and June annually, and he accepted. She opened the markets to him and she furnished him with gifts of silver and gold as well as envoys and ambassadors. The duration of the treaty was agreed upon for three years. Ransom and prisoners were released, and the *jizya* enforced.[65]

Irene was therefore compelled to demand a peace treaty from Hārūn al-Rashīd in order to restore stability within the Byzantine Empire and to safeguard her reign. Al-Rashīd at first refused the offer, but subsequently accepted it.[66] The interest that motivated Irene was similar to that which Muslims had taken into consideration in the past. Her other concern was to preserve the throne for her son, who was still quite young at that time. The people of the Byzantine Empire were not in favor of her decision however, and they resented her. As a result they transferred there support to her deputy, who succeeded her as emperor with the title Nicephorus I (r. 802-811).

When Nicephorus's reign was fully established and he was confident of his position, he violated the treaty of his predecessor, which had lasted only thirty two-months.[67] He then wrote a letter to al-Rashīd, which read,

From Nicephorus the emperor of Byzantine to Hārūnal King of the Arabs. Irene has parted with the castle, and contented herself with the pawn. She had paid you money, the double of which thoroughly should have been paid to her. It was but a woman's weakness. Wherefore, return what you have taken from her or the sword shall decide. And good-bye (*Salaam*).[68]

As soon as this letter reached al-Rashīd, the latter replied with a letter addressed to Nicephorus I, which read,

In the Name of God, the Most Gracious, the Most Merciful, from the servant of God Hārūn, Commander of the Faithful to Niqfūr (Nicephorus), Byzantine dog. I have read the letter, son of an unbelieving mother. The answer is for your eye to see, not for your ear to hear.[69]

Nuwayrī relates what followed:

As soon as al-Rashīd's letter reached Nicephorus I, he became worried and consulted his deputies until al-Rashīd attacked the Byzantine Empire and occupied part of its territory. He fought the Byzantine army and took booty and prisoners until he reached Constantinople. Then Nicephorus I commanded his army to set the road on fire, but this did not stop al-Rashīd from his goal: he went through it along with his followers. The news reached Nicephorus I and he [instead] sent him gifts, obeyed his order, and paid him personal tribute. Then al-Rashīd withdrew after Nicephorus I resumed payment of what had been given to al-Rashīd by Empress Irene … As soon as Nicephorus I felt secure, however, he took advantage of that ceasefire (*hudna*) and violated the treaty as he did earlier … As soon as the news reached al-Rashīd he engaged in a difficult battle with the Byzantine forces until he won by using heavy machinery, such as the mangonel (*manjanīq*), and the people demanded safe conduct (*amān*) from him, which he granted them. [70]

The details of these treaties between the Hārūn al-Rashīd and the Byzantine emperors Irene and her successor Nicephorus I are not described in much detail or even in chronological order in the sources consulted. A survey of the works of historical writers shows that their main interest was to reflect on what had caused these treaties to be concluded as well as the consequences for those who violated them. Although historians report that al-Rashīd took the same diplomatic path as the Prophet during the negotiations over the Ḥudaybiya treaty, especially in terms of accepting gifts and making peace with non-Muslims in the vicinity, there were differences. In the Prophet's case the Meccans recognized the seriousness of the Muslims' demand to make the pilgrimage to Mecca, and therefore, no blood was spilled. In the case of al-Rashīd, on the other hand, a serious challenge was posed to him by Nicephorus I in contrast to the arrangements mutually agreed upon by al-Rashīd and Irene. The challenges, and especially the violation of the treaty by Nicephorus I, led to a major battles that cost many lives on both sides. In the end, the Muslims defeated Nicephorus's forces and claimed victory. The Byzantines then asked for safe conduct and this was granted to them on their terms. Al-Rashīd won out on the battlefield, whereas the Prophet succeeded using the diplomatic approach; while the outcome of both treaties was almost the same, one resulted in the loss of many lives, and the other did not.

According to al-Ṭabarī, Nicephorus, after agreeing to the treaty between himself and Hārūn al-Rashīd, wrote a letter himself to the latter, asking him to escort his son's future wife, to whom he was engaged, one of the bondwomen (*jāriya*) or young girls from Byzantine territory (under Hārūn's authority). If you can assist me, then let it be. In addition Niqfūr send Hārūn a gift (*surādiq*). Hārūn al-Rashīd replied to his request endowing that young woman with perfume and sent along with Niqfūr's messenger special scents, dates, antidote and raisins. In return Niqfūr sent him heavy load of Islamic *darāhim* (fifty thousand), a hundred garments, two hundred draperies, twelve tailors, four hunting dogs and three workhorses. They exchanged promises and conditions not to cause any hostilities or damages to Hirqila ... [71]

D. An Ayyubid Period Treaty

The third example chosen for examination is the series of treaties drawn up during Ayyūbid rule, in particular the treaty agreed to by the fourth Ayyūbid Sulṭān, Malik al-Kāmil (1218-1238), and the Crusaders. It is important to mention also that the well known Ṣalāḥ al-Dīn al-Ayyūbī (Saladin, 1169-93),[72] had concluded a peace treaty in 1191 with Richard the Lionhearted (1157-1199), by which Jerusalem itself, the most respected city of the Crusaders, was officially surrendered to the Muslims forces, who in turn promised to allow unarmed Christian pilgrims to perform their religious duties unmolested.[73] This peace agreement failed to end the hostilities in the area; the Crusaders engaged in further military action to liberate Jerusalem from Ayyūbid rule. A fifth Crusade by King Andrew of Hungary in response to a call by Pope Innocent sailed not directly toward Jerusalem, but rather for Damietta in Egypt.[74] This was a careful studied strategy by the Crusaders aimed at defeating the Ayyūbids in their home first and then proceeding to Jerusalem. In this way Jerusalem could be captured without any actual combat or bloodshed or they intended to trade territories.[75]

The Crusaders' strategy was very successful in the initial stages. In 1218, they landed near Damietta[76] and started military operations against the city.[77] Al-Kāmil suspected, that the Crusaders might capture Damietta which they did after a siege that lasted two years,[78] and then march toward Cairo afterwards. If they did so, this might end Ayyūbid rule in Egypt.[79] He [al-Kāmil] realized that a good way to distract the Crusaders' attention from Damietta was to offer to make peace and cede to them Jerusalem on the condition that they withdraw from Egyptian soil. The Crusaders, however, rejected al-Kāmil's peace initiative and pressed their military initiative against Damietta, which eventually surrendered in 1219.[80] Al-Kāmil reportedly pleaded again with the Crusaders to spare Egypt and offered to cede other territories in Palestine.[81] The Crusaders rejected his pleas and marched toward Cairo, refusing/precluding to make any sort of peaceful settlement.[82]

Al-Kāmil, left with no choice except to fight the battle, was forced to meet, the Crusaders. In the summer of 1221, as they neared al-Manṣūra,[83] al-Kāmil, desperately desiring to avoid engaging his forces in a battle that could be ruinous not only to his own regime but also to the entire household of Islam (*dār al-Islām*), had a brilliant idea.[84] He ordered all dikes and dams on the Nile to be broken, so that the yearly flood would inundate the enemy and cut off its supply lines.[85] His plan was a great success, and the Crusaders, had to retreat in disarray.[86] Al-Kāmil's plan and its outcome led to the withdrawal of the Crusaders from Egypt in defeat. As well, they lost their sole opportunity to restore Jerusalem to Christian rule.[87] The Crusaders demanded safe conduct (*amān*) from al-Kāmil and they agreed to the *hudna* (ceasefire) on the basis of the abstention of the parties concerned from hostilities against each other. [88]

Information on the ceasfire concluded between the French and Malik al-Kāmil is scattered throughout the sources. However, Ibn Iyās (d. 1524) provides a summary of what the both parties agreed upon:

When the French realized their defeat, they sent a messenger to al-Malik al-Kāmil to seek safe conduct (*amān*) on the condition that they would leave Damiettia and withdraw from it to their own lands. Both parties agreed on the conditions to leave with each other hostages from among their relatives. Both agreed to release all the prisoners that were taking prisoners of war since the time of al-Naṣir Ṣalāḥ al-Dīn Yūsuf ibn Ayyūb. Both swore upon these conditions. The truce was concluded and signed by Malik al-Kāmil and the French. The French king sent twenty kings as a hostage to al-Malik al-Kāmil and Malik al-Kāmil sent his son prince Najm al-Dīn along with a group of princes to the French king. Upon this the French handed back the city of Damietta to the Muslims and released all of the prisoners, as they had agreed, from since the time of al-Malik al-Nāṣir Ṣalāḥ al-Dīn Yūsuf, while Malik al-Kāmil released all of the French prisoners.[89]

The duration of this truce is not mentioned in Ibn Iyās; al-Nuwayrī, however, states that it was to last for eight years.[90] When news of the defeat of the French in Damietta reached Europe, Frederick II (r. 1215-1250) of Germany agreed in 624/1227 to lead an army to the region to regain Jerusalem from the Muslims and to rid the Crusaders of the shame of their defeat. Frederick II reached Acre in September, 624/1228 [91] and proceeded toward Jaffa.[92] During that time Malik al-Kāmil found himself confronted with a rebellion against his rule led by his brother al-Malik al-Ashraf in Syria. Now he was faced with the threat of Frederick II. Fearing a possible alliance between his brother and the Crusader forces in Syria that might cost him his rule in Egypt, he immediately asked to negotiate a peace settlement with Frederick.[93]

Frederick II was fully informed of the abilities of Malik al-Kāmil, demonstrated in the 618/1221 battle to defend Damietta from French occupation that lasted a year, ten months and twenty-four days.[94] Because the outcome of a battle attack in Jersusalem was not certain, he did not create too many difficulties in the course of accepting the settlement that was offered to him by Malik al-Kāmil. Frederick II simply demanded the restoration of Jerusalem and also several other cities that the Muslims had previously captured from the Christians.[95] Malik al-Kāmil agreed to the conditions demanded by Frederick, and they signed a ceasefire (*hudna*) for a duration of ten years.[96] The agreement between the two leaders was thus concluded successfully.[97]

The decision of Malik al-Kāmil to negotiate a settlement with the Crusaders may be viewed as a sign of weakness on the part of a weak ruler, who in doing so betrayed the Islamic cause. The Imam is the chief representative and spokesman of the Muslims and is responsible for safeguarding the Muslim community from any threat or foreign attacks. In this case, Malik al-Kāmil, having responsibility for the Muslim community in Egypt and faced with current political and military threats, made a tactical decision to seek a peace-settlement with the Crusaders. In so doing he preserved Egypt from a serious threat that might have been fatal to his regime and Muslim interests. A number of jurists of the classical period in fact approved of this action, and one finds a consensus supporting Malik al-Kāmil's decision.[98] In this respect, Malik al-Kāmil deserves credit for having made a wise decision; one which saved the Ayyūbid regime from a possible collapse during his reign. His decision to sign a treaty in which he agreed to hand over Jerusalem for ten years might be viewed from a number of perspectives, but, in reality, al-Kāmil perpetrated this act out of political expediency. Since he feared hostilities from his Syrian relatives, and above all his brother, al-Kāmil needed Frederick's military support. Although Jerusalem's religious status was far from uppermost in al-Kāmil's mind,[99] many classical and contemporary scholars support Malik al-Kāmil's decision and refer to him as one of the leading Ayyūbid rulers.[100] In addition, this treaty owed a debt to the Ḥudaybiya agreement, though there are notable differences. Malik al-Kāmil's political decision to seek peace-agreement with non-Muslims was in accordance with divine legislation and permitted by the existing legal precedents.[101] Taking the circumstances of the day into consideration, Malik al-Kāmil did not stray from the principle of Islamic teachings.

E. An Ottoman Period Treaty

The last treaty that we will examine here is one that was negotiated by the Ottoman ruler Sulaeiman the Magnificient (926-74/1520-1566) - - known in the West as Sulaymān the Magnificent - - and the King of France, Francis I. (r. 1515-1547) This treaty, known as the Treaty of Amity and Commerce, was signed 1535.

Sulaeiman had an enigmatic personality but he was an able administrator; during his reign the Ottoman Empire experienced its golden age and ranked foremost among world powers in terms of both military and political influence. He ruled the Empire for a remarkably long reign of forty-six years, between 1520-1566.[102] He was a brilliant strategist and an acclaimed legislator.[103] He was surnamed Qānūnī "lawgiver", because he showed wisdom as a legislator, not in the sense of an innovator, but as a regulator and restorer of balance.[104] He was also known as "*ghāzī*" ("conqueror"), and assured success by leading his army in person.[105] During his reign, he initiated ten campaigns against Europe and three others in Asia.[106] He also grasped the strategic importance of Hungary, which became the scene of numerous clashes between the Ottoman Empire and Europe.[107] Under his reign, the imperial borders of the Ottoman Empire were extended to their furthest limits.[108]

Among the sources that provide a record of this treaty is the work *Middle East and North Africa in World Politics: A Documentary Record*, by J. C. Hurewitz. This book contains a translation of the French text of the official treaty, which is comprised of sixteen articles.[109] The aim in this section is to discuss and analyze this particular treaty and to evaluate its validity according to the Islamic tradition in general and its relation to the Ḥudaybiya treaty.

Sulaymān's reign was marked by extraordinary historical events, not the least of which was the 1535 treaty with France. The question that imposes itself, however, is: How did relations between the French and the Ottoman Empire in the time of Sulaymān's reign develop?

In 1519, the Habsburg Charles V and Francis I of France were candidates for the throne of the Holy Roman Empire, and both candidates promised to mobilize all of Europe's forces against the Ottomans.[110] When the electors chose Charles V for the position in 1521, the two European rulers went to war with each other. While Europe was thus divided, Sulaeiman took advantage and marched his forces toward Belgrade, which was the gateway to Central Europe; indeed, the Ottoman sources frequently refer to Belgrade as "the gate to Hungary."[111] Belgrade fell to Sulaeiman's troops on the 29th of August 1521. It is important to note here that Suleiman, as a brilliant politician, had seized an opportunity, as he was convinced that it was not in the interest of the Ottoman Empire that Europe should be dominated by single power.[112] In January of the following year Suleiman captured Rhodes, the key to the eastern Mediterranean, from the Knights of St. John, but he was forced to abandon this territory after a long and terrible siege.[113] When in 1525 Charles V took Francis I prisoner, the latter, through his ministers, turned to the Ottoman Empire for help, believing that the only hope of guaranteeing the independence of the European states against Charles V lay in a French-Turkish alliance.[114] In 1526, Francis's ambassador informed Suleiman that if Francis were to accept Charles's conditions, the Holy Roman Emperor would become the "ruler of the world."[115]

This prospect did not appeal to Suleiman, so he decided to oppose Charles's ambitions by mobilizing his large forces and advancing towards Hungary. On August 28th, 1526, he occupied Buda and Srem and forced the Hungarian Diet to elect his candidate John Zapolya as King. In the following year, the Hungarian partisans of the Habsburgs responded by electing Charles V's brother Archduke Ferdinand as King of Hungary; he in turn occupied Buda and expelled John Zapolya. In September 1529, Suleiman once more invaded Hungary and again enthroned John Zapolya in Buda as an Ottoman vassal. Zapolya agreed to pay an annual tribute and accepted a Janissary garrison in the citadel. When Ferdinand again entered Hungary in 1531 and besieged Buda, Suleiman responded the following year by leading a large army into Hungary which advanced as far as Guns, some sixty miles from Vienna. This was the military strategy adopted by Sulaymān by which he hoped to force Charles V into battle.[116]

Charles recognized Sulaymān's military strategy for what it was, and ordered his admiral Andrea Doria to take Coron in the Morea from the Ottomans. Suleiman countered this with an attempt to open a second front in the Mediterranean and placed all of his Ottoman naval forces under the command of the famous Turkish corsair and conqueror of Algeria, Khayruddīn Barbarossa, appointing him *kapudanī deryā* (grand admiral) with orders to cooperate with the French. Thus, beginning in 1531, French-Ottoman cooperation against a common enemy began to emerge, although a formal alliance was not forged until later in his rule. During that time, Sulaiman granted the French were friendly nation-status and freedom of trade within the Empire. Both parties, represented by their ambassadors, agreed orally on the military and political details of the alliance, which was kept secret.[117] Their strategy to defeat Charles V was to consist in a French maneuver matched by a complementary action undertaken by Suleiman's forces: in 1537 the French were to invade Italy from the north while Ottoman forces attacked from the south. In that year Suleiman's forces reached Valona in Albania and besieged the Venetian-held ports, where a French fleet assisted the Ottomans. In 1538 the French concluded a peace treaty with Charles V, but Francis maintained his secret policy of alliance with the Ottomans. This gave Charles an opportunity to resume his siege of Tunis, which was captured in 1535; however, in 1538, Khayruddīn Barbarossa defeated a fleet under Charles's admiral Andrea Doria at Preveza, leaving him undisputed master of the Mediterranean.[118]

In the interim John Zapolya had died, and Ferdinand once again invaded Hungary. Suleiman responded by sending forces again into Hungary with the aim to bringing Hungary under Ottoman rule – indeed, he intended to make it an Ottoman province under a *beylerbey* (governor-general of a province). Around two years later, in 1543, Suleiman sent a fleet of 110 galleys under the command of Barbarossa to assist Francis. The combined Franco-Ottoman fleet besieged Nice, and the Ottoman fleet wintered in the French port of Toulon. A small French artillery unit also joined the Ottoman army in Hungary. However, this cooperation was not effective, especially because of worsening relations with the Safavids in Iran. Therefore, Suleiman decided that the best policy would be to establish a state of peace on his western front. In 1547, he concluded an armistice with Ferdinand, which also included Charles V and France. The treaty allowed Ferdinand to keep part of Hungary, which would remain in his possession in return for a yearly tribute of thirty thousand ducats paid to the Ottoman state.[119]

In the years 1547-1555, wars broke out again in Europe, and these events led to the assassination of Ferdinand by the Ottomans. Then, in expanding his control over Transylvania, Suleiman established a new *beylerbeylik* (province) of Temesvar, in southern Transylvania. The new king of France, Henry II (r. 1547-1559), came to the throne and realized the need for maintaining an Ottoman alliance against Charles V. At the same time, Suleiman found a natural ally in the collectivity of German Protestant princes, who also opposed Charles

V. This semi-coalition led to the official recognition of Protestantism by the Habsburgs. Suleiman wrote a letter to the German princes, urging them to support France and also demanding that, if the Ottoman army entered Europe, they should be granted amnesty. In this letter, Suleiman indicated the similarities between Protestantism and Islam.[120]

Suleiman's intention resembles that of the earlier al-Malik al-Kāmil, in that both sought to maneuver the diplomatic situation for both religious and political gains. His political ambition was to keep Europe divided and prevent the potential of a united crusade against the Ottomans. On the religious plane, Suleiman sought to shift all the battles to outside Muslim-dominated territory, in order to protect its inhabitants from the ravages of war. However, his political motives come across as being much stronger than the religious ones, since upon securing the western front he immediately sent troops to the eastern front, which was under threat from Iran. His quick reaction prevented war from breaking out, and he was able to conclude a treaty with the Safavids. We noted above, on the basis of Donald Little's observation, that Malik al-Kāmil's decision to cede Jerusalem in a treaty was a sign that religious considerations were not his prime concern at the time. The same may be said of Suleiman's political stance towards Europe, though ultimately all his actions may be seen as a defence of Islamic territory. Needless to say, after his death in 1566 the Ottoman Empire began to decline and suffered an acute loss of status on the international stage. Halil Inalcik states that "up to 1595 there was no question of international politics, which did not somehow involve the Ottomans."[121] Indeed, the Ottoman Empire during the reign of Suleiman was recognized as one of the most powerful participants in international affairs.

The question that can then be raised is the following: If Suleiman was more of a politician than a religious leader, then to what extent did Islamic jurisprudence or Muslim jurists affect his decisions regarding the welfare of the community? According to both modern and medieval sources, Suleiman was a leader who functioned as both a statesman and a servant of the Sacred Law.[122] The Muftī that occupied the position during the reign of Sulaymān was Abū Su'ūd, one of the most distinguished intellectuals in the history of the Ottoman Empire.[123] According to Colin Imber, who has written a special study of the career of Abū Su'ūd, Shaykh al-Islam (expounder of Islamic law) chief Muftī to Suleiman, this can clearly seen in the case of the annexation of Hungary upon the death of its king in 1541. Suleiman converted it into a province under an Ottoman *beylerbey* and subject to Ottoman law.[124] Since Ottoman land tenure and taxation rules emerged gradually in different Ottoman provinces, such as Rumelia. it came into existence through custom and "piecemeal" legislation.[125] Since there was no uniform practice or complete account of its underlying norms, there was a need for legislation to be introduced into the system. In this matter, Suleiman consulted Abū Su'ūd, who in earlier cases, such as in Buda, provided the material for Suleiman's New Qānūn in the "Law Book," for enactment as an Imperial decree.[126]

There is no doubt that Suleiman recognized the importance of the Muftī's position during his reign; therefore, in granting any concessions to *ḥarbīs*, he always considered to prescriptions of law of the Ḥanafī school.[127] Abū Su'ūd even became a close personal friend of Sulaymān, and during the latter's reign held the two most important if not the highest ranking legal offices. The first post was that of military judge of Rumelia in 1537, and the second the most important and highest rank in legal tradition, that of Shaykh al-Islām, in 1545. Furthermore, he was always close by Suleiman both in the capital and on military campaigns.[128]

The treaty between the Ottoman Empire and France allowed Suleiman to gain more time to accomplish his desire of keeping Europe divided. Furthermore, this treaty contributed to his success in preventing additional warfare with the neighboring Safavids. Suleiman was aware of the circumstances that might emerge if he did not conclude a treaty with France. Therefore, this treaty had a great impact and contributed to both political and economic success and accomplishments during his reign.[129] When the new King of France, Henry II, came to the throne, he maintained the Ottoman alliance because of its vital importance, especially against Charles V.[130] The French alliance was the cornerstone of Ottoman foreign policy in Europe.[131]

Although the treaty remained a draft only, it was observed in practice. Further discussions on its capitulation provisions were carried on between the French ambassador, J. de La Forest, and Ibrahim Pasha.[132] Because Ibrahim Pasha carried out these negotiations over the treaty without Suleiman's consent, however, he was executed.[133] This draft treaty, as finally drawn up by de la Forest, bears the imprint of a treaty concluded between two equal parties. This was the sole example of such a treaty among "capitulations" (all the others of which were granted as unilaterally conceded *'ahdnāmes*).[134] This draft treaty of capitulation contains conditions and serves the interest of both parties. In substance, it embodies a fair and just spirit, suggesting that power is distributed equally among both parties. It is likewise fair in terms of religious matters, since it acknowledges both parties' religious beliefs and legal systems; this is best seen, for example, in the cases where it stipulates that if someone of either party commits a violation, he will be persecuted in accordance with his own judicial system and then duly punished. It granted merchants the freedom to advertise their merchandise with only limited restrictions. The treaty sets forth the opportunities for both parties to participate in the exchange of economic goods. Both parties benefited from the revenues that resulted from this treaty. As well, to a certain degree, it allowed both cultures to learn about each other and undoubtedly contributed to a better understanding between the Ottoman Empire and the European powers.[135]

In the long run, there were both positive and negative conseguences of this treaty that affected the Empire itself. Once it opened its markets to Europe, the Ottoman Empire gradually lost its significance and political impact, especially during the reign of Salīm III (ca. 1798). The Ottoman Empire gradually slipped into a decline, until the Empire itself was abolished and Turkey became a republic in 1924.[136]

What is demonstrated in the treaties surveyed above is a pattern of consistency in resolving international disputes and facilitating international contract, despite the specific circumstances in each case. Much of this consistency is owed to the model provided by the treaty of Ḥudaybiya of 628 C.E. Both the letter and the spirit of this agreement informed all subsequent pacts, determining what conditions could be set as well the justifications needed for either agreeing to or breaking them.

Although some of the actual details of the treaties agreed to in the period under study are sketchy in terms of details, they can be seen to fulfill in each case the limits and demands put forward by theorists of Islamic law. Thus, in addition to satisfying the rules on contracts, they also obeyed the prime directive of *maṣlaḥa*, i.e., that whatever is agreed to in a treaty must be in the best interests of the Muslim community. Much of the discussion by contemporary and later critics of individual treaties can be seen in fact to revolved around this issue, and most of the reactions are positive – an indication in itself that these documents conformed to legal precedent.

The different attitudes on the part of Muslim and non-Muslim states towards treaties during this period are illustrated by almost casual violations of agreements by the Byzantines and other European powers, and the carefully justified responses by the various Muslim rulers, who took pains to consult experts in Islamic law before making decisions of such legal import. Of course, the Muslim sources consulted take pains to outline these justifications, but one cannot imagine them approving a decision based on utilitarian considerations – a common enough motive for treaty breaking in European history.

Conclusion

The evolution of *'ilm al-siyar* owes much to the work of prominent jurists beginning in the second half of the second Islamic century, in particular those of the Ḥanafī school, among whom Abū Ḥasan al-Shaybānī was the most outstanding contributor. Shaybānī's era coincided with the intial period of the codification of Islamic law, which saw the appearance of treatises that provided guidance to later jurists. In addition, he was among the leading jurists to combine the approaches of both the Medinas and Kufas schools, especially in the spheres of *ḥadīth* and *ra'y*.

Shaybānī was also among the first jurists to incorporate *'ilm al-siyar* as a branch of law, since the roots of the former are derived from and based on revelation. Among the characteristics of *siyar* are its stability and flexibility in dealing with new developments that confront Muslims. As a part of *fiqh*, *siyar* has often been employed in order to deal with significant issues, such as the conduct of Muslims and their relations with non-Muslims, with the *dār al-Islām* and *dār al-ḥarb*. It ensures that the relations between Muslim and non-Muslim powers are not solely based on war or peace, but on the principle that *da'wa* (conveying the message of Islam) be given prime consideration.

Siyar also determines the status of the *ahl al-dhimma* as part of *dār al-Islām* under the terms of an everlasting safe conduct (*amān*), even though the agreement stops short of bestowing Muslim identity and full membership in the Muslim community on the *dhimmī*. Nevertheless, *dhimmis* are granted full rights, such as the right to practice their own faith freely, and full respect, honor and protection. At the same time, certain obligations were required of them, such as payment of *jizya*. By contrast, the *musta'min* who resides within *dār al-Islām* on a temporary basis do not enjoy the status of *dhimmī*. Their rights and obligations are based on agreements that most of the time comes under the purview of Islamic law, such as business transactions or commercial law, but even these are extremely fair. Criminal acts by the by *musta'min* are deferred, since they are under the temporary agreement or safe conduct, as long as the contract (*'aqd*) is valid. Even if the *musta'min* status of an individual should expire, Muslims are urged to assist them should they need additional time to fulfill their obligations within *dār al-Islām*.

With regard to the treaties or *mu'āhadāt* between Muslims and non-Muslims, works on *siyar* and in particular that of Shaybānī devote much attention to the problem of their conclusion, duration, validity, conditions and whatever might render them void. What makes a treaty, or *mu'āhada*, valid according to *siyar* is the consideration of the interest of *dār al-Islām* and the nature of its relations with *dār al-ḥarb*. The most noticeable issue is the emphasis on honoring and fulfilling the conditions of the treaty and the warning against treachery and injustice. Moreover, in the event that hostilities take place between Muslims and non-Muslims, Muslims must always observe the pronouncements and conduct of the Prophet in his battles, meaning that they have to follow his example and thus should not be the first to open hostilities. In keeping with this principle, fighting should be considered a last resort, especially when *jizya* can be imposed in order to avoid bloodshed or continued hostilities. Every effort must be made by the commanders of the opposing parties to reach an agreement that leads to a temporary cessation of hostilities, an armistice, a cease-fire, covenant or pledge.

All of the post-Ḥudaibiyya treaties examined in the previous chapters, namely the treaties concluded during the reigns of 'Abd al-Malik ibn Marwān, Hārūn al-Rashīd, Malik al-Kāmil and Suleiman the Magnificent, were drawn up in consultation with jurists. Their legal opinions were vital to these caliphs, who were bound to follow the commands of the Sharī'a and Islamic tradition. Without seeking legal advice regarding their conduct, their legitimacy as rulers would have been in question. Therefore, as long as Muslim leaders followed Islamic teachings along with the consultation and support of jurists, their conduct could be regarded as valid. Contemporary jurists generally agreed with the need for Muslims to maintain peaceful relations with their fellow human beings, including non-Muslim communities. As long as relations between Muslims and non-Muslims favour the respective interests of both parties, they should be cherished, honored and followed in this world. This lesson from the past can still contribute to improving relations between nation states, whether they are Muslim or non-Muslim.

The nature of Muslim - non-Muslim relations can not however be defined solely as based on the circumstances of peace or war, since the types of relationship that Muslims have with others depend on the conditions and status of non-Muslims and their reactions to Islam. Since the essential purpose of Islamic preaching is to introduce Islam to non-Muslims free of any compulsion, it is up to the non-Muslims to accept or reject the faith. Only if the non-Muslim is determined to reject Islam and at the same time demonstrate a hostile attitude towards Islam wills the relations be based on retaliation and the outcome of that retaliation will determine the norm of the subsequent relations.

The Islamic treaties concluded between Muslims and non-Muslims were meant to exemplify the principles of fairness, justice and protection. Ever since the time when the Islamic state was in a position of power and non-Muslims were obliged to demand safe conduct from Muslims, these safe conducts were granted without setting any precondition that the non-Muslims had to change their religion. Muslims were obligated to provide a peaceful environment for the non-Muslims whether *musta'min* or *ahl al-dhimma*, in terms of their lives, belongings and religious practices. Treaties in Islam were one of the most important instruments to establish such relations with non-Muslims. This was in fact the early practice of the Prophet, whose treaties with non-Muslims where implemented, honored and respected in all of their conditions, without any betrayal, deceit or violation. Concluding treaties between Muslims and non-Muslims thus became a common practice throughout Islamic history. While it is true that public interest was never far from the minds of Muslims who concluding their treaties with non-Muslims, this was achieved without any deception as it was addressed and made known to the other party of the treaty through the negotiation process. This was common practice among Muslim leaders and representatives of Islamic community, who strove to serve the interests of Islam first in addition to safeguarding the well being of Muslims in general.

The Muslim scholars responsible for the evolution of the Islamic legal system, such as Shaybāni, lived mostly during the Abbasid period. It is commonly accepted among modern scholars that this was the golden age of all the fields of Islamic science, including law. As seen in the works of the scholars from this period consulted throughout this study, the sources of Islamic jurisprudence and rulings were the essential elements from which they derived their opinions regarding any given matter, despite the error of some. This is not because they intended to introduce restrictions; rather they searched for a solution to any giving problem by exercising *ijtihād*. Shaybānī, the master architect of the branch of *siyar* (Muslim conduct of public law), al-Awzāʿī, al-Thawrī, Fazārī, and others strove to elaborate the matters necessary to establishing sound relations with non-Muslims. The field of *siyar* encompasses such concepts as *ahl al-dhimma*, *'aqd al-dhimma*, *amān*, *musta'min*, *ṣulḥ*, *muwāda'a*, *dār al-Islām*, *dār al-ḥarb* and *mu'āhada*, each of which contains regulations on the validity, duration and violation of conditions in conformity with its purposes. At the core of all these elements is the relation between *dār al-Islām* and *dār al-ḥarb*. Essential to the success of the above types of treaties was loyalty to the contractual obligation and avoidance of betrayal, treachery and oppression.

Islamic literature on treaties contains much material that can contribute to improving the relations among nations, as well as being useful in avoiding bloodshed, hatred and mistrust among present-day nation states. Modern international law, which evolved largely in the sixteenth century under the guiding hand of Grotius, known as the father of international law, was a law developed in suited to Christian nations.[137] Many modern non-Muslim scholars, such as Khadduri, Krousa and Boregitshal, admit on the roots of modern international that many elements of the latter system were derived from the works of Muslim jurists, in particular, the *Siyar* of Shaybānī. They even agree that Shaybānī deserves the title of the "father" of modern public International law.[138]

In closing, it may be useful to recall that, since ancient times, nations have employed contracts known as treaties for a variety of purposes, and Islam is no exception. Treaties are an essential aspect of Islamic international law, for they help Muslim nations to regulate the many different aspects of their relations with non-Muslim states. Since an Islamic nation is a part of the world community, this entails maintaining productive contracts with other members of the international community. Muslim jurists active in the field of *siyar* realize that evidence from both the Qur'ān and the Sunna of the Prophet favored co-existence and peaceful relations with non-Muslims were of prime importance in their texts; hence, as we have seen in this study of the historical evolution of treaties, Muslims were commanded by the sacred text to adhere to all treaty pledges. According to the Islamic sources that were consulted for this study, furthermore, Muslim nations observed their treaties, unless the other party had first broken a pledge.

Early Muslim scholars and jurists set the pattern for later jurists and rulers[139] to follow, stipulating the conditions that are needed to conclude any type of treaty with non-Muslims. The consensus of Muslim jurists throughout Islamic history was that the Ḥudaibīyya treaty should be seen as the underlying model for all latter treaties. In order for a treaty to be finalized, it has to pass through certain stages, beginning with the determination by one of two or more parties involved in a dispute or a related matter to pursue a treaty. Once they have agreed to talk, then the process of determination of the conditions of that treaty will be the subject of their negotiations. If they are able to agree on conditions, then the two parties proceed to the actual drafting of that treaty. Finally, signatures, the date and the name of witnesses should be affixed, after which both parties must strive to put the treaty into practice. This process must be pursued in a spirit of reconciliation; if any is based on compulsion or inequality, the treaty will be rendered void.

Muslim jurists stated that the core of making a treaty is a question of honor. The fulfillment of all of the elements in the treaty to their fullest is imperative. This is the attitude that is needed in today's world, since many recent treaties lack any balance between the parties involved; indeed, the more powerful party will determine the conditions and the role for the other party. Therefore, the treaties concluded in the modern world should be based on the Islamic model which honors, respects and fulfills the interests of both parties involved. Modern international law can learn much from the Islamic model, which would improve the relations between treaty-making states in the world today.

The Qur'ān, as always, is the ultimate reference that Muslims look to for guidance. Therefore, let the final words in this study be the Qur'anic passages that embody the core purpose of this study: "But if they incline to peace, you also incline to it, and [put your] trust in Allah."[140]

I hope this study contributes to a new understanding of the conduct of treaties in early Islamic history and that it may shed some light on the nature of treaties among nation-states in the contemporary period. It is to be hoped that it will lead to deeper reflection on the ongoing disputes and hostilities in many parts of this world; especially the Middle East, and in particular the Palestinian-Israeli dispute.

1 *Sharḥ al-Siyar al-Kabīr*, 5:1780; *Badā'i' al-Ṣanā'i'*, 7:108; Māwardī, *al-Ḥāwī*, 19:113; Ramlī, *Nihāyat al-Muḥtāj*, 8: 106; Ibn Qudāma, *al-Mughnī*, 8: 459; *Fatḥ al-Qadīr*, 4: 293.
2 Sami, Hanna, ed. *Medieval and Middle Eastern Studies* (Leiden: E. J. Brill, 1972), 51-52.
3 Ṭabarī, *Tarīkh*, 3: 608-609; Muḥammad Ḥamīdallāh, *Majmū'at al-Wathā'iq al-Siyāsiyya*, 268-269.
4 Ṭabarī, *Tārīkh*, 4: 104-109.
5 Balādhurī, *Futūḥ al-Buldān*, 159-160; Mas'ūdī, *Murūj al-Dhahab*, 5: 224; Ibn al-Farrā', *Rusul al-Mulūk*, 106, 152, 155.
6 Balādhurī, *Futūḥ al-Buldān*, 159; Ibn Farrā', *Rusul al-Mulūk*, 152.
7 For the text of this treaty see Muḥammad Ḥamīdallāh, *Majmū'at al-Wathā'iq al-Siyāsiyya*, 345.
8 'Umar was asked to perform his prayer inside the church but he refused to do so because he was afraid that the Muslims would later claim this church for their own on that basis. He believed that this might also lead to a common practice among Muslims of taking over churches.
9 Muḥammad Ḥamīdallāh, *Majmū'at al-Wathā'iq al-Siyāsiyya*, 345-346; Balādhurī, *Futūḥ al-Buldān*, 2: 383; Abu 'Ubayd, *Amwāl*, 97-98.
10 Ibid., 340.
11 *Majmū'at al-Wathā'iq al-Siyāsiyya* , 341, 418, 474, 487-488; Abū Yūsuf, *Kharāj*, 42-45; Balādhurī, *Futūḥ al-Buldān*, 1: 28.
12 Balādhurī, *Futūḥ al-Buldān*, 197.
13 Ibid., 159; Ibn al-Farrā', *Rusul al-Mulūk*, 152; Sarakhsī, *Sharḥ al-Siyar al-Kabīr*, 1: 97; and idem *Mabsūṭ*, 10: 92; Abū 'Ubayd, *Amwāl*, 290.
14 Mas'ūdī, *Murūj al-Dhahab*, 5: 224; Balādhurī, *Futūḥ al-Buldān*, 160.
15 Ibn al-Farrā', *Rusul al-Mulūk*, 106; 155; F. W. Buckler, *Harun'l-Rashid and Charles the Great* (Cambridge: The Mediaeval Academy of America, 1931) , 43-47.
16 Majid Khadduri, *War and Peace in the Law of Islam*, 234.
17 James Brundage, *The Crusaders: A Documentary History* (Milwaukee: Marquette University Press, 1962), 185-186; Carole Hillenbrand, *The Crusaders: Islamic Perspectives* (Edinburgh: Edinburgh University Press, 1999), 310, 392-397; al-Maqrīzī, *Tārīkh al-Duwal wa al-Mulūk*; see also, P. M. Holt, "Baybars Treaty with the Lady of Beirut in 667/1269", in *Crusade and Settlement*, ed. P.W. Edbury (Cardiff, 1984), 255; al-Qalqashandī, *Subḥ al-A'shā*, 14: 40-42.
18 E. Ashtor, *A Social and Economic History of the Near East in the Middle Ages* (London, 1976); D. Abulafia,"The Role of Trade in Muslim-Christian Contact During the Middle Ages", in *The Arab Influence in Medieval Europe*, eds. D. A. Agius and R. Hitchcock (Reading 1994) 1-24.
19 J. C. Hurewitz, *The Middle East and North Africa in World Politics: A Documentary Record*, 1 *European Expansion, 1535-1914* (New Haven and London: Yale University Press, 1975) 1-5.
20 See Appendix (A) for the full text of this treaty. Muḥammad Ḥamīdallāh, *Majmū'at al-Wathāiq al-Siyāsiyya*, 57; and idem, the *Muslim Conduct of State*, 265-268.
21 Ch. Pellat, "Hilf al-Fuḍūl", *Encyclopaedia of Islam*, new edition, 3: 389, Muḥammad Ḥusayn Haykal, *The Life of Muhammad* (*Ḥayāt Muḥammad*), translated by Ismā'il R. Fārūqī (Indianapolis: American Trust Publications, 1976) 57-56; W. Montgomery Watt,

Muhammad at Mecca (Oxford: Clarendon Press, 1952), 13-16; Ibn Hishām, *Sīra*, 1: 133-135; Ibn Sa'd, *Ṭabaqāt*, 1: 42;

22 Muḥammad Ḥusayn Haykal, *The Life of Muhammad* (*Ḥayāt Muḥammad*) 57; Ch. Pellat, "Hilf al-Fuḍūl", *Encyclopaedia of Islam*, new edition, 3: 389.

23 For more details on the peace treaties drawn up by the Arabs in the pre-Islamic era, see Irfan Kawar, "The Arabs in the Peace Treaty of A. D. 561", *Arabica*, 3, (1982?) 181-213; regarding the Muslims who participated in or heard about Ḥilf al-Fuḍūl in the pre-Islamic era, see W. Montgomery Watt, *Muhammad at Mecca* (Oxford: Clarendon Press, 1952).

24 Ḥudaybiya was a valley a short day's journey from Mecca. This valley was the center of a local cult with a well and a sacred tree. A modest village afterwards arose here surrounding by lands rich in subterranean water. See the *Encyclopaedia of Islam*, 1913-1936 3, (1987) 328-329; Ibn Sa'd, *Ṭabaqāt al-Kubrā*, 2: 95-96. The Ḥudaybiya treaty is referred to by several terms in jurisprudence and the *Maghāzī* literature, being described as a *muwāda'a,musālama, hudna,* etc. See Ibn Qudāmā, *al-Mughnī*, 10: 522; Ibn Humām, *Fatḥ al-Qadīr*, 5: 466; al-Ramlī, *Nihāyat al-Muḥtāj*, 8: 102.

25 Ibn Ḥajar al-'Asqalānī, *al-Iṣāba*, 1: 94; Wāqidī, *al-Maghāzī*, 2: 61-112; Ibn Sa'd, *Ṭabaqāt*, 2: 95; Ibn Hishām, *Sīra*, 3: 332.

26 Muḥammad Ḥusayn Haykal, *The Life of Muhammad* (*Ḥayāt Muḥammad*) 179-183.

27 See the following for additional information and details: W. Montgomery Watt, *Muhammad Prophet and Statesman* (London: Oxford University Press, 1961) 124-126; *Muhammad At Medina* (London: Clarendon Press, 1966), 10-16; Muḥammad Ḥusayn Haykal, *The Life of Muhammad*, 216-241, 242-248, and 299-316; Antonie Wessels, *A Modern Arabic Biography of Muḥammad* (Leiden: E. J. Brill, 1972), 162-164Ibid., 299-316.

28 Ibid., 317-318.

29 Ibid.

30 Ibid., 340-343.

31 Ibn Hishām, *Sīra*, 2: 314-315; Ibn Sa'd, *Ṭabaqāt*, 2: 96-97; Maqrīzī, *Imtā' al-Asmā'*, 1: 289-291; Ṭabarī, *Tafsīr*, 29: 86.

32 Ibn Sa'd, *Ṭabaqāt*, 2: 96-97; Maqrīzī, *Imtā' al-Asmā'*, 1: 289-291; Ṭabarī, *Tafsīr*, 29: 86;

Muḥammad Ḥusayn Haykal, *The Life of Muhammad* (*Ḥayāt Muḥammad*), 345-353.

33 Ibn Qayyim al-Jawziyya, *Zād al-Ma'ād*, 3: 287.

34 Ṭaḥāwī, *Muskhil al-Āthār*, 7: 302; Shawkānī, *Nayl al-Awṭār*, 8: 35; Ghazālī, *Wajīz*, 2: 196; *'Iqd al-Jawāhir al-Thamīna*, 1: 480; *Kashshāf al-Qinā'*, 3: 99-100; *al-Mubdi'*, 3: 393; Shāfi'ī, *al-Umm*, 4: 201; *al-Muhadhdhab wa 'l-Majmū'*, 18: 87; *al-Mughnī*, 10: 595. According to al-Ṭabarī, there was a consensus among scholars regarding the status of emissaries. They must be well treated, respected and welcomed by their host in order to maintain the process of negotiations. If the emissaries are harmed or mistreated, this might cause further hardship throughout the negotiations. Therefore, Muslims must take this into consideration while there are negotiations, even if the emissaries insult them. An example of this is when the Prophet received a messenger from the Meccans. The latter insulted the Prophet, and the Prophet's companions were very angry at his words. They were about to react to his statements, then the Prophet commanded them to honor and welcome the messenger without any harm for the sake of reaching an agreement with the Meccans. This became the customary practice among Muslims in their treatment of emissaries. Ṭabarī, *Ikhtilāf al-Fuqahā'*, 32.

35 Ibid.

36 See Aḥmad Bashmīl, *Ṣulḥ al-Ḥudaybiya*, 280-200.
37 Ibn Kathīr, *al-Bidāya wa al-Nihāya*, 4:210-214; Ṭabarī, *Tārīkh*, 2: 620-644; Ya'qūbī, *Tārīkh*, 2: 35-37; Imran N. Hosein, "Diplomacy in Islam," *Muslim Education Quarterly* 3, 3 (1986), 70.
38 Ṭabarī, *Tārīkh*, 2: 620-644; Ya'qūbī, *Tārīkh*, 2: 35-37; Imran N. Hosein, "Diplomacy in Islam." *Muslim Education Quarterly*, 3, 3 (1986), 70. In addition to the classical historical sources that deal with the conduct of the Prophet during his lifetime, see the following: Montgomery Watt, *Muhammad: Prophet and Statesman* (London: Oxford University Press, 1961); idem, *Muhammad at Medina* (Oxford, England: Clarendon Press, 1956); Muhammad Husayn Haykal. *The Life of Muhammad.*
39 Muḥammad Ḥusayn Haykal, *The Life of Muhammad*, 400-408.
40 Ibid., 356.
41 Mas'ūdī, *Murūj al-Dhahab*, 3: 42. 'Abd al-Malik's brother 'Abd al-'Aziz ruled Egypt forcefully and suppressed the rebellions.
42 Mas'ūdī, *Murūj al-Dhahab*, 5: 226.
43 H. A. R. Gibb, "'Abd al-Malik Ibn Marwān," *Encyclopaedia of Islam*, new edition, 1: 76.
44 Mas'ūdī, *Murūj al-Dhahab*, 11: 299
45 Mas'ūdī, *Murūj al-Dhahab*, 5: 225-226; H. A. R. Gibb, "'Abd al-Malik Ibn Marwān," *Encyclopaedia of Islam*, new edition, 1 (1960) 76-77.
46 Ṭabarī, *Tārīkh*, 6: 150; Mas'ūdī, *Murūj al-Dhahab*, 11: 299; Balādhurī, *Futūḥ al-Buldān*, 160.
47 Ṭabarī, *Tārīkh*, 6: 150; see also Mas'ūdi, *Murūj al-Dhahab*, 11: 299; Nuwayrī, *Nihāyat al-Arab*, 11: 77, 109; Sir William Muir, *The Caliphate: Its Rise Decline and Fall* (Oxford: The Religious Society, 1891) 353. The phrase "every *jum'ā*" cannot mean "every Friday" and hence every week. It can only mean a specific "*jum'a*", perhaps a specific one in a month, or occasion of some other "gathering."
48 Mas'ūdī, *Murūj al-Dhahab*, 11: 299; H. A. R. Gibb, "'Abd al-Malik Ibn Marwān," *Encyclopaedia of Islam*, new edition, 1, 76.
49 Mas'ūdī, *Kitāb al-Tanbīh wa 'l-Ishrāf*, 312-317.
50 Nuwayrī, *Nihāyat al-Arab*, 21: 109.
51 Sarakhsī, *Sharḥ al-Siyar al-Kabīr*, 5: 1689; and idem, *Mabsūṭ*, 10: 86; Kasānī, *Badā'i' al-Ṣanā'i'*, 9: 4324; *Fatḥ al-Qadīr*, 4: 293; *Tabyīn al-Ḥaqā'iq*, 3: 245-246; *al-Baḥr al-Rā'iq*, 5: 85; Abū Yūsuf, *Kharāj*, 224-225; *al-Fatāwā al-Hindiyya*, 2: 196; Jaṣṣāṣ, *Aḥkām al-Qur'ān*, 3: 69; Ghazālī, *Wajīz*, 2: 203; Shāfi'ī, *al-Umm*, 4: 110-112; Māwardī, *Aḥkām al-Sulṭāniyya*, 52.
52 Mas'ūdī, *Murūj al-Dhahab*, 5: 224-226; H. A. R. Gibb, "'Abd al-Malik Ibn Marwān," *Encyclopaedia of Islam*, new edition, 1 (1960 77, Sir William Muir, *The Caliphate: Its Rise Decline and Fall* (Oxford: The Religious Society, 1891), 354.
53 The work of F. W. Buckler regarding the relationships between Hārūn al-Rashīd and Charles the Great is well documented. We need not repeat the details here. See, F. W. Buckler, *Harūn al-Rashīd and Charles the Great* (Cambridge: The Mediaeval Academy of America, 1931) 1-42.
54 Al-Dhahabī, *Siyar A'lām al-Nubalā'*, 9: 290.
55 See al-Khaṭīb al-Baghdādī, *Tārīkh Baghdād*, 1: 119; and 1: 70.
56 Abū Yūsuf, *Kharāj*, 48-49, 93-94, 114-119, 142-148.
57 Suyūṭī, *Tārīkh al-Khulafā'*, 286.
58 Ibn Khaldūn, *Muqaddima*, 1: 26-29.

59 Albert Hourani, *A History of the Arab Peoples* (Cambridge: Harvard University Press, 1991), 196.
60 See Mas'ūdī, *Murūj al-Ḍhahab*, 3: 275-278; Ṭabārī, *Tārīkh*, 8: 63; Ibn Khaldūn, *Muqaddima*, 1: 26-29; Aḥmad Amīn, *Ḍuḥā al-Islām*, 2: 104.
61 Suyūṭī, *Tārīkh al-Khulafā'*, 266-276,270-271, 287-297, 283, 293-297; *Tanwīr al-Ḥawālik*, 1: 11; *Sharḥ al-Zarqānī 'alā al-Muwaṭṭa'*, 1: 6.
62 Buckler, *Harun'l-Rashid and Charles the Great* 14-15, 17.
63 Ibid., 32.
64 Ibid., 17
65 Ṭabarī, *Tārīkh*, 3: 504 and 8: 152-153; see also Ibn Kathīr, *al-Bidāya wa al-Nihāya*, 10: 147
66 Mas'ūdi, *Murūj al-Dhahab*, 4: 287-414; *al-Aghānī*, 17: 44; Ṭabarī, *Tārīkh*, 6: 510-512; Nuwayrī, *Nihāyat al-Arab*, 22: 151-152; F. Omar, "Hārūn al-Rashīd" *Encyclopaedia of Islam*, new edition, 3: 232-234.
67 Ibn Kathīr, *al-Bidāya wa 'l-Nihāya*, 10: 150.
68 Nuwayrī, *Nihāyat al-Arab*, 22: 151-152; Sir William Muir, *The Caliphate: Its Rise Decline and Fall* (Oxford: The Religious Society: 1891) 474.
69 Muir, *The Caliphate: Its Rise Decline and Fall*, 474.
70 Nuwayrī, *Nihāyat al-Arab*, 22: 155-157; *al-Aghānī*, 17:44; Ṭabarī, *Tārīkh*, 8: 308 and 3: 696; Aḥmad Zakī Ṣafwat, *Jamharat Rasā'il al-'Arab fī al-'Uṣūr al-'Arabiyya al-Zāhira*, 3: 275-276; Muir, *The Caliphate: Its Rise Decline and Fall*, 474.
71 Ṭabarī, *Tārīkh*, 8: 321-322.
72 In Egypt, the Fatimids continued to rule until 1171, when they were deposed by Ṣalāḥ al-Dīn al-Ayyūbi, a military leader of Kurdish origin. The change of rulers brought with it a change of religious alliance. The Fatimids belonged to the Ismā'īlī branch of Shī'ism, but Ṣalāh al-Dīn was a Sunnī, and he was able to mobilize the strength and religious fervour of Egyptian and Syrian Muslims in order to defeat the European Crusaders who had established Christian states in Palestine and on the Syrian coast at the end of the eleventh century. The Ayyūbid dynasty founded by Ṣalāh al-Dīn ruled Egypt from 1171-1252, Syria to 1260, and part of western Arabia to 1229. Albert Hourani, *A History of the Arab Peoples*, 84.
73 James Brundage, *The Crusaders: A Documentary History* (Milwaukee: Marquette University Press, 1962), 185-186; for more details see, *The Crusade of Richard the Lionhearted*, ed. and trans. by John L. LaMonte (New York: Columbia University Press, 1941).
74 Nuwayrī, *Nihāyat al-Arab*, 29: 98.
75 For more details regarding the status of Jerusalem and the Crusaders, see Carole Hillenbrand, *The Crusaders: Islamic Perspectives* (Edinburgh: Edinburgh University Press, 1999); R. C. Smail, *The Crusaders in Syria and Holy Land* (New York and Washington: Praeger Publication, 1973).
76 Damietta: is an old and strategic coastal city near the north of the Eastern branch of the Nile River. It was strategically important because it provided an ideal position from which the French and Byzantine could attack Egypt. The crusaders first occupied Damietta in 647 A. H., during the rule of Malik al-Ashraf. Al-Ẓāhir Baybars was the one who prevented the French from passing through Damietta. Al-Malik al-Kāmil redeemed Damietta from the French occupation. See, *Mu'jam al-Buldan*, 2: 314-315; Ibn 'Abd al-Ẓāhir, *al-Rawḍ al-Ẓāhir*, ed. A. A. al-Khuwaytir (Riyadh, 1976), 386-387; P. Thorau, *The Lion of Egypt*, trans. P.M. Holt (London: Longman, 1992) , 207.
77 Qalqashandī, *Ṣubḥ al-A'shā*, 5: 389-392.

78 Nuwayrī, *Nihāyat al-Arab*, 29: 94; Ibn Iyās, *Kitāb Tārīkh Miṣr*, 1: 79.
79 Ibn Iyās, *Kitāb Tārīkh Miṣr*, 1: 88.
80 Ibid., 94-95.
81 Qalqashandī, *Ṣubḥ al-A'shā*, 5: 389-390.
82 Ibid., 92.
83 Qalqashandī, *Ṣubḥ al-A'shā*, 5: 389.
84 Ibn Iyās, *Kitāb Tārīkh Miṣr*, 1: 79.
85 Qalqashandī, *Ṣubḥ al-A'shā*, 5: 390; Ibn Kathīr, *al-Bidāya wa al-Nihāya*, 13: 76.
86 Qalqashandī, *Ṣubḥ al-A'shā*, 5: 390; Ibn Iyās, *Kitāb Tārīkh Miṣr*, 1: 79.
87 Qalqashandī, *Ṣubḥ al-A'shā*, 5: 389-390.
88 Nuwayrī, *Nihāyat al-Arab*, 29: 113-114; Qalqashandī, *Ṣubḥ al-A'shā*, 5: 390; Ibn Iyās, *Kitāb Tārīkh Miṣr*, 1: 79.
89 Ibn Iyās, *Kitāb Tārīkh Miṣr*, 1: 79-80.
90 Nuwayrī, *Nihāyat al-Arab*, 29: 117.
91 Ibid., 117-118; Some scholars claim that the relationship between al-Malik al-Kāmil and Frederick was well-established. According to the sources, Frederick was very interested in philosophy, mathematics and geometry. He once sent a mathematical problem to al-Kāmil, seeking an answer. Al-Malik al-Kāmil passed this problem to his advisor Shaykh 'Alam al-Din Qayṣar ibn Abī al-Qāsim, when solved it, and sent the solution to Frederick. He was please with their solution. It has also been said that he was very interested in Islamic civilization and was exposed to Islam more than any other of the Crusader rulers. For more details on the relations between Frederick and al-Malik al-Kāmil see the following: M ayrī, *Nihāyat al-Arab*, 29: 150-151.
91 Ibid., 151.
91 Ibn Wāṣil, *Mufārrij al-Kurūb*, ed., J. al-Shayyāl (Cairo, 1953-7) 4:242-245; Ibn Hafiẓ al-Ḥamawī, *al-Tārīkh al-Mansūrī*, ed. A. Dudu (Damscus,1982) 176-177.
91 See comments by earlr scholars on similar event, Ṭabarī, *Ikhtilāf al-Fuqahā'*, 14-21; Abū Yūsuf, *Kharāj*, 207-214; Sarakhsī, *Sharḥ al-Siyar al-Kabīr*, 4: 2-86; Shāfi'ī, *al-Umm*, 4: 103-124; Kāsānī, *Badā'i' al-Ṣanā'i'*, 7: 108-110; Majid Khaddurī, *Islamic Law of Nations: Shaybānī's Siyar* (a portion of *Kitāb al-Aṣl*) (Baltimore: Johns Hopkins University Press, 1966) chapter 5; Hans Kruse, "al-Shaybānī on International Instruments," *Journal of Pakistan Historical Society*, 1 (1953) 90-100.
91 D. P. Little, "Jerusalem under the Ayyūbids and Mamlūks 1197-1516 A.D.", in *Jerusalem in History*, ed. K. J. Asali (London, 1989) 180.
91 Ḥasan Ibrahīm Ḥasan and Aḥmad al-Ṭanṭāwī, *Tārīkh al- 'Uṣūr al-Wusṭā*, 183-184.
91 Q. 8: 63.
If they incline to peace, you also incline to it, and (put your) trust in Allāh. Verily, He is the All-Hearer, the All-Knower.
91 Roger Bigelow Merriman, *Suleiman the Magnificent: 1520-1566* (New York: Cooper Square Publication, 1966), 27-48; Albert Howe Lyber, *The Government of the Ottoman Empire in the time of Suleiman the Magnificent* (Cambridge: Harvard University Press, 1913) , 26-28, 56-58; Halil Inalcik, *The Ottoman Empire: The Classical Age, 1300-1600*, translated by Norman Itzkowitz and Colin Imber (London: Weidenfeld and Nicolson, 1975), 23-34; M.A. Cook, eds. V.J. Parry, H. Inalcik, A. N. Kurat and J.S. Bromley, *A History of the Ottoman Empire to 1730* (Cambridge: Cambridge University Press, 1976), 91-92, 101-102 and 159; Norman Itzkowitz, *Ottoman Empire and Islamic Tradition* (Chicago and London: The University of Chicago Press, 1980) 34-36; G. Veinstein, "Suleyman," *The Encyclopaedia of Islam*, new edition, 9: 832-842.

91 Albert Howe Lyber, *The Government of the Ottoman Empire in the Time of Suleiman the Magnificent*, 26-27, 32, 159-161; Roger Bigelow Merriman, *Suleiman the Magnificent: 1520-1566*, 147-148, 157-165.
91 Ibid.
91 Halil Inalcik, *The Ottoman Empire: The Classical Age 1300-1600*, trans. Norman Itzkowitz and Colin Imber (London: Weidenfeld and Nicolson, 1973), 57-58; Norman Itzkowitz, *Ottoman Empire and Islamic Tradition* (Chicago and London: The University of Chicago Press, 1980), aqrīzī, *Tārīkh al-Duwal wa 'l-Mulūk*, ed. M.F. al-Shayyāl, (1986) 1-2; Ibn Wāṣil, *Mufārrij al-Kurūb*, iv: 242; D. Abulafia. *Frederick II: A Medieval Emperor* (London, 1988), 439.
92 Nuwayrī, *Nihāyat al-Arab*, 29: 150; al-Dhahabī, *Tārīkh al-Islam wa Wafayāt al-Mashāhīr wa 'l-A'lām*, 4:17-18.
93 Ibid., 4: 18; Ibn Iyās, *Kitāb Tārīkh Miṣr*, 1: 80; Qalqashandī, *Ṣubḥ al-A'shā*, 5: 390; Ibn al-Athīr, *al-Kāmil fī al-Tārīkh*, 12: 320-321; Manṣūrī, *Tārīkh*, 73; *Dhayl al-Rawḍatayn*, 102; *Tārīkh al-Zamān*, 252; *Mufarrij al-Kurūb*, 1: 254-257; *Bidāya wa 'l-Nihāya*, 13: 76-77; Maqrīzī, *Kitāb al-Sulūk li-Ma'rifat Duwal al-Mulūk*, 1: 186-187.
94 Ibn Iyās, *Kitāb Tārīkh Miṣr*, 1: 80.
95 Nuwayrī, *Nihāyat al-Arab*, 29: 150-151.
96 Ibid., 151.
97 Ibn Wāṣil, *Mufārrij al-Kurūb*, ed., J. al-Shayyāl (Cairo, 1953-7) 4:242-245; Ibn Hafiẓ al-Ḥamawī, *al-Tārīkh al-Mansūrī*, ed. A. Dudu (Damscus,1982) 176-177.
98 See comments by earlr scholars on similar event, Ṭabarī, *Ikhtilāf al-Fuqahā'*, 14-21; Abū Yūsuf, *Kharāj*, 207-214; Sarakhsī, *Sharḥ al-Siyar al-Kabīr*, 4: 2-86; Shāfi'ī, *al-Umm*, 4: 103-124; Kāsānī, *Badā'i' al-Ṣanā'i'*, 7: 108-110; Majid Khaddurī, *Islamic Law of Nations: Shaybānī's Siyar* (a portion of *Kitāb al-Aṣl*) (Baltimore: Johns Hopkins University Press, 1966) chapter 5; Hans Kruse, "al-Shaybānī on International Instruments," *Journal of Pakistan Historical Society*, 1 (1953) 90-100.
99 D. P. Little, "Jerusalem under the Ayyūbids and Mamlūks 1197-1516 A.D.", in *Jerusalem in History*, ed. K. J. Asali (London, 1989) 180.
100 Ḥasan Ibrahīm Ḥasan and Aḥmad al-Ṭanṭāwī, *Tārīkh al- 'Uṣūr al-Wusṭā*, 183-184.
101 Q. 8: 63.
If they incline to peace, you also incline to it, and (put your) trust in Allāh. Verily, He is the All-Hearer, the All-Knower.
102 Roger Bigelow Merriman, *Suleiman the Magnificent: 1520-1566* (New York: Cooper Square Publication, 1966), 27-48; Albert Howe Lyber, *The Government of the Ottoman Empire in the time of Suleiman the Magnificent* (Cambridge: Harvard University Press, 1913) , 26-28, 56-58; Halil Inalcik, *The Ottoman Empire: The Classical Age, 1300-1600*, translated by Norman Itzkowitz and Colin Imber (London: Weidenfeld and Nicolson, 1975), 23-34; M.A. Cook, eds. V.J. Parry, H. Inalcik, A. N. Kurat and J.S. Bromley, *A History of the Ottoman Empire to 1730* (Cambridge: Cambridge University Press, 1976), 91-92, 101-102 and 159; Norman Itzkowitz, *Ottoman Empire and Islamic Tradition* (Chicago and London: The University of Chicago Press, 1980) 34-36; G. Veinstein, "Suleyman, " *The Encyclopaedia of Islam*, new edition, 9: 832-842.
103 Albert Howe Lyber, *The Government of the Ottoman Empire in the Time of Suleiman the Magnificent*, 26-27, 32, 159-161; Roger Bigelow Merriman, *Suleiman the Magnificent: 1520-1566*, 147-148, 157-165.
104 Ibid.
105 Halil Inalcik, *The Ottoman Empire: The Classical Age 1300-1600*, trans. Norman Itzkowitz and Colin Imber (London: Weidenfeld and Nicolson, 1973), 57-58; Norman

Itzkowitz, *Ottoman Empire and Islamic Tradition* (Chicago and London: The University of Chicago Press, 1980), 34-35.
106 Roger Bigelow Merriman, *Suleiman the Magnificent: 1520-1566*, 210-219, 220-223, 275-276; Norman Itzkowitz, *Ottoman Empire and Islamic Tradition* (Chicago and London: The University of Chicago Press, 1980), 35.
107 Roger Bigelow Merriman, *Suleiman the Magnificent: 1520-1566*, 257-259, 262-264, 267-268, 272-273.
108 Albert Howe Lybyer, *The Government of the Ottoman Empire in the Time of Suleiman the Magnificent*, 93-95; Roger Bigelow Merriman, *Suleiman the Magnificent: 1520-1566*, 210-223; G. Veinstein, "Suleyman, " *The Encyclopaedia of Islam*, new edition, 9: 832-842; Itzkowitz, *Ottoman Empire and Islamic* Traditio, 34-35; *The Middle East and North Africa 1995* (London: Europa, 1995), 909.
109 J. C. Hurewitz, *The Middle East and North Africa in the World Politics: A Documentary Record*, I, European expansion, 1535-1914, second edition (New Haven and London: Yale University Press, 1975). 1.
110 Inalcik, *The Ottoman Empire: The Classical Age 1300-1600*, 35.
111 Colin Imber, *Ebu's-Su'ud: The Islamic Legal Tradition* (Stanford: Stanford University Press, 1997) 4.
112 Ibid.
113 Ibid.
114 Itzkowitz, *Ottoman Empire and Islamic Tradition*, 34-35; Inalcik, *The Ottoman Empire: The Classical Age 1300-1600*, 35.
115 Halil Inalcik, *The Ottoman Empire: The Classical Age 1300-1600*, trans. Norman Itzkowitz and Colin Imber, 35.
116 Ibid.
117 Ibid.
118 Ibid.
119 Ibid., 37.
120 Ibid.
121 Ibid., 35.
122 Albert Howe Lyber, *The Government of the Ottoman Empire in the Time of Suleiman the Magnificent*, 212.
123 Albert Howe Lyber, *The Government of the Ottoman Empire in the Time of Suleiman the Magnificent*, 212; see also, Uriel Heyd, "Some Aspects of the Ottoman Fetva," *Bulletin of the School of Oriental and African Studies*, no. 32 (1969) 35-56.
124 Imber, *Ebu's-Su'ud: The Islamic Legal Tradition*, 122.
125 Ibid., 12
126 Ibid., 122
127 Inalcik, "Imtiyāzāt," *The Encyclopaedia of Islam*, new edition 3: 1179-1199.
128 Imber, *Ebu's-Su'ud: The Islamic Legal Tradition*, 11 and 15.
129 Inalcik, "Imtiyāzāt," *The Encyclopaedia of Islam*, new edition 3: 1179-1199.
130 Inalcik, *The Ottoman Empire: The Classical Age 1300-1600*, 37.
131 Ibid.
132 Ibid., 137; Inalcik, "Imtiyāzāt," *The Encyclopaedia of Islam*, new edition 3: 1179-1199.
133 Ibid.
134 Ibid.
135 Ibid; J. C. Hurewitz, *The Middle East and North Africa in World Politics: A Documentary Record*, 1 *European Expansion, 1535-1914* (New Haven and London: Yale

University Press, 1975) 1-5; ses Albert Howe Lyber, *The Government of the Ottoman Empire in the Time of Suleiman the Magnificent*, 212-220.
136 Inalcik, "Imtiyāzāt," *The Encyclopaedia of Islam*, new edition 3: 1179-1199.
137 Majid Khadduri, *War and Peace in the Law of Islam*, 276.
138 See Marcel A. Boisard, "On the Probable Influence of Islam on Western Public and International Law," *International Journal of Middle Eastern Studies* (1980) 11: 429-450; *Humanism in Islam*, 149; D. de Santillana, *Law and Society in the Legacy of Islam*, eds., Thomas Arnold and Alfred Guillaume, 310; Muhammad Ṭal 'at Ghunaymī, *The Muslim Conception of International Law and the Western Approach*, 85; Hans Kruse, "The Foundation of Islamic International Jurisprudence," *Journal of the Pakistan Historical Society* 3 (1955): 231 and "The Islamic Doctrine of International Treaties," *Islamic Quarterly* (1954) 1: 152-158; Muḥammad Ḥamidallāh, *The Emergence of Islam*, 105-107.
139 See Wael B. Hallaq, *A History of Islamic Legal Theory: An Introduction to Sunnī Uṣūl al-Fiqh*, 9.
140 Q. 8: 61.

Appendix

The Treaty of Ḥudaybiya[1]

1. With Thy Name Oh God!
2. This is what was agreed upon between Muḥammad, son of 'Abdullah and Suhail, son of 'Amr.
3. They both agreed to put down fighting on the part of the people for ten years, during which period the people were to enjoy peace and refrain from fighting with each other
4. And whereas whoever of the companions of the Muḥammad, comes to Mecca on Hajj or 'Umra (pilgrimage), or in quest of the bounty of God, (i.e. commerce) en route to Yemen or Ṭā'if, such shall be in security regarding his person and property. And whoever comes to Medina, from among the Quraysh, en route to Syria or Iraq seeking bounty of God, such shall be in security regarding his person and property.
5. And whereas whoever comes to Muḥammad from the Quraysh without the permission of his guardian, he (i.e. the Prophet) will hand him over to them; and whoever comes to the Quraysh from amongst those who are with Muḥammad, they will not hand him over to him.
6. And that between us is a tied-up breast (i.e. bound to fulfill the terms), and that there shall be no secret help violating neutrality and no acting unfaithfully.
7. And that whoever likes to enter the league of Muḥammad and his alliance, may enter into it; and those whose likes to enter the league of Quraysh and their alliance, may enter it. And thereupon sparge the tribe of Khuzā'ah and said: We are in the league with Muḥammad and his alliance; and up sprang the tribe of Banu Bakr and said: We are in the league with the Quraysh and their alliance.
8. And that thou (Muḥammad) shall return from us (Quraysh) in this year and enter not in our midst; and that when it is the coming year, we shall go out from thee and thou shall enter with thy companions and stay three nights, with thee being the weapon of the rider: having swords at the side, thou shall not enter with what is other than them (swords).
9. And that the animals of sacrifice (brought by thee) will be slaughtered where we found them (i.e. in Ḥudaybiya) and thou shall not conduct them to us (in Mecca). (Probably seal of Muḥammad and seal of Suhail).
10. Witnesses of the Peace (*Ṣulḥ*).

Muslims side: Abu Bakr, 'Umar, 'Abd al-Raḥman ibn 'Awf, 'Abdallah ibn Suhail ibn 'Amr, Sa'd ibn Abī Waqqās, Maḥmūd ibn Maslama, etc.

Quraysh side: Mikrāz ibn Ḥafs and Ḥuwaiṭib (both clansmen of Suhails)

Scribe: 'Alī ibn Abī Ṭalib.

Glossary

AḤKĀM (sing. *ḥukm*): rulings, regulations, legislation

Ahl al-Dhimma: non-Muslim subjects of the Islamic state

AHL AL-ḤARB: subjects of enemy territory

AHL AL-KITĀB: non-Muslims who possess a scripture

AL-MITHL BI 'L-MITHL: quid pro quo

AMĀN: pledge of security, safe conduct, peaceful relationship, temporary safety

'AQD: contract

ÁQD AL-AMĀN: pact of safeguard

BĀṬIL: void; invalid

BĀGHĪ (PL. BUGHĀT): dissenter, rebel

BAYT AL-MĀL: public treasury

ḌAMĀN: responsibility; liability; suretyship

DĀR: house; abode; territory

DĀR AL- 'AHD: territory in covenant with Islam

DĀR AL-ḤARB: territory of war (enemy territory)

DĀR AL-ISLĀM: territory of Islam

DĀR AL-ṢULḤ: territory at peace with Islam

DA'WA: invitation to adapt to Islam

DHIMMA: protection (care as a duty of conscience obligation)

DHIMMI: non-Muslim who are protected by a treaty of surrender

DIRHAM: silver unit of the Arab monetary system during most of the Islamic Middle Ages

DIYA: financial compensation (cash payment or some form or transferred wealth) for wounds or loss of life, blood money for voluntary or involuntary homicide which can be paid by a convict to the relative of the victim as satisfaction

FATWA: legal opinion by a Muftī or *mujtahid* pronounced on specific points often as a result of petition or inquiry

FAY': booty, spoil of war acquired from the enemy without actual fighting

FIDYA: ransom payment of cash for relinquishing of entitlement to debt, e.g. a wife's giving up offer dowry in exchanged of divorce

GHĀZĪ: warrior

GHANĪMA: booty, spoil of war

Ghazwa: raiding, invasion, military expedient or campaign

ḤADD (pl. ḥudūd): fixed penalties for certain crimes

ḤAQQ: right and obligation

'IBĀDĀT: religious observances

IJMĀ': general consensus in the matters of Sharī'a laws of the people of the first three successive generations after the death of the Prophet, it is the third source in Islamic jurisprudence

IJTIHĀd: exercise of legal reasoning (*ra'y*) for the derivation of an independent judgment (*ḥukm*)

Ikhtilāf: differences of opinion among jurists

'ILLA: effective reasoning employed in the exercise of *raý* (legal opinion) in the four schools of thought in Islamic jurisprudence in various forms

IMĀm: leader, caliph, supreme authority of the state

IMĀn: faith, beliefs

ISNĀd: ascription, racing the chain of authorities in a *ḥadīth*

ISTAJĀra: asks or seeks your protection or refuge

ISTA'MANA: asks or seeks your pledge of safety, to seek assurance or protection

JIZYA: poll tax

KĀFIR: infidel, unbeliever

KĀTIB 'Adl: notary public

KHARĀJ: land tax levied on lands deemed to be owned by the state but left in the possession of individuals

KHIYĀNA: embezzlement, treason, betrayal

KHUMS: a twenty- percent levy imposed on certain types on wealth

MAGHĀZĪ: conduct of battles

MAṢLAḤa: an element of public interest which permits deviation of the applicable legal principles; what is beneficial or expedient

MAṢLAḤA MURSALA: not explicitly supported by the text (*naṣṣ*)

MĪTHĀq: covenant

MU'ĀHADA: treaty, conclusion of truce

MU'ĀMALĀT: mutual relations (of Muslims with other nations)

MUFTĪ: jurisconsult, learned person appointed to give authoritative answers on questions of law and casuistry

MUHĀdana: peace agreement

MUḤADDITH: (pl. *muḥaddithūn*), *ḥadīth* collectors

MURTADD: apostate

MUQĀḌĀT: institution of legal proceedings (against)

MUSHRIK: (pl. *mushrikūn*): polytheist, unbeliever

MUSTA'MIN: an enemy alien who has been given (*amān*), the promise of security or safe conduct given to an enemy or alien by Muslims

MUWĀDA'A: peaceful treaty and contracts to stop the hostilities

NAṢṢ: text (Qur'ān), also used for texts (wordings) of *ḥadīth* and *fiqh*

QĀḌĪ: judge

QĀṬI': certain

QIṢĀṢ: penalty, punishment

QITĀL: fighting, battle

QIYĀS: doctrine of systematic reasoning which seeks the *'illa* (effective reasoning) in a given judgment (*ḥukm*) on the basis of the Qur'ān, Sunna, *ijmā'* and *qiyās*

RAHN: security, hostage

RASŪL: emissary, messenger, apostle

SHARĪ'A: laws in Islamic jurisprudence based on four sources, the Qur'ān, Sunna, *ijmā'* and *qiyās*

SHARṬ (pl. *shurūṭ*): stipulations in contract or treaty or in a given judgment *(ḥukm*)

SHARṬ ṢAḤĪḤ: valid condition

SHARṬ FĀSID: irregular condition

SHARṬ BĀṬIL: invalid or null condition

SĪRA (PL. *SIYAR*): biography; course; conduct of the state

SIYĀSA SHAR'IYYA: administrative state organizations and public institutions

ṢULḤ: peace treaty, agreement

SUNNA: custom of precedent based on the Prophet's acts and sayings

ṬABAQĀT: biographies of jurists arranged by "classes" or generations, subject of special works

TA'WĪL: individual interpretation of a religious or legal doctrine

'USHR: tithe, tax levied on lands held in absolute ownership duties

WADĪ'A:**Error! Bookmark not defined.** deposit

WATHĪQA. (pl. *wathā'iq*), document

Bibliography

A. Primary Sources:

Abū Barakāt, Majd al-Dīn (d. 625/1228). *Al-Muḥarrar fī al-Fiqh 'alā Madhhab Aḥmad ibn Ḥanbal.* With *al-Nukat wa-Fawā'id al-Sunna 'alā Mushkil al-Muḥarrar* of Shams al-Dīn Muḥammad Ibn Miflīḥ al-Maqdisī (d. 762). Eds. Muḥammad Ḥasan Ismā'īl and Aḥmad Muhrawwī. Riyadh: Maktabat al-Ma'ārif, 1985.

Abū al-Nu'aym, Aḥmad ibn 'Abdullāh al-Iṣbahānī (d. 430/1038). *Ḥilyat al-Awliyā' wa-Ṭabaqāt al-Aṣfiyā'.* Beirut: Dār al-Kitāb al-'Arabī, 1400/1979.

Abū Su'ūd, Muḥammad ibn Muḥammad al-'Imādī al-Ḥanafī (d. 982/1574-5). *Irshād al-'Aql al-Salīm 'ilā Mazāyā al-Kitāb al-Ḥakīm.* Beirut: Dār al-Fikr, 1400/1979.

Abū 'Ubayd, al-Qāsim ibn Sallām (d. 224/837). *Al-Amwāl.* Ed. Muḥammad Khalīl Harās. Doḥa: al-Shaykh 'Abdallah al-Anṣārī, 1987.

Abū Ya'lā, Muḥammad ibn al-Ḥusayn ibn Muḥammad al-Farrā' al-Baghdādī (d. 458/1066). *Al-Aḥkām al-Sulṭāniyya.* Ed. Muḥammad Ḥāmid al-Fiqī. Cairo: Maṭba'at Muṣṭafā al-Bābī al-Ḥalabī, 1356/1937.

________*Al-Mu'tamad fī Uṣūl al-Dīn.* Ed. Wadī' Zaydān Ḥaddād. Beirut: Dār al-Mashriq, 1394/1974.

________. *Rusul al-Mulūk wa man Yaṣluḥ lil-Risāla wa 'l-Sifāra.* Ed. Ṣalāḥ ibn al-Dīn al-Munajjid. Cairo: Maṭba'at Lajnat al-Ta'līf wa 'l-Tarjama wa 'l-Nashr, 1366/1947.

Abū Yūsuf, Ya'qūb ibn Ibrāhīm ibn Ḥabīb al-Anṣārī (d. 182/798-9). *Al-Āthār.* Ed. Abū al-Wafā' al-Afghānī. Cairo: Dār al-Kutub al-'Ilmiyya, 1355/1936.

________. *Ikhtilāf Abī Ḥanīfa wa Ibn Abī Layla.* Ed. Abū al-Wafā' al-Afghānī. Cairo: Maṭba'at al-Wafā', 1358/1939.

________. *Al-Kharāj.* Medina: al-Maṭba'a al-Salafiyya, 1392/1972.

________. *Al-Radd 'alā Siyar al-Awzā'ī.* Ed. Abū al-Wafā' al-Afghānī. Cairo: Lajnat Iḥyā' al-Ma'ārif al-Nu'māniyya, 1357/1938.

'Alī ibn Abī Ṭālib (d. 61/661). *Nahj al-Balāgha.* Ed. Muḥammad 'Abduh. Beirut: Dār al-Balīgha, 1405/1985.

Ālūsī al-Kerbir, Abū al-Faḍl al-Shihāb Maḥmūd Ibn 'Abdullah al-Baghdādī (d. 1270 H.). *Rūḥ al-Ma'ānī fī Tafsīr al-Qur'ān wa 'l-Sab' al-Mathānī.* Ed. 'Alī Bārī 'Aṭiyya. Beirut: Dār al-Kutub al-'Ilmiyya, 1994-1996.

Āmidī, Sayf al-Dīn Abū al-Ḥasan 'Alī ibn Abī 'Alī (d. 631/1233). *Al-Iḥkām fī Uṣūl al-Aḥkām.* Cairo: Mu'assasat al-Ḥalabī, 1378/1958.

'Arāqī, Zayn al-Dīn Abū al-Faḍl 'Abd al-Raḥīm ibn al-Ḥusayn (d. 806/1404). *Takhrīj Aḥādīth Iḥyā' 'Ulūm al-Dīn.* Along with *Takhrīj al-Zubaydī and al-Subkī.* Riyāḍ: Dār al-'Āṣima, 1408/1987.

Aṣfahānī, Shams al-Dīn Abū al-Thanā' Maḥmūd ibn 'Abd al-Raḥmān ibn Aḥmad (d. 749/1349). *Bayān al-Mukhtaṣar Sharḥ Mukhtaṣar ibn al-Ḥājib.* Ed. Muḥammad

Muẓaffar Baqā. Mecca: Markaz al-Baḥth al-'Ilmī bi Jāmi'at Umm al-Qurā, 1406/1985.

'Ayāḍ Ibn Mūsa, Abū al-Faḍl 'Iyāḍ ibn Mūsa al-Yaḥṣubī al-Mālikī (d. 544/1149). *Mashāriq al-Anwār 'alā Ṣiḥāḥ al-Āthār.* Cairo: Dār al-Turāth, 1977.

'Aynī, Badr al-Dīn Abū Muḥammad Maḥmūd ibn Aḥmad al-Ḥalabī (d. 855/1451). *Al-Bināyya Sharḥ al-Hidāya.* Beirut: Dār al-Fikr, 1400/1979.

________. *'Umdat al-Qārī Sharḥ Ṣaḥīḥ al-Bukhārī.* Beirut: Dār al-Fakr, n.d.

________. *Kashf al-Qinā' 'an Muhimmāt al-Asāmī wa al-Kunā.* Ed. Aḥmad Muḥammad Nimr al-Khaṭīb. Jidda: Markaz al-Nashr al-'Ilmī, 1994.

Azharī, Muḥammad ibn Aḥmad (d. 370/980-1). *Al-Zāhir fī Gharīb Alfāẓ al-Shāfi'ī.* Ed. Samīḥ Abū Maghlī, Majdī 'Alī al-Ash'arī. Ámman: Dār al-Fikr, 1999.

Bābartī, Kamal al-Dīn Muḥammad ibn Maḥmūd (d. 786/1384). *Al-'Ināya 'alā al-Hidāya,* published in the margin of Ibn Humām. *Fatḥ al-Qadīr*, *Ḥāshiyat Sa'dī Chalabī*, Qāḍī Zādā. *Natā'ij al-Afkār fī Kashf al-Rumūz wa al-Asrār.* Cairo: Muṣṭafā al-Bābī al-Ḥalabī, 1970.

Ba'lī, Badr al-Dīn Muḥammad ibn 'Alī al-Ḥalabī (d. 777/1375). *Mukhtaṣar al-Fatāwā al-Miṣriyya li Ibn Taymiyya.* Ed. 'Abd al-Majīd Salīm. Cairo: Maṭba'at al-Sunna al-Muḥammadiyya, 1368/1948.

Ba'lī, Abū 'Abdallah Muḥammad Shams al-Dīn ibn Abī al-Fatḥ al-Ḥanbalī (d. 709/1309). *Al-Muṭli' 'alā Abwāb al-Muqni'.* Along with *Mu'jam Alfāẓ al-Fiqh al-Ḥanbalī* by Muḥammad Bashīr al-Idlibī. Beirut: al-Maktab al-Islāmī, 1981.

Baghawī, Muḥyī al-Sunna Abū Muḥammad al-Ḥusayn ibn Mas'ūd al-Farrā' al-Shafi'ī (d. 510/1117). *Ma'ālim al-Tanzīl.* Eds. Muḥammad al-Nimr, 'Uthmān Jum'a Ḍamīriyya, Sulaymān al-Ḥursh. Riyadh: Dār al-Ṭība, 1414/1993.

_______. *Maṣābīḥ al-Sunna.* Ed. 'Abd al-Raḥmān Mar'ashlī. Beirut: Dār al-Ma'rifa, 1407/1986.

_______. *Sharḥ al-Sunna.* Ed. Shu'ayb al-Arna'ūṭ, Beirut: al-Maktab al-Islāmī, 1403/1982.

Bahūtī, Manṣūr ibn Yūnus ibn Idrīs (d. 1051/1641-2). *Kashshāf al-Qinā' 'alā Matn al-Iqnā'.* Mecca: Maṭba'at al-Ḥukūmiyya, 1394/1974.

Bājī, Abū al-Walīd Sulaymān ibn Khalaf ibn Sa'd ibn Ayyūb al-Andalusī (d. 494/1081). *Al-Muntaqā Sharḥ al-Muwaṭṭa'.* Beirut: Dār al-Kitāb al-'Arabī, 1331/1912.

_________. *Al-Ta'dīl wa al-Tajrīḥ li-man Kharraja 'anhu al-Bukhārī fī al-Jāmi' al-Ṣaḥīḥ.* Ed. Aḥmad Labzar. Rabaṭ: al-Mamlakah al-Maghribiyya, Wizarat al-Awqaf wa 'l-Shu'ūn al-Islāmiyya, 1991.

Balādhurī, Aḥmad ibn Yaḥya ibn Jābir (d. 279/892-3). *Futūḥ al-Buldān.* Ed. Ṣalāḥ al-Dīn Munajjid. Beirut: Dār al-Kutub al-'Ilmiyya, 1398/1977.

Bayḍāwī, Nāṣir al-Dīn Abū al-Khayr 'Abdullah ibn 'Umar al-Shīrāzī (d. 685/1286-7). *Anwār al-Tanzīl wa Asrār al-Ta'wīl.* Beirut: Dār al-Fikr, 1305/1887.

_______. *Al-Ghāya al-Quṣwā fī Dirāyat al-Fatwā.* Ed. 'Alī Muḥyī al-Dīn al-Qara Daghī. Dammam [Saudi Arabia]: Dār al-Iṣlāḥ, 1982.

Bayhaqī, Abū Bakr Aḥmad ibn al-Ḥusayn ibn 'Alī (d. 458/1066). *Al-Sunan al-Kubrā.* Ed. Muḥammad 'Abd al-Qādir. Beirut: Dār al-Ma'rifa, 1346/1927.

_______. *Al-Sunan al-Ṣughrā.* Ed. Bahjat Yūsuf Aḥmad Abu al-Ṭayyib. Beirut: Dār al-Jīl, 1995.

Bujayramī, Sulaymān ibn 'Umar ibn Muḥammad (d. 1221/1806-7). *Ḥāshiyat al-Bujayramī 'alā al-Minhāj,* Cairo: n.p., 1309/1891.

Bukhārī, 'Alā' al-Dīn 'Abd al-'Azīz ibn Aḥmad (d. 730/1330). *Kashf al-Asrār 'an Uṣūl Abī al-Ḥasan 'Alī ibn Muḥammad ibn Ḥasan al-Bazdawī.* Ed. Muḥammad al-Mu'taṣim bi-Allah al-Baghdādī. Beirut: Dār al-Kitāb al-'Arabī, 1997.

Dabūsī, 'Ubaydallah ibn 'Umar ibn 'Īsā (d. 430/1038). *Ta'sīs al-Naẓar.* Cairo: Maṭba'at al-Imām, 1972.

Dāmād Afandī, Shaykh Zādah 'Abd al-Raḥmān ibn Muḥammad ibn Sulaymān (d. 1078/1667). *Majma' al-Anhur fī Sharḥ Multaqā al-Abḥur.* In the margin of Ḥaṣkafī. *Durr al-Muntaqā fī Sharḥ al-Multaqā.* Beirut: Dār Iḥyā' al-Turāth al-'Arabī, 1986.

Dardīr, Abū al-Barakāt Aḥmad ibn Muḥammad ibn Aḥmad al-'Adawī al-Mālikī (d. 1201/1786-7). *Al-Sharḥ al-Ṣaghīr 'alā Aqrab al-Masā'il.* With the margin of *Ḥāshiyat al-Ṣāwī.* Cairo: Maṭba'at 'Īsā al-Ḥalabī, n.d.

_______. *Al-Sharḥ al-Kabīr 'alā Mukhtaṣar Khalīl.* With *Ḥāshiyat al-Dasūqī,* and *Taqrīrāt al-Shaykh 'Allīsh.* Cairo: Maṭba'at 'Īsā al-Ḥalabī, n.d.

Dhahabī, Abū 'Abdallāh Shams al-Dīn Muḥammad ibn Aḥmad ibn 'Uthmān (d. 748/1347-8). *Al-Muntaqā min Minhāj al-I'tidāl.* Ed. Muḥib al-Dīn Khaṭīb. Cairo: al-Maṭba'a al-Salafiyya, 1374/1954.

________. *Siyar A'lām al-Nubalā'.* Ed. Shu'ayb al-Arnā'ūṭ. Beirut: Mu'assasat al-Risāla, 1402/1981.

________. *Tadhkirat al-Ḥuffāẓ.* Ed.'Abd al-Raḥmān al-Mu'allmī. Beirut: Dār Iḥyā' al-Turāth, n.d.

________. *Tārīkh al-Islām wa Wafayāt al-Mashāhīr wa al-A'lām.* Ed. 'Abd al-Salām Tadmurī. Beirut: Dār al-Kitāb al-'Arabī, 1411/1990.

Dasūqī, Muḥammad ibn Aḥmad ibn 'Arafa (d. 1230/1815). *Ḥāshiyat al-Dasūqī 'alā Sharḥ al-Kabīr li-Abī al-Barakāt Aḥmad al- Dardīr.* Cairo: Maṭba'at 'Īssā al-Ḥalabī, 1800.

Fashnī, Aḥmad ibn Ḥijāzī Shihāb al-Dīn (d. 978/1570). *Mawāhib al-Ṣamad fī Ḥall Alfāẓ al-Zubad.* Ed. 'Abdullah Ibrāhīm al-Anṣārī. Doḥa: al-Shu'ūn al-Dīniyya, 1400/1979.

Fayyūmī, Abū al- 'Abbās Aḥmad ibn Muḥammad al-Muqrī (d. 770/1368). *Al-Miṣbāḥ al-Munīr fī Gharīb Sharḥ al-Kabīr li'l Ramlī*. Ed. 'Abd al-'Aẓīm al-Shinnāwī. Beirut: Dār al-Kutub al-'Ilmiyya, 1978.

Fīrūzābādī, Majd al-Dīn Muḥammad ibn Ya'qūb al-Shīrāzī (d. 817/1414-5). *Baṣā'ir dhawī al-Tamyīz fī Laṭā'if al-Kitāb al-'Azīz*. Ed. Álī al-Najār. Cairo: Maṭba'at al-Nahḍa, 1405/1984.

______. *Al-Qāmūs al-Muḥīṭ*. Ed. Ṭāhir Aḥmad al-Zāwī. Beirut: 'Ālam al-Kutub, 1971.

Ghazālī, Abū Ḥamīd Muḥammad ibn Muḥammad al-Ṭūsī (d. 505/1111). *Ma'ārij al-Quds fī Madārij Ma'rifat al-Nafs*. Ed. Maḥmūd Bījū. Damascus: Dār al-Albāb, 1989.

______. *Al-Wajīz fī Madhhab al-Imām al-Shāfi'ī*. Beirut: Dār al-Ma'rifa, 1399/1978.

Ḥājjī Khalīfa, Muṣṭafa ibn 'Abdallah (d. 1067/1656-7). *Kashf al-Ẓunūn 'an Asāmī al-Kutub wa al-Funūn*. Baghdād: Maktabat al-Muthannā, n.d.

Ḥākim, Abū 'Abdullah Muḥammad ibn 'Abdullah al-Naysābūrī (d. 405/1014). *Ma'rifat 'Ulūm al-Ḥadīth*. Ed. al-Sayyid Mu'aẓẓam Ḥusayn. Medina: al-Maktaba al-'Ilmiyya, 1397/1976.

Ḥaṣkafī, 'Alā' al-Dīn Muḥammad ibn 'Alī (d. 1088/1677-8). *Al-Durr al-Mukhtār Sharḥ Tanwīr al-Abṣār*. With *Ḥāshiyat Ibn 'Ābidīn*. Cairo: Dār al-Ṭibā'a, 1328/1910.

Ḥaṭṭāb, Abū 'Abdullah Muḥammad ibn Muḥammad al-Mālikī (d. 954/1547). *Taḥrīr al-Kalām fī Masā'il al-Iltizām*. Beirut: Dār al-Gharb al-Islāmī, 1404/1983.

Haythamī, Aḥmad ibn Muḥammad ibn Ḥajar al-Makī (d. 974/1547). *Al-Fatāwā al-Kubrā*. Printed with *Fatāwā al-Ramlī* of Shams al-Dīn Muḥammad ibn Aḥmad ibn Ḥamza (d. 1004) in the margin. N.p.: Maṭba'at al-Mashhad al-Ḥusīnī, 1392/1972.

________. *Tuḥfat al-Muḥtāj Sharḥ al-Minhāj*. Beirut: Dār Ṣādir, n.d.

Haythamī, Nūr al-Dīn 'Alī ibn Abū Bakr (d. 807/1405). *Mawārid al-Zamān 'alā Mawārid Sawā'id Ibn Ḥibbān* (d. 965). Ed. Shu'ayb al-Arnaūṭ, Muḥammad Riḍwān 'Irqsūsī. Beirut: Mu'assasat al-Risāla, 1993.

Ḥuṣnī, Taqī al-Dīn Abū Bakr ibn Muḥammad al-Ḥusaynī (d. 829/1427). *Kifāyat al-Akhyār fī Ḥall Ghāyat al-Ikhtiṣār*. Ed. 'Abdallah Ibrāhīm al-Anṣārī. Doḥa: al-Shu'ūn al-Dīniyya, n.d.

Ibn 'Abd al-Ẓāhir, Muḥyī al-Dīn. *Al-Rawḍ al-Zāhir fī Sīrat al-Malik al-Ẓahir*. Ed. A. A. al-Khauwaytir. Riyadh: n.p., 1976.

Ibn 'Ābidīn, Muḥammad Amīn ibn 'Umar al-Dimashqī al-Ḥanafī (d. 1252/1836-7). *Ḥāshiyat Radd al-Muḥtār 'alā al-Durr al-Mukhtār*. Cairo: Maṭba'at Muṣṭafa al-Ḥalabī, 1386/1966.

Ibn 'Abd al-Barr, Abū 'Amr Yūsuf ibn 'Abdallah ibn Muḥammad 'Abd al-Barr ibn 'Āṣim al-Nimrī al-Qurṭubī (d. 463/1070-1). *Al-Durar fī Ikhtiṣār al-Maghāzī wa al-Siyar.* Ed. Shawqī Ḍayf. Beirut: Dār al-Ma'ārif, 1403/1982.

_______. *Al-Istī'āb fī Ma'rifat al-Aṣḥāb.* Ed. 'Alī al-Bajāwī. Beirut: Dār Iḥyā' al-Turāth al-'Arabī, 1328/1910.

_______. *Al-Kāfī fī Fiqh Ahl al-Madīna.* Ed. Muḥammad Walīd Mādīk. n.p.: Maṭba'at al-Hudā, 1399 /1978.

_______. *Al-Tamhīd limā fī al-Muwaṭṭa' min al-Ma'ānī wa 'l-Asānīd.* Ed. Muṣṭafa ibn al-'Alawī. Morocco: Wizārat al-Awqāf, 1387/1967.

Ibn 'Abd Rabbih Abū 'Amr Aḥmad ibn Muḥammad (d. 940/1564). *Kitāb al-'Iqd al-Farīd.* Eds. Aḥmad Amīn, Aḥmad al-Zayyār and Ibrāhīm al-Ibyārī. Beirut: Dār al-Kitāb al-'Arabī, 1982.

Ibn 'Abd al-Salām, Abū Muḥammad, 'Abd al- 'Azīz (d. 660/1263). *Qawā'id al-Aḥkām fī Maṣāliḥ al-Anām.* Cairo: Maktabat al-Kuliyyāt al-Azhariyya, 1388/1968.

Ibn Abī Ḥātim, 'Abd al-Raḥmān ibn Muḥammad ibn Idrīs al-Tamimī ibn Mundhir al-Ḥanzalī al-Rāzī. *Kitāb al-Jarḥ wa al-Ta'dīl.* Beirut: Dār al-Kutub al-'Ilmiyya, 1980.

Ibn Abū al- 'Izz, Ṣadr al-Dīn 'Alī ibn Muḥammad ibn 'Alī al-Dimashqī (d. 792/1355-6). *Sharḥ al-'Aqīda al-Ṭaḥāwiyya.* Ed. Shu'ayb al-Arnā'ūṭ. Beirut: Mu'assasat al-Risāla, 1408/1987.

Ibn Abī Shayba, 'Abdallah ibn Muḥammad (d. 235/848). *Al-Muṣannaf fī al-Aḥādīth wa 'l-Āthār.* Ed. Muḥammad 'Abd al-Sallām Shāhīn. Beirut: Dār al-Kutub al-'Ilmiyya, 1995.

Ibn Ādam, Yaḥyā ibn Sulaymān al-Qurashī (d. 203/802-3). *Al-Kharāj.* Ed. Aḥmad Muḥammad Shākir. N.p.: al-Maktaba al-Salāfiyya, 1384/1964.

Ibn al- 'Arabī, Abū Bakr Muḥammad ibn 'Abdullah ibn 'Arabī al-Ishbīlī (d. 543/1148). *Aḥkām al-Qur'ān.* Ed. 'Alī Muḥammad al-Bajāwī, Cairo: Maṭba'at 'Īsā al-Ḥalabī, 1394/1974.

_______. *Qānūn al-Ta'wīl.* Ed. Muḥammad al-Sulaymānī. Beirut: Mu'assasat 'Ulūm al-Qur'ān, 1406/1985.

Ibn 'Arafa, Muḥammad ibn 'Arafa al-Warghamī al-Tūnisī (d. 803/1400). *Mukhtaṣar ibn 'Arafa.* With *Sharḥ al-Raṣāṣ al-Attī.* Beirut: Dār al-Gharb al-Islāmī, 1993.

Ibn 'Asākir, Abū al-Qāsim 'Alī ibn Ḥasan (d. 573/1177). *Tārīkh Madīnat Dimashq.* Ed. 'Umar Gharāma al-'Umarī. Beirut: Dār al-Fikr, 1417/1996.

Ibn al-Athīr, 'Alī ibn Muḥammad ibn Muḥammad (d. 630/1232-3). *Usd al-Ghāba fī Ma'rifat al-Ṣaḥāba.* Ed. Muḥammad Ibrāhīm al-Bannā. Beirut: Dār al-Sha'b, 1970.

_______. *Al-Kāmil fī al-Tārīkh.* Beirut: Dār al-Kitāb al-'Arabī, 1400/1979.

_______. *Al-Nihāya fī Gharīb al-Ḥadīth wa al-Āthār.* Cairo: al-Maṭba'a al-Khayriyya, 1322/1904.

Ibn ʻAṭiyyā, ʻAbd al-Ḥaqq ibn ʻAṭiyyā al-Andalusī (d. 548/1154). *Al-Muḥarrar al-Wajīz fī Tafsīr al-Kitāb al-ʻAzīz.* Eds. ʻAbdullah Ibrāhīm al-Anṣārī and al-Fārūqī. Dūḥa: Tubiʻa ʻalá nafaqat al-Shaykh Khalifah ibn Ḥamād al-Thānī, 1398/1977.

Ibn al-Azraq, Abū Muḥammad ʻAbdallah ibn al-Azraq al-Andalusī (d. 896/1492). *Badāʼiʻ al-Silk fī Ṭabāʼiʻ al-Mulk.* Ed. Muḥammad ʻAbd al-Karīm. Tunisia: al-Dār al-ʻArabiyya lil-Kitāb, 1400/1979.

Ibn al-Bazzāz, Ḥāfiẓ al-Dīn Muḥammad ibn Muḥammad al-Kardarī al-Ḥanafī (d. 827/1424). *Al-Fatāwā al-Bazzāziyya.* With the margin of *al-Fatāwā al-Hindiyya.* Būlāq: al-Maṭabaʻa al-Amīriyya, 1310/1892.

Ibn al-Daybaʻ, Wajīh al-Dīn ʻAbd al-Raḥmān ibn ʻAlī (d. 944/1536). *Ḥadāʼiq al-Anwār wa- Maṭāliʻ al-Asrār fī Sīrat al-Nabī al-Mukhtār.* Ed. ʻAbdullah ibn Ibrāhīm al-Anṣārī. Doha, Maṭbaʻat M. H. al-Kutūbī, 1979.

Ibn Farḥūn, Burhān al-Dīn Ibrāhīm ibn ʻAli (d. 799/1396). *Tabṣirat al-Ḥukkām fī Uṣūl al-Aqḍiya wa-Manāhij al-Aḥkām.* Cairo: Maktabat al-Kuliyyāt al-Azhariyya, 1406/1985.

Ibn Fāris al-Qazwīnī, Abū al-Ḥusayn Aḥmad ibn Fāris ibn Zakariyyā (d. 395/1004). *Majāmiʻ Maqāyīs al-Lugha.* Ed. ʻAbd al-Salām Muḥammad Hārūn. Beirut: Dāt al-Fikr, 1979.

Ibn al-Ghars, Badr al-Dīn Muḥammad ibn Khalīl al-Miṣrī (d. 894/1489). *Al-Fawākih al-Badriyya fī al-Aqḍiya al-Ḥukmiyya.* Printed with its *Sharḥ al-Majānī al-Zahriyya* of Muḥammad Ṣāliḥ ibn ʻAbd al-Fattāḥ al-Jārim. Cairo: Maṭbaʻat al-Nīl, 1326/1908.

Ibn Ḥabīb, Abū Jaʻfar Muḥammad ibn Ḥabīb ibn ʻAmr al-Hāshimī al-Baghdādī (d. 245/859-60). *Al-Muḥabbar.* Beirut: Dār al-Āfāq al-Jadīda, n.d.

Ibn Ḥajar, Aḥmad ibn ʻAlī ibn Muḥammad al-ʻAsqalānī (d. 852/1449). *Fatḥ al-Bārī fī Ṣaḥīḥ al-Bukhārī.* Eds. ʻAbd al-ʻAzīz ibn Bāz and Muḥammad Fuʼād ʻAbd al-Bāqī. Beirut: al-Maṭbaʻa al-Salāfiyya, n.d

________. *Al-Iṣāba fī Tamyīz al-Ṣaḥāba.* Ed. ʻAlī Muḥammad al-Bajāwī. Cairo: Maktabat al-Nahdha, 1392/1972.

________. *Tahdhīb al-Tahdhīb.* Beirut: Dār al-Fikr, 1404/1983.

Ibn Ḥanbal, Aḥmad ibn Muḥammad ibn Ḥanbal al-Shaybānī (d. 241/855-6). *Faḍāʼil al-Ṣaḥāba.* Ed. Waṣiyuallah ʻAbbas. Mecca: Markaz al-Baḥth al-ʻIlmi, n.d.

________. *Musnad.* Cario: al-Maktab al-Islāmī, 1405/1984.

Ibn Ḥayyān, Abū ʻAbdullah Muḥammad ibn Yūsuf (d. 654/1246). *Tafsīr al-Baḥr al-Muḥīṭ.* Cairo: Maṭbaʻat al-Saʻāda, 1328/1911.

Ibn Ḥazm, Abū Muḥammad ʻAli ibn Aḥmad ibn Saʻīd (d. 456/1064). *Al-Iḥkām fī Uṣūl al-Aḥkām.* ed. ʻAbd al-ʻAzīz Aḥmad ibn Aḥmad. Cairo: Maktabat Āṭif, 1978.

_______. *al-Fiṣal fī al-Milal wa al-Ahwā' wa al-Niḥal.* Eds. Muḥammad Ibrāhīm Naṣr, 'Abd al-Raḥmān 'Amīra. Riyadh: Sharikat Maktabāt 'Ukāẓ, 1402/1981.

_______. *Marātib al-Ijmā'.* With Ibn Taymiyya *Naqd Marātib al-Ijma'.* Beirut: Dār al-Kutub al-'Ilmiyya, n.d.

_______. *Al-Muḥallā.* Ed. Aḥmad Muḥammad Shākir. Beirut: Dār al-Turāth, 1392/1972.

Ibn Hishām, Abū Muḥammad 'Abd al-Malik ibn Hishām ibn Ayyūb al-Ḥimyarī (d. 218/833). *Al-Sīra al-Nabawiyya.* Ed. Muṣṭafa al-Saqqā. Cairo: Maktabat al-Kulliyyāt al-Azhariyya, 1391/1971.

Ibn Hubayra, Abū al-Muẓaffar Yaḥyā ibn Muḥammad (d. 560/1169). *Al-Ifṣāḥ 'an Ma'ānī al-Ṣiḥāḥ.* Riyadh: al-Mu'assasa al-Sa'īdiyya, n.d.

Ibn Humām, Kamāl al-Dīn Muḥammad ibn 'Abd al-Wāḥid al-Sīwāsī (d. 861/1456-7). *Fatḥ al-Qadīr 'alā 'l-Hidāya.* With the margin of *Ḥāshiyat Qāḍī Zadah.* Beirut: Dār Iḥyā' al-Turāth al-'Arabī, 1986.

al-Iṣbahānī, Abū Nu'aym Aḥmad ibn 'Abdullah (d. 430/1039). *Ḥilyat al-Awliyā'.* Beirut: Dār al-Kitāb al-'Arabī, 1400/1979.

Ibn al-'Imād, 'Abd al-Ḥayy ibn 'Imād al-Ḥanbalī (d. 1089/1678-9). *Shadharāt al-Dhahab fī Akhbār man Dhahab.* Beirut: Dār Iḥyā' al-Turāth, n.d.

Ibn Isḥāq, Muḥammad ibn Isḥāq ibn Yasār al-Muṭṭalibī (d. 151/786). *Sīrat Ibn Isḥāq al-Mubtada' wa 'l-Mab'ath wa al-Maghāzī.* Ed. Muḥammad Ḥamidullah. Rabāṭ [Morocco]: Ma'had al-Dirasāt wa al-Abḥāth lil-Ta'rīb, 1976.

Ibn Iyās, Muḥammad ibn Aḥmad al-Ḥanafī al-Miṣrī (d. 930/1524). *Kitāb Tārīkh Miṣr.* Cairo: al-Maṭba'a al-Kubrā al-Āmīriyya, n.d.

Ibn Jamā'a, Badr al-Dīn (d. 733/1332-3). *Taḥrīr al-Aḥkām fī Tadbīr Ahl al-Islām.* Ed. Fu'ād 'Abd al-Mun'im. Doha: Maṭbū'āt Ri'āsat al-Maḥākim al-Shar'iyya, 1407/1986.

Ibn al-Jawzī, Abū al-Faraj 'Abd al-Raḥmān ibn 'Alī al-Qurashī al-Baghdādī (d. 597/1201). *Sīrat 'Umar ibn al-Khaṭṭāb.* Cairo: al-Dār al-Qawmiyya li Ṭibā'a wa al-Nashr, n.d.

Ibn Juzayy, Muḥammad ibn Aḥmad al-Gharnāṭī (d. 741/1342). *Al-Qawānīn al-Fiqhiyya* "Qawānīn al-Aḥkām al-Shar'iyya". Eds. Ṭāhā Sa'd and Muṣṭafa al-Ḥamawī. Cairo: 'Ālam al-Fikr, 1395/1975.

Ibn Kathīr, Abū al-Fidā' 'Imād al-Dīn Ismā'īl (d. 774/1372). *Al-Bidāya wa al-Nihāya.* Riyadh: Maktabat al-Ma'ārif, 1966.

_______. *Tafsīr al-Qur'ān al-'Aẓīm.* Beirut: Dār al-Fikr, 1400/1979.

_______. *Tuḥfat al-Ṭālib bi Ma'rifat Aḥādīth Mukhtaṣar Ibn al-Ḥājib.* Ed. 'Abd al-Ghanī ibn Ḥmīd al-Kibīsī. Mecca: Dār Ḥarā', 1406/1985.

Ibn Khaldūn, 'Abd al-Raḥmān al-Maghribī (d. 808/1406). *Al-Muqaddima*, "Muqaddimat Tārīkh Ibn Khaldūn". Beirut: Dār al-Kitāb al-Lubnānī, 1981.

Ibn Khallikān, Abū al-'Abbās Shams al-Dīn Aḥmad ibn Muḥammad (d. 681/1282). *Wafayyāt al-A'yān wa-Anbā' Abnā' al-Zamān*. Ed. Muḥammad Muḥyī al-Dīn 'Abd al-Majid. Cairo: Maktabat al-Nahḍa al-Maṣriyya, 1367/1948.

Ibn Māja, Muḥammad ibnYazīd al-Qazwīnī (d. 275/886-7). *Sunan Ibn Māja*. Ed. Muḥammad Fu'ād 'Abd al-Bāqī. Beirut: Maṭba'at 'Īsā al-Ḥalabī, 1972.

Ibn Mammatī, Sharaf al-Dīn Abū al-Makārim ibn Abū As'ad ibn al-Muhadhdhab (d. 606/1209). *Kitāb Qawānīn al-Dawāwīn*. Ed. Azīz Suryāl Aṭiyya. Cairo: Maktabat Madbūlī, 1991.

Ibn Manẓūr, Abū al-Faḍl Jamāl al-Dīn Muḥammad ibn Mukarram al-Anṣārī (d. 711/1311). *Lisān al-'Arab*. Beirut: Dār Ṣādir, 1992.

Ibn Miflīḥ al-Maqdisi, Abū 'Abdallah Shams al-Dīn Muḥammad (d. 763/1362). *Al-Ādāb al-Shar'iyya wa 'l-Minaḥ al-Mar'iyya*. Eds. Shu'ayb al-Arnā'ūṭ and 'Umar al-Qayyām. Beirut: Mu'assasat al-Risāla, 1996.

_______. *Al-Furū'*. Ed. 'Abd al-Laṭīf Muḥammad al-Subkī. Beirut: 'Ālam al-Kutub, 1981.

Ibn Miflīḥ, Abū Isḥāq Burhān al-Dīn Ibrāhīm ibn Muḥammad (d. 884/1479-80). *Al-Mubdi' Sharḥ al-Muqni'*. Beirut: Dār al-Kutub al-'Ilmiyya, 1997.

Ibn al-Mundhir, Abū Bakr ibn Ibrāhīm al-Naysābūri (d. 318/930). *Al-Ijmā'*. Ed. Abū Ḥamād Ḥanīf. Riyadh: Dār al-Ṭība, 1402/1981.

Ibn Murtaḍā, Aḥmad ibn Yaḥyā al-Yamānī (d. 840/1437). *Al-Baḥr al-Zakhkhār al-Jāmi' li Madhāhib 'Ulamā' al-Amṣār*. Beirut: Dār al-Kitāb al-Islāmī, n.d.

Ibn al-Nadīm, Muḥammad ibn Isḥāq ibn Muḥammad al-Shī'ī (d. 438/1046). *Al-Fihrist*. Beirut: Dār al-Ma'rifa, n.d.

Ibn al-Najjār, Muḥammad ibn Aḥmad ibn 'Abd al-'Azīz al-Fatūḥī (d. 972/1536-7). *Sharḥ al-Kawkab al-Munīr*. Eds. Muḥammad al-Zuḥaylī, Nazīh Ḥammād. Mecca: Markaz al-Baḥth al-'Ilmī, 1408/1987.

Ibn Nujaym, Zayn al-Dīn Ibrāhīm al-Ḥanafī (d. 969/1563). *Al-Ashbāh wa al-Naẓā'ir*. Cairo: Mu'assasat al-Ḥalabī, 1378/1958.

_______. *Al-Baḥr al-Rā'iq Sharḥ Kanz al-Daqā'iq*. Beirut: Dār al-Ma'rifa, 1311/1893.

_______. *Rasā'il Ibn Nujaym*. Ed. Khalīl al-Mays. Beirut: Dār al-Kutub al-'Ilmiyya, 1400/1979.

Ibn Qāḍī Samāwna, Maḥmūd ibn Ismā'īl (d. 823/1440-1). *Jāmi' al-Fuṣūlayn*, with the margin of "Ḥāshiyat al-Fawā'id al-Khayriyya". Cairo: al-Maṭba'a al-Azhariyya, 1300/1882.

Ibn al-Qāṣṣ, Abu al-'Abbas Aḥmad ibn Abī Aḥmad al-Ṭabarī (d. 335/946). *Adab al-Qāḍī.* Ed. Ḥusayn al-Jabūrī. Ṭā'if [Saudi Arabia]: Maktabat al-Ṣiddīq, 1409/1988.

Ibn Quṭlūbghā, Abu al-Fidā' Zayn al-Dīn Qāsim al-Ḥanafī (d. 879/1471). *Tāj al-Tarājim.* Ed. Muḥammad Khayr Yūsuf. Damascus: Dār al-Qalam, 1413/1992.

Ibn Qayyim al-Jawziyya, Shams al-Dīn Muḥammad ibn Abū Bakr al-Dimashqī (d. 751/1350-1). *Aḥkām Ahl al-Dhimma.* Ed. Ṣubḥī al-Ṣāliḥ. Beirut: Dār al-'Ilm li'l-Malāyīn, 1401/1980.

______. *I'lām al-Muwaqqi'īn 'an Rabb al-'Ālamīn.* Ed. Muḥammad Muḥyī al-Dīn 'Abd al-Majīd. Beirut: Dār al-Sa'āda, 1374/1954.

______. *Zād al-Ma'ād fī Hudā Khayr al-'Ibād.* Eds. Shu'ayb and 'Abd al-Qādir al-Arnā'ūṭ. Beirut: Mu'assasat al-Risāla and Dār al-Fikr, 1392/1972.

Ibn Qudāma, Abū Muḥammad Muwaffaq al-Dīn 'Abdallāh ibn Aḥmad (d. 630/1233-4). *Al-Kāfī fī Fiqh al-Imām Aḥmad ibn Ḥanbal.* Beirut: al-Maktab al-Islāmī, 1399/1979.

______. *Al-Mughnī Sharḥ Mukhtaṣar al-Kharqī.* With *Sharḥ al-Kabīr.* Beirut: Dār al-Fikr, 1404/1983.

Ibn Qudāma, Shams al-Dīn 'Abd al-Raḥmān ibn Abī 'Omar (d. 682/1256). *Al-Sharḥ al-Kabīr.* Beirut: Dār al-Fikr, 1404/1983.

Ibn Qutayba, Abū Muḥammad 'Abdallāh ibn Muslim al-Dīnawarī (d. 286/891-2). *'Uyūn al-Akhbār.* Beirut: Dār al-Kitāb al-'Arabī, 1343/1925.

Ibn Raf'ā, Abū al-'Abbās Najm al-Dīn al-Anṣārī (d. 710/1310). *Al-Iḍāḥ wa al-Tibyyān fī Ma'rifat al-Mikyāl wa 'l-Mīzān.* Mecca: Manshūrāt Markaz al-Baḥth al-'Ilmī, 1400/1979.

Ibn Rajab, Abū al-Faraj 'Abd al-Raḥmān (d. 795/1392-3). *Al-Qawā'id fī al-Fiqh.* Ed. Ṭāha 'Abd al-Ra'ūf Sa'd. Cairo: Maktabat al-Kulliyyāt al-Azhariyya, 1392/1972.

Ibn Rushd, Abū al-Walīd Muḥammad ibn Aḥmad ibn Rushd [grand father] (d. 520/1122). *Al-Bayān wa 'l-Taḥṣīl.* Eds. Muḥammad Ḥajjī and 'Abdallāh ibn Ibrāhīm al-Anṣārī. Beirut: Dār al-Gharb al-Islāmī, 1404/1983.

______. *Al-Muqaddimāt al-Mumahhidāt li-Bayān ma Iqtadathu Rusūm al-Mudawwana min al-Aḥkām al-Shar'iyya.* Ed. Muḥammad Ḥajjī. Beirut: Dār al-Gharb al-Islāmī, 1408/1987.

Ibn al-Rushd, Muḥammd ibn Aḥmad ibn Rushd al-Qurṭubī [grand son] (d. 595/1198). *Bidāyat al-Mujtahid.* Beirut: reprint of Ṭab'at Musṭafā al-Ḥalabī, 1401/1980.

______. *Al-Kashf 'an Manāhij al-Adilla fī 'Aqā'id al-Milla.* Printed within *Faṣl al-Maqāl.* Ed. Muḥammad 'Amāra. Cairo: Dār al-Ma'ārif, 1977.

Ibn Sa'd, Muḥammad ibn Sa'd (d. 230/844-5). *Al-Ṭabaqāt al-Kubrā.* Beirut: Dār Ṣādir, 1377/1958.

Ibn Ṣalāḥ, Abū ʿUmar ʿUthmān ibn ʿAbd al-Raḥmān al-Shahrazūrī (d. 643/1245). *ʿUlūm al-Ḥadīth.* Ed. Nūr al-Dīn ʿAṭṭār. Beirut: Dār al-Fikr, 1404/1983.

Ibn Ṣanʿāʾī, Muḥammad ibn Ismāʿīl (d. 1132/1721). *Subul al-Salām.* Cairo: Maṭbaʿat al-Ḥalabī, 1950.

Ibn Shāsh, Jalāl al-Dīn ʿAbdullah ibn Najm (d. 616/1219). *ʿIqd al-Jawāhir al-Thamīna fī Madhahib ʿĀlim al-Medina.* Ed. Muḥammad Abū al-Ajfān. Beirut: Dār al-Gharb al-Islāmī, 1415/1994.

Ibn al-Ṣiddīq, Aḥmad ibn Muḥammad al-Husaynī (d. 1380/1960). *Al-Hidāya bi-Takhrīj Aḥādīth Bidāyat al-Mujtahid.* With *Bidāyat al-Mujtahid wa-Nihāyat al-Muqtaṣid* of Ibn Rushd. Ed. al-Marʿashlī. Beirut: ʿĀlam al-Kutub, 1407/ 1986.

Ibn Ṭāhir al-Baghdādī, Abū Manṣūr ʿAbd al-Qāhir ibn Ṭāhir al-Tamīmī al-Baghdādī (d. 429/1037). *Uṣūl al-Dīn.* Istanbūl: Madrasat al-Ilāhiyyāt, 1346/1927.

Ibn Taymiyya, Aḥmad ibn ʿAbd al-Ḥalīm ibn ʿAbd al-Salām (d. 728/1327-8). *Majmūʿ Fatāwī Shaykh al-Islām Ibn Taymiyya.* Ed. ʿAbd al-Raḥmān ibn Qāsim. Ribāṭ [Morocco]: Maktabat al-Maʿārif, 1400/1979.

_______. *Naẓariyyat al-ʿAqd.* Ed. Muḥammad Ḥāmid al-Fiqī. N.p: Maṭbaʿat al-Sunna al-Muḥamadiyya, 1368/1948.

_______. *Al-Siyāsa al-Sharʿiyya fī Iṣlāḥ al-Rāʿī wa al-Raʿiyya.* Ed. Muḥammad al-Mubārak. Beirut: Dār al-Kutub al-ʿArabiyya, 1368/1948.

Ibn Wāsil, Jamāl al-Dīn Muḥammad (d. 1298/1882). *Mufārrij al-Kurūb fī Akhbār banī Ayyūb.* Ed. J. al-Shayyāl. Cairo: Maṭbaʿat Idārat Iḥyāh al-Turāth al-Qadīm, 1953.

Ibn Zanjawayh, Ḥamīd ibn Zanjawayh al-Ārtdhī al-Nisāʾī (d. 251/866). *Al-Amwāl.* Ed. Shākir Dhīb Fayyāḍ. Riyād: Markaz al-Malik Fayṣal li ʾl-Buḥūth wa ʾl-Dirāsat al-Islāmiyya, 1406/1985.

Jaṣṣāṣ, Abū Bakr Aḥmad ibn ʿAlī al-Rāzi (d. 370/980). *Aḥkām al-Qurʾān.* Cairo: Dār al-Fikr, 1980.

________. *Mukhtaṣar Ikhtilāf al-ʿUlamāʾ of Ṭaḥāwī.* Ed. ʿAbdallāh Nadhīr Aḥmad. Beirut: Dār al-Bashāʾir al-Islāmiyya, 1416/1995.

________. *al-Fuṣūl fī al-Uṣūl.* Ed. ʿAhīl al-Nashmī. Kuwait: Wizārat al -Awqāf wa ʾl-Shuʾūn al-Islāmiyya, 1405/1984.

Jawharī, Ismāʿil ibn Ḥamād (d. 393/1003). *Tāj al-Lugha wa-Ṣiḥāḥ al-ʿArabiyya.* Ed. Aḥmad ibn ʿAbd al-Ghāfūr ʿAṭār. Beirut: Dār al-ʿIlim lil-Malayīn, 1979.

Jurjānī, al-Sayyid ʿAlī ibn Muḥammad ibn ʿAlī al-Sharīf (d. 816/1416). *Al-Taʿrīfāt.* Ed. Ibrāhīm al-Ibyārī. Beirut: Dār al-Kitāb al- ʿArabī, 1405/1984.

Juwaynī, Abū al-Maʿālī ʿAbd al-Malik ibn ʿAbdallāh [Imām al-Ḥaramīn] (d. 478/1089). *Ghiyāth al-Umam fī Iltiyāth al-Ẓulam.* Ed. ʿAbd al-ʿAẓīm al-Dhīb. Doha: al-Shuʾūn al-Dīniyya, 1400/1979.

Kafawī, Abu al-Baqā' Ayyūb ibn Mūsā al-Ḥusaynī (d. 1094/1675). *Al-Kulliyyāt*. Ed. 'Adnān Darwīsh, Muḥammad al-Miṣrī. Damascus: n.p, 1982.

Karābīsī, As'ad ibn Muḥammad ibn al-Ḥasan al-Naysābūrī (d. 245/860-1). *Al-Furūq*. Ed. Muḥammad Ṭamūm. Kuwait: Wizārat al-Shu'ūn al-Islāmiyya, 1402/1981.

Kasānī, 'Alā' al-Dīn Abu Bakr ibn Mas'ūd al-Ḥanafī (d. 587/1191). *Badā'i' al-Ṣanā'i' fī Tartīb al-Sharā'i'*. Beirut: Dār al-Kutub al-'Ilmiyya, 1406/1968

Khaṭṭīb al-Baghdādī, Abū Bakr Aḥmad ibn 'Alī (d. 463/1072). *Tārīkh Baghdād*. Beirut: Dār al-Kitāb al-'Arabi, n.d.

Khaṭṭābī, Abū Ḥamad ibn Muḥammad ibn Ibrāhīm (d. 338/942). *Gharīb al-Ḥadīth*. Ed. 'Abd al-Karīm al-'Izbāwī. Mecca: Markaz al-Buḥūth al- 'Ilmiyya, 1402/1981.

Khallāl, Abū Bakr Aḥmad ibn Muḥammad (d. 311/923). *Aḥkām Ahl al-Milal min al-Jāmi' li-Masā'il al-Imām Aḥmad*. Ed. Sayyid Kusūri. Beirut: Dār al-Kutub al-'Ilmiyya, 1414/1993.

Khaṣṣāf, Abū Bakr Aḥmad ibn 'Amr al-Shaybānī (d. 261/873-4). *Adab al-Qāḍī*. With *Sharḥ al-Jaṣṣāṣ*. Ed. Farḥāt Ziyāda, Cairo: American University, 1978.

Khuwārizmī, Abū al-Mu'ayyad Muḥammad ibn Maḥmūd (d. 665/1238-9). *Jāmi' al-Masānīd, Masānīd Abū Ḥanīfa*. Ed. 'Alī al-Qāri'. Beirut: Dār al-Kutub al-'Ilmiyya, 1405/1984.

Khuwārizmī, Jamāl al-Dīn Abū Bakr. *Mufīd al-'Ulūm wa-Mubīd al-Humūm*. Cairo: Maṭba'at al-Sa'āda, 1330/1910.

Al-kiyā Harāsī, 'Alī ibn Aḥmad (d. 504/1110). *Aḥkām al-Qur'ān*. Eds. Musa Muḥammad 'Alī and 'Izzat 'Aṭiyya. Cairo: Dār al-Kutub al-Ḥadītha, 1974.

Kurdarī, Ḥāfiẓ al-Dīn ibn Muḥammad (d. 827/1018-9). *Manāqib Abī Ḥanīfa*. Beirut: Dār al-Kitāb al-'Arabī, 1401/1980.

Laknawī, Muḥammad 'Abd al-Ḥayy ibn Muḥammad 'Abd al-Ḥalīm (d. 1304/1887). *Al-Nāfi' al-Kabīr liman Yuṭāli' al-Jāmi 'al-Ṣaghīr*. Karachi: Idarat al-Qur'ān wa 'l-Ulūm al-Islāmiyya, 1987.

_______. *Al-Ta'līq al-Mumajjad 'alā Muwaṭṭa' Muḥammad*. Damascus: Dār al-Qalam, 1412/1991.

_______. *Al-Fawā'id al-Bahiyya fī Tarājim al-Ḥanafiyya*. With *Kitāb A'lām al-Akhyār* of Kafawī Maḥmūd ibn Sulayman. Banares: Maktabat Nadwat al-M'ārif, 1967.

Maḥallī, Jalāl al-Dīn Muḥammad ibn Aḥmad (d. 864/1360-1). *Sharḥ Minhāj al-Ṭālibīn*. Cairo: Maṭba'at al-Ḥalabī, 1375/1955.

Mālik ibn Anas (d. 179/795). *Al-Mudawwana. Riwāyat Saḥnūn*. Beirut: Dār Ṣādir, reprint of Maṭba'at al-Sa'āda, 1323/1905.

Manjūr, Aḥmad ibn 'Alī (d. 995/1587). *Sharḥ al-Muntakhab 'ilā Qawā'id al-Madhhab.* Ed. Muḥammad al-Shanqīṭī. Cairo: Dār Iḥyā' al-Kutub al-'Arabiyya, n.d.

Maqrīzī, Taqi al-Dīn Aḥmad ibn 'Alī (d. 845/1441-2). *Imtā' al-Asmā'.* Ed. Maḥmūd Muḥammad Shākir. Doha: al-Shu'ūn al-Dīniyya, 1401/1981.

______. *Al-Khiṭaṭ al-Maqrīziyya, al-Mawā'iẓ wa al-I'tibār bi-Dhikr al-Khiṭaṭ wa 'l-Āthār.* Beirut: Dār al- 'Irfān, n.d.

______. *Al-Sulūk li Ma'rifat Duwal al-Mulūk.* Ed. Muṣṭafā Ziyāda. Cairo: Lajnat al-Ta'līf wa 'l-Tarjama wa 'l-Nashr, 1958.

Mardāwī, Abū al-Ḥasan 'Alī ibn Sulaymān (d. 885/1480-1). *Al-Inṣāf fī Ma'rifat al-Rājiḥ min al-Khilāf.* Ed. Muḥammad Ḥāmid al-Fiqī. Beirut: Dār Iḥyā' al-Turāth al-Islāmī, 1400/1980.

Marghinānī, Burhān al-Dīn 'Alī ibn Abī Bakr (d. 593/1196-7). *Al-Hidāya Sharḥ Bidāyat al-Mubtadī.* With *Fatḥ al-Qadīr.* Cairo: Maṭba'at al-Bābī al-Ḥalabī, 1315/1897.

Mas'ūdī, Abū al-Ḥasan 'Alī ibn Ḥasan (d. 346/957-8). *Murūj al-Dhahab wa-Ma'ādin al-Jawhar.* Ed. Muḥammad Muḥyī al-Dīn 'Abd al-Ḥamīd. Cairo: Maktaba al-Tijāriyya al-Kubrā, 1373/1958.

________. *Al-Tanbīh wa 'l-Ishrāf.* Beirut: Dār al-Hilāl, 1981.

Mawṣlī, Abū al-Faḍl 'Abdallāh ibn Maḥmūd ibn Wadūd (d. 683/1286). *Al-Ikhtiyār li-Ta'līl al-Mukhtār.* Cairo: Maṭba'at Muṣṭafa al-Ḥalabī, 1371/1951.

Māwardī, Abū al-Ḥasan 'Alī ibn Muḥammad ibn Ḥabīb al-Baṣrī (d. 450/1058). *Adab al-Qāḍī.* Ed. Muḥyī Hilāl Sarḥān. Baghdād: Maṭba'at al-'Ānī, 1392/1972.

______. *Al-Aḥkām al-Sulṭāniyya.* Cairo: Maṭba'at Muṣṭafā al-Babī al-Ḥalabī, 1393/1973.

______. *Al-Ḥāwī al-Kabīr.* Eds. Maḥmūd Maṭrijī, Yasīn Nāṣir Maḥmūd al-Khaṭīb, 'Abd al-Raḥmān al-Aḥdal... et al. with "Bahjat al-Ḥāwī," Urjūzat al-Wardī, vol. 18. Beirut: Dār al-Fikr, 1414/1995.

______. *Qawānīn al-Wizāra wa-Siyāsat al-Mulk.* Beirut: Dār al-Ta'līf, 1993.

Mīdānī, 'Abd al-Ghanī ibn Ṭālib al-Ghunaymī al-Dimashqī (d. 1298/1884). *Al-Lubāb Sharḥ al-Kitāb.* Damascus: Dār al-Ḥadīth, n.d.

Munāwī, Muḥammad ibn 'Abd al-Ra'ūf (d. 1031/1621). *Fayḍ al-Qadīr Sharḥ al-Jāmi' al-Ṣaghīr.* Beirut: Dār al-Ma'rifa, 1398/1977.

________. *Al-Tawqīf 'alā al-Muhimmāt al-Ta'ārīf.* Ed. Muḥammad Riḍwān al-Dāya. Beirut: Dār al-Fikr, 1410/1989.

Mundhirī, Abū Muḥammad Zakī al-Dīn 'Abd al- 'Aẓīm ibn 'Abd al-Qawī (d. 656/1258). *Al-Targhīb wa 'l-Tarhīb min al-Ḥadīth al-Sharīf.* Ed. Muṣṭafa 'Imāra. Beirut: Dār al-Kutub al-'Ilmiyya, 1986.

Muslim, ibn al-Ḥajjāj al-Qushayrī al-Nīsābūrī (d. 261/875). *Ṣaḥīḥ Muslim.* Ed. Muḥammad Fu'ād 'Abd al-Bāqī. Beirut: Maṭba'at 'Īsā al-Ḥalabī, 1374/1954.

Muṭarrizī, Abū al-Fatḥ Nāsir al-Dīn (d. 610/1213-4). *Al-Mughrib fī Tartīb al-Mu'rib.* Eds. Maḥmūd Fākhūrī, 'Abd al-Ḥamīd Mukhtār. Aleppo: Maktabat Usāma ibn Zayd, 1399/1978.

Nasafī, Najm al-Dīn 'Umar ibn Muḥammad ibn Aḥmad Abū Ḥafṣ (d. 537/1143). *Ṭilbat al-Ṭalaba.* Ed. Khalīl al-Mīs. Beirut: Dār al-Qalam, 1406/1985.

Nawawī, Abū Zakariyyā Muḥyī al-Dīn Yaḥyā ibn Sharaf (d. 676/1277-8). *Al-Majmū' Sharḥ al-Muhadhdhab.* Beirut: Dār al-Fikr, 1405/1975.

_______. *Rawḍat al-Ṭālibīn.* Damascus: al-Maktab al-Islāmī, 1405/1984.

_______. *Sharḥ Ṣaḥīḥ Muslim.* Beirut: Dār al-Kitāb al-'Arabī, n.d.

_______. *Tahdhīb al-Asmā' wa 'l-Lughāt.* Beirut: Dār al-Kutub al-'Ilmiyya, n.d.

Niẓām al-Dīn (d. 1070/1658-9). *Al-Fatāwī al-Hindiyya fī Madhhab al-Imām Abū Ḥanīfa.* Cairo: al-Maktabah al-Islāmiyya, 1310/1892.

Nuwayrī, Abū al- 'Abbās Aḥmad ibn 'Abd al-Wahhāb ibn Muḥammad Shihāb al-Dīn (d. 733/1332-3). *Nihāyat al-Arab fī Funūn al-Adab.* Ed. 'Alī Muḥammad al-Najāwī. Cairo: al-Hay'a al-Miṣriyya al- 'Āmma li l-Kitāb, 1396/1976.

Qāḍī Khān, Fakhr al-Mawlā Ḥasan ibn Manṣūr al-Uzjandī al-Farghānī (d. 592/1196). *Al-Fatāwī al-Khāniyya of Qāḍī Khān.* Printed with the margin of *al-Fatāwī al-Hindiyya.* Iṣtanbūl: al-Maktaba al-Islāmiyya, n.d.

Qalqashandī, Abū al- 'Abbās Aḥmad ibn 'Alī (d. 821/1418-9). *Ṣubḥ al-A'shā fī Ṣinā'at al-Inshā'.* Cairo: Wizarat al-Thaqāfa wa 'l-Irshād, n.d. and Beirut: Dār al-Kutub al-'Ilmiyya, 1407/1987.

Qarāfī, Abū al- 'Abbās Aḥmad ibn Idrīs (d. 684/1285-6). *Al-Aḥkām fī Tamyīz al-Fatāwī 'an al-Aḥkām wa-Taṣarufāt al-Qāḍī wa al-Imām.* Ed. Maḥmūd 'Arnūs. Rabāṭ [Marocco]: Wizarat al-Awqāf li-Shu'ūn al-Dīniyya, 1974.

_______. *Al-Furūq.* With the margin of *'Umdat al-Muḥaqqiqīn* of Ibn al-Shāṭṭ. Beirut: Dār al-Ma'rifa, n.d.

_______. *Sharḥ Tanqīḥ al-Fuṣūl.* Cairo: Maktabat al-Kulliyyāt al-Azhariyya, 1393/1973.

Qināwī, Qāsim (d. 978/1570). *Anīs al-Fuqahā'.* Ed. Aḥmad 'Abd al-Razzāq al-Kubīsī. Jidda: Dār al-Wafā', 1406/1985.

Qirwānī, Abū Muḥammad 'Abdallāh ibn Abū Zayd (d. 386/986). *Al-Risāla al-Fiqhiyya.* Ed. Al-Hādī Ḥamū. Qatar: Dār Iḥyā' al-Turāth al-Islāmī, 1406/1985.

Qurṭubī, Abū 'Abdallāh Muḥammad ibn Aḥmad al-Anṣārī (d. 671/1273). *Al-Jāmi' li-Aḥkām al-Qur'ān.* Cairo: Dār al-Kutub al-Miṣriyya, 1369/1950.

Quṭb, Sayyid ibn Ibrāhīm (d. 1387/1966). *Fī Ẓilāl al-Qur'ān.* Beirut: Dār al-Shurūq, 1397/1976.

Rāfiʿī, ʿAbd al-Karīm ibn Muḥammad al-Qazwīnī (d. 623/1226). *Fatḥ al-ʿAzīz Sharḥ al-Wajīz.* Beirut: Dār al-Fikr, 1417/1996.

Rāghib, Abū al-Qāsim Ḥusayn ibn Muḥammad al-Iṣfahānī (d. 502/1108-9). *Mufradāt al-Qur'ān.* Ed. Muḥammad Sayyid Kīlānī. Cairo: Maṭbaʿat Muṣṭafa al-Ḥalabī, 1381/1961.

Raḥībānī, Muṣṭafa ibn Saʿd al-Dimashqī (d. 1243/1827). *Maṭālib Ūlī al-Nuhā fī Sharḥ Ghāyat al-Muntahā.* Damascus: al-Maktab al-Islāmī, 1380/1960.

Rakbī, Baṭṭāl ibn Aḥmad ibn Sulaymān (d. 633/1235-6). *Al-Naẓm al-Mustaʿdhab fī Tafsīr Gharīb Alfāẓ al-Muhadhdhab.* Ed. Muṣṭafā ʿAbd al-Ḥafīẓ Sālim. Mecca: al-Maktaba al-Tijāriyya, 1408/1987.

Ramlī, Khayr al-Dīn (d. 1081/1614). *Al-Fatāwī al-Khayriyya li-Nafʿ al-Bariyya.* Ed. Ibrāhīm ibn Sulaymān. Isṭanbūl: al-Maṭbaʿa al-ʿUthmāniyya, 1311/1893.

Raṣṣāʿ, Abū ʿAbdallāh Muḥammad al-Anṣārī (d. 894/1489). *Sharḥ Ḥudūd ibn ʿArafa* "al-Hidāya al-Kāfiya al-Shāfiya". Ed. Muḥammad Abu¯al-Ajfān. Beirut: Dār al-Gharb al-Islāmī, 1993.

Rāzī, Fakhr al-Dīn Muḥammad ibn Ḍiyā' al-Dīn (d. 604/1208). *Mafātīḥ al-Ghayb.* Beirut: Dār al-Fikr, 1405/1984.

________. *Iʿtiqādat Firaq al-Muslimīn wa 'l-Mushrikīn.* Cairo: Maktabat al-Nahḍa, 1356/1938.

Riḍā, Muḥammad Rashīd (d. 1354/1935). *Tafsīr al-Manār.* Cairo: Maktabat al-Qāhira, 1373/1953.

Sibṭ ibn Jawzī, Abū al-Muẓaffar Yūsuf ibn Furʿalī (d. 1257/1841). *Āthār al-Inṣāf fī Āthār al-Khilāf.* Ed. Naṣir al-ʿAlī al-Khalīfī. Cairo: Dār al-Salām, 1408/1987.

Ṣafadī, Ṣalāḥ al-Dīn Khalīl ibn Aybak (d. 764/1363). *Al-Wāfī bi al-Wafiyāt.* Berlin [Germany]: Das arabische Buch, 1999; Damascus: Dār Saʿd al-Dīn, 1999.

Saḥnūn, ʿAbd al-Salām ibn Saʿīd al-Tanūkhī (d. 240/854). *Al-Mudawwana of Mālik.* Beirut: Dār Ṣādir, 1323/1905.

Sakhāwī, Muḥammad ibn ʿAbd al-Raḥmān Shams al-Dīn (d. 903/1497). *Al-Iʿlān bi al-Tārīkh li-man Dhamma al-Tārīkh.* Ed. Franz Rosenthal, translated into ʿArabic by Ṣāliḥ Aḥmad ʿAlī. Beirut: Mu'assasat al-Risāla, 1986.

Samʿānī, Abū Saʿd ʿAbd al-Karīm ibn Muḥammad ibn Manṣūr al-Tamīmī (d. 562/1168). *Al-Ansāb.* Ed. Muḥammad ʿAwāma. Beirut: Sharikat al-Fajr al-ʿArabī, 1396/1976.

Samnāwī, Abū al-Qāsim ʿAlī ibn Muḥammad ibn Aḥmad al-Raḥabī (d. 499/1106). *Rawḍat al-Quḍā wa-Ṭarīq al-Najā.* Ed. Ṣalāḥ al-Dīn al-Nāhī. Amman: Dār al-Furqān, 1404/1983.

Samarqandī, 'Alā' al-Dīn Abū Bakr Muḥammad ibn Aḥmad (d. 539/1143). *Mīzān al-Uṣūl*. Ed. Muḥammad Zakī 'Abd al-Barr. Doḥa: Maṭābi' al-Doḥa, 1404/1983.

_______. *Tuḥfat al-Fuqahā'*. Ed. Muḥammad Zakī 'Abd al-Barr. Beirut: Dār al-Kutub al-'Ilmiyya, 1405/1984.

Ṣan'ānī, Abu al-Bakr 'Abd al-Razzāq Ibn Humām ibn Nāfi' (d. 211/827). *Al-Muṣannaf fī al-Ḥadīth*. Along with *Kitāb al-Jāmi'* of Mu'ammar ibn Rashīd al-Azdī, riwayat 'Abd al-Razzaq al-San'ānī. Ed. Naṣr al-Dīn al-Ahar. Beirut: Dār al-Kutub al-'Ilmiyya, 2000.

Sarakhsī, Abū Bakr Muḥammad ibn Aḥmad ibn Sahl (d. 483/1090). *Al-Mabsūṭ*. Beirut: Dār al-Ma'rifa, 1324/1906.

_______. *Al-Nukat Sharḥ Ziyādāt al-Ziyādāt of Imām Muḥammad ibn Ḥasan*. With *Sharḥ al-'Attābī*. Beirut: 'Alam al-Kutub, 1406/1985.

_______. *Sharḥ al-Siyar al-Kabīr*. Ed. Muṣṭafā Zayd with the commentary of Muḥammad Abū Zahra. Cairo: Maṭba'at Jāmi'at al-Qāhira, 1958.

_______. *Sharḥ al-Siyar al-Kabīr*. Eds. Ṣalāḥ al-Munajjid and 'Abd al-'Azīz Aḥmad. Cairo: Maṭba'at Sharikat al-I'lānāt al-Sharqiyya, 1971.

_______. *Uṣūl al-Sarakhsī*. Ed. Abū al-Wafā' al-Afghānī. Karachi: Lajnat Iḥyā' al-Ma'ārif al-Nu'māniyya, 1372/1952.

Shāfi'ī, Muḥammad ibn Idrīs (d. 204/819-20). *Aḥkām al-Qur'ān*. Ed. 'Abd al-Ghanī 'Abd al-Khāliq. N.p.: Nashr 'Izzat al-'Aṭṭār al-Ḥusaynī, 1371/1951.

_______. *Musnad al-Shāfi'ī*. Ed. 'Azat al-'Aṭār. Beirut: Dār al-Kutub al-'Ilmiyya, 1980.

_______. *Al-Risāla*. Ed. Aḥmad Shākir. Beirut: Dār al-Turāth, 1399/1978.

_______. *Al-Umm*. With *Mukhtaṣar al-Muzanī* (d. 264 H.). Cairo: Maṭba'at al-Sha'b, 1321/1903.

Shahrastānī, Muḥammad 'Abd al-Karīm (d. 548/1153). *Al-Milal wa 'l-Niḥal*. On the margin of Ibn Ḥazm, *al-Fiṣal fī al-Milal wa 'l-Niḥal*. Cairo: al-Maṭba'a al-Adabiyya, 1317/1888.

Sha'rānī, 'Abd al-Wahhāb ibn Aḥmad ibn 'Alī (d. 973/1565). *Al-Mīzān al-Kubrā*. Cairo: Maṭba'at Muṣṭafa al-Ḥalabī, 1359/1940.

Sharqāwī, 'Abdullah ibn Ḥijāzī (d. 1237/1812). *Ḥāshiyat al-Sharqāwī 'alā al-Taḥrīr*. Cairo: al-Maṭba'a al-'Āmira, 1290/ 1873.

Shāṭibī, Abū Isḥāq Ibrāhīm ibn Mūsā al-Gharnāṭī (d. 790/1388). *Al-Muwāfaqāt fī Uṣūl al-Sharī'a*. Ed. 'Abdallāh Darāz. Beirut: Dār al-Ma'rifa, n.d.

Shawkānī, Muḥammad ibn 'Alī b. Muḥammad (d. 1250/1834). *Irshād al-Fuḥūl 'ilā Taḥqīq al-Ḥaqq min 'Ilm al-Uṣūl*. Cairo: Maṭba'at Muṣṭafa al-Ḥalabī, 1356/1937.

_______. *Nayl al-Awṭār Sharḥ Muntaqā al-Abḥār*. Cairo: Maṭba'at Muṣṭafā al-Ḥalabī, 1391/1971.

_______. *Al-Sayl al-Jarrār al-Mutadaffiq 'alā Ḥadā'iq al-Azhār*. Ed. Maḥmūd Ibrāhīm Zāyid. Beirut: Dār al-Kutub al-'Ilmiyya, 1405/1984.

Shaybānī, Muḥammad ibn Ḥasan (d. 189/804). *Al-Aṣl* "Mabsūṭ". Ed. Abū al-Wafā' al-Afghānī. Karachi: Maṭba'at Idārat al-Qur'ān, n.d.

________. *Al-Ḥujja 'alā Ahl al-Madīna*. Ed. Mahdi al-Kīlāni. Beirut: 'Ālam al-Kutub, 1385/1965.

________. *Al-Jāmi' al-Kabīr*. Ed. Abū al-Wafā' al-Afghānī. Cairo: Nashr Lajnat al-Iḥyā' al-Ma'ārif al-Nu'māniyya, n.d.

________. *Al-Jāmi' al-Ṣaghīr*. With the margin of *al-Nāfi' al-Kabīr* of Abū al-Ḥusunāt al-Laknawī. Karachi: n.d.

________. *Kitāb al-Siyar of Shaybānī* (chapters of "Siyar" from "Kitāb al-Aṣl"). Ed. Majid Khadduri. Beirut: al-Dār al-Muttaḥida li 'l-Nashr, 1975.

________. *Al-Siyar al-Kabīr*, with the commentary of Sarakhsī. Ed. Ṣalāḥ al-Dīn al-Munajjid. Cairo: Maṭba'at Sharikat al-I'lānāt al-Sharqiyya, 1391/1971.

________. *Al-Siyar al-Ṣaghīr*, within *al-Mabsūṭ* of Sarakhsī. Beirut: Dār al-Ma'rifa, 1406/1985.

________. *Ziyādāt al-Ziyādāt*. With the margin of *Sharḥ al-Sarakhsī and al-'Attābī.* Beirut: 'Alam al-Kutub, 1406/1985.

Shīrāzī, Abū Isḥāq Ibrāhīm ibn 'Alī. (d. 476/1080). *Al-Muhadhdhab fī Fiqh al-Imām al-Shāfi'ī*. Beirut: Dār al-Ma'rifa, 1379/1959.

_______. *Ṭabaqāt al-Fuqahā'*. Baghdād: al-Maktaba al-'Arabiyya, 1356/1937.

Subkī, Abū al-Ḥasan 'Alī ibn 'Abd al-Kāfī (d. 756/1355). *Fatāwī al-Subkī*. N.p.: Maktabat al-Qudsī, 1356/1937.

________. *Al-Jāmi' al-Ṣaghīr min Ḥadīth al-Bashīr al-Nadhīr.* With *Fayḍ al-Qadīr.* Beirut: Dār al-Ma'rifa, 1391/1971.

________. *Takmilat al-Majmū' Sharḥ al-Muhadhdhab*. Printed with Nawawī, *Majmū'*. Cairo: Maṭba'at al-'Āṣima, 1966.

Suyūṭī, Jalāl al-Dīn 'Abd al-Raḥmān ibn Abū Bakr (d. 911/1505). *Al-Ashbāh wa 'l-Naẓā'ir fī Qawā'id wa Furū' al-Shāfi'iyya*, Cairo: Maṭba'at Muṣṭafa al-Ḥalabī, 1378/1958.

_______. *Al-Durr al-Manthūr fī al-Tafsīr bi 'l-Ma'thūr*. Beirut: Dār al-Fikr,1403/1982.

_______. *Al-Ḥāwī li l-Fatāwī*. Cairo: Maṭba'at al-Sa'āda, 1378/1958.

_______. *Al-Itqān fī 'Ulūm al-Qur'ān*. Ed. Muḥammad Abū al-Faḍl. Cairo: al-Hay'a al-Maṣriyya al-'Āma, 1974.

_______. *Ṭabaqāt al-Mufassirīn*. Ed. 'Alī Muḥammad 'Umar. Cairo: Maktabat Wahba, 1976.

_______. *Tārīkh al-Khulafā'*. Ed. Muḥyī al-Dīn 'Abd al-Majīd. Cairo: Maṭba'at al-Sa'āda, 1371/1952.

Ṭabarī, Abū Ja'far Muḥammad ibn Jarīr (d. 310/923). *Ikhtilāf al-Fuqahā'*, "Kitāb al-Buyū'". Ed. Fredrick Kern. Beirut: Dār al-Kutub al-'Ilmiyya, n.d.

_______. *Ikhtilāf al-Fuqahā'* "Kitāb al-Jihād wa al-Jizya wa Aḥkām al-Muḥāribīn". Ed. Joseph Schacht. Leiden, 1933.

_______. *Tārīkh al-Rmam wa 'l-Mulūk*. Ed. Muḥammad Abū al-Faḍl. Beirut: Dār al-Ma'ārif, 1979.

Taftazānī, Sa'd al-Dīn Mas'ūd ibn 'Umar (d. 793/1390). *Al-Talwīḥ 'alā al-Tawḍīḥ Sharḥ al-Tanqīḥ*. Cairo: Maṭba'at Ṣubīḥ, 1377/1957.

Tahānāwī, Muḥammad 'Alī al-Fārūqī (fl. 1745). *Kashshāf Iṣṭilāḥāt al-Funūn*. Ed. Luṭfī 'Abd al-Badī'. Beirut: Dār Ṣādir, 1382/1962.

Ṭaḥāwī, Abū Ja'far Aḥmad ibn Muḥammad ibn Salāma (d. 321/933). *Mukhtaṣar al-Ṭaḥāwī*. Ed. Al-Afghānī. Beirut: Maṭba'at Dār al-Kitāb al-'Arabī, 1370/1950.

______. *Sharḥ Ma'ānī al-Āthār*. Ed. Muḥammad Sayyid Jād al-Ḥaqq. Cairo: Maṭba'at al-Anwār, 1387/1967.

Ṭarabulsī, 'Alī ibn Khalīl (d. 844/1437-8). *Mu'īn al-Ḥukkām fīma Yataraddad Bayn al-Khiṣmayn min al-Aḥkām*. Cairo: Maṭba'at Muṣṭafa al-Ḥalabī, 1393/1973.

'Uthmānī, Abū 'Abdallāh Muḥammad ibn 'Abd al-Raḥmān al-Dimashqī (d. 780/1376) *Raḥmat al-Umma fī Ikhtilāf al-A'imma*. Eds. 'Alī Sharbajī and Nūrī Qāsim. Beirut: Mu'assasat al-Risāla, 1994.

Wāḥidī, Abū al-Ḥasan 'Alī ibn Aḥmad al-Wāḥidī al-Naysābūrī (d. 468/1074). *Asbāb al-Nuzūl*. Ed. Aḥmad Ṣaqr. Jidda: Dār al-Qibla li 'l-Thaqāfa al-Islāmiyya, 1407/1986.

Wāqidī, Abū 'Abdallāh Muḥammad ibn Wāqid al-Islāmī al-Madanī (d. 207/822). *Kitāb al-Maghāzī*. Ed. Marsden Jones. London: Oxford University Press, 1966.

Wansharishī, Abū al- 'Abbās Ahmad ibn Yaḥya (d. 914/1508). *Al-Mi'yār al-Mu'rib 'an Fatāwī Ulamā' Ifrīqiyā wa 'l-Maghrib*. Ed. Muḥammad Ḥajjī. Beirut: Dār al-Gharb al-Islāmī., n.d.

Yāfi'ī, Abū Muḥammad 'Abdallāh ibn As'ad al-Yamānī (d. 768/1309). *Mir'āt al-Jinān wa 'Ibrat al-Yaqdhān*. Beirut: Mu'assasat al-A'lāmī, n.d

Ya'qūbī, Aḥmad ibn Isḥāq ibn Ja'far ibn Wahhāb al-Ya'qūbī al-Baghdādī (d. 292/905). *Tārīkh al-Ya'qūbī*. Ed. Khalīl al-Manṣūr. Beirut: Dār al-Kutub al-'Ilmiyya, 1419/1999.

Yāqūt, Shihāb al-Dīn Abū 'Abdallāh Yāqūt al-Ḥamawī al-Rūmi al-Baghdādī (d. 626/1229). *Mu'jam al-Buldān*. Beirut: Dār Ṣādir, 1376/1956.

Zabīdī, Muḥammad Murtaḍā (d. 1205/1790). *'Uqūd al-Jawāhir al-Munīfa fī Adillat al-Imām Abū Ḥanīfa*. Ed. 'Abdallāh Hāshim al-Yamāmī. Cairo: Maṭba'at al-Shubukshi, n. d.

_______. *Tāj al-'Arūs*. Beirut: Maktabat al-Ḥayāt, n.d.

Zamakhsharī, Abu al-Qāsim Jārallāh Maḥmūd ibn 'Umar (d. 538/1144). *Asās al-Balāgha*. Beirut: Dār Ṣādir, 1385/1965.

_______. *Al-Kashshāf 'an Ḥaqā'iq al-Tanzīl wa 'Yūn al-Aqāwīl fī Wujūh al-Ta'wīl*. Cairo: al-Bāb al-Ḥalabī, 1367/1948.

Zarkashī, Badr al-Dīn Muḥammad ibn 'Abdallāh (d. 794/1395). *Al-Burhān fī 'Ulūm al-Qur'ān*. Ed. Muḥammad Abū al-Faḍl Ibrāhīm. Cairo: Maṭba'at 'Isā al-Ḥalabī, 1391/1971.

________. *Al-Burhān fī 'Ulūm al-Qur'ān*. Beirut: Dār al-Ma'rifa, 1391/1972.

________. *Al-Mu'tabar fī Takhrīj Aḥādīth al-Minhāj wa 'l-Mukhtaṣar*. Ed. 'Abd al-Majīd al-Salafī. Kuwait: Dār al-Arqam, 1404/1983.

________. *Al-Manthūr fī al-Qawā'id*. Ed. Taysīr Fā'iq. Kuwait: Wizārat al-Awqāf wa al-Shu'ūn al-Islāmiyya, 1402/1981.

Zarqānī, Muḥammad ibn 'Abd al-Bāqī ibn Yūsuf al-Miṣrī (d. 1122/1710-1). *Sharḥ Muwaṭṭa' Mālik*. Beirut: Dār al-Ma'rifa, 1398/1977.

Zayd ibn 'Alī, Imām Abū al-Ḥasan Zayd ibn 'Ali ibn Ḥusayn ibn 'Alī ibn Abī Ṭalib (d. 122/740). *Majmū' fī al-Fiqh*, edited by Eugenio Griffine under the title "Corpus Iurus di Zayd Ibn 'Ali. Milano: Liberia Della Real Cassia, 1919.

_______. *Musnad al-Imām Zayd*. Ed. 'Abd al-'Azīz ibn Isḥāq al-Baghdādī. Beirut: Dār al-Kutub al-'Ilmiyya, 1981.

Zayla'ī, Fakhr al-Dīn 'Uthmān ibn 'Alī (d. 743/1340-1). *Tabyīn al-Ḥaqā'iq Sharḥ Kanz al-Daqā'iq*. with the margin of *Ḥāshiyat al-Shalabī*. Cairo: n.p., 1313/1895.

B. Secondary Sources:

'Abd al-Baqī, Muḥammad Fu'ād. *Al-Mu'jam al-Mufahras li-Alfāẓ al-Qur'ān al-Karīm*. Cairo: Maṭābi' al-Sha'b, 1378/1958.

'Abd al-Qādir, 'Alī Ḥasan. *Naẓra 'Amma fī Tārīkh al-Fiqh al-Islāmī*. Cairo: Maktabat al-Qāhira al-Ḥadītha, 1956.

'Abd al-Salām, Ja'far. *Qawā'id al-'Alāqāt al-Dawliyya fī al-Qānūn al-Duwalī wa al-Sharī'a al-Islāmiyya*. N.p.: Maktabat al-Salām al-'Ālamiyya, 1401/1980.

_______. *Sharṭ Baqā' al-Shay' 'alā Ḥālih*. Beirut: Dār al-Kitāb al-Árabī, 1970.

Abel, A. "Dār al-Ḥarb," *The Encyclopaedia of Islam*, new edition, vol. 2. Leiden: E. J. Brill, 1965: 126.

________. "Dār al-Islam," *The Encyclopaedia of Islam*, new edition, vol. 2. Leiden: E. J. Brill, 1965: 127-128.

________. "Dār al-Sulḥ" *The Encyclopaedia of Islam*, new edition, vol. 2. Leiden: E. J. Brill, 1965: 131.

Abū Ḥabīb, Sa'dī. *Mawsū'at al-Ijmā' fī al-Fiqh al-Islāmī*. Damascus: n. p., 1996.

Abū Zahra, Muḥammad Muḥammad (d. 1394 H.) *Al-Jarīma wa al-'Uqūba fī al-Fiqh al-Islāmī*. Beirut: Dār al-Fikr al-'Arabī, 1976.

_________. *Al-'Alāqāt al-Dawliyya fī al-Islam*. Cairo: Dār al-Qawmiyya li-Ṭibā'ā, 1964.

_________. *Al-Mulkiyya wa Naẓariyyat al-'Aqd fī al-Sharī'a al-Islāmiyya*. Beirut: Dār al-Fikr, 1977.

_________. *Uṣūl al-Fiqh*. Cairo: Dār al-Fikr al-'Arabī, 1377/1957.

Alūsī, Muḥammad Shukrī. *Bulūgh al-Arab fī Ma'rifat Aḥwāl al-'Arab*. Beirut: Dār al-Kutub al-'Ilmiyya, 1304/1886.

Albānī, Muḥammad Nāṣir al-Dīn. *Irwā' al-Ghalīl fī Takhrīj Aḥādīth Manār al-Sabīl*. Beirut: al-Maktab al-Islāmī, 1979.

Amīn, Aḥmad. *Ḍuḥā al-Islām*, Beirut: Dār al-Kitāb al- 'Arabī, 1388/1966.

Armazānī, Najīb. *Al-Shar' al-Duwali fī al-Islām*. Damascus: Maṭba'at ibn Zaydūn, 1349/1930.

Arnold, Thomas. *Al-Da'wa ilā al-Islam*. Translated by Ḥasan Ibrāhīm. Cairo: Maktabat al-Nahḍa al-Miṣriyya, 1390/197 [translation of *Preaching of Islam*].

'Askarī, Abū Hilāl al-Ḥasan ibn 'Abdallāh. *Al-Furūq al-Lughawiyya*. Ed. Muḥammad Bāsil 'Uyūn al-Sūd. Beirut: Dār al-Kutub al-'Ilmiyya, 2000.

Asyūṭī, Muḥammad Ibn Aḥmad al-Minhājī. *Jawāhir al-'Uqūd wa-Mu'īn al-Quḍat wa al-Shuhūd*. n.p.: Maṭba'at al-Sunna al-Muḥamadiyya, 1374/1954.

'Aṭṭār, Aḥmad 'Abd al-Ghafūr. *Al-Diyānāt wa 'l-'Aqā'id fī Mukhtalif al-'Uṣūr*. Mecca [Saudi Arabia]: n.p., 1401/1981.

'Awdah, 'Abd al-Qādir. *Al-Tashrī' al-Jinā'ī al-Islāmī Muqārana bi 'l-Qānūn al-Waḍ'ī*. Beirut: Dār al-Turāth al-'Arabī, 1977.

'Azzām, 'Abd al-Raḥmān. *Al-Risāla al-Khālida*. Beirut: Dār al-Shurūq, 1969.

'Azmī, Muḥammad Muṣṭafa. *Minhāj al-Naqd 'ind al-Muḥaddithīn: Nash'atuh wa-Taṭawwuruh*, followed by "Tamyīz al-Tamyīz" by Abu Ḥusayn Muslim ibn al-Ḥājj al-Quysharī al-Nisābūrī. Riyadh: Maktabat al-Kawthar, 1990.

Baron, S.A. Kroff. "An Introduction to the History of International Law," *American Journal of International Law*, vol. 18 (1924) 248-260.

Bashīr, Muḥammad 'Uthmān. *Aḥkām al-Kharāj fī al-Islām*. Kuwait: Dār al-Arqam, 1406/1985.

Bashmīl, Muḥammad Aḥmad. *Ṣulḥ al-Hudaibiyya*. Beirut: Dār al-Fikr, 1390/1970.

Boisard, Marcel A. "On the Probable Influence of Islam on Western Public and International Law," *International Journal of Middle Eastern Studies*, vol. 11 (1980) 429-450.

________. *Humanism in Islam*. Indianapolis: The American Trust Publication, 1988.

Brockelman, Carl. *Tārīkh al-Adab al-'Arabi*, trans. 'Abd al-Ḥalīm al-Najjār. Cairo: Dār al-Ma'ārif, 1977.

Brundage, James. *The Crusaders: A Documentary History*. Milwaukee: Marquette University Press, 1962.

Buckler, F. W. *Harun al-Rashid and Charles the Great*. Cambridge: The Medieval Academy of America, 1931.

Cahen, Claude. "Ayyubids," *The Encyclopaedia of Islam*, second edition, vol. 1. Leiden: E. J. Brill, 1960: 796-807.

Clayer, Nathalie. "'Ushr," *The Encyclopaedia of Islam*, new edition, vol. 10. Leiden: E. J. Brill, 2000: 917-919.

Ḍamīriyyī, 'Uthmān Jum'a. *Al-Islām wa 'Ilāqatihi bi al-Sharā'i' al-Ukhrā*. Tā'af: Dār al-Fārūq, 1410/1989.
________. *Manhaj al-Islam fī al-Ḥarb wa 'l-Salām*. Kuwait: Dār al-Arqam, 1402/1981.

Dennett, Daniel C. *Conversion and the Poll Tax in Early Islam*. Cambridge: Harvard University Press, 1950.

Disuqī, Muḥammad. *Al-Imām Muḥammad ibn al-Ḥasan al-Shaybānī wa-Atharuhu fī al-Fiqh al-Islāmī*. Doḥa [Qaṭar]: Dār al-Thaqāfa, 1987.

Fahd, T. "Ṣābi'a," *The Encyclopaedia of Islam*, new edition, vol. 8. Leiden: E. J. Brill, 1993: 675-678.

Faranjiyya, Najīb and Albert Rīḥānī. *Al-Mawsū'a al-'Arabiyya*. Beirut: Dār al-Rīḥānī, 1955.

Gaber, Moḥamed Ḥosny. *The Early Islamic State with Special Reference to the Evolution of the Principles of Islamic International Law*. Unpublished Ph. D. dissertation, Political Science, International Law and Relations. Washington: The American University, 1962.

Ghaḍbān, Munīr Muḥammad. *Fiqh al-Sīra al-Nabawiyya*. Mecca: Ma'had al-Buḥūth wa Iḥyā' al-Turāth al-Islāmī, 1410/1989.

Ghānim, Muḥammad Ḥāfiẓ. *Mabādi' al-Qānūn al-Duwalī al-'Āmm*. Cairo: n.p., 1964.

Ghathīth, Muḥammad 'Ali. *Al-Sharq wa 'l-Gharb min al-Ḥurūb al-Ṣalībiyya ilā Ḥarb al-Suwīs*. Cairo: al-Dār al-Qawmiyya li 'l-Ṭibā'a wa al-Nashr, n.d.

Ghunaymī, Muḥammad Ṭal'at. *Aḥkām al-Mu'āhadāt fī al-Sharī'a al-Islāmiyya*. Alexandria: Munsha'at al-Ma'ārif, 1977.
________. *Qānūn al-Salām fī al-Islām*. Alexandria: Munsha'at al-Ma'ārif, 1988.
________. *The Muslim Conception of International Law and the Western Approach*. The Hugue: Martinus Nijhoff, 1968.

Gibb, H. A. R. "'Abd al-Malik B. Marwān," *The Encyclopaedia of Islam*, new edition, vol. 5. Leiden: E. J. Brill, 1960: 76-77.

Goitein, Shlomo Dov. *Jews and Arabs: Their Contacts through the Ages.* New York: Schocken Books, 1964.

Gottschalk, H. L. "Al-Kāmil," *The Encyclopaedia of Islam*, new edition, vol. 4. Leiden: E. J. Brill, 1960: 520-521.

Haig, T. W. "Al-Malik al-Kāmil," *The Encyclopaedia of Islam*, new edition, vol. 1. Leiden: E. J. Brill, 1987: 204-205.

Ḥājj, 'Abd al-Ḥamīd. *Al-Nuẓum al-Duwaliyya wa 'l-Sharī'a al-Islāmiyya.* N.p.: Ma'had al-Dirāsāt al-Islāmiyya, 1395/1975.

Hallaq, Wael B. *A History of Islamic Legal Theory: An Introduction to Sunnī Uṣul al-Fiqh.* Cambridge: Cambridge University Press, 1997.

Ḥamād, Nazīh. *Mu'jam al-Muṣṭalaḥāt al-Iqtiṣādiyya fī Lughat al-Fuqahā'.* Virginia: al-Ma'had al-'Ālamī lil Fikr al-Islāmi, 1414/1993.

Ḥamawī, Muḥammad Ibn 'Alī. *Al-Tārīkh al-Mansūrī: Talkhīṣ al-Kashf wa 'l-Bayān fī Ḥawādith al-Zamān.* Ed. A. Dudu. Damascus: Majma' al-Lugha al-Arabiyya, 1982.

Ḥamīdallāh, Muḥammad. *Dawlat al-Islam wa 'l-'Ālam*, translated into Arabic by Fatḥī 'Athmān. Cairo: Silsilat al-Thaqāfa al-Miṣriyya, 1382/1962.

________. *The Emergence of Islam.* Ed. and trans. by Afzal Iqbal. Islamabad: Islamic Research Institute, 1993.

________. *Majmū'at al-Wathā'iq al-Siyāsiyya li 'l 'Ahd al-Nabawī wa 'l-Khilāfa al-Rāshida.* Beirut: Dār al-Irshād, 1969.

________. *The Muslim Conduct of the State*, third edition. Lahore: Islamic Research Institute, 1954.

Hanna, Sami. Ed. *Medieval and Middle Eastern Studies: In Honour of Aziz Suryal Atiya.* Leiden: E. J. Brill, 1972.

Ḥasan, 'Abd al-Fattāḥ. *Mīthāq al-Umam wa 'l-Shu'ūb fī al-Islām.* Kuwait: Maktabat al-Manār, 1966.

Ḥasan, Ibrāhīm Ḥasan. *Tārīkh al-Islam al-Siyāsī wa 'l-Dīnī wa 'l-Thaqāfī wa al-Ijtimā'ī.* Beirut: Dār al-Jalīl, 1411/1990.

Ḥasan, Muḥammad 'Abd al-Ghanī. *Al-Mu'āhadat wa 'l-Mu'āhadāt fī Tārīkh al-'Arab.* Cairo: Maktabat Miṣr, 1966.

_______. *Al-Tarājim wa 'l-Siyar.* Cairo: Dār al-Ma'ārif, 1955.

Haykal, Muḥammad Ḥusayn. *The Life of Muḥammad*, translated by Ismā'īl Rāgī A. al-Fārūqī. Indianapolis: American Trust Publications, 1976.

Heyd, Uriel. *Ottoman Documents on Palestine*. 1552-1615. Oxford: Clarendon Press, 1960.

________. *Studies in Old Ottoman Criminal Law*. Oxford: Clarendon Press, 1973.

Hilālī, Muḥammad Taqi al-Dīn and Muḥammad Muḥsin Khān. *Interpretation of the Meaning of the Noble Qur'ān in the English Language*. Riyadh: Dār al-Salām, 1996.

Hillenbrand, Carole. *The Crusaders: Islamic Perspectives*. Edinburgh: Edinburgh University Press, 1999.

Holt, P. M. *Early Mamluk Diplomacy (1260-1290) Treaties of Baybars and Qalāwūn with Christian Rulers*. Leiden: E. J. Brill, 1995.

Ḥomoud, Moḥammad 'Alī Naṣir. *Diplomacy in Islam*. Jaipur: Printwell, 1994.

Hosein, Imrān N. "Diplomacy in Islam: Treaties and Agreements an Analysis of the Treaty of Hudaibiyah," *Muslim Education Quarterly*, 3, 3 (Spring, 1986) 67-85.

Hourani, Albert. *A History of the Arab Peoples*. Cambridge: Harvard University Press, 1991.

Humphreys, R. Stephen. *Islamic History: A Framework for Inquiry*. Princeton: Princeton University Press, 1991.

_______. *From Saladin to the Mongols: The Ayyubids of Damascus, 1193-1260*. New York, 1977.

Hurewitz, J. C. *Al-Maghāzī al-Ūlā wa Mu'allifūhā*, translated by Ḥusayn Naṣr. Cairo: Maṭba'at Muṣṭafa al-Ḥalabī, 1369/1949.

_______. *The Middle East and North Africa in World Politics: A Documentary Record*, vol. 1, European Expansion, 1535-1914. New Haven and London: Yale University Press, 1975.

Imām, Muḥammad Kamāl. *Al-Ḥarb wa 'l-Salām fī al-Fiqh al-Duwalī al-Islāmī*. Cairo: Dār al-Ṭibā'a al-Muḥammadiyya, 1399/1978.

Imber, Colin. *Ebu's-Su'ūd: The Islamic Legal Tradition*. Stanford: Stanford University Press, 1997.

Inalcik, Khalil. "Dār al- 'Ahd," *The Encyclopaedia of Islam*, new edition, vol. 2. Leiden: E. J. Brill, 1965: 116.

________. "Imtiyāzāt," *The Encyclopaedia of Islam*, vol. 3. Leiden: E. J. Brill, 1971: (1197-1189).

________. *The Ottoman Empire: The Classical Age 1300-1600*, translated by Norman Itzkowitz and Colin Imber. London: Weidenfeld and Nicolson, 1973.

Ismā'īl, Pasha. *Īḍāḥ al-Maknūn fī al-Dhayl 'alā Kashf al-Ẓunūn*. Ed. Kātib Chelebī. Baghdād: Maktabat al-Muthannā, 1945-1972.

________. *Hadīyat al-'Ārifīn, Asmā' al-Mu'allifīn wa-Āthār al-Muṣannifīn.* Baghdād: Maktabat al-Muthanna, 1951.

Itzkowitz, Norman. *Ottoman Empire and Islamic Tradition.* Chicago and London: The University of Chicago Press, 1972.

Jabūrī, 'Abdallāh Muḥammad. *Fiqh al-Imām al-Awzā'ī.* Baghdād: Maṭba'at al-Irshād, 1397/1976.

Juraysha, 'Alī. *al-Mashrū'iyya al-Islāmiyya al-'Ulyā.* N.p.: Maktabat Wahbī, 1396/1976.

Kassim, Husian. "Treaties (Muwāda'a) and Mutual Relations (Mu'āmalāt) of Muslims with other Nations," *The American Journal of Islamic Social Sciences*, vol. 5, no.2 (1988).

Kawar, Irfan. "The Arab in the Peace Treaty of A. D. 561,"*Arabica*, vol. 3. Leiden: E. J. Brill, 1956: 181-213.

Kawtharī, Muḥammad Zāhid ibn Ḥasan. *Bulūgh al-Amānī fī Sīrat al-Imām Muḥammad ibn Ḥasan al-Shaybānī.* Cairo: Maktabat Dār al-Hidāya, 1985.

Khaddūrī, Majīd. "Hudna," *The Encyclopaedia of Islam*, new edition, vol. 6. Leiden: E. J. Brill, 1971: 246--247.

________. *The Islamic Law of Nations.* Baltimore: The Johns Hopkins Press, 1966

________. "Maṣlaḥa," *The Encyclopaedia of Islam*, new edition, vol. 6. Leiden: E. J. Brill, 1971: 738-740.

________. *al-Qānūn al-Duwalī al-Islāmī* "Kitāb al-Siyar li 'l-Shaybāni". Beirut: al-Dār al-Muttaḥida li 'l-Nashr, 1975.

________. *War and Peace in the Law of Islam.* Baltimore: The Johns Hopkins Press, 1955.

________. and Herbert J. Liebesny. *Law in the Middle East: Origin and Development of Islamic Law.* Washington, D. C.: Middle East Institute, 1955.

Khafīf, 'Alī. *Mukhtaṣar Aḥkām al-Mu'āmalāt al-Shar'iyya.* Cairo: Maṭba'at al-Sunna al-Muḥammadiyya, 1949.

________. *Al-Ḍamān fī al-Fiqh al-Islāmī.* Cairo: Jāmi'at al-Duwal al-'Arabiyya, 1970.

Khalāf, 'Abd al-Wahāb. *Al-Siyāsa al-Shar'iyya.* Beirut: Dār al-Anṣār, 1397/1976.

Khamīs, Ibrāhīm...et al. *Al-Mu'jam al-Wasīṭ.* Beirut: Dār Iḥyā'al-Turāth al-Árabī, n.d.

Kruse, Hans. "The Islamic Doctrine of International Treaties," *Islamic Quarterly*, vol. 1 (1954) 152-158.

________. "The Notion of Siyar," *Journal of Pakistan Historical Society*, vol. 2 (1954) 16-25.

________."Al-Shaybānī on International Instruments," *Journal of Pakistan Historical Society*, (1953) vol. 1: 90-100.

LaMonte, John L. *The Crusade of Richard the Lionhearted.* Ed. and trans. New York: Columbia University Press, 1941.

Landau, J. M. "Mu'āhada," *The Encyclopaedia of Islam,* new edition, vol. 7. Leiden: E. J. Brill, 1993: 250-253.

Lapidus, Ira M. *A History of Islamic Societies.* Cambridge: Cambridge University Press, 1988.

Lewis, Bernard. *The Middle East: 2000 Years of History from the Rise of Christianity to Present Day.* New York: Scribner, 1995.

Little, D. P. "Jerusalem under the Ayyūbids and Mamlūks, 1197-1516 AD". In Jerusalem *in History.* Ed. Kāmil Jamil Asali (London: Kegan Paul International, 1989) 177-200.

Lybyer, Albert Howe. *The Government of the Ottoman Empire in the Time of Suleiman the Magnificent.* Cambridge: Harvard University Press, 1913.

Lyons, M. C. and David Jackson. *Saladin: The Politics of the Holy Land.* Cambridge: Cambridge University Press, 1982.

Madkūr, Muḥammad Salām. *Madkhal al-Fiqh al-Islāmī.* Cairo: Dār al-Nahḍa al-'Arabiyya, 1976.

________. *al-Fiqh al-Islāmī: Madkhal wa 'l-Amwāl wa 'l-Ḥuqūq wa 'l-Mulkiyya wa al-'Uqūd.* Cairo: Dār al-Nahḍa al-'Arabiyya, 1959.

Maḥmaṣānī, Subḥī. *Falsafat al-Tashrī' al-Islāmī,* "The Philosophy of Jurisprudence in Islam," translated by Farhat J. Ziadeh. Lieden: E. J. Brill, 1961.

________. *Al-Qānūn wa 'l-'Alāqāt al-Dawliyya fī al-Islam.* Beirut: Dār al-'Ilm li 'l Malāyīn, n.d.

Maḥmūd, 'Abd al-Ghanī. *al-Taḥaffuẓ 'alā al-Mu'āhadāt al-Dawliyya fī al-Qānūn al-Duwalī al-'Amm wa 'l-Sharī'a al-Islāmiyya.* Cairo: n.p., 1986.

Manṣūr, 'Alī 'Alī. *Al-Sharī'a al-Islāmiyya wa 'l-Qānūn al-Duwalī al-'Āmm.* n.p.: al-Majlis al-A'lā li 'l-Shu'ūn al-Islāmiyya, 1395/1974.

Mar'ashlī, Nadīm and Usāma. *Al-Ṣiḥāḥ fī al-Lugha wa 'l-'Ulūm.* Beirut: Dār al-Ḥaḍāra al-'Arabiyya, 1395/1981.

Murqus, Sulaymān. *Naẓarīyat al-'Aqd.* Cairo: Dār al-Nashr li 'l-Jam'iyyāt al-Khayriyya, 1956.

Maraghlī, 'Abdallāh Muṣṭafā. *Al-Tashrī' al-Islāmī li-ghayr al-Muslimīn.* Cairo: Dār al-Adab, 1900.

Merriman, Roger Bigelow. *Suleiman the Magnificent, 1520-1566.* New York: Cooper Square Publishers, 1966.

Mont Tesquieu, Baron de. *The Spirit of the Law*, vol. 1. New York: Appleton and Co., 1900.

Muḥammad, Abū al-Faḍl Ibrāhīm, and 'Alī Muḥammad al-Bajī. *Ayyām al-'Arab fī al-Islam*. Beirut: Dār al-Jalīl, 1408/1988.

Muḥammad, Aḥmad Abū al-Wafā'. *Al-Mu'āhadāt al-Duwaliyya fī al-Sharī'a al-Islāmiyya*. Beirut: Dār al-Nahḍa al-'Arabiyya, 1410/1989.

Munjjid, Ṣalāḥ al-Dīn. *Al-Nuẓum al-Diplomāsiyya fī al-Islam*. Beirut: Dār al-Kitāb al-Jadīd, 1983.

Muir, William. *The Caliphate: Its Rise Decline and Fall*. Oxford: The Religious Society, 1891.

Mūsā, Muḥammad Yūsuf. *Al-Amwāl wa-Naẓariyyat al-'Aqd fī al-Fiqh al-Islāmī*. Beirut: Dār al-Kitāb al-'Arabī, 1952.

________. *Al-Tashrī' al-Islāmī wa-Atharuhu fī al-Fiqh al-Gharbī*. Beirut: Dār al-Qalam, 1960.

Muṣṭafā, Nadia Muḥammad. *Al-Muqaddima al-'Āmma li-Mashrū' al-'Alāqāt al-Dawliyya fī al-Islam*. Cairo: al-Ma'had al-'Ālamī li 'l-Fikr al-Islamī, 1996.

Mutwalī, 'Abd al-Ḥamīd. *Al-Islām wa-Mabādi' Niẓām al-Ḥukm*. Alexandria: Mansha'at al-Ma'ārif, 1976.

An-Na'im, Abdullahi Ahmed. *Toward an Islamic Reformation: Civil Liberties, Human Rights, and International Law*. New York: Syracuse University Press, 1990.

Naṣr, Ḥasan. *Nash'at al-Tadwīn al-Tārīkh 'ind al-'Arab*. Cairo: Maktabat al-Nahḍa al-Miṣriyya, n.d.

Omar, F. "Hārūn al-Rashīd" *Encyclopaedia of Islam*, new edition, vol. III. Leiden: E. J. Brill, 1971: 232-234.

Parry, V. J., H. Inalcik, A. N. Kurta and J. S. Bromley. *A History of the Ottoman Empire to 1730*, edited with an Introduction by M. A. Cook. Cambridge: Cambridge University Press, 1976.

Pellat, Ch. "Ḥilf al-Fuḍūl," *the Encyclopaedia of Islam*, new edition, (Leiden: E. J. Brill, 1971) 3: 389.

Qāsim, 'Awn al-Sharīf. *Nash'at al-Dawla al-Islāmiyya 'ala 'Ahd Rasūl Allāh: Dirāsa fī Wathā'iq al-'Ahd al-Nabawī*. Beirut: Dār al-Kitāb al-Lubnānī, 1981.

Rabbāṭ, Idmun. *Al-Wasīṭ fī al-Qānūn al-Dusturī al-'Amm: Min Ajl Naẓariyya fī al-Qānūn al-Duwalī al-Islāmī*. Beirut: Dār al- 'Ilm li 'l-Malāyīn, 1965.

Rahbī, 'Abd al- 'Azīz ibn Muḥammad. *Fiqh al-Mulūk wa-Miftāḥ al-Ratāj al-Murṣad 'alā Khizānat Kitāb al-Kharāj.* Baghdād: Ri'āsat Dīwān al-Awqāf, 1973.

Rayyis, Muḥammad Ḍiyā' al-Dīn. *Al-Kharāj wa 'l-Nuẓum al-Māliyya li-Dawlat al-Islām.* N.p.: Dār al-Anṣār, 1977.

Rustum, Asad. *Muṣṭalaḥ al-Tārīkh 'ind al-Muslimīn.* Beirut: al-Maktaba al-'Aṣriyya, 1966.

Ṣa'īdī, Ḥāzim 'Abd al-Muta'ālī. *Al-Naẓariyya al-Islāmiyya fī al-Dawla.* Beirut: Dār al-Nahḍa al-'Arabiyya, 1397/1976.

Ṣafar, Ḥasan Muḥammad. *Al-Madhāhib al-Fiqhiyya al-Islāmiyya: Nash'at al-Madhāhib wa-Manahij Fiqh Rijālatuhu wa-Maṣādiruhum wa Dawruhum.* N.p. [Saudi Arabia]: Dār al-Ittiḥād al-'Arabī, 1992.

Ṣafwat, Aḥmad Zakī. *Jamharat Rasā'il al-Arab fī 'Uṣūr al-'Arabiyya al-Zāhira.* Cairo: Maṭba'at Muṣṭafā al-Bābī al-Ḥalabī, 1356/1937.

Salem, Elie. "Arab Reforms and the Reinterpretation of Islam," *The Muslim World,* (October, 1965) 311-320.

Sanhūrī, Nādiyah and Tawfiq 'Abd al-Razzāq Shāwī. *Fiqh al-Khilāfa wa-Taṭawwuruhā li-Tuṣbiḥa 'Uṣbat Umam Sharqiyya.* Cairo: al-Hay'a al-Maṣriyya al-'Āmma, 1989.

Sanūsī, Aḥmad Ṭaha. *Fikrat al-Jinsiyya fī al-Tashrī' al-Islamī.* Cairo: Miṣr al-Mu'āṣira, 1957.

Schacht, Joseph. "Abu 'l-Su'ūd," *The Encyclopaedia of Islam,* new edition, vol. 1. Leiden: E. J. Brill, 1960: 152.

________. "Amān," *The Encyclopaedia of Islam,* new edition, vol. 1. Leiden: E. J. Brill, 1960: 429-430.

________. *An Introduction to Islamic Law.* Oxford: Clarendom Press, 1964.

________. *The Origins of Muḥammadan Jurisprudence.* Oxford: Clarendom Press, 1953.

Shabīr, Muḥammad 'Othmān. *Aḥkām al-Kharāj fī al-Fiqh al-Islāmi.* Kuwait: Dār al-Arqam, 1406/1985.

Shaltūt, Maḥmūd. *Al-Islam 'Aqīda wa-Sharī'a.* Beirut: Dār al-Shurūq, n.d.

Shanqīṭī, Aḥmad ibn Muḥammad al-Mukhtār al-Jaknī. *Mawāhib al-Jalīl.* Ed. 'Abdallah Ibrāhīm al-Anṣārī. Doḥa: n.p., 1403/1982.

Sharīf, Ja'far 'Alī al-Qurayshi. *The Customs of Mussulmans of India,* trans. Gerhard Andreas Herklots. New Delhi: Asian Education Service, 1991.

Sezgīn, Fu'at. *Tārīkh al-Turāth al-'Arabī,* trans. Maḥmūd Fahmī Ḥijāzī. Riyadh: Ṭab' Idārat al-Thaqāfa wa 'l-Nashr Jāmi'at al-Imām Muḥammad ibn Su'ūd, 1403/1982.

Smail, R. C. *The Crusaders in Syria and Holy Land.* New York and Washington: Praeger Publication, 1973.

Subāʿī, Muṣṭafā Ḥusnī. *Al-Sunna wa-Makānatuha fī al-Tashrīʿ al-Islāmī*, second edition. Beirut: al-Maktab al-Islāmī, 1398/1977.

Sufyānī, ʿUbayd ibn Muḥammad. *Aḥkām al-Diyār: Dār al-Islam wa-Dār al-Kufr.* Istanbul: al-Maktaba al-Islamiyya, n.d.

Sulṭān, Ḥamid. *Aḥkām al-Qānūn al-Duwalī fī al-Sharīʿa al-Islāmiyya.* Cairo: Dār al-Nahḍa al-ʿArabiyya, 1986.

Tabātabāʾi, Hossein Modarressi. *Kharāj in Islamic Law.* London: Anchor Press, 1983.

Ṭaḥāwī, Sulaymān. *Al-Sulutāt al-Thalāth fī al-Dasātīr al-Muʿāṣira fī al-Fikr al-Islāmī.* Beirut: Dār al-Fikr, n.d.

The Cambridge Encyclopaedia of the Middle East and North Africa, Cambridge: Cambridge University Press, 1988.

Thorau, Peter. *The Lion of Egypt: Sultan Baybars I and the Near East in the Thirteenth Century.* trans. P.M. Holt. London; New York: Longman, 1992.

Ṭurayqi, ʿAbdallāh ibn Ibrāhīm ibn ʿAlī. *Al-Istiʿāna bi-ghayr al-Muslimīn fī al-Fiqh al-Islāmī.* Riyadh [Saudi Arabia]: Muʾassasat al-Risāla, 1993.

ʿUmar, Nāṣir Sulayman. *Al-ʿAhd wa ʾl-Mīthāq fī al-Qurʾān al-Karīm.* Riyadh: Dār al-ʿĀṣima, 1992.

Veinstein, G. "Sulaymān," *the Encyclopaedia of Islam*, new edition, vol. 9. Leiden: E.J. Brill, 1997: (832-842).

Waṣfī, Muṣṭafā Kamāl. *Al-Mashrūʿiyya fī al-Niẓām al-Islāmī.* Cairo: Maṭbaʿat al-Amāna, 1390/1970.
________. *Muṣanafat al-Nuẓum al-Islāmiyya.* N.p.: Maktabat Wahbī, 1397/1976.

Watt, Montgomery. *Muhammad Prophet and Statesman.* Oxford: Oxford University Press, 1961.
________. *Muhammad at Mecca.* Oxford: Clarendon Press, 1968.
________. *Muhammad at Medina.* Oxford: Clarendon Press, 1962.

Wessels, Antonie. *A Modern Arabic Biography of Muḥammad.* Leiden: E. J. Brill, 1972.

Ye'or, Bat. *Islam and Dhimmitude: Where Civilization Collide.* New Jerssy: Fairleigh Dickston University Press, 2002.

Zirikilī, Khayr al-Dīn ibn Maḥmūd ibn Muḥammad al-Dimashqī (d. 1396 H.). *Al-Aʿlām.* Beirut: Dār al-ʿIlm li ʾl-Malāyīn, 1408/1986.

Zarqā, Aḥmad. *Sharḥ al-Qawā'id al-Fiqhiyya.* Beirut: Dār al-Gharb al-Islāmī, 1403/1982.

Zarqānī, Muḥammad 'Abd al- 'Aẓim. *Manāhil al-'Arfān fī 'Ilūm al-Qur'ān.* Beirut: Dār al-Fikr, n.d

Zaydān, 'Abd al-Karīm. *Aḥkām al-Dhimmiyyīn wa 'l-Musta'manīn fī Dār al-Islam.* Beirut: Mu'assasat al-Risāla, 1396/1976.

_______. *Majmū'at Buḥūth Fiqhiyya.* Beirut: Mu'assasat al-Risāla, 1402/1981.

Zuḥaylī, Wahba. *Āthār al-Ḥarb fī al-Fiqh al-Islāmī.* Beirut: Dār al-Fikr, 1401/1981.

________. *Al-'Alāqāt al-Dawliyya fī al-Islam.* Beirut: Dār al-Fikr, 1403/1984.

Biographical Note

Labeeb Ahmed Bsoul, born, raised and educated through secondary school in the city of Nazareth-Palestine. Educated in the U.S.A. California State University in S.F. obtained undergrad and graduate degrees in International Relations with honor and Ph.D. from McGill University in Montreal- Canada. Taught at St. Mary's University, Dalhouies University in Halifax-Canada and United Arab Emirates University, currently teaching at Qatar University in the History Department. Area of specialty and expertise are in modern and contemporary history, International Relations, Middle East and Islamic studies and, Islamic International Law (*Siyar*).

www.ingramcontent.com/pod-product-compliance
Ingram Content Group UK Ltd.
Pitfield, Milton Keynes, MK11 3LW, UK
UKHW020125290926
15471UKWH00003B/296

9 780761 838982